FALFUR

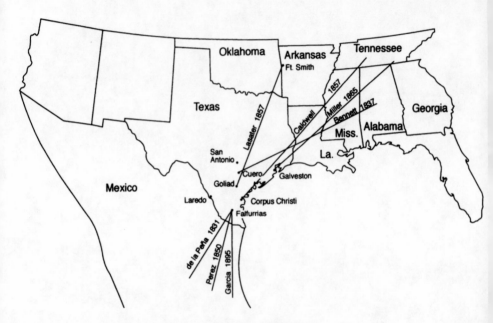

Courtesy Cartographic Service Unit of the Department of Geography at Texas A&M University

Falfurrias

Ed C. Lasater and the Development

of South Texas

By

DALE LASATER

TEXAS A&M UNIVERSITY PRESS

College Station

Library of Congress Cataloging in Publication Data

Lasater, Dale, 1943–
    Falfurrias : Ed C. Lasater and the development of South
Texas.

    Bibliography: p.
    Includes index.
    1. Lasater, Edward Cunningham, 1860–1930.
2. Falfurrias Region (Tex.)—Biography. 3. Ranchers—
Texas—Falfurrias Region—Biography. 4. Falfurrias Region
(Tex.)—History. I. Title.
F394.F17L375   1985   976.4'476 [B]   84-40130
ISBN 0-89096-209-X (cloth); 0-89096-830-6 (pbk.)

ISBN-13: 978-0-89096-830-7 (pbk.)

Manufactured in the United States of America
THIRD PRINTING, 2007

To the memory of
Albert Lasater Maher,
who loved the Falfurrias country,
and for
Peggy Lasater Clark,
who shared this dream with me.

Contents

List of Illustrations   ix

Acknowledgments   xi

Introduction: A Train to Katherine   xiii

Part 1. Wilderness to Empire

1. Seven Families: The Road to Texas   3
2. Distant Shores, Forgotten Names   18
3. All the Land That Joins   37
4. Mary Miller Moves to La Mota   54
5. The End of the Line   70
6. Between Archie and Don Manuel   94
7. Jersey Cows at Heart's Delight   120
8. The Bottom Line   132

Part 2. Loma Blanca: Sentinel of Passage

9. Mr. Swift and Mr. Hoover   153
10. After Versailles: Peace and Panic   183
11. Ranch Brats and Shetland Ponies   207
12. By the Order of the Judge   227
13. The Ninety-Eighth Year   247
14. A Train to Oklahoma   261

Epilogue   266

Appendix. Financial Reports, Ed C. Lasater, 1910–14   269

Bibliography   277

Index   289

List of Illustrations

Ed C. Lasater, circa 1890 *following page 62*

Edward C. Lasater Family Tree

Mary Gardner Miller Family Tree

Susan Dismukes Cunningham

Edward Cunningham

Sarah Jane Cunningham Lasater

Albert Hezekiah Lasater

Col. Edward Hall Cunningham

Ada Lasater Caldwell

Thomas Lasater

Lois Lasater Terrell

Ed C. Lasater, circa 1890

Martha (Patti) Bennett Lasater

John M. Bennett and son, John

Ed C. Lasater, Jr.

Mary Miller Lasater

Ed C. Lasater, 1905

Garland Burleigh Miller

Mary Gardner Miller

Ed Lasater with son Albert, 1904

Lasater children with governess, 1913

La Mota ranch house *following page 126*

Living room at La Mota

Tom and Lois Lasater at their father's office

Garland and Tom riding ponies at the Playhouse

Albert, Garland, Tom, Mary, and Ed Lasater, circa 1915
Albert, Lois, Tom, Ed, and Garland, circa 1915
Tom with pony, circa 1915
Albert, Garland, and Lois in pony cart
The cousins, 1929
Ed Lasater with Lois, circa 1917
Ed C. Lasater, 1929
La Loma Blanca, 1912
Picnic group at La Loma Blanca, circa 1912
Falfurrias, circa 1910
Falfurrias Mercantile Company, circa 1910
Original Falfurrias Creamery, circa 1907
Second Falfurrias Creamery, built in 1925
Lasater cotton gin   *following page 254*
Falfurrias, 1910
Falfurrias State Bank Building
1911 real estate brochure
"Land of Heart's Delight" promotional brochure
Lasater subdivision advertisement
Registered Herefords on Lasater Ranch, circa 1920
T. S. Proctor at creamery, circa 1920
Jersey cows at Cabezas Blancas dairy
Early Falfurrias Creamery butter carton
L. D. Miller, Sr., 1929
Richard G. Miller, circa 1899
Early-day milking, circa 1910
Lasater advertisement for Brahman cattle, 1921

Acknowledgments

THIS book was incubated during many years of fireside stories, casual conversations, visits, and interviews. The book was written in 1982, the 150th anniversary of Albert H. Lasater's birth near Fort Smith, Arkansas, and the 100th anniversary of his purchase with his son, Ed C. Lasater, of a ranch near Oakville, in Live Oak County, Texas.

I am indebted to Ed Lasater's three children who survived him. His daughter, Lois Lasater Maher, expressed a keen interest in seeing this book written, and prior to her death, gave me enthusiastic encouragement. Without the complete cooperation and generous assistance of his two sons, Garland M. Lasater and Tom Lasater, I could not have written the book. I am deeply grateful to each of them.

Four others merit special mention and special thanks: Florence Schuetz, General John M. Bennett, Jr., Barney Bowie Holland, and Duke Phillips III. Only true friends could have contributed what they did to this project.

My wife, Janine Vidal de Moragas Lasater, and my two sons, Alex and Tom, lived with this project on a daily basis during the final two years. They traveled with me, analyzed with me, listened to me, held me up, rejoiced with me, and patiently humored me as the book took shape.

All the events recorded in the book took place more than fifty years prior to its writing. A major fire and the flooding occasioned by a Gulf Coast hurricane, events separated by some four decades, both contributed to the loss of important records related to this story. But natural disasters and the lapse of time were at least partially compensated by the willing cooperation of those who had knowledge of the early days of the Falfurrias country. Many such people generously opened their files and searched their memories to help assemble the material used in this book. In addition to those who consented to be interviewed, and who are thus listed in the bibliography, those persons who assisted me in many ways, large and small, include:

Eva Avery, Eleanor Bennett, the late John M. Bennett, Lois Boyd, Carolyn Brimer, Robert C. Cage, Mr. and Mrs. Clay Caldwell, Noella Caldwell, Mr. and Mrs. Robert Caldwell, the late Sarah Caldwell, Mrs. Larry Casey, Mr. and Mrs. Watt M. Casey, Jr., Sara Clark, Mr. and Mrs. William A. Clark, Mary Whatley Clarke, Mr. and Mrs. A. A. Cosby, Mr. and Mrs. L. O. Dallas, Gilbert Denman, Leroy Denman, Mr. and Mrs. Thomas Drought, the late Emily Edwards, Mr. and Mrs. George Ellis, Vi Foulks, Mr. and Mrs. Alfredo García, Judge and Mrs. Joe B. García, Mr. and Mrs. Julián García, Burleigh Gardner, William B. Gardner, Jr., Mr. and Mrs. Gorgonio Garza, William W. Green, Gene M. Gressley, and Ron Jenkins.

Also William R. Johnson, Dan Kilgore, Thomas H. Kreneck, Carolyn Kampmann Lasater, Mr. and Mrs. Edward A. Lasater, the late Mary C. Lasater, Mr. and Mrs. L. M. Lasater, Sally W. Lasater, Starling R. Lawrence, Mr. and Mrs. Abel Mayorga, Owen N. McKinney, Jr., Bradford F. Miller, Mr. and Mrs. L. D. Miller, III, Mr. and Mrs. John C. Miller, Mr. and Mrs. Gardner B. Miller, Helen Mary Miller, Calixto Mora, Josephine Bennett Musgrave, Joe Nicholson, Doug Perkins, Jimmie R. Picquet, David Rainey, Mary Ratteree, Milton E. Robinowitz, Marcelo Silva, James A. Tinsley, Lourdes Treviño Treviño, Miriam Wagenschein, Susan Wagner, Cecilia Walker, and Hendrick Woods.

To all these, and to many others not here recorded by name, who gave suggestions, provided helpful leads, and offered encouragement, I extend warmhearted thanks.

Introduction:

A Train to Katherine

He is a man who has attained success in his business. He
is esteemed by all who know him as a man of character,
integrity and ability.
—Governor Dan Moody

In every sense of the word, he was a cattle king.
—W. W. Sterling

THE young man peered out the window as the train moved north-
ward across the flat coastal plain. In the moonlight he could see the
darkened prairie, and he squinted as he tried to make out the clumps
of trees, or maybe they were cattle grazing in the distance. The rancher
had said he would meet him when the train stopped at Katherine, and
they would have a brief visit. The young man had applied for the job of
teaching the rancher's children. It sounded like interesting work; now
they would discuss the details to see if they could work out a satisfactory arrangement.

The train lurched and appeared to be slowing down, but it continued moving forward. It seemed to take forever to get to this place.
The young man was certain they had not passed Katherine because he
had made it clear when he boarded the train that he needed to stop
there. He saw a small lake which had caught water after the recent
rain. The train lurched again and appeared to be stopping. He pressed
his forehead to the window and looked out. There was no light, but he
could see some cattle-loading pens near the tracks. When the train
stopped, the young man walked out onto the platform.

A man approached him from the other side. Behind him the young

man could see a cart hitched to a team and the outline of another figure. The two men shook hands and introduced themselves. The rancher
said he had only two questions for the prospective teacher.

"Can you ride a horse?"

The young man replied that he could.

"Can you shoot a gun?"

Again the answer was affirmative.

The rancher told the young man he was hired, with two conditions: "You will never be without a gun, and you will never let my children out of your sight."[1]

The deal was made. Before the train pulled away from Katherine,
the rancher had jumped off the platform, seated himself in the cart,
and disappeared into the darkness.

Hilario García turned the team down a trail that led west from the
railroad tracks. The cart was headed to San Tomás, where one of the
corridas (cow outfits) was camped near an artesian well. They had not
gone far when Hilario could see the rancher's hand waving in a quick
back-and-forth motion. "Let it move along, Hilario; let it move along,"
the rancher said in Spanish. "We may catch the men before they leave
camp."[2]

It was daylight by the time the cart reached San Tomás, and the
cowboys had already left. Hilario turned the team north and then back
to the west past a large area of sand dunes. Even in the early cool, the
team was hot and lathered with sweat by the time they reached Lucero. While Hilario was hitching up a fresh team of horses, the rancher
walked over to a mesquite tree and picked up a phone. He tried to
reach J. O. Terrell at the Central Trust Company in San Antonio. Terrell was not at the bank. He called Ike Pryor, but the colonel had already departed for the meeting they were both going to attend in
Washington, D.C., at the end of the week.

The rancher did catch Peter McBride at the mercantile store in
Realitos. McBride had shipped fifteen cars of cattle that morning. The
rancher told McBride that he would be in Realitos that evening, and
they would look at the steers in La Golona trap together the following
day. With the recent rain it might pay to hold them a little longer. The

---

[1] Interviews, Tom Lasater, January 12, 1980, and Gardner B. Miller, July 22, 1981.

[2] Interview, Juan Maldonado, July 13, 1981.

rancher hated to sell cattle on a market like this; prices would probably be higher in a couple of months.

As the cart moved along in a northeasterly direction toward the Barrosa camp, the rancher gazed at some of the Brahman-cross cows in Los Muertos pasture. The best cattle he had seen for this country, he thought. At Barrosa, while Hilario changed teams again, the rancher called a banker in National Stockyards, Illinois. He was going to need to borrow some more money if he decided to hold the steers.

North of Barrosa the cart passed Rancho del Novillo where Plácido Maldonado and his small grandson were gentling some of the Brahman bulls the rancher had recently bought.[3] Farther north, the Jersey cows were all grazing south of the barn as they passed the dairy at Cabeza Blanca on the way into town.

In Falfurrias the rancher stopped by his office and then went by the bank to see Richard Miller before making a brief stop at the railroad depot. An employee in the Falfurrias Mercantile Company saw the cart head west along Rice Street, pulled by a fresh team. He had worked there two years, but he had not yet met his employer. "Some day I will," he thought, "but not today. He's moving too fast."[4]

Early one morning in 1923, Harriett Miller heard the screaming again. She turned on a light and began talking softly to her husband. The screaming stopped, but L. D. Miller was shaking when he sat up in bed. His brothers Garland and Richard were both dead; brother Rob's health was failing rapidly. Sister and her husband had been forced into a receivership. Now Helen desperately needed help.[5]

When Richard's widow Helen had called him that fall, L. D. Miller thought he had heard it all before. The situation at the Falfurrias State Bank had continued to deteriorate and had become critical. Only a few weeks before he got involved with Helen's problems at the bank, Sister had called. L. D. knew as soon as she began talking that she was distraught. She had tried to tell him something about some stock certificates, but she could not complete the sentence. She needed his assistance. Could he come to Falfurrias?[6]

[3] Ibid.
[4] Interview, Albert W. Dale, August 25, 1971.
[5] Interview, Gardner Miller, July 22, 1981.
[6] Interview, Laurence D. Miller, Sr., September 22, 1971.

Miller had caught the next train to Falfurrias. Now he was going there again, to that little South Texas town at the end of the railroad line. During the long ride from Oklahoma, L. D. had time to ponder the events of the past few years. What was there about that country? He had spent the unhappiest years of his life there, and his luck had improved dramatically since he had left. But he also remembered its charm and its beauty, at least after a rain. He recalled the day his brother-in-law took Harriett and him for a ride in the carriage just after they were married. They had driven out to La Fruta. The country was lush and green; he had never seen a prettier sight.[7]

L. D. Miller did not know what would happen next. But he was headed to Falfurrias, and he would do whatever he could.

An artesian well pouring forth a high-volume fountain of water graced the cover of a 1906 brochure. Inside, colorful prose described in glowing terms the advantages of land ownership and life in general in the Falfurrias area. It was a land whose capacity to produce cattle, cotton, corn, fruit, and vegetables was unexcelled. Winters were mild, and the heat from the summer sun was moderated by cool gulf breezes. The climate was ideal for livestock and for agriculture and had a beneficial effect on many of the most common ailments: "In short, there is no healthier section of the United States, or of the world, so far as we know."[8] The final disclaimer was hardly noticed.

This was an area where a man could support a family by owning a small farm. For a few dollars down, and a few more each month, a man could lead an independent and productive life. "How would you like to live where snow, blizzards, cold winters and big coal bills are unknown, where flowers bloom and vegetables grow all winter?" The sleek bulletin posed that and other leading questions to residents of northern and midwestern states. "How would you like to have a business of your own, . . . a business that never feels panics and bank failures, a business that would keep you out in the open, where you could breathe the fresh air and live next to nature?"[9] Many home seekers responded positively to those questions, and the special trains carried them south to look. Some of them returned with their families and all their possessions, to stay.

[7] Ibid.
[8] *Falfurrias, Texas Wants You.*
[9] *Falfurrias Bulletin.*

It was a wonderful country, a Garden of Eden. This was a productive region, where man and beast could live comfortably without pestilence or plague. Or was it? Early reports on this paradise had termed it a desert; some had called it uninhabitable. As late as 1871, on Ross's map of Texas and the Indian Territory, the area was identified only as an undeveloped region populated by herds of wild cattle and horses.[10]

The rancher had come to this place before the turn of the century. He had seen promise here and had decided to bet his future on this sandy land where the mesquite trees provided shade along creeks with names like Los Olmos, Palo Blanco, and Baluarte. The rancher wore a beard to protect his skin from the blistering sun. His beard was red, and the early settlers called him "El Colorado de Los Olmos"—"the Red One from Olmos Creek."[11]

The cart carrying the rancher in 1915 was heading west from Falfurrias across the Copita prairie. He observed his cattle and his pastures as the cart skimmed across the sand. The cart hit a hole and bounced, and then later, as they crossed a creek, the cart ran over a fallen log, nearly throwing the passengers out.[12] After a few minutes of smooth riding, the rancher was again moving his hand back and forth rapidly, letting Hilario know that they needed to maintain the maximum speed.

At the annual Linden Grove Jersey sale a few years before, many people in the crowd took note of the rancher. "Who is this man from Falfurrias?" several asked. When he started to bid on an animal he was the last to stop, and he started often. He reportedly owned a beef cattle ranch in Texas, and he was establishing a dairy operation as well. When the sale ended, the Texan had bought a large herd of Jersey cattle that included more males than females. Either he had a big operation or he was confused. "That man must be starting a bull dairy," one bystander laughed.[13]

"El Colorado" and his companion moved rapidly across the pastures as they headed west and north. Even so it was dark when they set

[10] *Falfurrias Facts*, June 30, 1939; *Ross's New Corrected County & Rail Road Map of Texas and Indian Territory* (Saint Louis: E. H. Ross, Western Map Emporium, 1871), copy in Author's Files.

[11] John M. Bennett, "Notes on Ed C. Lasater," 1967, Author's Files.

[12] William Warren Sterling, *Trails and Trials of a Texas Ranger*, p. 16; Interview, Juan Maldonado, July 13, 1981.

[13] Hugh G. Van Pelt, "The Man from Falfurrias," *Field Illustrated*, March, 1924, p. 12.

out with a fresh team to cross the last few miles of El Colorado's ranch between Sejita and Realitos. The rancher could occasionally make out an animal or a familiar landmark. In the evening cool, he thought of the years he had spent in this area. They had been active years, filled with strenuous work, with opportunities, and with problems. It had all been worthwhile. This was a wonderful country; it was indeed the Land of Heart's Delight.

Many years later when John Miller's phone rang in Oklahoma City, Falfurrias no longer had rail service. The trains that had come south from Alice and west from Riviera had all made their last run. Only the oldtimers could remember where Katherine had been. Sister had been dead for twenty-five years and her husband for more than forty. But there were memories, some of them still intense despite the lapse of time.

John picked up the phone and began answering his father's questions. L. D. Miller was insistent. Finally John said, "Let me put him on; he's right here," and he handed the phone to the visitor, who was having dinner.

"I got your letter and I have been thinking about it. Why would you want to write a book about this?" L. D. Miller asked.

"It's an interesting story," the visitor replied.

"No, it's not. It's a terrible story, a tragic one. I wish I could forget it. Please do not come to see me. I don't want to discuss it. I don't want to remember," Miller said.

The visitor had driven many miles to get there and did not want to miss the opportunity. "I will be in Okmulgee tomorrow, and I will look forward to seeing you," he replied.

"Dad's funny," John Miller said after the phone conversation ended. "Living alone, he gets to thinking about things and gets all worked up. But maybe he'll talk. You never know about Dad."[14]

[14] Interviews, L. D. Miller, September 21, 1971, and John C. Miller, September 21, 1971.

PART 1
Wilderness to Empire

CHAPTER 1

Seven Families:

The Road to Texas

People who come to Texas these days are preachers or
fugitives from justice or sons of bitches. Which one of
those fits you?

—Richard King, ca. 1850

Ed Lasater's parents moved to Texas three years before his birth in
1860. He grew up near Goliad, north of the Nueces River. In 1881 he
rode his horse south across that river, as far as Los Olmos Creek, perhaps farther.[1] More than a decade later when he again headed south,
he rode to the white hill. From the top of that rise he could see into the
distance, and he could dream of the future. He liked the country that
stretched out before him, and he was excited by its potential. He would
own that white hill, and he would own all the land surrounding it.

Lasater had ridden his horse into the southern extremity of what
was then called the Great American Desert, a desolate expanse of
sandy prairie with scattered oak trees and mesquite brush, traversed
every few miles by dry stream beds. The territory between the Nueces River and the Rio Grande was part of Mexico until Texas won its
independence in 1836; for the following twelve years the area was the
center of a lengthy dispute over sovereignty. Prior to the war that
settled the dispute, some questioned the advisability of fighting at all.
After one early inspection tour, a Major Gaines summarized his negative view of the area: "The country below the Nueces is poor, sterile,
sandy and barren. . . . The only tree we saw was the mesquite tree,
and very few of these. . . . The whole country may be truly called a

---

[1] Edward H. Caldwell, "Notes and Facts in the Life of E. H. Caldwell," Corpus
Christi, 1934, p. 35.

perfect waste, uninhabitable. . . . The country is not now and never can be of the slightest virtue."[2]

Even after the Treaty of Guadalupe Hidalgo in 1848 permanently established the boundary between Texas and Mexico on the Rio Grande, the exact status of this part of southern Texas continued to be blurred, at least in the minds and speech of many who lived there. Mexican inhabitants in this area often referred to it as "medio Mexico"—half Mexico. Many horsemen crossing the hot, arid region wondered if it were an asset or a liability. One offered a solution: "So we fought the Mexicans and took this God forsaken land away from them. I am in favor of fighting them again and making them take it back."[3]

Indians inhabited this part of Texas until well into the nineteenth century. In fact most of the territory south and west of San Antonio belonged to the Indians in the period before the Civil War. Government troops headquartered in that city had trouble holding down depredations.[4]

During the Civil War, the troops were withdrawn, and the frontier line actually receded. The troops returned at the end of the war, putting renewed pressure on the Indians.[5] Behind the troops came an increasing flow of settlers, a flow that would ultimately drive the Indians forever from this sandy land.

Texas' population grew from a few thousand in 1821 when Stephen F. Austin brought his colonists to Columbus and Washington-on-the-Brazos to more than three million in 1900.[6] Among those who made their way into Texas during the nineteenth century were seven families whose lives would become intertwined to varying degrees in that isolated region south of the Nueces. Business deals, marriage, and other events over the years would link these families as their paths crossed in that area where Los Olmos Creek winds its way toward Baffin Bay and where the Palo Blanco and Baluarte creeks carry floodwaters into the Laguna de Loma Blanca (White Hill Lake).[7]

[2] *Falfurrias Facts*, June 30, 1938.

[3] William Warren Sterling, *Trails and Trials of a Texas Ranger*, p. 23.

[4] Marilyn McAdams Sibley, *George W. Brackenridge: Maverick Philanthropist*, p. 90.

[5] Ibid.

[6] Walter Prescott Webb and H. Bailey Carroll, eds., *The Handbook of Texas*, I, 331.

[7] Los Olmos meant The Elms; Palo Blanco (white stick) refers to the hackberry

It is not known into which of Richard King's classifications the head of each of the seven families fits—preachers, fugitives, or others. Details of their lives before journeying to Texas are sketchy in most cases. But all were willing to leave behind their former lives in order to face the uncertainties that awaited them in this frontier area. For each of these families, opportunity outweighed risk.

From Mexico came the de la Peñas, the Pérezes, and the Garcías. The Bennetts, Lasaters, Caldwells, and Millers came from states to the north and east. These families had a variety of individual reasons for making the move to Texas. For most of them, the opportunity Texas offered was closely associated with the availability of land that could be secured at little or no cost. This land could be used to pasture cattle and horses, to grow crops. The land tendered a positive and prosperous future, and the search for that future brought these families to Texas.

Some of them made their way toward South Texas in a series of moves over a period of years; others came directly. The region they came to was known by a series of names. One family came to the northern part of the Mexican state of Tamaulipas; one moved to the Republic of Texas. Two families settled in the southern part of the twenty-eighth state before the Civil War, while three moved to Texas after that war. They came on horseback, in buggies, on boats, and in trains.

While international boundaries were being established, and later while county lines were being drawn and re-drawn to suit a variety of whims and exigencies, one or more members of each of these families came to that place which one colorful, symbolic, and mysterious name described best: they came to the Falfurrias country.

In 1831, Ignacio de la Peña submitted an application to the government of Tamaulipas for a tract of land lying between the Rio Grande and the Nueces River. The tract ran north and west from a point on the western edge of the Laguna de Loma Blanca. The boundary lines went in and out of chaparral and timber, across creeks and lagoons, and over stretches of open prairie. The claim covered a rectangular block of

---

tree; Baluarte means bulwark or defense. Laguna de Loma Blanca (White Hill Lake) was the original name of Salt Lake, located southeast of Falfurrias. This lake was referred to as Laguna de Loma Blanca on all early surveys, deeds, and abstracts and as late as a von Blucher map of the Falfurrias Jersey Dairy Company lands made in 1911.

land, measuring more than thirteen miles north and south and more than five miles east and west: ten leagues of land, 44,284 acres.[8]

The same year a group of surveyors sent by the state of Tamaulipas surveyed the land. The decree giving title to this tract to Ignacio de la Peña was finalized on December 9, 1831. The grant was named Los Olmos y Loma Blanca.[9] De la Peña took possession of this property less than five years before the Battle of San Jacinto gave birth to the Republic of Texas. The changes precipitated by the events of that war made four additional steps over the following thirty-nine years necessary to perfect his title.

The first step was accomplished when the original decree signed by the governor of Tamaulipas was filed of record in 1849. At that time the U.S. Consul at Matamoros authenticated the signatures of the governor, the secretary, and the surveyor.[10] Twelve years later, the district court of Starr County, Texas, issued a Decree of Confirmation confirming de la Peña and his heirs as owners of the Los Olmos y Loma Blanca grant and stating that: "The title to the above described tract of land is forever settled, rested, and adjusted as between the State of Texas and the said Ignacio de la Peña."[11]

This decree describes at least one of the problems encountered by de la Peña and his family between 1831 and 1861: "Possession of said land . . . has been uninterrupted up to the present day, except when Ignacio de la Peña or his heirs have been driven therefrom by the incursion of hostile Indians; and whenever it became safe to return to the said land the heirs of Ignacio de la Peña did so. . . ."[12]

It is interesting to note how Texas, having taken over sovereignty of the land, recognized title to the land just as Tamaulipas would have.

---

[8] Deed Records, Starr County, Book B, pp. 234–39.

[9] Ibid. The white hill (*loma blanca*) gave its name to two Mexican land grants in this area: the Los Olmos y Loma Blanca, awarded to Ignacio de la Peña in 1831, and a grant which joined it on the east, the Loma Blanca grant. The latter grant was awarded to Francisco Guerra Chapa in 1831. This grant included most of the lake as well as the white hill on the northeastern side of the lake. A common misconception holds that all the land grants in South Texas were Spanish. Only four of the grants touching Brooks County were granted by the Spanish crown to Spanish subjects, between 1798 and 1808. The majority were granted to Mexican citizens by the State of Tamaulipas, between 1827 and 1835. See Virginia H. Taylor, *Index to Spanish and Mexican Land Grants*.

[10] Deed Records, Starr County, Book B, pp. 234–39.

[11] Minutes of District Court, Starr County, Book B, pp. 33–36.

[12] Ibid.

The 1861 decree stated that de la Peña had complied with all the laws of Tamaulipas, that his claim originated in good faith, and that "the said claim would have matured into a perfect title under the laws, usages and customs of said State of Tamaulipas had its sovereignty over the same not passed to and been vested in the Republic and State of Texas."[13] The method of perfecting title thus provided one constant in a region where shifting international boundaries resulted in changes of other laws and customs.

Even the fees remained the same. The decree assessed the de la Peña family the same amount they would have had to pay had Texas not emerged victorious at San Jacinto twenty-five years earlier. The Decree of Confirmation ordered de la Peña to pay three hundred dollars to the General Land Office of Texas as the price for the ten leagues— "which amount he would have had to pay to the State of Tamaulipas had not the sovereignty of the soil changed. . . ."[14]

Almost four decades after the surveyors marked the boundaries of de la Peña's claim, his heirs secured the final document that perfected their title. The State of Texas issued a patent in March, 1870, which confirmed their ownership of the Los Olmos y Loma Blanca grant. The patent described this tract as "ten leagues of land on the Palo Blanco and San Antonio Creeks, and the Laguna de Loma Blanca, sixty miles southeast of Corpus Christi, sixty-eight and one half miles north, thirty-two degrees east of Rio Grande City."[15] After thirty-nine years, the title was official, secure, and permanent.

During the years in which de la Peña and his family were perfecting the title to their grant, three more of the seven families made their way into Texas. The Bennett family was the first to arrive. Stephan Bennett was the head of a clan that moved to Texas from Alabama in 1837. The Bennetts made the trip west in a wagon train with several other families who had banded together for protection. They settled near Cuero, in DeWitt County.[16]

Six-year-old John M. Bennett was among the family members in that migration to the frontier. Born in the same year that Ignacio de la Peña received the Los Olmos y Loma Blanca grant, the young Bennett

[13] Ibid.
[14] Ibid.
[15] Deed Records, Nueces County, Book P, pp. 541–42.
[16] Interview, John M. Bennett, Jr., July 24, 1981.

grew up with the Republic of Texas. Between 1846 and 1848, Bennett and a brother contracted to haul supplies to General Zachary Taylor during the Mexican War.[17] After that war, the disputed area between the Nueces River and the Rio Grande was recognized by both countries as part of Texas.

When the northern cattle drives started after the Civil War, Bennett became a trail boss. He drove herds up the Chisholm Trail for several owners, among them George W. Brackenridge, a San Antonio banker. After Bennett had made a number of drives, Brackenridge advised the young cowman to take his own herd up the trail and loaned him twenty-five thousand dollars for that purpose. Bennett drove his herd to the northern market, and after paying his debts and all his expenses, he had a twenty-five-thousand-dollar profit.[18]

The money earned in that venture gave Bennett the capital necessary to quit the trail and to launch his own business career. After his last drive, Bennett stated that he would leave the rigors of the trail, the Indians, rustlers, stampedes, bad weather, and flooding rivers to others. He decided that he would loan money; someone else could borrow it and take those risks.[19]

John Bennett married Elizabeth Bonneau Noble and moved to Sweet Home, in Lavaca County. He used the profit from his last trail drive to found a bank in Yoakum, and in 1875 he purchased a ranch in Jackson County in partnership with George W. West.[20] Bennett maintained an active interest in ranching, but the banking business proved to be his true calling.

In 1850, thirteen years after Stephan Bennett led a wagon train into Texas from Alabama, Sabas Pérez moved his family into Hidalgo County from Camargo, Tamaulipas. The treaty that established the U.S.-Mexican border on the Rio Grande did not stop the flow of settlers from south of the river. This frontier area of Texas continued to attract immigrants from Mexico as well as from states to the north and east.

Like Bennett and many others, Pérez came motivated by pastoral considerations. He came to graze cattle on part of the Loma Blanca

---

[17] John M. Bennett, Jr., *Those Who Made It*, p. 5.
[18] Interview, John M. Bennett, Jr., July 24, 1981.
[19] Interview, Garland M. Lasater, February 21, 1981.
[20] *Texas Family Land Heritage Registry*, (1975), p. 33.

grant. This grant ran north from the Laguna de Loma Blanca, and de la Peña's Los Olmos y Loma Blanca grant served as its western boundary.[21] Pérez later purchased land on the south side of the lake and established a permanent home on what became known as the Loma Blanca Ranch.[22]

One year after John Bennett's birth in Alabama in 1831, Albert Hezekiah Lasater was born in Arkansas. Orphaned as a young boy, he was raised by a half-sister and her husband, a merchant who had business interests in Arkansas and New Orleans. In 1856 he married Sarah Jane Cunningham in Van Buren, Arkansas, and the following year Lasater and his young bride made the move to Texas.[23] Lasater's oldest child later described that move, which took place because of Lasater's health. The trip was made by ambulance, with servants and household goods following by wagon: "They camped out until they reached Dallas, Texas, but spent each night thereafter in hotel or private home . . . because it was not considered safe to be abroad with their valuables after night."[24] Albert and Sarah Jane Lasater spent their first few months in Texas with her brothers, Edward and Thomas Cunningham, who had moved to Texas from Arkansas the preceding year and had started a livestock operation in Bexar County on Cibolo Creek.[25]

In early 1858, the Lasaters moved to Goliad, where their first child, Ada, was born. Later that same year, the family moved to a property called Valley Farm, located eighteen miles above Goliad on the San Antonio River. The Lasaters spent seven years on this place, and their two sons were born there—Edward Cunningham in 1860 and Thomas in 1863. Ada Lasater recalled the years at Valley Farm as happy ones for the children: "For months we never saw anyone besides the family. Papa loved to tell or read stories, and every night he took us on his knees or lay in front of the fire with one of us in each arm."[26]

[21] *Falfurrias Facts*, November 19, 1981.

[22] Transcribed Deed Records from Hidalgo County, Brooks County, Book I, pp. 454–55, 542.

[23] Ada Lasater Caldwell, "Recollections," p. 1. Albert H. Lasater was born July 19, 1832. His half-sister, Ada Parks, was married to John Henry (ibid., p. 5).

[24] Ibid., p. 1.

[25] A. J. Sowell, *History of Fort Bend County, Texas*, p. 349. Sowell places the Cunninghams on Martinez Creek; Ada Caldwell places them on Cibolo Creek. Both creeks are in Bexar County, Texas.

[26] Caldwell, "Recollections," p. 1. Albert Lasater also liked to read novels. One

Lasater immigrated from Arkansas in the days of the black slave and the open range. His principal business during his first years in Texas was raising horses and mules, and he normally ran between one and two thousand head.[27] Grazing the open range was a typical practice in those days. Most livestock men in Texas prior to the Civil War ranged their herds on unoccupied public lands.[28]

The dislocations caused by the Civil War ended that isolated, pastoral life at Valley Farm. At the end of the war, Lasater lost his livestock "during the readjustment period."[29] Lasater was not alone in that plight; many settlers lost their holdings in the confusion following the war. Postwar conditions brought legions of displaced people into the state, including "thieves and cut-throats, . . . and with the decline of the buffalo, recreant skinners and cattle rustlers were roaming the far-reaching open ranges, driving off cattle by the score."[30]

In 1865, Lasater cashed in what he had left and moved his family back to Goliad, where he established a mercantile business. He became a wholesale and retail dealer in dry goods, groceries, and hardware.[31] A newspaper advertisement said that Lasater would sell low for cash or that he would exchange his wares for wool, hides, bacon, and other country produce. Lasater was also prepared to ship cotton, wool, hides, and pecans to any city or commission merchant.[32]

The de la Peñas, Bennetts, Pérezes, and Lasaters, then, had all moved to Texas before the Civil War. That protracted conflict changed

---

evening Ada saw him sitting by the fireplace reading, with tears streaming down his cheeks. Concerned, she asked her father what was wrong. "A man loves a woman," was the reply (interview, Garland M. Lasater, February 21, 1981).

[27] Ed C. Lasater, "What I Did When I Lost $130,000 Farming," *Farm and Fireside*, March, 1919, quoted in Lasater, "Meat Packer Legislation," statement before the Committee on Agriculture, U.S. House of Representatives, March 1, 2, 3, and 6, 1920, p. 204, in Edward C. Lasater Collection, Eugene C. Barker Texas History Center, University of Texas, Austin.

[28] Edward Everett Dale, *The Range Cattle Industry: Ranching on the Great Plains from 1865 to 1925*, p. 5.

[29] J. Marvin Hunter, *The Trail Drivers of Texas*, p. 886.

[30] Mary Whatley Clarke, *A Century of Cow Business*, p. 2.

[31] Lasater, "Meat Packer Legislation," p. 204.

[32] The Lasater ad appeared on an undated and unidentified newspaper page, which included an ad placed by Norton and Deutz of San Antonio that makes reference to the Texas State Fairs of 1870 and 1871.

the course of many lives, and conditions existing in the eastern states after the war prompted many more settlers to make the journey west. Texas continued to attract new residents from Mexico as well in the decades after the Civil War. Julián García reached the same conclusion many southerners did: Texas offered greater opportunities than those existing in his native state. Before the end of the century he moved his family from Tamaulipas into the area near Los Olmos Creek.[33]

Texas was a place for new beginnings. The Millers and the Caldwells were two Tennessee families who decided that the prospects on the Texas frontier appeared more promising than in the South: "No one can realize the distressing conditions the South had to face, and the apparent hopeless fate that seemed unbearable at the close of the war and afterwards during the Reconstruction period."[34]

Garland Burleigh Miller and his family knew the Caldwells in Tennessee. In 1865, Miller decided that the future lay in Texas and moved from Fayetteville, Tennessee, to Galveston.[35] One of Miller's business ventures was an investment beginning in 1880 in Colonel Edward Cunningham's sugar plantation in Fort Bend County. Cunningham and Miller were among those who met in 1890 at the Cotton Exchange Building in Houston to form the Texas Sugar Growers' Association. Miller's involvement with Cunningham ended in 1898, after Cunningham built a sugar refinery and began experiencing business reverses.[36]

Garland Miller was a businessman whose expansive approach to life was illustrated some years after his move to Texas. He called his family together for a serious discussion in which he detailed how the family's income at that time was not keeping pace with the family's ex-

---

[33] Interview, Hilario García, Jr., March 22, 1982. About 1890, Julián García moved from Matamoros to the Beeville area, where extensive vegetable farming was carried out at that time. In the mid 1890s, Julián García again moved from Mexico to Texas. This time he settled near Los Olmos and brought with him his two young sons, Nicolás and Hilario. Julián went to work for Ed Lasater at the Rancho de los Mesquites; his eight-year-old son, Hilario, was first employed by Lasater as a shepherd at la Fruta. At that time he earned fifty cents a day (ibid).

[34] E. H. Caldwell, "Notes," p. 7.

[35] Interview, L. D. Miller, Sr., September 22, 1971; W. H. Miller, *History and Genealogies of the Families of Miller, Woods, Harris, Wallace, Maupin, Oldham, Kavanaugh and Brown*, p. 137.

[36] Interview, L. D. Miller, Sr., September 22, 1971; William R. Johnson, "A Short History of the Sugar Industry in Texas," *Texas Gulf Coast Historical Association Publications*, vol. 5, no. 1 (April, 1961): 51.

penses. Instead of the expected exhortation, however, he concluded his comments by stating that they were simply going to have to earn more money. Such was the spirit and outlook of one who went to Texas.[37]

W. E. Caldwell was a man who fit unashamedly into one of Richard King's categories: he was a Presbyterian minister. A devout and dedicated Christian, Caldwell was also concerned with the worldly future of his seven sons and one daughter. The area around his parish in Bethany, Tennessee, was decimated after the war, and he decided to make a trip to Texas in 1871 to have a firsthand look at this reputed land of promise. He evidently liked what he saw, and he accepted the call of the Presbyterian Church in Corpus Christi, moving his family there in 1872.

Caldwell's oldest son, Edward, was the last family member to reach Corpus. He later described the trip, which began on a train that went from Tennessee to Huntsville, Alabama, to Grenada, Mississippi, and thence to New Orleans. Another train carried him to Morgan City, Louisiana, at that time the terminus of the Southern Pacific Railroad. There Caldwell boarded a steamer for Galveston, where he took another for Indianola. A sailboat used for mail delivery carried him on the last leg of his journey to Texas.[38]

On Sunday after Edward Caldwell's arrival in Corpus, the family all gathered for breakfast and prayers. Afterward the Reverend Caldwell told the assembled family members they would have to live down the reputations of some of their ancestors, among them pirates and robbers. He expressed the hope that each new family member would make a name for himself in this new country.[39]

W. E. Caldwell's oldest son, Edward, had little trouble adapting himself to life on the margin of nineteenth-century civilization. After short stints in city jobs, he had concluded that a life on the range held the most attraction. In particular, he decided that the sheep business offered the greatest prospect for financial reward, and he set out to determine the most practical way to get started.[40]

[37] Interview, Gardner Miller, July 22, 1981.
[38] E. H. Caldwell, "Notes," pp. 16–18.
[39] Interview, Sarah Cunningham Caldwell, June 26, 1971.
[40] Edward Caldwell's description of his experience with sheep ranching near Realitos, Texas, appears in Caldwell, "Notes," pp. 25–39.

In 1875, Caldwell made a wide swing through South Texas on horseback to visit ranches and to study sheep industry conditions. As Caldwell described it, the whole country was open, and raiding parties from both sides of the Rio Grande could rob stores, or steal horses and cattle, and then move their stolen property across the river into Mexico before they could be overtaken. Little assistance was available from authorities in either the United States or Mexico.

On the road between Laredo and Corpus, Caldwell passed a settlement called Borjas, located near Realitos in Duval County.[41] There, in 1875, Caldwell and his brother Willie leased a twenty-five-thousand-acre ranch. The consideration was fifty dollars annual cash rent, with the additional stipulation that they remove all the Mexican squatters and their flocks from the land. By the end of the year, the ranch was free of squatters, and, according to Caldwell, they had friendly relations with all their Mexican neighbors, "but we felt it necessary to be always well-armed and watchful, and making frequent demonstrations of our ability to draw quick and shoot straight."[42]

On March 27, 1875, Caldwell and his brother purchased twelve hundred ewes for twelve hundred dollars and moved them to the ranch at Borjas. The Caldwells' move into livestock proved to be a good one; for the next five years, they realized a steady profit and high returns. The wool, sheared twice a year, paid all the overhead and operating expenses. Half of the lamb crop (which averaged 75 percent) was sold to buy Merino bucks, which were introduced to improve the grade of the wool. That left a net increase in the flock of nearly 40 percent each year.

Sheep were profitable and the frontier environment was an added attraction for young men like Caldwell: "There was enough real danger and adventure in such conditions to appeal to the younger generation who appreciated a thrill, and I must confess it had a strong appeal to me at the time."[43]

Caldwell recounted numerous instances of bandit raids and stolen horses. The only Indian incursion during his years in the Realitos area

---

[41] "Borjas was on the main line of travel between Corpus and Laredo. Ox carts from the interior of Mexico, passengers on the buckboard mail line, and a lot of salesmen each way. . . . The traveling public was so glad to find a place where company, food, water and cots could be found that we had lots of company. . . ." (E. H. Caldwell, "Notes," p. 30).

[42] Ibid., p. 25.

[43] Ibid., p. 24.

occurred in 1878 when a group of some forty Indians stole several hundred horses from ranchers in the area. Eleven Anglos and ten Mexicans set out after the raiders in an attempt to recover the stock. The Indians sent part of their group ahead with the horses; the remainder followed behind and had several encounters with Caldwell and his fellow ranchers, who abandoned the pursuit after an unsuccessful seventy-five-mile chase. Caldwell learned later that these were Kickapoo Indians from the Santa Rosa Mountains in Mexico.

A pamphlet published in Corpus Christi shortly after that raid provides some insight into the reactions provoked by the event, and the attitudes fostered by such an incident. The report described the peaceful, law-abiding pioneers who resided in the area and who followed their flocks and herds "which roam over wide-spreading savannas, through the lovely valleys, across the hills, or scatter far over the great expanses of our grander prairies." This pleasant pastoral life and the prosperity the settlers had secured were destroyed "with a fury of a hurricane," and many precious lives were "ruthlessly sacrificed to sate the hate of the remorseless Mexican bandit, as well as to gratify his hellish greed and that of his allies, the Indian brutes whom he gives shelter and a home. . . ." The pamphlet included such statements as: "Our cry is for justice. Mexico should make atonement and her savages should be expelled." It concluded with the plea that "our cry shall not come before them in vain, and that you . . . will redress our grievous wrongs."[44]

Despite such reports and pleadings, assistance from governments on either side of the Rio Grande was sporadic at best. Those who chose to live in that area south of the Nueces had to rely on themselves and on their neighbors to protect their persons and their property. From time to time the Caldwell brothers had other young men living with them on the Borjas ranch. These men provided both company and additional protection. They pastured their own flocks at no cost, but shared in the living expenses. Caldwell's description of the ultimate fate of several of these young men provides a stark summary of life in the ranch country near Realitos in the 1870's: "Six of the seven were dead long ago: two were drowned in swollen rivers, one died of con-

⁴⁴ "The Mexican and Indian Raid of '78," *Texas State Historical Association Quarterly*, vol. 5, no. 3 (January, 1902): 212–15.

sumption, one of disease contracted from exposure, one killed by Indians, one got into trouble with the law and had to leave the country, dying in a foreign land."[45]

Edward Caldwell had first become interested in the sheep business while observing the financial transactions of sheep men at the bank in Corpus Christi where he worked as a bookkeeper. Albert Lasater developed a similar interest from his vantage point as a Goliad merchant dealing with wool and other farm products. In 1878, three years after the Caldwell brothers leased the Borjas ranch, Albert Lasater entered the sheep business with the purchase of a ranch in Atascosa County.[46]

Caldwell had met the Lasater family in 1876 while visiting his parents in Goliad, where they had moved from Corpus. At least he had met Miss Ada, the Lasaters' eldest daughter. Life in Texas during the last half of the nineteenth century was often violent and for some short, but Caldwell's account of his four-year pursuit of Miss Ada illuminates the pleasant side of life on the Texas frontier.[47]

Caldwell first met Ada Lasater while she and several other friends were playing a game of croquet with Caldwell's sister in Goliad. Ada had just returned from school in Oxford, Ohio. Caldwell, struck by her fairness, thought she was from the north, "where the wind didn't spoil their fresh complexions." In an effort to ingratiate himself, he stated that he would never marry a Texas girl. Ada responded to his mistaken assumption by affirming that she would never marry a sheep man.

In spite of that exchange, Caldwell found Ada's personality so pleasing and her looks so attractive that it was love at first sight. He was stymied by his opening statement and by other circumstances: "Everything was against me. She heard me say that I wouldn't marry a Texas girl. She was engaged to another. The more I tried to modify my aversion to Texas girls, the deeper I got into trouble."

Caldwell returned to the Borjas ranch, in love but with little hope regarding the outcome of that romance. His sister and other friends

---

[45] E. H. Caldwell, "Notes," p. 27.

[46] E. H. Caldwell, "Life and Activities of Edward Cunningham Lasater," Corpus Christi, 1937, p. 5.

[47] Edward Caldwell's account of his courtship of Ada Lasater appears in his "Notes," pp. 31–34.

kept him apprised of Ada's activities as he went about the business of ranching in Duval County. More than two years passed before he received the unexpected but welcome news that Ada's engagement had been terminated.

He immediately set out on horseback to see Ada. Since their first meeting, Ada's father had joined the ranks of the sheep men for whom she had expressed such disdain. When Caldwell arrived at the Lasaters' ranch in Atascosa County, Sarah Jane Lasater told him that her daughter was visiting at the home of their neighbors, the Tom family. Mrs. Lasater sent her son Ed to their home to tell Ada that she had company.[48]

Edward Caldwell found Ada as lovely as ever. In the course of his visit, they made plans for Ada to visit his sister in Goliad during the Christmas holidays, 1879. He would be there as well.

In December, while Caldwell and Ada were both in Goliad, he posed the question. After a long buggy ride, and after attending a church service and prayer meeting together, Ada gave Caldwell the response he sought. Before leaving Goliad, they agreed that Caldwell would go to the Atascosa ranch in March to ask for her parents' consent to the marriage.

In March, 1880, Caldwell again rode his horse from Borjas to the Lasaters'. He and Albert Lasater went outside to discuss the matter. Lasater was very lame with rheumatism, and he sat down on a log in front of the house. Caldwell proceeded to tell him of "my love for his daughter, of my present prosperity and future prospects fully and frankly, and asked his direct answer, yes or no. I did not offer to help him up until he said yes, and he could not get up without help."[49]

---

[48] The ranch Albert Lasater purchased in Atascosa County in 1878 was in the vicinity of present-day Campbellton. The Lasater ranch was near a ranch owned by Ellen Campbell Tom, an enterprising lady from Donegal, Ireland, who, beginning in 1876, put together 50,000 acres of Texas ranchland (*Texas Family Land Heritage Registry*, [1978].) After Ed Lasater rode over to the neighbors', the Tom family said that the young visitor should come over to their place if he wanted to see Ada. Ed Lasater insisted on her returning, though, and escorted her home. Caldwell later commented, "That was the most important thing that Ed Lasater did for me, finer than all the other things he did for me in later life." (Caldwell, "Notes," p. 32).

[49] After returning to his ranch at Borjas, Caldwell built what he described as "a three room California box-style house." Caldwell and one of his brothers went to Benavides, the terminus of the Texas Mexican Railway. His encounter with four of the principals involved in the construction of that railway took place there. After loading all the furniture for the new house on the wagon, the Caldwells found they were hopelessly

The wedding was set for November 16 but was later postponed to December 16 because of bad weather. Edward's father, the Reverend William E. Caldwell, performed the marriage ceremony, which took place in the Lasaters' ranch home. Edward and Ada then set off in a new buggy with a two-horse team, with Edward's brother Patton following in an open buckboard with the baggage.

The first night was spent at Oakville at Nation's Hotel; the second, with friends on the San Antonio River. On the third day the newlyweds arrived in Cuero, where they spent the remainder of their honeymoon with Edward's parents. On December 27, Edward and Ada departed for the Borjas ranch.

They made the trip in five days, averaging about thirty miles a day, with overnight stops in Goliad, Beeville, Lagarto, and San Diego. Cold weather and snow made travel slow and uncomfortable. At Beeville, Edward carried Ada into the hotel in his arms to keep her out of the snow. The following day, they stopped several times at homes along the road to warm bricks to place under their feet. At San Diego, buckets of charcoal fire and hot irons could not take the chill out of their bones.

On a cold New Year's Day, 1881, Edward and Ada Lasater Caldwell left San Diego for the last leg of their trip to Borjas, to begin their married life together on a sheep ranch northwest of Realitos.

---

mired in the sand: "While we were working to get started, I looked back at the depot and saw Mr. Lott's private car on the track with Captain Richard King, R. Holbein, Mr. Lott and Captain Mifflin Kenedy on the platform watching our vain efforts to get off. Captain King called out for us to wait, that they would help us. He came right over with the others, and with the four millionaires, one at each wheel, the wagon was started. We couldn't stop to say thank you for fear we would be stalled again." (Caldwell, "Notes, p. 33).

CHAPTER 2

Distant Shores, Forgotten Names

> The Anglo-Saxon laced this soil with his own and with
> other men's blood; it would take his bones, and monstrous
> artifacts, and still remain.
>
> —T. R. Fehrenbach

IT was 1685 when the Frenchman stopped on the hill and looked out over the green fields. This land had been his father's. Now it was his, and he had thought it always would be, but these were uncertain times. How could he leave this place? He continued on over the hill to the gathering. Together with his neighbors he would pray. How could the King do such a thing? Surely prayer would provide the answer and would produce a solution.[1]

Before the year was over, the Frenchman had left behind those green fields. Along with scores of his fellow Huguenots, he had set out on the long journey to the New World. His name reflected a life connected with the land: Lasaterre (literally translated: "there his land"). When they arrived in the southeastern part of the United States, immigrants with that name once again earned their living from the land. The name changed in the New World. It became, among other variations, Lasater, Laseter and Lassiter.[2]

---

[1] France's King Louis XIV revoked the Edict of Nantes in 1685. That edict, issued in 1598, had restored to French Huguenots their full civil rights and had given them freedom to worship. The revocation of that edict made life intolerable for French protestants and within a few years some four hundred thousand of them had emigrated from France (Lucian J. Fosdick, *The French Blood in America*, pp. 38, 39, 54, 56).

[2] The French Huguenot connection, the derivation of the name Lasater, and the subsequent detail of soldiers with that surname who fought in the Civil War all come from George Thomas Lasater, *Members of the Lasater Family and Variations of the Family Name Serving in the Civil War*.

These people spread out across the country, and by the time of the Civil War their names appeared on the military records of most states. A majority fought for the Confederacy. From Tennessee, sixty-seven Lasaters (and variations) are listed on the Confederate States Army rolls, and six on the United States Army records. One of the Confederate soldiers from Tennessee, Thomas Lasater, was captured by Union forces at Kemper Barracks, Kentucky. Later he was moved to Camp Chase, Ohio, and then to Camp Douglas, Illinois. The final report states that Lasater died in 1864 of smallpox. Another Tennessee Confederate, Benjamin Lasater, survived the war and moved to Crowley, Tarrant County, Texas, where he applied in 1922 for a pension under the Indigent Soldier of the Confederacy Act. The application was rejected because his oath of allegiance was taken prior to April 9, 1865.

Many Lasaters had moved west before the Civil War started. Thirty-six Lasaters from Arkansas and fifteen from Texas appear on the Confederate rolls. A William A. Lasater enlisted in the United States Army in 1863 at Fort Smith, Arkansas. A pension claim shows that he was injured when his horse threw him a year later near Dardanelle, Arkansas.

Did that Frenchman's blood run in Ed Lasater's veins? Were any of those soldiers related to his family? Ed Lasater did not know and was too busy to care. Surveying his domain while riding over the country surrounding the white hill, moving along rapidly over the sand in a two-horse cart on the way to check his herds at Encino, or talking to a foreman at La Mota in the shade of the oak trees where Lipan Indians had once found rest and solace, he looked only to the future. His actions and his vision were unencumbered by the past.

Genealogy for Ed Lasater went only as far as Tennessee, and even that much was hazy. One of his wife's cousins had traced her family back to England in the tenth century and had concluded that they had been aristocrats.[3] But not Ed Lasater. When pressed for details, he would only say that the family had been run out of Tennessee many years ago for stealing some horses. And then he would laugh.[4]

After moving from Fort Smith, Arkansas, to Texas in 1857, Albert

---

[3] Gertrude Gardner Turner to Tom Lasater, February 9, 1974.
[4] Interview, Tom Lasater, November 9, 1980.

H. Lasater, Ed Lasater's father, became one of the first members of the Masonic Lodge in Goliad.[5] That fact lends at least a semblance of credibility to the idea that his forebears descended from Protestant immigrants.[6] Despite that tenuous connection, the Lasater past is all hypothesis. Albert Lasater did not pass on to his children any details regarding either the family's life in Arkansas or the activities and whereabouts of the Lasaters in earlier years.

Sarah Jane Cunningham, Ed Lasater's mother, provided a more complete outline of her family's history before its arrival in Arkansas. She was the daughter of Susan T. Dismukes and Edward Cunningham, whose grandfather, Richard Cunningham, lived from 1727 to 1797 at "Church Hill" Parish Maghera, near Dundrum Bay in County Down, Ireland. Richard Cunningham was a member of the Grand Lodge of Dublin. His son, Richard, Jr., took part in an uprising against the British and, assisted by the Freemasons, escaped with his family to America. They arrived in Charleston, South Carolina, around 1790 and later moved to Cumberland County, Virginia. His son Edward lived in Tennessee and then moved to Arkansas, where he married and where his daughter Sarah Jane was born at Osage Prairie in 1837.[7]

Sarah Jane Cunningham was a "charming and lovable person. She was good looking and had personality. She was always attractively dressed, immaculate."[8] When she was nineteen, Sarah Jane married Albert Lasater. The following year, the young couple moved to Texas, where their four children were born.

The Lasaters' son Tom and the youngest daughter, Lois, had their father's dark hair and coloring. Ada and Ed inherited their mother's

---

[5] Interview, Garland M. Lasater, February 21, 1981. Lake Newell Porter was sheriff of Brooks County from 1919 to 1922. His father, S. P. Porter, had moved from Mississippi to Goliad, Texas, in the 1850s. There S. P. Porter and Albert Lasater were both Freemasons, working their way up through the ranks at the same time (interview, Matt Gouger, March 20, 1982).

[6] "It was natural that French protestants who came to America should be favorable to Freemasonry, this being an institution that had been put under ban by the same Roman Catholic Church which had so bitterly oppressed them and driven them into exile" (Fosdick, *The French Blood in America*, p. 386).

[7] Edward Cunningham, *The Descendants of Richard Cunningham*, pp. 100, 104, 152, 244, 248; family records from the files of Sarah Cunningham Caldwell, in possession of Clay Caldwell, Corpus Christi.

[8] Interview, John M. Bennett, February 24, 1967.

blond hair and blue eyes. Ed's complexion was ruddy and his beard was red.[9] "Put your trust in your auburn-faced boy," Ed reassured his mother during a horse-trading venture in the East, adding: "I have just been figuring. It will take 125 feet of snow to cover me all up, and even then my auburn beard may melt it before Spring."[10]

Ed's sister Ada later remembered her two brothers' fighting constantly: "Tom was a great tease, and played jokes on young and old alike. Ed could not bear teasing." Ada also remembered her brother Ed as being self-reliant and unselfish. As a boy of ten, he drove a wagon and a team of horses twenty-eight miles from Goliad to Victoria to accommodate a salesman who did not know the way. The salesman paid the young boy ten dollars for his help, the first money he had ever earned. Ed returned home very pleased. He gave the ten dollars to Ada, saying he wanted her to buy a ring for herself. "As the jeweler had nothing that fit me, he made a plain gold ring and we were both very happy with it," Ada recalled.[11]

Albert Lasater moved his family from Valley Farm to Goliad after the Civil War. There his son Ed got his brief taste of school. When he was nine, he attended Miss Ocea Hughes's private school, and later he studied at the Aranama school for one year. At twelve, Ed enrolled in a public school. That was the first year boys had been allowed to attend: "The free school had been open to girls for several years and the girls were much further advanced than boys of the same age. . . . Ed studied for the love of it, . . . history, Latin and mathematics were his favorite subjects."[12]

When Ed was sixteen, his family became concerned about his health and decided that he should spend a year in the outdoors, working on Murray Brown's farm near Goliad. The change proved beneficial. The young Lasater gained strength and was ready to return to school. He was a serious student, and he was already making plans, big plans, for the future: "My ambition was to be a lawyer. With the enthusiasm

[9] Ibid.; interview, Sarah Cunningham Caldwell, June 26, 1971.

[10] Ed C. Lasater to Sarah Jane Lasater, October 9, 1887, Lasater Files, in possession of Garland M. Lasater, Falfurrias.

[11] Ada Lasater Caldwell, "Recollections," p. 1.

[12] Ibid.

and exuberance of youth I dreamed of being the first lawyer in the land. My father was dubious. . . . He hinted that perhaps I was not strong enough to lay the entire legal world at my feet."[13]

About this time Albert Lasater's health began to fail. For this reason, the elder Lasater suggested that Ed spend one more year "roughing it," promising his son that he could resume his schooling the following year. Ed obeyed his father's wish, but he did not give up his dream of further study: "The law seemed to beckon me; I yearned for college life."[14]

His hopes were never to be fulfilled, however. His father's health continued to decline, and Ed was called upon to look after Albert Lasater's sheep venture.[15] Ed's academic training had ended. He left the classroom behind and began to learn something about handling sheep from his new associates, the Mexican shepherds. Ed respected the ability of his companions on the range: "I know of no better shepherds than the Mexicans. . . . The control they can acquire over a flock of sheep is remarkable."[16]

Ed Lasater responded to his family's need and devoted himself to the family's sheep business. But forty years later he still remembered his reaction to the frustration of his youthful ambition: "I felt as though I was losing out on everything I desired most in life. I could think of nothing but my brilliant career at the bar. . . . I have often regretted the fate which led me from the path I longed to follow."[17]

Lasater's nature was positive. His college career was ended before it had a chance to begin, but he found other challenges and other rewards. His new life took him "out into the open, under the stars, where I had time to think and to study nature. . . . Instead of finishing

[13] Ed C. Lasater, "What I Did When I Lost $130,000 Farming," *Farm and Fireside* (March, 1919), quoted in Lasater, "Meat Packer Legislation," statement before the Committee on Agriculture, U.S. House of Representatives, March 1, 2, 3, and 6, 1920, p. 205, in Edward C. Lasater Collection, Eugene C. Barker Texas History Center, University of Texas, Austin.

[14] Ibid.

[15] Ibid. Garland Lasater related that during Ed Lasater's years in the sheep business, he would take flocks out to the Tilden and Cotulla area to fatten them during the summer grazing period. Lasater would keep a Mexican shepherd with each flock and would go around checking on them and taking them supplies (interview, Garland Lasater, February 21, 1981).

[16] Ed C. Lasater, "Meat Packer Legislation," p. 205.

[17] Ibid.

my education at college, my final degrees were taken in various camps between the Rio Grande and the Kansas line."[18]

During the time when he was learning the sheep business, Ed Lasater made a trip to the Realitos area to visit Edward Caldwell. Caldwell had purchased a 12,000-acre ranch adjoining the Duval County ranch he had leased earlier. He had decided in 1880 that the time was right to buy land: "Prices were bound to go up; fences were being built all around, and free pasturage was rapidly disappearing."[19]

Caldwell was in the midst of moving his home from Borjas to his new property with twelve yoke of oxen. In Ada's absence, he did not have time to cook for his brother-in-law, but in anticipation of Lasater's visit, Caldwell prepared a large supply of oatmeal. He ate it with condensed milk and accompanied this meal with coffee.

Caldwell offered Lasater oatmeal for breakfast the morning after his arrival. Lasater said that he did not eat oatmeal and did not drink coffee. The same exchange took place at lunch. At supper, Lasater accepted the coffee but still refused the oatmeal. The following day Caldwell was relieved when his brother-in-law relented: "By evening the second day he had acquired a taste for oatmeal and learned to like it fine."[20]

That 1881 visit was probably Lasater's first look at the country around Realitos. He was twenty-one that year, when he rode his horse over the grasslands along the Los Olmos Creek, several miles west of where it winds its way southeasterly across Ignacio de la Peña's grant. Lasater may have ridden farther south toward the Palo Blanco Creek, or east to the big lake. Circumstances had ended his schooling early and his plans for a legal career.[21] Perhaps on this visit he already glimpsed a different future, one that would lead him back to Los Olmos Creek and to the Loma Blanca.

The years during which Edward Caldwell and the Lasaters raised sheep were the last years of the big northern cattle drives. The trail

[18] Ibid.

[19] Edward H. Caldwell, "Notes and Facts in the Life of E. H. Caldwell," Corpus Christi, 1939, p. 31.

[20] Ibid., p. 35.

[21] Edward Everett Dale, *The Range Cattle Industry: Ranching on the Great Plains from 1865 to 1925*, p. 14.

drives began at the end of the Civil War, when Texas was a vast reservoir overflowing with cattle. In 1867, a three-year-old steer was worth less than ten dollars per head in Texas. That same steer would bring thirty-eight to forty dollars in Kansas and Illinois and as much as seventy to eighty dollars in the East. The trail drive began as a means of getting the Texas cattle to the markets, and between 1866 and 1885 Texas cowboys drove more than 250,000 head north each year.[22]

John Bennett, Sr., was one of many young men from South Texas who accumulated his initial capital by driving herds to northern markets. Dillard R. Fant, who grew up near the Lasaters in Goliad County, took some 200,000 head up the trail during the years he engaged in the business.[23] E. R. Rachal and his brothers took a herd north in 1871: "We went from the mouth of the Nueces River to Ellsworth, Kansas without opening a gate."[24]

The years 1882–85 have traditionally been described as the boom years of the western cattle industry. The boom was followed by a bust; the glamor of rising prices and large profits disappeared during nearly a decade of declining markets. Cattlemen throughout the western range area were hurt financially: "The great depression in the ranching industry and the consequent distress of most men engaged in it after 1885 was almost, if not entirely, as apparent in Texas as on the northern plains."[25]

Financial difficulties had overtaken the Texas sheep raisers several years earlier. In 1880, Caldwell thought he could see the end of the profitable years in the sheep business approaching, and in that year he began making the switch from sheep to cattle. The year 1882 was very dry in Duval County. There was no surface water on Caldwell's ranch,

[22] Ibid., p. 43.

[23] J. Marvin Hunter, ed., *The Trail Drivers of Texas*, p. 517. Colonel Isaac T. Pryor, who worked closely with Lasater in the state and national cattle associations during the first two decades of the twentieth century, estimated that a herd on the trail would move between 450 and 500 miles per month. Pryor estimated that it cost $500 per month to move a herd of 3,000 head (ibid., p. 367).

[24] Ibid., p. 809. E. R. Rachal returned by rail from Kansas City to New Orleans via Saint Louis. From New Orleans he traveled by boat to Texas. Rachal, his sons Ed Rachal, Jr., and Frank C. Rachal, and his nephew Frank S. Rachal were all early Falfurrias area residents (ibid.).

[25] Dale, *The Range Cattle Industry*, p. 117.

and he dug three wells, "while we were fencing the 12,000 acres of lovely open valley grasses." The wells did not produce sufficient water for his flocks, however, and Caldwell was forced to drive them to Charco Redondo, a watering hole near the southern Duval County line. There he found thousands of sheep that had been forced off other ranches for the same reason.[26]

By 1883, every factor had conspired against the sheep man. "The sheep business from every standpoint was in a desperately depressed condition. Drought, disease, and the low price of wool had forced many out of business."[27] Before the spring shearing that year, sheep were worth $2.00 per head. Later in the spring, Caldwell got no response to his offer to sell for $1.25 per head. In June, no buyers could be found at any price in the Realitos area. Caldwell concluded that the only solution was to drive his flocks north in search of a buyer. He took his sheep to Abilene, passing through Pearsall, Kerrville, and San Angelo on the way. In Abilene he found a buyer and liquidated his remaining sheep.[28]

While Caldwell was making that 525-mile drive, he received word from Ada that her father had died in Oakville in July, 1883. At the time of Albert Lasater's death, Ada was in San Antonio with her mother, who was staying in Edward Cunningham's home while Lois went to school there.

Ed and Tom buried their father in Oakville. Ed made the two-day ride on horseback to inform his mother. When Sarah Jane Lasater saw her son, she asked immediately, "How is your Papa?" Ed replied, "All is well with Papa."[29]

---

[26] E. H. Caldwell, "Notes," pp. 35–36.

[27] Edward H. Caldwell, "Life and Activities of Edward Cunningham Lasater," Corpus Christi, 1937, p. 5.

[28] E. H. Caldwell, "Notes," p. 38. Caldwell later recalled that trip with pleasure: "The memory of that drive of over five hundred and twenty-five miles is a delightful one. We had all sorts of experiences, but all the time we were seeing a wonderful undeveloped country, enjoying the best of health, all in the open . . ." (ibid.).

[29] Ibid., p. 39; Ada Lasater Caldwell, "Recollections," p. 4. Emily Edwards stated in a taped interview that Ed Lasater's father, Albert, was "killed on the ranch." Evan Anders wrote that Albert Lasater was "murdered" in 1883 (interview, Emily Edwards, February 25, 1967; Evan M. Anders, "Bosses Under Siege: The Politics of South Texas during the Progressive Era" [Ph.D. diss., University of Texas at Austin, 1978], p. 117). These two statements evidently confuse Albert Lasater's death with that of his father,

Albert Lasater had purchased a ranch near Oakville in 1882, and had moved his family to that Live Oak County property after selling his ranching interests in Atascosa County.[30] Lasater's assets at the time of his death consisted of about 7,000 acres of land and 3,000 head of sheep. His debts, largely to William Koehler and company, exceeded the value of his assets by about $30,000.[31]

The sheep business was in a depressed state. Wool had declined in value from thirty cents to six cents per pound. Ed Lasater cashed in his father's sheep by fattening them and shipping them to the Chicago market. There he realized sixty cents per head for the sheep his father had purchased for six dollars per head several years earlier.[32]

This experience discouraged the young Lasater, and he decided to turn the mortgaged property over to the noteholders. On the way to San Antonio to do this, he overtook a herd of horses being driven to that city to be sold. Lasater bought the horses and drove them on to San Antonio where he sold them at a handsome profit. With that money, he was able to pay the loan company the accrued interest, and he assumed responsibility for his father's remaining indebtedness.[33]

His uncle, Colonel Edward Cunningham, played a vital role in launching the young Lasater's business career. The livestock operation Cunningham had started in Bexar County in 1856 was interrupted by his service in the Civil War. Cunningham organized and commanded a company called the Mustang Greys, which became part of General

who was murdered in Arkansas when Albert was a young boy. Albert's mother died shortly afterward, and he was raised by his half-sister, Ada Parks (Mrs. John) Henry, a merchant in Van Buren, Arkansas, and later in New Orleans (notes written by Ada Lasater Caldwell, June 16, 1930, in Edward C. Lasater Collection, Eugene C. Barker Texas History Center, University of Texas, Austin). According to Sarah Caldwell, Albert Lasater died of a heart attack (interview, Sarah Caldwell, June 26, 1971). His remains were later moved from Oakville to the Bennett-Lasater burial plot in San Antonio (John M. Bennett to Sarah Caldwell, August 7, 1937, in Caldwell Files, Corpus Christi).

[30] Deed Records, Live Oak County, Book G, pp. 266, 356–57. The deed describes part of the Live Oak County property as follows: "Beginning at an Elm marked X, the upper corner of the Santiago McGlovin grant of one league and the lower corner of the said William O'Docharty two leagues at a point of rocks on the east bank of the Nueces River."

[31] Letter dictated by Ed C. Lasater, "To My Children," n.d., in the handwriting of Mary Miller Lasater, in Lasater Files, Falfurrias.

[32] Ibid.

[33] E. H. Caldwell, "Life and Activities," p. 6.

Hood's Fourth Texas Brigade. When the war was over, Cunningham returned to Texas and purchased five sugar plantations in Fort Bend County. His extensive operations later earned him a reputation as "the Texas Sugar King."[34]

Shortly after Albert Lasater's death, Cunningham took his twenty-three-year-old nephew into the San Antonio National Bank and introduced him with the statement "I will endorse this young man for anything he wants." In the following years, Ed Lasater used his uncle's endorsement for up to $40,000 at a time.[35]

Colonel George W. Brackenridge founded the San Antonio National Bank in 1866.[36] Unlike Cunningham, who had a distinguished career in the Confederate Army, Brackenridge had joined the Union forces during the war. After the war, as a Republican in a largely Democratic area, Brackenridge was an enigma in more than one way. He was an unusual man to be a central figure in South Texas financial circles during the last half of the nineteenth century: "Melancholy and introspective, he was subject to spells of insomnia during which he sometimes sat for hours at his organ, filling the night with classical music."[37]

Brackenridge's personality may have been a curiosity, but the colonel's bank was actively and aggressively involved in financing the Texas range cattle industry during the trail drive days and in later years: "Brackenridge counted among his valued patrons some of the best known cattlemen of the era—Mifflin Kenedy, Richard King, Shanghai Pierce, Charles Goodnight, J. R. Blocker, Lafayette Ward, and Ben Q. Ward."[38]

The San Antonio National Bank extended liberal credit terms to Texas cattlemen; this practice kept Brackenridge constantly at odds with the bank examiners and in continual correspondence with the

---

[34] *San Antonio Daily Express*, July 3, 1891; A. J. Sowell, *History of Fort Bend County, Texas*, pp. 348–49. Ed Cunningham was wounded fourteen times during the war and his brother Thomas was killed in an encounter General Robert E. Lee called one of the most brilliant charges in the Civil War. In that battle, the Confederates turned McClellan's right flank and saved Richmond (ibid.).

[35] Ed C. Lasater, "To My Children."

[36] Marilyn McAdams Sibley, *George W. Brackenridge: Maverick Philanthropist*, p. 80. The bank charter issued July 30, 1866, was the fourth national bank charter in Texas (ibid., p. 92).

[37] Ibid., p. 11.

[38] Ibid., p. 98.

comptroller of the currency: "The examiners regularly paid homage to his business acumen and good management, but they just as regularly complained of his 'excessive loans' to cattlemen."[39]

Brackenridge's form of banking was highly personal. He relied more on the borrower's character than on the collateral offered as security.[40] Brackenridge evidently saw sufficient character as well as some promise in Ed Lasater. After first loaning the young trader money on his uncle's endorsement, Brackenridge continued to work with Lasater after he accumulated property and credit of his own. Thirty years after Cunningham introduced his nephew, Brackenridge's San Antonio Loan and Trust Company would arrange for Lasater one of the first million-dollar bonds issued on a Texas ranching operation.[41]

The big loans, however, would come later. Before Lasater could begin accumulating property of his own, he had his father's debts to settle, and he had to begin generating some income. Having liquidated his family's sheep interests, Lasater commenced trading in livestock and became a cattle buyer, associated with several commission houses in Fort Worth and Kansas City. This work took Lasater all over South Texas as he contracted cattle for delivery to northern buyers.[42] Lasater traveled as far east as New York and Connecticut trading horses. Letters he wrote to his mother in 1887 provide a few details about those trading ventures and on the young Ed Lasater's approach to life. He took a herd of horses to the East, and he moved them from one town to another trying to sell them: "At Watkins [New York] I squandered some of my hard-earned dollars in printer's ink, advertised my sale most thoroughly, talked until I could rival Ingersoll for eloquence in expatiating upon the good points of a Texas horse." But weather interfered at Watkins, and his sale had to be postponed. Lasater was able to make a few sales by private treaty, but his horses were selling at a slower pace than he had expected. He assured his mother that he was still at work despite some disappointments: "I have been a little discouraged but not whipped, or as Tom [his brother] would express it, 'slightly disfigured but still in the ring.'"[43]

[39] Ibid., p. 99.

[40] Ibid., p. 97.

[41] Deed of Trust Records, Brooks County, vol. 2, pp. 115–45; interview, Garland Lasater, February 21, 1981.

[42] Interview, Garland Lasater, February 21, 1981.

[43] Ed C. Lasater to Sarah Jane Lasater, October 9, 1887.

Lasater was still on the East Coast when he turned twenty-seven on November 5, 1887. That day found him in Woodbury, Connecticut, trying to "sell six Texas plugs to these 'nutmeg' Yankees." He was approaching the end of his eastern horse-trading venture, and he happily anticipated its conclusion: "If, within the next few days I can persuade them to buy my horses, there won't be a particle of the feeling of unappreciated genius within my heart."[44]

In each communication written to Sarah Jane Lasater from the East, her son expressed confidence in his ability and exhibited an optimistic outlook. While telling his mother about the various complications encountered, he continually assured her of his faith in himself and in the future: "Put your trust in your auburn-faced boy. . . . He is going to get there, yes, and with both feet."[45]

After seven years of trading cattle and horses, Ed Lasater finished paying off the debts he assumed after his father's death. In 1890, Lasater and his brother Tom formed a partnership with J. T. Aycock of New Orleans. This partnership, called Aycock and Lasater Bros., operated a livestock commission business that shipped cattle from South Texas to the New Orleans market.[46] The firm's history was cut short by an unexpected event.

South Texas was a frontier area in the last quarter of the nineteenth century. Edward Caldwell wrote of the isolation and dangers that were part of life on a Texas ranch during that period. The frontier conditions created a lawless situation that spawned widespread violence and frequent killings. In 1891, Texas newspapers reported one incident after another in which area residents resorted to arms to settle disputes. That year the LaSalle County Law and Order League passed a resolution stating: "crime has prevailed in some localities in our state to such an extent as to deter immigration, to intimidate capital and to depreciate property values. . . ."[47] In June, 1891, the *San Antonio*

[44] Ed C. Lasater to Sarah Jane Lasater, November 6, 1887.
[45] Ed C. Lasater to Sarah Jane Lasater, October 9, 1887. Sarah Jane Lasater maintained the home on the ranch near Oakville for her two sons and her daughter Lois from Albert Lasater's death in 1883 until 1887. That year she moved to Corpus Christi to live with her daughter Ada's family. (E. H. Caldwell, "Life and Activities," p. 9).
[46] E. H. Caldwell, "Life and Activities, p. 7; *San Antonio Daily Express*, June 21, 1891.
[47] *San Antonio Daily Express*, July 25, 1891.

Daily Express reported that the city's Board of Trade voiced the sentiments of the area in endorsing Governor Hogg's attempts to curb lawlessness: "No community in the state will stand closer . . . to the Governor in his efforts to enforce the laws against carrying deadly weapons and to punish murderers. . . ."[48]

That same month, a story from the border reported a "sensational affair," the discovery of a plot to assassinate a Mexican governor who was visiting in Laredo. A few days earlier, W. C. Bowen, the editor of the *Cotulla Ledger*, was killed and his brother wounded. Bowen, whose body was riddled with bullets, had "waged a conspicuous war on the lawless elements of southwestern Texas," and his murder created quite an uproar in that locality.[49]

Ed Lasater was in Pearsall, Texas, on June 19, 1891, when he received word that his brother Tom had been killed. A Neel Ricks had shot Tom on the Lasater property at Oakville, and a number of conflicting versions of the incident were reported in papers during the following days.[50] Two days after the shooting, the *San Antonio Daily Express* stated that Ricks had been in Ed Lasater's employ for several years. The article further commented that Tom Lasater was reported to be "a peaceable and quiet citizen" and that "so far as can be learned, there is nothing detrimental to the record of Ricks, but he was supposed to be quick on the trigger and usually 'fixed for emergencies'." The story added that the "better element" of Live Oak County was known to be opposed to the practice of "shooting it out."[51]

The following day J. M. Dobie, a rancher from Lagarto, brought to the paper a firsthand version of Tom's killing. Ed Lasater had hired Ricks only until his brother returned from Alabama, where the Lasaters were pasturing cattle. When Tom returned to the ranch at Oakville, he and Ricks got into a dispute about who was in charge. Tom went into town, returning the following day with the deputy sheriff.

---

[48] Ibid., June 29, 1891.

[49] Ibid., June 10 and June 19, 1891. The June 19 story alleged that the governor "would have been assassinated for a paltry $300." Alfred Allee and Jasper Lyons were accused of Bowen's murder. Allee surrendered himself to authorities, and Lyons was arrested a few days later by Captain James A. Brooks's company of Texas Rangers (ibid., July 16, 1891).

[50] Ibid., June 20, 1891.

[51] Ibid., June 21, 1891.

The killing took place with both Lasater's and Ricks's friends claiming the other shot first.[52]

One week after the killing, a story reported that there was "some talk of bad blood developing between friends of the two men, but Captain McNelly's company of fifteen rangers are present at Oakville to prevent any outbreak, and things are reported to be quiet." Several days later, a group of Oakville residents wrote the *San Antonio Daily Express* denying that Tom Lasater's friends had attempted to incite mob violence against Neel Ricks. The letter was signed by the county sheriff, two deputy sheriffs, the assessor, the county clerk, and twenty-five other citizens of Oakville.[53]

Whatever the facts were in that killing, such events occurred frequently and were indicative of conditions in Texas at the time.[54] After Tom Lasater's death, Colonel C. M. Rogers of Austin wrote the San Antonio paper that he had known Lasater well and that he regretted his death. He went on to express his opinion about why such incidents occurred: "There seems to be prevalent among cattlemen . . . a mistaken notion that the man who is left in charge of a big ranch should be a desperate character." Rogers stated that "the dangers are great and the opportunities for dispute and trouble between neighboring ranchmen numerous, . . ." but he argued that this was all the more reason for replacing arms with amicable and intelligent settlement of disputes.

---

[52] Ibid., June 22, 1891. Dobie further stated in that article that Ricks was reported "to have shot a colored man on the ranch last year, at which time he was befriended and assisted out of the difficulty by Ed Lasater." A telegram from Ed Lasater attached to the article in the *Express* included this statement: "The killing took place on the ranch and not in the town of Oakville. My brother had entire and complete control of my interests in Live Oak County at the time of his killing. He discharged Neel Ricks from his employ the day previous to the killing."

[53] Ibid., June 26, 1891, and July 4, 1891. After a trial, Ricks was apparently set free. Ed Lasater was determined to find Ricks and avenge his brother's death. Edward Caldwell intervened and convinced Lasater not to pursue that course of action (interview, Garland M. Lasater, April 9, 1981). Ten years after Tom Lasater's death, Walter Nations shot and killed Ricks in Alice, Texas (*Alice Echo*, January 24, 1901).

[54] A number of different versions of this incident were passed down through the family. One related that Tom Lasater returned unexpectedly from Mississippi and found the men at the Oakville ranch putting their brand on Lasater cattle. Returning to the ranch the next day with the deputy sheriff, he was shot in the back. Another story has Tom killed by a horse thief he was pursuing (interviews, John M. Bennett, February 24, 1967; Sarah Caldwell, June 26, 1971; Tom Lasater, November 9, 1980).

The newspaper called Rogers a "pioneer in requiring his men to lay aside their pistols while drawing pay within his enclosures."[55]

Ed Lasater lost his partner and only brother in 1891. The following year on December 28, he started his own family with his marriage to Martha (Patti) Noble Bennett, the daughter of John Bennett, Sr., of Sweet Home. Shortly after that marriage, both the Bennetts and the Lasaters moved to San Antonio. The young couple's first son, Edward, was born there on November 17, 1893.[56] As Ed Lasater's business interests developed in the area south of the Nueces River over the next several years, he and his young bride would live in Corpus Christi, on the Shaeffer ranch near Alice, and at La Mota—La Mota de Falfurrias.[57]

The year 1883 was one of transition for several of the seven families who moved to Texas from Mexico, Alabama, Arkansas, and Tennessee. Albert Lasater died that year, the same year that his eldest daughter and her husband, Edward Caldwell, sold their ranch near Realitos and moved to Corpus Christi to start a new life. It was a disastrous year in the sheep business. Cattlemen were still enjoying a boom period, however, and that year one group of Texas cowboys drove three thousand steers north from the Bennett and West ranch in Jackson County to Colorado and Nebraska.[58]

[55] *San Antonio Daily Express*, June 24, 1891.

[56] E. H. Caldwell, "Life and Activities," p. 9. Ed Lasater later rented a residence in Corpus Christi alongside the home of Edward and Ada Lasater Caldwell.

[57] Ibid. Correspondence from Ed Lasater in the H. P. Drought and Co. files gives his address in the following places: San Antonio (1895), Corpus Christi (1898), Realitos (1899), and Falfurrias (1902). *La Mota* in this context means a mott of trees. The Reverend W. E. Caldwell wrote in a letter shortly after moving to Corpus Christi: "All this with a ride to the country and a romp in the shade of a mott of trees, with the broad prairie spread out on one side and the waters of the bay on the other. . . ." In a footnote, Caldwell explained that *mott* was a word peculiar to Texas, of Spanish origin, and meant "little grove" (Margaret Lasater Clark, *On This Bluff: Centennial History, 1867–1967, First Presbyterian Church*, p. 31). La Mota de Falfurrias was (and is) a prominent grove of very large live oaks located on the western boundary of de la Peña's Los Olmos y Loma Blanca grant. The term *La Mota* was used to describe other locations in the area as well. Another account of early life in the area refers to "the rural settlement called Mota de Olmos near Benavides in Duval County" (Priscilla L. Buckley and William F. Buckley, Jr., eds., *W.F.B.—An Appreciation*, p. 11).

[58] Hunter, *The Trail Drivers of Texas*, p. 802. The author of this chapter, J. A. Humphries, does not state which of the northern trails they took, but he does say that it could have been called the "River Route" because they forded every major river of any

South and west of Bennett's ranch, below the Nueces River, a partition decree issued just before Christmas in 1883 put the court's stamp of approval on the property lines that divided the two tracts awarded to Ignacio de la Peña in 1831: the Los Olmos and the Los Olmos y Loma Blanca grants.[59] The divisions established by that decree underscored the passage of time, the temporary role of those who serve as stewards of the soil, and the ebb and flow in the worldly fortunes of those whose lives are linked, sometimes almost inextricably, with the land.

Official decrees and confirmations spanning three different governments gave de la Peña and his descendants good title to fifteen leagues of land, a little more than sixty-six thousand acres. However, even before the Texas patents were issued in 1870, de la Peña's heirs had begun to sell off their father's claim.

In 1862 Ignacio de la Peña's son, Ignacio, Jr., sold one of the three leagues that he inherited. The sale price was five hundred dollars, or about eleven cents an acre.[60] Within seven years after the Texas patent was granted, the younger de la Peña sold his remaining holdings in two transactions.[61] His total revenue from his share of the two grants, 13,272 acres, was eighteen hundred dollars.

Several de la Peña descendants experienced what many other landowners did during the last two decades of the nineteenth century in that sandy region: during periods of falling sheep markets and drought they simply had no money, not even enough to pay taxes. Among those whose properties were sold at public auction for delinquent taxes were two of de la Peña's grandsons. The county tax collector sold ranches belonging to José Angel Hinojosa and Juan de la Garza in

---

importance in the area: the San Antonio, Guadalupe, San Marcos, Colorado, Brazos, Red River, Cimarron, and Arkansas (ibid.).

[59] The Los Olmos grant was a five-league tract that joined Los Olmos y Loma Blanco on the west. Los Olmos was originally awarded to Juan Antonio Canales, but it was patented to de la Peña along with the Los Olmos y Loma Blanco in 1870 (Virginia H. Taylor, *Index to Spanish and Mexican Land Grants*, p. 58). Ignacio de la Peña also applied for and received title to a grant several miles west of the Los Olmos tract. It was called "Los Magueyes de Palo Blanco," and had originally been petitioned for in 1808 by his father. De la Peña was awarded the grant in 1831 (ibid.).

[60] Deed Records, Starr County, Book D, pp. 6–7. This property was sold to Diego García, father of Matías García Saldaña.

[61] Ibid., pp. 397–99, and Book E, p. 366. These two leagues were sold to Benito García and Manuel García Canales.

1881 for back taxes totalling $31.55 and $50.29, respectively. Such sales took place with considerable frequency, but in these two cases, as in most others, the properties were returned to their owners within the two-year period allowed for redemption.[62]

By 1883 only one-half of the fifteen leagues granted to Ignacio de la Peña in the Los Olmos and the Los Olmos y Loma Blanca tracts remained in the hands of his heirs and their families. The partition decree issued on December 21 of that year shows that only three of de la Peña's heirs owned land in the two grants: Juan de la Garza and his brother Bernardo, grandsons of de la Peña, owned two leagues; Tomasa Hinojosa, a granddaughter, owned one and one-half leagues. In addition, Tomasa's husband, Matías García Saldaña, had purchased four leagues, which brought the family total to seven and one-half leagues. The other half of the acreage in the two grants was owned in 1883 by Manuel García Canales (two leagues), C. C. Lewis (one league), Benito García (one and one-half leagues) and Henry Seeligson (three leagues).[63]

In the years following that 1883 partition, the evolution of the financial status of Matías García and his wife can be surmised from three consecutive mortgages, which placed a steadily increasing debt load against their property. The first was a $4,000 loan in 1886 which was due in seven years.[64] Despite the extended period allowed for payment, García paid off that note in one year and increased his indebtedness with a loan of $10,000 arranged by a San Antonio loan company.[65]

The same year that García transacted this note, Ed Lasater was on the East Coast selling horses. He wrote his mother from Ovid, New York: "While the prospects are not flattering for big profits in this speculation, I don't think there is any possibility for a loss."[66] If in fact Ed Lasater returned to Texas with a profit after that trip, he finished the year ahead of most of his fellow livestock men.

Out west the cattle industry had plunged into another of its periodic crises, and the price decline that began in the mid-1880s was producing increasingly negative and discouraging news. Early in 1887, after the failure of the two-million-dollar Dolores Land and Cattle

---

[62] Deed Records, Starr County, Book G, pp. 124–26.
[63] Deed Records, Starr County, Book F, pp. 674–77.
[64] Trust Deed Records, Starr County, Book A, pp. 108–10.
[65] Ibid., pp. 172–80.
[66] Ed C. Lasater to Sarah Jane Lasater, October 9, 1887.

Company, "cattlemen became loathe to pick up their newspapers."[67] Later that same year, Swan Brothers, the largest cattle operators in Wyoming, announced a reorganization. Swan's collapse, trumpeted in front-page banner headlines, shocked cattlemen everywhere.[68]

Conditions were equally rough in South Texas, where low cattle and sheep prices continued over the next several years. The note Matías García signed in 1887 was due in payments spread over ten years, but once again he paid the debt early to make way for a larger mortgage. In 1889 García borrowed eighteen thousand dollars, this time mortgaging all of the property he and his wife owned in the two grants. That amounted to an indebtedness of seventy-two cents per acre. The loan, at ten percent interest, was due in ten years.[69]

Even that loan did not prove sufficient to sustain their operation. Four years later, in 1893, the county sheriff sold García's land in the Los Olmos y Loma Blanca grant to cover delinquent taxes of $449.05.[70] And then on March 27, 1895, García and his wife sold all of their holdings in these two grants, 25,709 acres, to John M. Bennett, Sr., and Ed C. Lasater for $1.00 an acre.[71]

Two years later Juan and Bernardo de la Garza became the last of de la Peña's heirs to sell their land in these two grants. In 1897 these de la Peña grandsons sold Ed Lasater a little more than two leagues, approximately nine thousand acres for fifty cents per acre.[72]

Sixty-six years after de la Peña had first applied for title to that isolated block of land in the area Major Gaines had called uninhabitable and fit for no useful purpose, the fifteen leagues in the Los Olmos and the Los Olmos y Loma Blanca grants passed out of his family's hands. De la Peña had seen more potential in this country than the

---

[67] Gene M. Gressley, *Bankers and Cattlemen*, p. 244.

[68] Ibid., p. 245.

[69] Trust Deed Records, Starr County, Book A, pp. 333–40.

[70] Deed Records, Starr County, Book P, p. 31. This property was redeemed by García in 1895 at the time he sold the property.

[71] Ibid., Book O, pp. 395–98. Various years have been given in articles and conversations to mark the date of Ed Lasater's first land purchase in the Falfurrias area. No deed record of any purchase could be located prior to the Matías García transaction in March, 1895. E. H. Caldwell also names that as the year of Lasater's first purchase (Ed. H. Caldwell, "Life and Activities," p. 10; E. H. Caldwell, "In Appreciation of Edward Cunningham Lasater," p. 6). Lasater's own statement corroborates the 1895 date (Lasater, "Meat Packer Legislation," p. 207).

[72] Transcribed Deeds from Starr County, Brooks County, IV, 499, and V, 60.

major had. For more than half a century de la Peña and his descendants lived on this property and pastured their livestock there until the elements and the collapse of the sheep business broke their hold on the land.

Now new money and new methods combined with youthful energy and optimism would once again go to work to make that land produce. But nature and the livestock markets would again and again test the staying power and the fortitude of those who ran their herds in the sand and brush of the country surrounding the stately promontory of Loma Blanca.

CHAPTER 3

All the Land That Joins

Texas cowmen have extended civilization, have advanced
commerce, have made the plains the home of wealth and
refinement and have made Texas what it is today.
                                    —1902 Oration in memory of Jim Loving

IN 1893 Edward Cunningham Lasater was thirty-three years old. He
had accumulated experience and credit, and he was ready for action:
"That was the very year I had chosen to become ambitious. I was determined to make a fortune. I could see no use postponing the matter
or in taking a number of years to do it; I proposed to make a fortune
right then."[1]

Early in 1893 Lasater laid the foundation for this fortune by contracting some twenty-five thousand head of cattle. A dry spell spread
over South Texas, and the cattle did not reach a marketable condition
on the range that spring as anticipated. In June financial panic engulfed
the country, and the cattle market plummeted. Ed Lasater had surveyed the terrain. He had studied the business, but when he had
plunged into it in 1893, his timing was faulty. "In that year another of
the periodic depressions that characterized the early economic history
of the United States descended, wreaking havoc on many of the nation's
banks."[2] Not only banks were hurt; the steel industry was depressed
and the spectacular failure of the Philadelphia and Reading Railroad
contributed to the economic dislocation.[3]

---

[1] Ed C. Lasater, "What I Did When I Lost $130,000 Farming," *Farm and Fireside*,
March, 1919, quoted in Lasater, "Meat Packer Legislation," statement before the Committee on Agriculture, U.S. House of Representatives, March 1, 2, 3, and 6, 1920,
p. 206, in Edward C. Lasater Collection, Eugene C. Barker Texas History Center, University of Texas, Austin.

[2] Marilyn McAdams Sibley, *George W. Brackenridge: Maverick Philanthropist*,
p. 90.

[3] Gene M. Gressley, *Bankers and Cattlemen*, p. 17.

In the cattle arena the depressed market that resulted from the panic was merely the final extension of the declining price levels that had characterized the livestock industry since the end of the boom period in the middle 1880s. The last northern trail drive originating in Texas was in 1885. That year cattle prices started down and went down almost continually for nine years. Animals that had been worth twenty-five dollars per head in 1884 dropped to six dollars per head in 1893.[4]

Caught in the middle of this widespread business crisis and faced with more obligations than he could meet, Lasater wrote his former partner, J. T. Aycock of New Orleans, on July 4, 1893. Lasater had contracted for an additional eight thousand head of cattle for delivery in August, but circumstances intervened: "The present tightness in money matters renders it impossible for me to comply with my engagements to receive and pay for same according to contract." Despite his predicament, Lasater remained optimistic and confident: "Now if you have any surplus cash that you want to put to work earning good interest, you can accomplish that end and help me out of a tight. . . . I know there is a fortune in carrying my deals."[5]

Aycock's response to Lasater's invitation to participate in his deal is not known. Instead of being able to dispose quickly and profitably of the cattle he had purchased, Lasater was forced to feed many of them through the following winter. That was an expensive proposition, and the cattle market in the spring of 1894 reached new low levels. When all of the cattle were sold, Lasater had done $800,000 worth of business. He lost all his capital, and instead of a quick fortune he had accumulated debts totaling some $130,000.[6]

The outlook was bleak for the young man who had aspired to be the nation's greatest lawyer and who had decided only twelve months earlier to make his fortune in one year. But his buoyant spirit carried the day: "the man who lets failure discourage him doesn't deserve to succeed. I went back at it hammer and tongs." Lasater's ambitious plans had been rudely buffeted, but in that painful financial experience he found purpose and resolve. "Whatever I possess today was built out of that failure," he wrote a quarter-century later. After more than a dec-

---

[4] J. Marvin Hunter, ed., *The Trail Drivers of Texas*, p. 368.

[5] Ed C. Lasater to J. T. Aycock, July 4, 1893, in Lasater Files, in possession of Garland M. Lasater, Falfurrias.

[6] Ed C. Lasater, "Meat Packer Legislation, pp. 206–207.

ade of criss-crossing South Texas on horseback, Lasater knew the land well, and he was confident of its productive capacity: "I still had faith in the country. . . . I knew the range was there; I felt sure the opportunity was there."[7]

Lasater concluded that the misfortune he had shared with other cattlemen in 1893 and early 1894 was merely a backdrop for the prosperity that lay ahead. He had simply picked the wrong year. Once again the young entrepreneur was "slightly disfigured but still in the ring." He remained confident and more determined than ever to succeed.

As 1894 drew to a close, Ed Lasater was ready to try again. He plunged back into the business on a bigger scale than ever, contracting thirty thousand head for delivery in the spring of 1895. At the same time he began buying property as rapidly as he could secure credit and locate willing settlers.[8]

In 1894 Ed Lasater rode onto the white hill and halted his horse. He looked out to the southwest across a wide expanse of cracked earth, white from the heavy salt content. It was not a lake then, just a dry bed where eddies of wind carried sand and salt back and forth across its parched surface. He had sent Bob Rice down from Live Oak County to have a look at this country. Rice had returned saying that he would not trade the west pasture of the Oakville Ranch for the entire area surrounding the tract where Ignacio de la Peña had settled more than sixty years earlier.[9]

But Ed Lasater had been there before; he had seen the lake when it was full. He knew how quickly that sandy land could blossom with a little rain. From that prominent rise he could see the future, and he was excited. He would own that white hill, and he would own all the land surrounding it.

Goliad was the scene of several pivotal events in the Texans' fight to separate their territory from Mexico. The independent character and the heroic courage Goliad symbolized deeply impressed young Ed Lasater. "My boyhood was thrilled with stories of the Texas fight for independence. I roamed over historic ground. The spirit of freedom

---

[7] Ibid., p. 206.
[8] Ibid., p. 207.
[9] Interview, Tom Lasater, January 12, 1980.

was in the air—boundless, buoyant freedom."[10] The independence and the optimism that filled the air in Goliad County appear to have motivated and inspired more than one future entrepreneur who rode his pony as a child along the banks of the San Antonio River. The area proved to be a spawning ground for men who enjoyed taking big risks in the cattle business. Five of the largest cattle operators in South Texas at the turn of the century were men who had grown up around Goliad: Dillard Fant (b. 1841), Cyrus Lucas (b. 1857), W. W. Jones (b. 1858), Ed Lasater (b. 1860), and Tom Coleman (b. 1861). Among them, they controlled several million acres of land, and they handled hundreds of thousands of head around the turn of the century.[11]

Goliad sits some fifty miles north and east of the Nueces River. South and west of that river, Starr and Duval counties in 1900 encompassed a wide territory in the center of a broad area of rangeland stretching to the Rio Grande. Before 1890 a majority of the surnames in the deed records of those two counties were of Spanish or Mexican origin. In the following decades the shift of ownership from the original Mexican landowners to Anglo cattlemen and farmers accelerated. Two sons of Goliad, Bill Jones and Ed Lasater, were among the most aggressive buyers in that area as the nineteenth century came to an end.

Jones and Lasater were born two years apart in Goliad County and grew up within a few miles of each other. As young cattlemen, they both headed south in search of broader horizons and they both focused their expansive ambitions on South Texas. But there the similarities ended.

Jones's father, Captain A. C. Jones, was sheriff of Goliad County in 1860. "He was a self-made man like so many sons of Texas, having no advantages in early life. His success was due to his unaided efforts, a keen business sagacity and a prompt and decisive way of taking hold of things."[12] The sheriff's son was a large, rough-talking man who drank heavily and was noted for his miserly ways. Bill Jones's crude manner

[10] Ed C. Lasater, "Meat Packer Legislation," p. 204.
[11] Hunter, *The Trail Drivers of Texas*, pp. 325, 515, 913, 937. The Fants moved to the Goliad area from South Carolina in 1852, the Joneses from East Texas in 1858, the Lasaters from Arkansas in 1858, the Lucases from Canada in 1859, and the Colemans before 1861.
[12] Ibid., p. 936.

survived an education that included study at Roanoke College in Salem, Virginia, and Poughkeepsie Business College in New York.[13]

Lasater, who did not drink, was largely self-educated. The sheep camps, which replaced his classroom instruction at an early age, did not harden his manner. He was an articulate man with a polished presence that belied his frontier upbringing and experience. "No doubt Ed Lasater would have made a great lawyer, a great engineer or a great banker," commented one observer, "because he is a natural student with a positive genius for details and for the mastery of big problems."[14]

Lasater was described in one article as the refined type of Texan who could pass for a university professor. The writer cautioned against concluding that Lasater was therefore not a fighter. "Living near the Mexican border where political feuds have been frequent, he has had to run a gauntlet of every possible danger and no one ever succeeded in putting anything over on Ed Lasater and getting by with it."[15]

Bill Jones operated his cattle business with a tight rein on expenditures. On a personal level he was so close with his cash that when he stopped at a cafe in Falfurrias for a cup of coffee, he would remove his chewing gum, stick it on the saucer, and use it again when he departed—that is, when he was not chewing tobacco and spitting freely in all directions, a trait that became legendary around the Nueces Hotel in Corpus Christi, which he owned.[16]

By contrast, Lasater spent freely and kept large amounts of money in constant circulation: "Everyone around Falfurrias that made money made it off Ed Lasater, because he was the only one who would spend anything."[17] Whatever stirred his interest activated his bank account and he poured funds into diverse projects, large and small, ever confident that he could locate a banker willing to lend him money until future profits could service the debt.

As their properties took shape, Jones's Alta Vista Ranch and Lasa-

---

[13] *Corpus Christi Caller-Times*, October 27, 1935.

[14] Everett Lloyd, "Ed C. Lasater: The World's Jersey King and His 300,000 Acre Kingdom," *National Magazine*, February, 1920; R. M. Gow, "Ed C. Lasater," *Jersey Bulletin*, March 26, 1930, p. 558.

[15] Lloyd, "Ed C. Lasater."

[16] Interview, Mrs. T. R. Bennett, July 31, 1981; and Tom Lasater, January 12, 1980.

[17] Interview, Dick McIntyre, July 19, 1981.

ter's Falfurrias Ranch shared a common boundary through miles of sandy pastures and mesquite bush. The extent of the personal mistrust and animosity between these two ranchers was illustrated by their placing on all gates between their ranches two separate chains with locks requiring the presence of a representative from each ranch whenever a gate was opened. And these two men, busy with extensive and far-flung operations, both took time personally to ride their common fenceline.[18]

For all their differences of personality and style, however, Lasater and Jones shared a strong attraction to the sandy country south of the Nueces. Evidently Captain Jones's only son inherited his father's prompt and decisive manner, and both the young Jones and Lasater were particularly decisive when it was a matter of buying land. Around the turn of the century, they both moved rapidly to acquire and to consolidate their holdings. Page after page in the deed records filed in the courthouses at Rio Grande City and San Diego record the details of the transactions that transferred title from earlier owners like Gonzáles, Sáenz, Izaguirre, Hinojosa, Falcón, Canales, Peña, Ramírez, Balboa, Martínez, Olivares, Moreno, Vela, Barrera, Leal, del Valle, Solís, Caballero, Longoria, Montalvo, and Salinas to Jones and Lasater.[19] Collecting deeds and putting the L— (Lasater) and the V—1 (Jones) on thousands of head were the consuming pastimes of these two energetic young cowmen from Goliad.

Of course, Lasater and Jones were not the only ones buying land. Nor did all the Mexican landowners in the area sell their holdings. The family of Sabas Pérez, who pastured cattle on the Loma Blanca grant

[18] Interview, Tom Lasater, July 21, 1981.
[19] Transcribed Deed Records from Starr County, Brooks County, vols. IV–VIII; Deed Records, Duval County, Books M–S. Title to numerous tracts of the land purchased by Lasater had to be cleared through litigation. This was partly due to the fact that many of the purchases were of small undivided interests in large properties. In one instance, Lasater had to purchase 13,284 acres twice. This land, in the Los Olmos grant, was purchased from the current owners in 1897 and again from the heirs of Juan Antonio Canales, the original grantee. See fn. 59, chapter 2. The confusion surrounding title to the Los Olmos grant, and the litigation which necessitated Lasater's double purchase is spelled out in Mildred Seaton, "Abstract of Lands Owned by Ed C. Lasater in Grants of Los Olmos and Los Olmos y Loma Blanca in Counties of Nueces, Duval, Hidalgo, Starr, Texas," Nueces County, December 19, 1904.

and who later bought property on the south side of the Laguna de Loma Blanca, continued the livestock operation that he had started in 1850.[20] Pilar Zarate Bayarena and Lázaro López bought land in 1848 and 1871, respectively, in grants near the tract awarded Ignacio de la Peña. Their descendants were among those operating in the vicinity of Lasater's ranch who managed to outlast market declines, drought, and the pressures of the financially aggressive Anglo ranchers.[21]

In the southern part of Starr County, the Guerra family effectively stalled the Anglo encroachment. Manuel Guerra, head of a family dynasty that controlled the county like feudal barons, was a descendant of José Alejandro Guerra, a surveyor for the Spanish crown who received two land grants in 1767. These grants lay on both sides of the Rio Grande in the vicinity of Mier, Tamaulipas, and Roma, Texas. Manuel Guerra, his brothers and other family members were expanding their land holdings in southern Starr County at the same time Lasater and Jones were acquiring extensive range properties farther north.[22]

Although Guerra, Jones, and many others were busy buying property and livestock in South Texas at the turn of the century, few men anywhere in Texas moved faster to put together a veritable empire of land and cattle than Ed Lasater did. On the heels of a major financial setback, he recognized a once-in-a-lifetime opportunity and lost no time in positioning himself to reap the maximum profit. Those who saw Lasater in San Antonio, Kansas City, or Chicago, where he went to borrow money, and judged him to be a lawyer or professor could hardly have imagined the aggressive young cowman in action in his home territory as he bought cattle and filed deeds at a frantic pace in the region that Major Gaines had called a perfect waste.

When Lasater decided to move, he moved fast. Five or six hours of sleep was all he required, and he often traveled at night to save time. John Bennett spent the winter and spring of 1900–1901 with Lasater.

[20] *Falfurrias Facts*, November 19, 1981.

[21] Texas Family Land Heritage Registry, 1974, p. 16, and 1978, p. 5.

[22] Jovita González, "Social Life in Cameron, Starr, and Zapata Counties" (M.A. thesis, Univ. of Texas, 1930), pp. 87–88; J. R. Monroe to C. M. Laughlin, April 3, 1906, Treviño Files, in possession of Florentino Treviño, Falfurrias; Transcribed Deed Records from Starr County, Brooks County, vols. IV–VI.

"I made trips at night with him in a two-horse cart from Realitos to La
Mota, always with a Winchester between us. He would get up at 3:00
a.m. and would go full-steam all day."[23]

Lasater had confidence in the country and he dedicated himself to
the task of assembling a large property from numerous small holdings.
He made many of his early purchases at one dollar an acre, the price
he paid Ignacio de la Peña's granddaughter for his first major purchase.
A substantial number of the properties he acquired prior to 1900 cost
even less, many of them fifty cents per acre.[24] A friend riding across
Lasater's property with him one day told him frankly that he was making a mistake in buying land in that area. There was not a sign of green
anywhere as they made their way across the acres of sandy pastures.
The ground was covered with dried-up grass, apparently dead and
worthless. Lasater got off his horse and picked up a runner, stripping
off the outer covering. To explain his confidence in the country's grazing
capacity, he held up for his friend a stem of succulent green grass several inches long.[25]

Lasater made one purchase after another as his large ranch took
shape. "To his credit it is known that no pressure was ever used to secure land from an unwilling owner, and those that would not sell at a
price satisfactory to him were in all cases given . . . access to roads
leading out of his pastures."[26] A young man in a hurry, he bought
everything that was available. "He treated the Mexicans fairly. He
bought them out at the going price, whatever it was. . . He would
never gouge anybody or out-trade anybody."[27]

Not everyone viewed Lasater's land purchases with the same respect. The son of one long-time associate recalled Lasater's land transactions with evident bitterness fifty years after his death: "He bought
and paid for it; he got it legally. But the Mexican families had to have

[23] John M. Bennett, "Notes on Ed C. Lasater," 1967. Three Bennetts with the same
name appear in this book. They will be referred to as follows: John M. Bennett, Sr.
(1831–1920); John M. Bennett (1878–1974); John M. Bennett, Jr., (b. 1908).

[24] Transcribed Deeds from Starr County, Brooks County, vol. IV, pp. 109–565, and
vol. V, pp. 4–665.

[25] Edward H. Caldwell, "Life and Activities of Edward Cunningham Lasater,"
pp. 10–11.

[26] Ibid., p. 12.

[27] Interview, John M. Bennett, February 24, 1967.

money to keep from starving. The gringo had money, so he got it for a song." [28] Lasater himself later described the low cost of his purchases with evident pride. He said that he had bought the land largely from Mexican families at prices equal to only 50 percent of the value the prior owners had placed on that land while trading it back and forth among themselves during the preceding generation. [29]

After his untimely plunge into the cattle market in 1893, Ed Lasater was left without capital and with a substantial debt. To accomplish his financial comeback and to finance the rapid program of land acquisition which he commenced in 1895, he needed extensive sources of credit. The capital required by Lasater and his contemporaries came from banks, trust companies, and other lending agencies. Most of the ranchers operating between the Nueces and the Rio Grande at the turn of the century availed themselves of substantial amounts of credit from a variety of sources. Manuel Guerra borrowed $5,000 from Joseph Bowling Company of New Orleans in 1896. As collateral he mortgaged seventeen hundred head of goats, twenty-five hundred head of sheep, and more than ten thousand acres of land. [30] Guerra and Lasater, archenemies on the Starr County political front, were among the many South Texas landowners around the year 1900 with loans outstanding from their acquisitive neighbor to the east, Henrietta M. King. [31]

Colonel George Brackenridge, the melancholy and introspective banker from San Antonio who had been Lasater's first credit source, continued to extend financial backing to area cattlemen. Though Brackenridge was a man of thought and a scholar in a country that placed a premium on action, few bankers were more active than the former Union colonel in financing the Texas cattle industry. Brackenridge's venturesome philosophy of banking prompted him to establish the San Antonio Loan and Trust Company in 1892. This company, founded under state laws and the first such trust organized in South Texas, had

[28] Interview, Judge John Morgan Brooks, April 8, 1981.

[29] Ed C. Lasater to Gilbert N. Haugen, quoted in Ed C. Lasater, "Meat Packer Legislation," p. 209.

[30] Transcribed Trust Deed Records from Starr County, Brooks County, vol. I, pp. 453–56.

[31] Ibid., pp. 500–48.

more freedom than his federally regulated bank to handle the cattle financing he found so attractive and profitable.[32]

Three of the firms most actively engaged in financing land transactions in South Texas at the turn of the century were D. Sullivan and Company, T. C. Frost, Banker; and H. P. Drought and Company. The Frost firm was organized in 1874; the Sullivan Company, in 1883; and the predecesor firm to H. P. Drought began operating in Texas in the early 1880s.[33]

The Drought Company developed an extensive loan business with landowners between the Nueces River and the Mexican border. That firm's operation typified the manner in which large quantities of foreign money were channeled into Texas between 1880 and 1920 to finance the ambitious undertakings of men like Bill Jones and Ed Lasater.

The firm that became H. P. Drought and Company in 1900 began its Texas business as Francis Smith, Caldwell and Company. This was a branch office of a lending agency headquartered in Memphis, Tennessee. Before moving to Texas, Francis Smith had worked in the Midwest, where he made loans secured by farmland for English and Scottish companies that had capital to invest. Evidently Smith's lending experience had produced mixed results for his clients. His move to Texas was motivated by a desire to seek a more profitable area for mortgage lending and also "to recuperate his impaired health by outing and traveling in open air. . . ." Smith, accompanied by a Spanish interpreter, personally made the inspections of prospective properties in Hidalgo, Duval, Starr, Zapata, and Webb counties.[34] After several years in Texas, Francis Smith, Caldwell and Company was dissolved. In 1890 Francis Smith brought H. P. Drought into his firm. Drought was a native of County Clare, Ireland, and was educated in London, Ontario. An attorney, he had already gained experience in the business of representing foreign investment firms before he and Smith joined forces.[35]

[32] Sibley, *George W. Brackenridge*, pp. 11, 99–100; *Southwest Texans*, p. 25A. The San Antonio Loan and Trust Company's first board of directors in 1892 included Franz Groos, H. D. Kampmann, T. C. Frost, and Ben A. Stribling (ibid.).

[33] John M. Bennett, Jr., *Those Who Made It*, p. 10; "Historical Memorandum," Drought Files, in possession of Thomas Drought, San Antonio; Transcribed Trust Deed Records from Starr County, Brooks County, vols. I and II.

[34] "Historical Memorandum," Drought Files.

[35] Interview, Thomas Drought, January 27, 1982.

Smith was enthusiastic about the opportunities for business in Texas and about the loans he and Drought could generate for their clients. In 1891 Smith wrote William Mackenzie in Dundee, Scotland, to assure him that his Texas business under Drought and Smith's direction would prove most satisfactory and would be an improvement over earlier deals in the Midwest that had gone sour. Smith summarized the situation for Mackenzie: "The lesson to be learned from the Indiana loans is: 1) avoid a hilly, stony country, 2) avoid wet lands and 3) avoid unprosperous localities and men."[36]

The Alliance Trust Company, Ltd., of Dundee, Scotland, and the American Freehold Land Mortgage Company of London were two of the fifteen or more firms that Drought and Smith represented in their lending business. For these and other firms Drought and Smith would typically arrange loans to Texas borrowers equal to 40 to 50 percent of the value of their patented land. The Texas firm received between 15 and 20 percent of the interest collected as their commission.[37]

One of Francis Smith's early loans was to Dillard R. Fant, who learned the livestock business as a young man in Goliad County.[38] In a letter to Mackenzie, Smith described Fant as "the richest stockman in this section of the country," but in subsequent correspondence Fant's character and approach to business had to be explained repeatedly to the English and Scottish lenders.[39] Fant had extensive business with Smith and Drought, who considered him an excellent credit risk, even though he was usually late in paying interest: "He is the kind of man who knows he is going to pay and is going to do so when it is convenient and is at a loss to understand why people should want money from him

[36] Francis Smith to William Mackenzie, May 26, 1891, Alliance Trust Letterbook, no. 1, Drought Files.

[37] Notation in loan registers, Drought Files. To facilitate and condense long-distance communication by cable, Smith devised a code for commonly used words and phrases involved with their mortgage loan business. Two frequent telegrams were "Send Gelding Inoculated," and "Need Gehenna testimony." Certain code words and their translations were: "gehenna," $25,000; "gelding," $50,000; "inoculated," what amount of money can you furnish in the next thirty days?; "inoculable," prospect for good loans justify a special effort to raise funds; "fountain," amount of your credit; and "testimony," early next week (Francis Smith to Holmes Ivory, December 5, 1884, United States Mortgage Co., no. 1).

[38] United States Mortgage Co., no. 1, Drought Files. Another early loan was to Ellen and W. E. Tom, Albert Lasater's neighbors when he entered the sheep business in Atascosa County in 1878.

[39] Francis Smith to William Mackenzie, May 25, 1891, Drought Files.

at any other time."[40] Fant was frequently out of town and often traveled to the Indian Territory and to Kansas City looking after his cattle interests. In an 1894 communication explaining Fant's overdue interest account, Smith tried to communicate an understanding of the Texas cowman's mentality to his English counterparts. He stated that Fant "in common with other cattlemen, at present is hard-up or at least is inclined to concentrate all his assets in cattle, expecting higher prices."[41]

Farther south, Smith made loans in the 1880s to Alejo de la Garza in Duval County and to Matías García in Starr County. These loans illustrated another recurring problem for their lenders: the length of the loans. Typically the borrowers would not take the loan for as long a period as the firm's English and Scottish clients requested. Smith and Drought frequently found themselves trying to persuade a client to approve a note that extended for a shorter than desired period. The de la Garza note, however, was a five-year note at 10 percent interest. The principals at the United States Mortgage Company of Scotland were undoubtedly pleased with their San Antonio agent when the Matías García note was negotiated. Ignacio de la Peña's granddaughter and her husband signed a note at 10 percent, payable in ten years.[42]

The following figures prepared by Francis Smith in 1897 give an overall summary of Drought and Smith's mortgage lending experience in Texas in the last two decades of the nineteenth century:[43]

Synopsis of Ranch Loans Made by F. Smith and Co.
from March 8, 1885 to January 7, 1897

Number	Acres	Loans	Average Loan per Acre
91 paid loans	759,740	$1,008,702	$1.32
111 loans in good standing	1,103,873	1,127,067	1.02

[40] Francis Smith to U.S. Mortgage Co., May 31, 1893, United States Mortgage Co., no. 3, Drought Files.

[41] Ibid., December 17, 1894.

[42] M. I. no. 1, Drought Files. Loan Number 6 was made to Matías García Saldaña and Number 10 to Alejo de la Garza. The latter was the father of Amado de la Garza, first sheriff of Brooks County.

[43] Francis Smith to Holmes Ivory, March 20, 1897, United States Mortgage Co., no. 3, Drought Files.

Number	Acres	Loans	Average Loan per Acre
9 loans slow on paying interest, but good	93,936	169,953	1.80
33 properties taken under foreclosure paying rental of 4%–5% on cost	427,168	485,442	1.13

The average acreage mortgaged to Francis Smith and Company was a little less than ten thousand acres. The average loan per acre was $1.17.

Francis Smith and Company made their first loan to Ed Lasater when he was thirty-one, four years before he made his move into the Falfurrias area. That loan was secured by the Live Oak County property that Lasater and his father had purchased in 1882. The first note Lasater signed in 1891 was a two-year note at 8.5 percent interest. That note was renewed two years later for five years at 8 percent. In the second transaction Lasater got a lower interest rate; the Scottish investors had their money placed for a longer period of time.[44]

In 1895 Lasater and his father-in-law, John Bennett, Sr., bought the Matías García tract of 25,709 acres; this purchase was financed by Francis Smith and H. P. Drought. Smith wrote William Mackenzie that his firm had dealt with Bennett and Lasater for a number of years and that he was certain that they would make good borrowers: "They own about 35,000 head of cattle. It is estimated that they will clear $80,000 on this year's business."[45]

In another letter written to the United States Mortgage Company regarding a second transaction later that year, Smith described his clients further: "The purchasers are both first-class cattlemen. Mr. Lasater has made and lost a great deal of money in the business, but is understood to be quite a considerable sum ahead. Mr. Bennett is reputed

[44] Alliance Trust Loan Register, no. 1, Drought Files.
[45] Francis Smith to William Mackenzie, July, 1895, Alliance Trust Co. correspondence, 1893–1896, Drought Files.

to be a wealthy man. We believe that he is." Smith concluded by telling his English clients that he considered this an "excellent loan."[46]

When Francis Smith first began loaning money in Starr and Duval counties, much of the land his company took as security was owned by the heirs of the original owners who had received grants from the Spanish and Mexican governments. The period during which Smith and Drought were most active was also the period which saw a major shift in ownership in Starr and Duval counties into the hands of Anglo ranchers. The attitudes and inclinations of these men and others who represented English and Scottish clients undoubtedly contributed to that change and facilitated the ambitions of the Anglo entrepreneurs. Ed Lasater recognized this when he began making plans for the major acquisition program he began in 1895.

His plans were given an impetus by the drought and low cattle markets of 1894. Many livestock raisers in that part of South Texas were devastated. Low prices and lack of foodstuffs were not the only problems; the shortage of stock water when the shallow wells dried up compounded the ranchers' plight and caused widespread livestock losses. Lasater saw a dependable water supply as a major key to success. "Now in a way, those Mexican grantees were no worse off than I was. I had one thing, however, which they did not have: confidence in my ability to provide a water supply." Lasater found that he could go into the old trench wells and by sinking the hole another sixty feet in depth he could secure enough volume to supply a four-inch pump. This would supply sufficient water for all the cattle that could graze in the immediate vicinity.[47]

Lasater also knew that the companies holding the notes from those ranchers who found themselves financially prostrate were still anxious to find reliable borrowers. "I canvassed the situation and came to the conclusion that the English companies from whom the Mexican ranchers had secured loans would want somebody to use those lands who could make them productive." Lasater had paid his dues in the cattle market. He was certain the timing was right, and he was ready. "I was confident I could do it. I had executive ability; certainly I knew the

[46] Francis Smith to U.S. Mortgage Co., June, 1895, Loan Register, no. 4, 1895–1897, Drought Files.
[47] Ed C. Lasater, "Meat Packer Legislation," pp. 206–207.

country and had faith in it. Faith in myself has helped me to do a lot of seemingly impossible things."[48]

Lasater's first decade of credit business with Smith and Drought was handled in a manner that was satisfactory to both parties. Lasater returned to H. P. Drought in 1901 with an application to borrow $130,000. That was far in excess of Drought's average South Texas real estate loan, and when approved it was one of the largest loans on Drought's books. But after ten years of observing this man from Los Olmos Creek, Drought had no doubts about the desirability of the loan, and he cabled William Mackenzie in Scotland: "It is of great importance that Lasater be done immediately."[49]

Drought's reasons were spelled out fully in a letter to Mackenzie and in a six-page memorandum accompanying another loan application. Lasater's security for this loan was 286,000 acres; 220,000 acres of that were deeded and 66,000 were leased at a low rate for five years. Drought liked the ranch Lasater had assembled in that section below the Nueces. "It is one of the best ranches in Texas. It is fenced and cross-fenced into several pastures. This ranch was partially improved when purchased by Mr. Lasater. Since then he has paid over $100,000 for additional improvements." Those improvements consisted of many miles of fence, thirty-four houses, seventy wells and windmills, and four or five artesian wells.[50]

At the time Lasater first made this loan application he had cattle on feed near Kansas City that he subsequently sold for $230,000. In addition, he sold cattle off his ranch for $100,000. That reduced his total indebtedness from $678,000 to $348,000. After those cattle sales, Lasater's ranch was stocked with 12,000 head of cattle, 500 horses, 60 mules, and 450 sheep. Drought valued all that livestock at $300,000.[51]

Drought liked the collateral Lasater offered to secure the loan, and

[48] Ibid., p. 207.

[49] H. P. Drought to William Mackenzie, March 21, 1901, Alliance Trust Letterbook 1898–1901, Drought Files. About the time this loan was transacted, Ed Lasater purchased the interest of John M. Bennett, Sr., in the land they had purchased together in 1895. The Quit Claim Deed filed of record does not give the terms of the transaction (Deed Records, Starr County, Book T, pp. 249–52).

[50] H. P. Drought to Walter Allnutt, June 12, 1901, American Freehold Land Mortgage Co. Loan Register, 1899–1905, Drought Files.

[51] Ibid.

he was effusive in his comments about the man behind the loan. "Of Mr. Lasater himself we cannot speak too highly; he is hard-working, industrious, frugal, thoroughly well versed in his business and in every respect a man worthy of confidence and credit."[52]

Drought thought one of Lasater's motives in seeking the new loan was related to the ambitions of the captain's widow, Henrietta M. King: "It may be our insinuating that Mrs. King would be exceedingly glad to get the land on which she has a mortgage that made him feel that he would like to have the loan in the hands of somebody else. . . ."[53]

Drought recommended the Lasater loan highly despite one negative consideration: Lasater would not take the loan for a fixed five-year term, as he anticipated retiring the debt in a shorter time. The loan was transacted in 1901 at 7 percent interest. It was payable in gold coin at H. P. Drought's San Antonio office five years later, but Lasater could pay off the loan after either three or four years if he so desired.[54] Drought was pleased with this loan and fully confident of his borrower, Ed Lasater: "His business matters are all in first class condition, he is an excellent businessman and we have every reason to believe that he will be as prosperous in the future as he has been in the past."[55]

Lasater secured credit and plenty of it from Drought and from other sources. By the time the senior John Bennett's son went to Falfurrias to spend a year with him, Lasater had also reaped very large profits from his cattle investments. The rebound in cattle prices that began in 1895 continued on a steady rise through 1900. Lasater bought and sold between ten thousand and twenty-six thousand head during each of those years. "I caught the speculators' profit in the advance. . . . Roughly speaking I made about $800,000 by handling large numbers of cattle when prices were advancing from a point below the cost of production. . . ."[56] As he made money, Lasater moved quickly to expand his land holdings, assembling in the process one of the largest ranch properties in Texas: "I laid the foundations then for the Falfurrias Ranch of today with its 350,000 acres."[57]

[52] Drought to Mackenzie, March 21, 1901, Drought Files.
[53] Ibid.
[54] Deed of Trust Records, Starr County, Book C, pp. 522–44.
[55] Drought to Allnutt, June 12, 1901, Drought Files.
[56] Ed C. Lasater, "Meat Packer Legislation," pp. 209–10.
[57] Ibid., p. 207

John Bennett rode the pastures stretching across the Los Olmos y Loma Blanca and adjoining grants with Ed Lasater the year before the Drought loan was transacted. He admired Lasater's grasp of his business and respected his standing in the livestock industry. Bennett was awed by the energy with which Lasater approached his work and was impressed by the stamina and courage he displayed in a harsh environment fraught with real personal danger. "He had one consuming weakness," Bennett later recalled, "he wanted to own all the lands that adjoined his ranch."[58]

In 1901 neither Lasater nor his bankers viewed that ambition as a weakness. Francis Smith and his partner, H. P. Drought, were astute financiers. Smith had learned back in Indiana the wisdom of avoiding stony country and unprosperous men. They found a good credit risk in Ed Lasater and they, like their borrower, saw the desire to own vast acreages of South Texas real estate as the natural response to the availability of cheap land during a very profitable period in the cattle industry. Lasater had placed his bet; it was a large one, and that time he was dealt a winning hand.

[58] John M. Bennett, "Notes," p. 3

CHAPTER 4

Mary Miller Moves to La Mota

When noonday's sun rides high above
This world's mad, moiling race,
Fair as at morn I see my love
And bless her saintly face.
—The 1898 *Cactus*, the University of Texas Yearbook

IN the spring of 1902, Ed Lasater met Garland Burleigh Miller's widow at Sugarland. He also became acquainted with her sons on the Cunningham plantation in Fort Bend County. Later that year Lasater accepted Mrs. Miller's invitation to visit in her Galveston home. There was one member of the family he had not met, her daughter Mary.[1]

When Lasater arrived at the Miller home in Galveston, Mrs. Miller led him into the entrance hall. From there they could see into the living room, where Mary Miller sat playing the piano. Lasater stood silently, listening to the music and observing Mary Miller. When the piece was completed, Lasater strode over to the piano and said, "I want you to be my wife." They were married on October 29, 1902, and Mary Miller left Galveston to make her home on a South Texas ranch.[2]

Ed Lasater had lost his entire first family in a series of events which were not uncommon on the Texas frontier. The first son, Edward, was born in San Antonio in 1893, and the second son, Bennett, was born in 1896. Early the following year Bennett developed a high

---

[1] Interview, Laurence D. Miller, Sr., September 22, 1971. L. D. Miller was fourteen when he met Ed Lasater at Sugar Land in 1902. Lasater invited him to ride around the plantation in a horse and buggy. When they reached a drainage canal, they had to make a decision and decided to try it: "We plunged in and landed in about four feet of water, then had to unhitch the horses and pull the buggy up on dry land" (ibid.).

[2] Ibid.; interview, Gardner B. Miller, July 22, 1981.

fever and died suddenly. In December of the same year, four-year-old Edward died of diphtheria.[3]

Patti Lasater's shock and grief over the loss of her two young sons weakened her health. Whether as a direct result of those deaths or because of a horseback riding accident, her physical condition deteriorated over the next three years.[4] By the summer of 1900, Ed Lasater's concern for his wife's health prompted him to take her to Colorado. Patti was expecting their third child, and he hoped she would gain strength by spending a cool summer in Denver, where they stayed in the Brown Palace Hotel.

A niece later described the letters Ed Lasater wrote to Patti's parents in San Antonio: "I read the letters with quiet admiration for a man who had such deep concern for his wife's health and well-being and such thoughtfulness for her caring parents." Lasater described every detail of the trip north, the view from their hotel window, the "bracing" air. "He had such hope at the beginning of their stay in Denver. . . . As time went on, he told of his concerns, but of course he tried to be cheerful." The change of climate did not prove sufficient to restore Patti's failing health. She died in Denver in August, 1900, during childbirth.[5]

G. B. Miller had died early in the year his only daughter married her cousin, Ed Lasater.[6] Thirty-seven years before, he had moved from

[3] Edward H. Caldwell, "Life and Activities of Edward Cunningham Lasater," p. 9; interview, Sarah Caldwell, June 26, 1971.

[4] Julián García related that according to his father, Hilario García, Patti Lasater's health crisis in 1900 was precipitated by a fall off a horse while working cattle on the ranch (Interview, Julián García, July 25, 1981).

[5] Josephine Bennett Musgrave to author, April 18, 1981, Author's Files, Colorado Springs. After Patti's death, Ed Lasater decided to resume his schooling and pursue his early ambition to study law. He made plans to attend a law school in Tennessee, but once again, his plans did not materialize (Interview, Sarah Caldwell, June 26, 1971).

[6] The mother of Sarah Jane Cunningham (Mrs. Albert Lasater) and Colonel Edward H. Cunningham was Susan T. Dismukes (d. 1855). Garland Burleigh Miller's mother was Sarah R. Dismukes (d. 1882). It is not known whether Susan and Sarah were sisters, or if they were more distant relations. On visits to Sugarland, Miller's children always addressed Cunningham's wife as "Cousin Narcissa" (Interview, L. D. Miller, Sr., September 22, 1971; notes from the files of Sarah Cunningham Caldwell, in possession of Clay Caldwell, Corpus Christi; W. H. Miller, *History and Genealogies*, p. 135).

Tennessee to Texas to seek his fortune. Miller and his brother Tom had both enlisted in the Confederate Army as teenage boys, and Tom, who had been captured and sentenced to be hanged, refused to take the Oath of Allegiance when the war ended. He and G. B. left for Texas in 1865. G. B. settled in Galveston, and Tom in Bastrop, where he was "assaulted with shotguns and pistols by two or three of his deadly enemies" and killed in 1867.[7]

G. B. Miller was eighteen years old when he reached Galveston. He went to work as a clerk with a Galveston company doing a general commission forwarding and receiving business and rose to be a partner in the firm.[8] Around the year 1880, Miller became involved financially with Edward Cunningham at Sugarland. For a number of years, he and his family spent a part of each year living on the sugar plantation there.[9]

Miller withdrew from the Cunningham firm in 1898.[10] Another of his business ventures was with the International Creosoting and Construction Company, which had plants in Beaumont and Texarkana and did extensive business in Latin America. Miller suffered a substantial financial loss during the Galveston hurricane and flood of 1900. His wife, daughter Mary, and youngest son L. D. were in Mexico during that devastating event.[11]

Two years before the storm, Mary Miller graduated as the valedictorian of her high school class in Galveston. The following fall she en-

[7] Miller, *History and Genealogies*, pp. 136–37. Thomas K. Miller was captured in Tennessee in 1863 and sentenced to be hanged. His mother went to Washington to plead his case to President Lincoln, who signed a pardon for Miller only a few hours before he was assassinated. President Johnson would not give Mrs. Miller the pardon. Miller's sister, working through Governor Brownlow, was successful in getting her brother a pardon in 1865 without his having to take the oath of allegiance (ibid., p. 136).

[8] Ibid., p. 137.

[9] Interview, L. D. Miller, Sr., September 22, 1971. G. B. Miller married Mary (Mamie) Gardner, daughter of Dr. R. C. Gardner in Fayetteville, Lincoln County, Tennessee (W. H. Miller, *History and Genealogies*, p. 137).

[10] Interview, L. D. Miller, Sr., September 22, 1971. Even though G. B. Miller withdrew from the Cunningham firm in 1898, he evidently maintained some involvement, either personal or financial, because his family continued spending time there until at least 1902. His oldest son, Garland Miller, became one of Ed Lasater's assistants during the period Lasater managed the plantation (ibid.; R. M. Curtis, *Falfurrias Facts*, undated).

[11] Interview, L. D. Miller, Sr., September 22, 1971; W. H. Miller, *History and Genealogies*, p. 137.

rolled in the University of Texas in the Class of 1902. She loved music, which played an important role throughout her life. She also demonstrated enough mathematical ability that one of her university professors urged her to continue her scholastic training in a postgraduate course in mathematics.[12]

Mary's brothers, Garland and Richard, were in the Class of 1901 at the university. So was Jamie Armstrong, whose family owned the ranch where the siding at Katherine would sit when the railroad was extended south from Sinton to Brownsville in 1903–1904.[13] The lifelong friendship that began at the university between Jamie Armstrong and Mary Miller was cemented further a few years later when they married John Bennett and Ed Lasater.

The circumstances that brought the Millers together with Ed Lasater at the Sugarland plantation two years after his first wife's death were not happy ones. A few years after building the state's largest sugar refinery in the last decade of the century, Colonel Edward Cunningham, the prosperous "Sugar King of Texas,"[14] began experiencing business reverses. By 1900 his difficulties had increased to a serious level. Ed Lasater responded to the call for financial assistance from the uncle whose name he bore and who had provided him with his first financial backing. As Cunningham's situation worsened, Lasater found himself heavily involved and increasingly compromised in terms of both time and money.[15]

Following his distinguished service in the Confederate Army during the Civil War, Colonel Cunningham had purchased five plantations

[12] Garland B. Miller, Jr., to Mary Miller, May 30, 1898; inscription in 1898 *Cactus*; interviews, L. D. Miller, September 22, 1971, Emily Edwards, February 25, 1967, and Holman Cartwright, May 10, 1971.

[13] The name Katherine was changed to Armstrong sometime between 1915 and 1920 (John M. Bennett, Jr., to author, February 16, 1982). The 1898 *Cactus*, yearbook of the University of Texas, was dedicated to Colonel George W. Brackenridge, Ed Lasater's first San Antonio banker. Another student in the Class of 1901 was Carl F. Groos, a member of another San Antonio banking family with which Ed Lasater did extensive business.

[14] *San Antonio Daily Express*, July 3, 1891.

[15] Interview, John M. Bennett, February 24, 1967; Ed C. Lasater, "To My Children," no date, Lasater Files, in possession of Garland M. Lasater, Falfurrias; William R. Johnson, "A Short History of the Sugar Industry in Texas," *Texas Gulf Coast Historical Association Publication* (April, 1961): 55.

totaling some 12,500 acres in Fort Bend County and had established a farming operation principally devoted to sugar cane. His plantation was situated on the Southern Pacific Railroad, and he built a fourteen-mile railway called the Sugarland Road connecting his property with the Gulf, Colorado and Santa Fe Railroad at Duke and with the International and Great Northern Railroad at Arcola.[16]

Slave labor was used on Texas sugar plantations until the Civil War. After the war, Texas planters turned to the leasing of convicts to replace the freed slaves. In 1875 Cunningham and L. A. Ellis, both extensive users of convict labor on their own plantations, secured a five-year lease on the entire Texas prison system. The state received $14.00 per month for each convict, and the lessees were permitted to sublease convicts to third parties. By the end of the century, Cunningham was the largest user of prison labor in the state. In 1880 he employed 133 convicts on his plantation, and by 1898 that number had risen to 233. Although the planters figured the cost of a convict to be $1.15 per day, somewhat higher than other available labor, the supply was constant and dependable.[17]

In the 1890s Cunningham expanded his operation, when he invested $1.5 million to build Texas' largest sugar refinery, one of the largest in the United States. This was housed in a nine-story wooden building, and Cunningham developed a hoist that could lift and dump a carload of cane on the inclined feeder that led to the crushers. The operation included a paper mill that made wrapping paper from the bagasse, the crushed cane fiber left over after the juice was extracted from the stalk. The town of Sugarland was built around the refinery. All the houses, stores, and businesses were owned by Cunningham's company.[18]

To supply his sugar refining operation, Cunningham grew cane on his own plantations and on land that he leased. He also purchased raw

[16] A. J. Sowell, *History of Fort Bend County, Texas*, pp. 348–50. Cunningham married Narcissa Brahan of Mississippi. Their children were: Edward, Eva, Susan, Thomas, and Narcissa. The Cunninghams lived in San Antonio in a large rock home near the military parade ground (ibid., p. 350; interview, Sarah Caldwell, June 26, 1971).

[17] William R. Johnson, "A Short History," pp. 39, 42, 43, 46.

[18] Ibid., pp. 55, 61; H. P. Drought to Walter Allnutt, June 21, 1901, American Freehold Land and Mortgage Co. Letterbook, 1899–1905, Drought Files, in possession of Thomas Drought, San Antonio.

sugar produced in Fort Bend and surrounding counties. Thus the refinery could be operated only on a seasonal basis, typically between 120
and 150 days each year. Cunningham's refinery operated profitably in
its early years, but three principal factors contributed to later operating losses: competition from foreign sugar, Cunningham's reluctance to
import raw sugar, and the deterioration of his plant's machinery.[19]

As operating losses mounted, Cunningham turned to his nephew,
Ed Lasater, for needed capital. Lasater began advancing funds to Cunningham in 1898 and continued advancing money until his uncle owed
him $300,000. Lasater borrowed $200,000 of that amount by putting
up his cattle as security to the Barse Livestock Commission Company,
and he obtained $100,000 on an unsecured note with Colonel Bracken-
ridge's San Antonio National Bank.[20]

In 1902 Ed Lasater submitted a loan application to H. P. Drought
on behalf of the Cunningham Sugar Company. Drought advised his
Scottish clients against the loan: "We think the property has a value
sufficient to justify the loan, but Colonel Cunningham has gotten to be
quite an old man and the son on whom he has been depending has not
turned out well and recently had a stroke of apoplexy." Drought added
that Cunningham "has been very much embarrassed owing to the
flood, the storm, a fire and a heavy and early freeze last year. Under all
these circumstances we felt we could not recommend anything like the
advance that was required. . . ."[21]

By 1904 Cunningham's business had deteriorated to such a level
that his creditors forced him into receivership. The court named Ed
Lasater receiver of the Cunningham properties. Lasater's first move
was to hire Edward P. Eastwick, Jr., a sugar refining expert from New
York, to examine the operation and to determine the necessary steps
for returning the company to profitability.[22] Eastwick's forty-page re-

[19] William R. Johnson, "A Short History," pp. 45, 62.

[20] Interview, John M. Bennett, February 24, 1967; Ed C. Lasater, "To My Children"; H. P. Drought to William Mackenzie, March 21, 1901, Drought Files.

[21] H. P. Drought to William Mackenzie, May 15, 1902, Drought Files. This letter
provides the only detail available about a suit filed by Henrietta M. King: "Within the
last few days, a suit has been brought by Mrs. King of Santa Gertrudis against Cunningham on a note of $53,000 and an application was made to put the property in the
hands of a receiver. This has been done and Mr. Lasater is the receiver."

[22] William R. Johnson, "A Short History," p. 62.

port described in detail the extensive renovations necessary to restore the plant to efficient operation. He estimated the repairs would cost more than $80,000.[23]

Lasater spent months commuting back and forth from his South Texas ranch to Sugarland, living in Houston's Rice Hotel while oversee-ing the Cunningham operation.[24] The company was reorganized and resumed operations in September, 1905, as Cunningham Sugar Com-pany. In the new corporation, Edward Cunningham was still the ma-jority stockholder, but real control lay with a vice-president who repre-sented the Lincoln Trust and Title Company, the corporation's principal financial backer.[25] Cunningham Sugar made a narrow profit in 1906, but the following year the company suffered a loss of $320,194. With the company again on the verge of bankruptcy, the seventy-two-year-old Cunningham decided to sell. I. H. Kempner of Galveston and W. T. Eldridge purchased a controlling interest in the company in 1908. Cunningham remained only as titular head and was dropped from the board of directors the following year.[26]

Lasater's involvement in the Cunningham situation appeared to some as a grand gesture, an act of loyalty to an uncle he admired greatly.[27] But bitterness between the two men grew out of Lasater's fi-nancial assistance to his uncle and his later role as court-appointed re-ceiver. Lasater's "act of sacrifice" alienated the Cunninghams, and rela-tions between the two families developed into the most vicious family feud South Texas had known up to that time.[28]

[23] Edward P. Eastwick, Jr., "Report on Sugar Factories Owned by Ed H. Cun-ningham & Co. (Ed C. Lasater, Receivor), Sugar Land, Texas," February 8, 1905, Impe-rial Sugar Company Records.

[24] Interviews, John M. Bennett, February 24, 1967; Tom Lasater, November 9, 1980.

[25] William R. Johnson, "A Short History," pp. 63–64.

[26] Ibid., pp. 66–69. "No record is available to indicate the price Kempner paid Cunningham for controlling interest in the company, but a stockholders meeting held on June 9, 1908, reflected the change in ownership" (Ibid., pp. 66–67).

[27] Interview, John M. Bennett (1878–1974), February 24, 1967.

[28] Ibid.; interview, L. D. Miller, Sr., September 22, 1971. Bennett added more de-tail to Drought's description of Cunningham's son, saying he was an alcoholic. Both Ben-nett and Miller credit Cunningham's daughter Eva with keeping the feud going between the Lasaters and the Cunninghams. The feelings were intense enough that some eighty years after the Cunningham properties were put into receivership, the grandchildren of Sarah Jane Cunningham Lasater's sister Mary refused to communicate the Cunningham side of the story to Ed Lasater's grandson.

Lasater's was a thankless role in a no-win situation. One observer said Lasater was a very disappointed man who felt his uncle had betrayed him.[29] There were other negative consequences of this enmity: "The Cunningham affair used up not only his financial means, but his energy as well. . . . It shortened his life. . . . The whole business made him very nervous and tense. . . . Just in the matter of time it was very expensive to him."[30]

No exact cost figures can be put on Lasater's expenditure of time and energy and his neglect of his own business interests. As an unsecured creditor of Cunningham Sugar Company, he lost the entire amount, some $300,000, which he had advanced to Cunningham between 1898 and 1902. The added financial burden of this additional debt load jeopardized Lasater's cattle operation and foreshadowed his own financial crisis two decades later.[31]

Ed Lasater began purchasing South Texas land in 1895 and continued buying and selling grazing cattle on a seasonal basis, handling between ten thousand and twenty-six thousand each year. In addition, the purchase of a large herd of brood cows marked a major new thrust in Lasater's business operation. This move led to the interest in cattle breeding and genetic improvement that became a major focus during the last half of his life.

Among the first cows he acquired was a herd of seven thousand that he contracted in the fall of 1894 from the Kenedy Pasture Company for delivery in the spring of 1895. These cows, predominantly of Shorthorn breeding (then called "Durham"), ranged from three to eight years old and cost seven dollars per head. Ed Lasater saw the cattle's value in terms of both market price and quality: "This was one of the best improved herds of cattle in Texas. The price was less than the hides were intrinsically worth."[32] Ed Lasater continued handling

[29] Interview, Sarah Caldwell, June 26, 1971.

[30] Interview, John M. Bennett, February 24, 1967. Bennett was familiar with the Lasater-Cunningham feud not just through his friendship with Ed Lasater. After spending a year working for Lasater (1900–1901), Bennett went to work in George Brackenridge's San Antonio National Bank. Brackenridge loaned Lasater on an unsecured note $100,000 of the money Lasater advanced to Cunningham.

[31] Interview, John M. Bennett, February 24, 1967.

[32] Ed C. Lasater to Gilbert N. Haugen, March 7, 1920, quoted in Ed C. Lasater, "Meat Packer Legislation," statement before the Committee on Agriculture, U.S. House

large numbers of grazing cattle for several years, and the large speculator's profit he realized provided a major share of the capital used in
his extensive land purchases. Kenedy's cows provided the original foundation for the long-range breeding program Lasater developed as he
stocked his ranges on a permanent basis.[33]

Ed Lasater established his headquarters near the west boundary
of de la Peña's Los Olmos y Loma Blanca grant between the Palo Blanco
and Baluarte creeks. It was a place distinguished by a grove of excep-
tionally large live oak trees; this grove or "mott," called La Mota de
Falfurrias, had been the headquarters of an earlier ranch. In July, 1895,
Jim Maupin moved a house from the old Copita pasture to La Mota for
Lasater to live in. There he and Patti Bennett spent a part of their married life.[34] Lasater never built a home on the ranch; the house from the
Copita pasture was the first of four wood frame dwellings he hauled
in and nailed together, connecting them with a series of wandering
porches and passageways.[35]

Southwest of La Mota was a little settlement called La Mota Vieja
(Old La Mota or "Old Town," which referred to old Falfurrias). There
were a small group of homes, a church, a school, and a branch of the

of Representatives, March 1, 2, 3, and 6, 1920, p. 209, in Edward C. Lasater Collection,
Eugene C. Barker Texas History Center, University of Texas, Austin.

[33] The Kenedy Ranch joined Ed Lasater's east boundary. Captain Mifflin Kenedy,
the ranch's founder, died in 1895, the year Ed Lasater began buying South Texas land and
the year he took delivery on the 7,000 Kenedy cows. In the early 1880s, in an effort to
improve his cow herd, Kenedy had bought some 12,000 head of young cattle, principally
Durham, to stock his property, "the largest pasture in the United States with the exception of the Maxwell Brothers in New Mexico" (*Corpus Christi Caller-Times*, January 18,
1959). Kenedy and Lasater were the Texas Honorees inducted into the National Cowboy
Hall of Fame in 1960 and 1961, respectively.

[34] James T. Maupin, "Sworn Affidavit," Falfurrias, August 11, 1938; Edward H. Caldwell, "Life and Activities," p. 11.

[35] Interview, L. D. Miller, Sr., September 22, 1971. Lasater was not the only
rancher in the area to use this method to construct his home. His ranching neighbor and
political enemy in Duval County, Archie Parr, perfected the system: "The house started
as a simple unadorned L-shaped affair, but it grew with the conception of each Parr child.
As the birth neared, ranch hands were given instructions to lasso yet another of the several small tenant shacks on the ranch and haul it unceremoniously into the yard. There it
was attached in one fashion or another to the main house. By the time that Atlee, the
youngest Parr child, arrived, even Archie's limited sense of architecture was rebelling.
Instead of attaching Atlee's room to the main house, the Parrs had left it freestanding in
the yard" (Dudley Lynch, *The Duke of Duval*, p. 3).

Ed C. Lasater, circa 1890, when he was about thirty years old. Courtesy Tom Lasater

Family Tree of Edward Cunningham Lasater

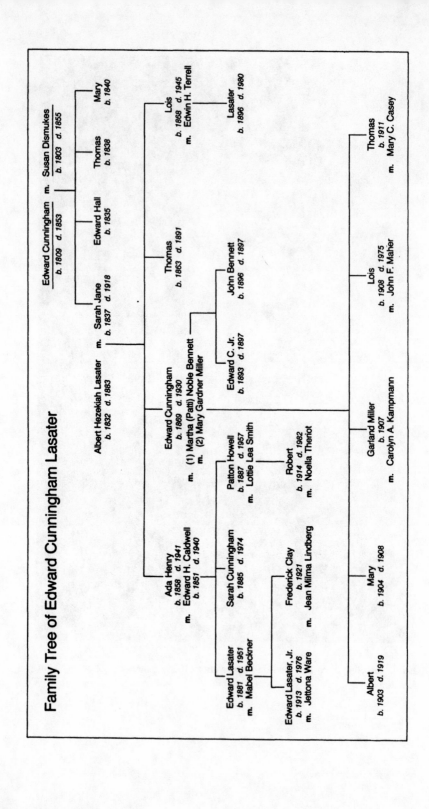

Family Tree of Mary Gardner Miller

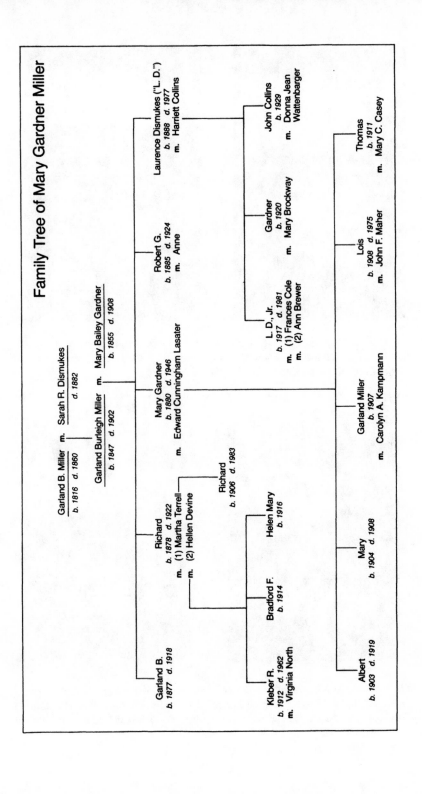

Left: Susan Dismukes Cunningham, mother of Sarah Jane Lasater and grandmother of Ed Lasater. Courtesy Noella Caldwell. *Right:* Edward Cunningham, father of Sarah Lasater. Courtesy Noella Caldwell

Left: Sarah Jane Cunningham Lasater, mother of Ed Lasater. Courtesy Tom Lasater. *Right:* Albert Hezekiah Lasater, father of Ed Lasater. Albert and his young bride, Sarah, moved from Arkansas to Texas in 1858. Courtesy Mary Caldwell Church

Left: Colonel Edward Hall Cunningham, Sarah Lasater's brother and Ed Lasater's uncle. He was known as the "Sugar King of Texas." Courtesy Imperial Sugar Company. *Right:* Ada Lasater Caldwell, 1899. Ed Lasater's sister, Ada, and her husband, Edward, operated a sheep ranch near Realitos before moving to Corpus Christi in 1883. Courtesy Sarah Cunningham Caldwell

Left: Thomas Lasater, Ed Lasater's brother, circa 1890. The brothers were partners in a cattle venture at the time of the younger Lasater's slaying in 1891. Courtesy Tom Lasater. *Right:* Lois Lasater Terrell, Ed Lasater's younger sister, circa 1890. Courtesy Sarah Cunningham Caldwell

Left: Ed C. Lasater, about the age of thirty, circa 1890. Courtesy Tom Lasater. *Right:* Martha (Patti) Bennett Lasater, Ed Lasater's first wife, circa 1890. Courtesy Noella Caldwell

Left: John M. Bennett, Sr., with his son, John, enjoying a cigar outside their adjacent San Antonio homes, circa 1906. Courtesy John M. Bennett, Jr. *Right:* Ed C. Lasater, Jr. (1893–97). Courtesy Noella Caldwell

Left: Mary Miller Lasater, Ed Lasater's second wife, in 1907. Courtesy G. M. Lasater. *Right:* Ed C. Lasater, 1905. Courtesy Tom Lasater

Left: Garland Burleigh Miller, Mary Lasater's father. Courtesy L. D. Miller III. *Right:* Mary Gardner Miller, Mary Lasater's mother. Courtesy L. D. Miller III

Ed Lasater with his son Albert at La Mota, 1904. Courtesy Tom Lasater

Lois, Albert, Tom, and Garland Lasater and Burleigh Gardner, with their governess, Miss Spears, 1913. Courtesy Tom Lasater

mercantile store Lasater had established earlier in Realitos.[36] Desiderio Treviño managed the store, and Bob Rice ran the post office in addition to carrying out other duties as a Lasater employee.[37] Frank Rachal, who had worked on the Chittim and Parr ranch, also went to work on the Lasater ranch and moved to Old Falfurrias, the first member of the Rachal family to settle permanently in the area. His young daughters attended school in that little settlement.[38]

Along with Bob Rice, who had worked with Lasater on his Oakville property, and Frank Rachal, Jim Maupin was one of the early arrivals on Lasater's ranch. Maupin was born in Missouri and moved with his family to Corpus Christi in 1875 when he was five years old. On June 15, 1895, he went to work for Lasater at a cow camp in the San Pedro de Charco Redondo grant in Duval County, where Lasater had leased some land. A year later he became Lasater's ranch foreman.[39]

Maupin first worked with Lasater immediately after he made his purchase from Matías García and was with Lasater as he profited from the cattle price recovery between 1895 and 1900 and poured those profits into numerous tracts of land adjoining his original purchase. "I took charge of the properties for him, repairing old fences or building new fences and frequently assisted in surveying the lands for him under the supervision of C. F. H. von Blucher of Corpus Christi, the surveyor doing the work."[40]

Lasater's headquarters was located at La Mota, and his ranch became known as the Falfurrias Ranch or Rancho Falfurrias. An abstract of the title contains the following reference to Lasater lands in the Santos García grant: "Beginning at the southeast corner of said Realitos

[36] Edward H. Caldwell, "Life and Activities," p. 11. The letterhead of Lasater's 1903 stationery indicates Lasater established his first mercantile store in Realitos. The Falfurrias store was originally a branch of that operation (Ed Lasater to J. M. Brown, May 27, 1903).

[37] Edward H. Caldwell, "Life and Activities," p. 11. R. H. Rice is credited with being Falfurrias' first postmaster (*Brooks County Golden Fiesta*, Falfurrias, 1961, p. 19).

[38] Interview, Edena Clere Scott Noll, July 20, 1981. Frank S. Rachal was born in 1868 on La Rosita Ranch near White Point, and married Anna Webster in Beeville in 1891. Their daughters were Lois Edena (m. J. R. Scott, Jr., in 1913) and Cecile Clere (m. Carl F. Hopper in 1922).

[39] Maupin, "Affidavit," p. 1; Lloyd N. Dyer, "The History of Brooks County," M.S. thesis, Texas College of Arts and Industries, 1938, p. 56.

[40] Maupin, "Affidavit," p. 1.

tract for a corner of this survey; thence south . . . along the south
boundary line of said Realitos town tract at 447 varas to center of road
to Falfurrias Ranch via La India. . . ." A later statement in the description of the same tract reads: "thence along the south side of said Clovis
Road . . . to the forks of said Clovis Road and the road from Realitos to
the Rancho Falfurrias via the Vela windmill. . . ."[41]

Ed Lasater was an independent thinker and formed his own judg-
ments about both issues and men. Bob Rice had been a boyhood friend
of Lasater's near Oakville and had worked on Lasater's property there.
Rice was in charge of repairs, largely of windmills, and also supervised
other aspects of Lasater's business. After Patti's death, Rice lived in
Lasater's home, and Lasater trusted him completely with his affairs.
Prior to moving to La Mota to work for Lasater, Rice had served time in
the penitentiary for murder. "No doubt Ed Lasater considered that the
man killed deserved it. It was characteristic of him to disregard public
opinion and to do what he thought was right."[42]

Other observers were not always impressed by the trust Ed Lasater put in his employees. The sons and daughter of his sister, Ada Caldwell, were frequent visitors at La Mota between 1895 and 1905. Ed
Lasater was on horseback from early morning until late at night, and
his niece recalls seeing employees "help themselves" to his possessions. She thought he needed protection from the people around him,
in whom he had complete confidence.[43]

Midway through the first decade of the twentieth century, Lasater had put together most of the ranch, which at its largest covered
some 350,000 acres. He had not yet gotten into the wide array of other
business enterprises that would develop in the following years, but he
already had an extensive operation and a large payroll. A series of news
items that mentioned various of Lasater's men in the *Alice Echo* imply

[41] Deed Records, Duval County, Book "P," pp. 429–30. This was part of a property
conveyed to Ed Lasater by Francis Smith on March 30, 1900. Lasater brought M. H.
(Mitt) Atkins from Oakville in 1898 to live at La India, an old ranch headquarters Lasater
purchased several miles south of Realitos (Interview, Dennis McBride, July 27, 1981;
Falfurrias Facts, June 15, 1934). A 1901 newspaper article contained the following description of a gathering at La India occasioned by the return of one of Atkins's sons, who
had been living in Mexico: "Elegant costume graced fair forms and the gentlemen were
dressed in full frock tail. They danced until sunrise" (*Alice Echo*, June 27, 1901).

[42] Interview, John M. Bennett, February 24, 1967.

[43] Interview, Sarah Caldwell, June 26, 1971.

a certain degree of confusion among employees and their roles: "R. H. Rice, boss of the Lasater Ranch at Falfurrias . . ." (March 3, 1904); "B. Temple Henry, manager of the Lasater enterprises . . ." (June 16, 1904); "James T. Maupin, chief caporal for the Lasater possessions . . ." (September 1, 1904); "J. J. Allen, superintendent of the Lasater possessions . . ." (November 3, 1904).

Those statements may represent just a reporter's choice of words, but they suggest strongly the unclear lines of authority, the overlapping responsibilities, the contradictory instructions, and other elements of faulty management that plagued Lasater's enterprises in later years.[44] "Ed Lasater was raised in an era when cattlemen had contact with only two types of people—his cowhands and his bankers," one early associate commented, adding, "He was a poor judge of men."[45] In some ranching operations, managerial and executive ability were not vital. But Ed Lasater conceived and implemented large and diverse undertakings. His subordinates often did not measure up to the confidence he had in them and were not prepared, either by education or by native talent, for the tasks and responsibilities he gave them.[46]

South Texas was a frontier when E. H. Caldwell went into the sheep business near Realitos in 1875, and it was still an area that offered both adventure and personal danger to those who ventured south of the Nueces at the turn of the century. Drinking was a favorite recreation in the area, and among those who indulged it was considered an insult to refuse an invitation to have a drink. Bars were not only places to socialize with one's friends and neighbors, however; they also provided an ideal setting for doing away with one's enemies. In the late night confusion which occurred when the lantern went out, many an early Texan lay dead while his assailants escaped unidentified and without fear of legal prosecution.[47] Ed Lasater did not drink, because of the additional risks incurred by those participating in that activity.

For similar reasons, Lasater never wore a gunbelt. He felt that not wearing one would prevent someone from shooting him and claiming it

---

[44] Interviews, L. D. Miller, Sr., September 22, 1971, Tom Lasater, November 9, 1980, G. M. Lasater, February 21, 1981, and W. B. Gardner, Jr., March 8, 1982.

[45] Interview, L. D. Miller, Sr., September 22, 1971.

[46] Ibid.; interviews, John M. Bennett, February 24, 1967; G. M. Lasater, February 21, 1981.

[47] Interview, Tom Lasater, May 1, 1979.

was done in self-defense, that Lasater had drawn first. But he did carry a Winchester rifle with him at all times in his cart, and although he did not carry a six-shooter, he was always accompanied by one or more heavily armed men.[48] As Lasater's holdings grew and as he became active politically, rumors of attempts on his life and threats to kidnap him or other members of his family abounded. The law and its agents were distant, and even then their dedication to seeing justice done was sometimes suspect. John Bennett was with Ed Lasater one day when they entered a neighbor's pasture where they rounded up a herd of cattle, cut out Lasater's strays and returned them to his ranch. As a result of this incident, Lasater was indicted for theft. A group of sheriff's deputies rode up to La Mota, where they found Lasater. They told him that he was under arrest and ordered him to mount a horse for the two-day ride to Rio Grande City, the county seat of Starr County. As they prepared to leave La Mota, several Texas Rangers happened by, and knowing the common method of dealing with an accused party in the course of a long horseback ride through brush country, they informed the deputies that they would accompany the group to Rio Grande City. When the trial began, Lasater demanded that the proceedings be conducted in English, and the case was dismissed.[49]

In November, 1882, Ada Lasater Caldwell was alone on the Borjas ranch with her infant son Edward when he became very sick. She stopped a group of Mexican horsemen who were passing by and prevailed on them to hitch two of their horses to a buggy so she could get into Realitos. There she caught the late-night train that went through en route from Laredo to Corpus Christi. Young Edward's life was saved, but the incident was a critical factor in Caldwell's decision to get out of ranching and go into business in Corpus Christi.[50]

Almost exactly twenty years later, Ed Lasater and his new bride got off the Texas-Mexican Railway at Realitos to begin their life together on a South Texas ranch. The young girl from Galveston and her husband were met by a carriage that carried them east to Cadena. Near there, where a chuckwagon was set up at a cow camp, they shared

[48] Interviews, John M. Bennett, February 24, 1967; L. D. Miller, Sr., September 22, 1971.

[49] Ibid.; John M. Bennett, "Notes on Ed C. Lasater," p. 1.

[50] Edward H. Caldwell," Notes and Facts in the Life of E. H. Caldwell," p. 37.

their first ranch meal before returning to the carriage to continue in a southeasterly direction, passing the water hole at Charco Redondo and crossing Palo Blanco Creek. It was nearly midnight when they reached the ranch headquarters, where the rambling collection of frame houses had been freshly painted and fixed up for the new bride's arrival and where the grove of massive live oak trees created somber and eerie figures in the moonlight.[51]

Later, Falfurrias would seem still primitive to Marybelle Bennett in 1916 when she arrived as a young bride. "I was scared. I thought we might be going to the jumping-off place," she recalled later. She remembered her husband's driving a car and dodging mesquite trees as they tried to maintain speed while crossing sandy pastures with no roads.[52] W. G. Schuetz moved his family from Nebraska to Falfurrias in 1912. His wife cried for two weeks after her first encounter with Falfurrias and Flowella, a real estate development several miles to the east.[53]

When Mary Miller first glimpsed the area a decade or more before the shocked reactions of those two ladies, the town of Falfurrias did not even exist. No one knows for certain, no documents or memories survive that record what she thought as she crossed mile after mile of grassland and passed the herds that carried her husband's brand. In that first morning's light she may have seen only the beauty of the live oak trees at La Mota, or she may have been impressed by the unbroken expanse of prairie dotted by mesquite trees, stretching out in all directions. She may have felt the isolation of that spot as well, far removed from the social whirl of Galveston and the intellectual atmosphere of Austin, where she had just spent four stimulating years.

The man Mary Miller married was an affable and gregarious individual who hit it off with her mother immediately when they met at Sugarland in the spring of 1902. Ed Lasater celebrated his forty-second birthday a week after marrying Mary Miller. He was twenty years her senior; throughout their married life, she addressed him as "Mr. Lasater."[54] He was in the prime of life when he began his second family, and

[51] Edward H. Caldwell, "Life and Activities," p. 13; interview, Tom Lasater, July 22, 1981.

[52] Interview, Mrs. T. R. Bennett, July 31, 1981.

[53] Interview, Florence Schuetz, April 9, 1981.

[54] Interviews, John M. Bennett, February 24, 1967, and L. D. Miller, Sr., September, 1971.

his land and livestock holdings had increased rapidly since he had made that first purchase along Los Olmos Creek seven years earlier. He was also endowed with a fiery temper, which could match the color of his beard and which did credit to his putative Irish ancestry. He was very excitable, and when working cattle, although he used no profanity, he would scream and yell and wave his hat while directing the work. That was quite a contrast to the Mexican cowboys, who could communicate almost anything across a milling, dusty herd using sign language.[55] Lasater's wrath would typically subside as quickly as the crisis of the moment had passed. In his home, Lasater had "the happy faculty of putting aside and forgetting all thoughts of business cares and worries. His cheerfulness and optimism were contagious and his presence carried with it the bright and humorous side of life."[56]

As the young bride of an established cattleman, Mary Miller was awed by the man who had walked with such purpose into the Millers' Galveston living room. As previously noted, she displayed above-average mathematical ability, and she was more dollars-and-cents conscious than her husband was. "Ed Lasater was not concerned with small things. It rather thrilled her . . . this romantic characteristic of his."[57]

Mary Miller loved music as well, but Ed Lasater had no use for it. John Bennett described an evening with Lasater: "We were in a big hotel in Saratoga and the orchestra played during the dinner hour. He asked me if I understood what they were trying to do. I explained the idea of music as well as I could." Lasater replied that to him it was just "a bunch of noise" and he could not understand why they insisted on playing while he and Bennett were trying to eat and converse.[58]

The isolation on that ranch where Mary Miller went to live with her husband would be broken in the years to come by the frequent visits of relatives and friends. One of Mary Miller's professors at the university, Dr. Caswell Ellis, an instructor of pedagogy, was one of the first to venture south of the Nueces to visit the young bride and her husband.

Ellis took the train south from Kingsville and got off at Katherine.

[55] Ibid.; interview, Tom Lasater, January 12, 1980.
[56] Edward H. Caldwell, "Life and Activities," p. 13.
[57] Interview, Emily Edwards, February 25, 1967.
[58] John M. Bennett, "Notes," p. 4.

There was no station there, only a siding and the pens used for loading cattle. It was dark when he stepped off the train at 4:00 A.M., and he stood alone on the platform for a few minutes after the train had disappeared before a man with a two-wheeled cart pulled up alongside and addressed him in Spanish. Ellis got into the cart, and the two headed west until they reached Pinole Lake, a sizable body of water fed by a large artesian well. The Mexican driver informed Ellis that he was to get out there and that Lasater would be by to pick him up later. The cart departed, and Ellis sat down by the lake to wait. Only after it became light did he notice a carriage parked a few hundred yards away. Ellis approached the carriage, apparently abandoned, which sat motionless on the silent prairie. Out of curiosity he raised one of the window curtains and looked inside, jumping back with surprise. Inside a man in full formal attire, frock coat, stiff collar, spats, handlebar moustache, and gloves sat as if frozen, staring straight ahead, with his arms extended forward grasping a walking stick. The man turned out to be a banker from the East who had also come to the Rancho Falfurrias for a visit.

Sometime later, Ed Lasater appeared suddenly out of the brush. The three men spent a long day touring the southern and central part of Lasater's holdings, stopping by various cow camps and changing teams at several points along the way. At 10:00 that night they arrived at La Mota, where Mary Lasater greeted her former professor and served her guests a large meal. After dinner, the men adjourned to the living room for cigars and a visit before retiring to bed. At 3:00 A.M. the visitors were awakened and advised that breakfast would be ready shortly. An hour later they were heading north toward Realitos to see the other end of the ranch. It had taken six hours to have two meals, a visit, and a night's sleep. As they left La Mota, Ellis turned to the banker and commented, "It damned sure doesn't take long to spend the night at that place."[59]

No, it did not take long to spend the night at La Mota. It did not take long for "El Colorado de los Olmos" to buy land or choose a wife, either. In fact, everything moved rapidly when you rode with that energetic young cowman from Goliad.

[59] Interview, Tom Lasater, January 12, 1980.

CHAPTER 5

The End of the Line

> Do you know that the Gulf Coast country of Texas is full
> of men who are in your position, men who faced the facts
> just like you are doing, and pulled up their stakes and
> moved to this wonderful country?
> —*Falfurrias Bulletin*, 1909

MAJOR Gaines would not have recognized the area below the Nueces River had he lived long enough to see the sleek brochures and to
read the astonishing reports of prosperity and productivity. The desolate wasteland he described after riding through the country north of
the Rio Grande River in the middle of the nineteenth century had
undergone a complete transformation. The sandy and barren land
Gaines rode through was attracting residents from a number of northern states who were drawn by a prolific flow of prose, which detailed in
the most expansive language the glories and economic potential of
northern Starr County.

The sterile country Gaines and his men had trekked across was
described in the early twentieth century as a flowering oasis, where a
wide variety of crops could be readily grown. It was a healthy climate,
and the weather and soil combined to produce abundant harvests of
cotton and corn, as well as most kinds of vegetables and fruits. The af-
firmations were all stated in superlatives, and the dramatic crop yields
were achieved almost effortlessly by colonists who recorded their experiences in notarized statements.[1]

The newfound glamor of the Falfurrias country was more literary
than real, at least in the beginning. The picture painted of the area in
the vicinity of Falfurrias before the real estate promoters recognized

---

[1] *About Falfurrias and Copita; Falfurrias, Texas Wants You; Falfurrias Bulletin.*

the potential for rapid profits remained unflatteringly reminiscent of the bleak assessment written by Major Gaines at the time of the Mexican War. One man who participated extensively in the railroad construction that took place in South Texas in the early years of the twentieth century seemed to echo the major's grim verdict as he described the wagon trains that hauled freight west and south from Corpus Christi to the border before the railroad's arrival: "It was no bed of roses to hit the miles of burning trail across desert stretches day in and day out, but when that semi-arid waste was stricken with drought and water holes dried up, hardships multiplied." The fate of the tough little burros who trudged back and forth across that inhospitable section of country symbolized the negative opinion of many who viewed the area from vantage points north and east of the Nueces River: "At such times the emaciated appearance of those beasts of burden showed something of a marvelous endurance and the awful punishment of the trail. . . . However, drought took its full toll as their whitened, sunbleached bones strewn along the way testified."[2]

Despite years of bad press on the Anglo side of the border, the area surrounding the land grants where Ignacio de la Peña pastured his herds attracted a small but continuous trickle of settlers, principally from south of the Rio Grande. And a series of ranches and small settlements were established in the decades before the trains made their way into South Texas, bringing the northern farmers who responded to the literary lure of the land promoters.

A hand-drawn map of Precinct No. 5 in northern Starr County, dating from about 1880, shows ranches owned by A. López and S. López on the north side of Baluarte Creek. Old Falfurrias is shown midway between Baluarte and Palo Blanco creeks, and close to the northeastern section of the country, near Los Olmos Creek, the settlement of Los Olmos or Paisano is located. Travel through this sandy country was slow and difficult. In 1883, a petition was presented to the Starr County Commissioner's Court asking that "a public road of the first class" be made from the Rio Grande River to Los Olmos.[3]

The Los Olmos community was a stop on the stage line between Santa Gertrudis and Rio Grande City, and the community at one time

[2] J. L. Allhands, *Gringo Builders*, p. 70.
[3] Minutes of Starr County Commissioner's Court, Book "A," p. 128.

had about three hundred inhabitants.[4] One of its principal stores was owned successively by three early residents: Homobono Garza, Camilo Pérez, and Lino Treviño. After the railroad from Corpus Christi to Laredo was completed in 1880, the mail was delivered on horseback • from Realitos. A horseman made the trip three times a week, leaving Realitos on Monday, Wednesday, and Friday and returning on Tuesday, Thursday, and Saturday. The rider's circuit also included Concepción, Santa Cruz, Old Falfurrias, and Delfino in Hidalgo County.[5]

The Word of God also came to Los Olmos on horseback. Father John Peter Bard, priest of the San Francisco de Paula Church in San Diego, Duval County, had a mesquite-country parish, which stretched from the Nueces River to the Baluarte Creek and included some two hundred ranches. He periodically went to perform marriages or baptisms at Los Olmos, where he stayed in the Treviño or Gonzáles homes.[6]

Padre Pedro, as Father Bard was called, was a native of the Basque provinces, where the spirit of rugged individualism had prepared him well for his missionary role on the Texas frontier. "He was frank, outspoken, of irreproachable character, indomitable will and inexhaustible energy. He was filled with zeal and pursuit of souls for God." Padre Pedro, a scholar and a linguist, had traveled extensively in a number of countries before settling permanently in South Texas. "Because of his kindness and solicitude for all the people of his far-flung mission . . . because of his selfless interest in the material and spiritual welfare of all his fellow men, he came to be loved and respected by all peoples of all faiths in the Southwest."[7]

Another Pedro also developed a large following in the vicinity of the boundary between Starr and Duval counties. In 1881, Pedro Jaramillo moved from Mexico to a ranch belonging to Julia Cuellar de García, near Los Olmos Creek. Jaramillo, who was universally known

[4] Rosa Treviño to Mrs. C. A. Downs, November 3, 1973, Brooks County Historical Commission Files. Old Falfurrias was first shown as a mail stop in 1900, according to mail route maps (Florence Schuetz to author, September, 1982).

[5] *Falfurrias Facts*, June 15, 1934; Allhands, *Gringo Builders*, p. 75; Lloyd N. Dyer, "The History of Brooks County" (M.S. thesis, Texas College of Arts and Industries, 1938) p. 24.

[6] Mrs. C. W. Bray, Mrs. C. A. Downs, and Miss Florence Schuetz, "Los Olmos," 1971, p. 5, Brooks County Historical Commission Files; Priscilla L. Buckley and William F. Buckley, Jr., *W.F.B.—An Appreciation*, pp. 10–11.

[7] Ibid.

as Don Pedrito, gradually acquired widespread fame as a healer, although he did not claim to possess any special powers. He explained that his mission was to help the afflicted through their faith in God's healing power. "En el nombre de Dios . . ." ("in the name of God") prefaced all his advice.[8]

By 1894, Don Pedrito was such a familiar figure in San Antonio, where he occasionally spent time receiving the sick and dispensing his cures, that the *San Antonio Daily Express* featured him in a story entitled, "Miracles of Don Pedrito." The article told how crowds of people went to Don Pedrito "to be relieved of all manner of aches and pains and many wonderful stories are told by witnesses as to the cures effected. . . ."[9]

Don Pedrito began his healing work simply by passing along household remedies to area residents. Most of his prescriptions cost little or nothing. Water was a favorite remedy, both hot and cold, either used in immersions or taken internally. Other common ingredients used in his cures included coffee, cheap alcoholic beverages, and native South Texas plants. His first patients were people of the nearby Los Olmos, Las Cabras, and La Parrita ranches.[10]

Padre Pedro was Spanish; Don Pedrito was a native of Guadalajara, Mexico. But Texas herself would produce another individual

---

[8] Samuel P. Nesmith, *The Mexican Texans*, p. 25; *Falfurrias Facts*, January 29, 1981.

[9] *San Antonio Daily Express*, April 8, 1894.

[10] *Falfurrias Facts*, January 29, 1981, and February 5, 1981. Don Pedrito was born near Guadalajara, Mexico, in the early years of the century—1827 or 1829 (*Falfurrias Facts*, January 29, 1981), or perhaps 1801 (*San Antonio Daily Express*, April 8, 1894). His funeral announcement after his death on July 3, 1907, indicates an 1829 birthdate. The announcement states that he was almost 78 years old (Florence Schuetz to author, September, 1982). Don Pedrito reportedly administered an early and informal welfare program. During the lengthy drought that began in 1893 and proved to be financially devastating for so many Starr County landowners, Don Pedrito fed many residents with his own food supplies and with stocks of corn and beans the state sent to him for distribution (*Falfurrias Facts*, February 1, 1981). Not everyone approved of him or his methods. The American Medical Association pressed charges against the healer, but a federal judge in Corpus Christi dismissed the case because Don Pedrito charged no fees in dispensing his prescriptions and cures (*Falfurrias Facts*, February 12, 1981). Seven decades after his death, a steady stream of visitors continues to make their way to the simple shrine located at Los Olmos, some expressing gratitude for cures given to forebears, some to invoke his spirit for the health or safety of loved ones today (*Falfurrias Facts*, February 12, 1981).

whose influence would be widely felt in the area. Goliad was not only the spawning ground for a number of Texas' largest livestock entrepreneurs, it was also the birthplace of Ignacio Zaragoza, a man who became one of Mexico's most revered heroes after his defeat of the French forces at Puebla on May 5, 1862. Zaragoza clubs sprang up in various Texas cities and towns in honor of that pivotal victory.[11] One such Sociedad Ignacio Zaragoza was formed in Los Olmos on January 24, 1886.

Early members of this mutual aid society, a club with "moral, progressive and philanthropic" aims, were Lino Treviño, Leocadio Flores, Damaso López, Albino Salinas, Eusebio Ríos, and Francisco Garza. Those unfamiliar with the historical evolution of the disputed area south of the Nueces River might have been surprised by some of the language included in the opening resolution adopted by those original members, who lived one hundred miles north of the Mexican border: "Those who found this club are and will continue to be Mexicans who maintain their rights as such."[12]

In the Treaty of Guadalupe Hidalgo in 1848, Mexico relinquished her claim to the territory north of the Rio Grande, thus resolving the longstanding border dispute between the United States and Mexico. But the governments that made that agreement were both far removed from the sandy pastures along Los Olmos Creek. Fifty years after that treaty was signed, Padre Pedro, Don Pedrito, and the Sociedad Ignacio Zaragoza were living symbols of the dominant influences and characteristics of life between the Nueces and the Rio Grande.

The peaceful rural tranquility and the predominantly Mexican lifestyle found in the area along Los Olmos Creek before 1900 were destined to change. After the turn of the century, new means of transportation and a new influx of Anglo settlers interrupted the established pattern of life in northern Starr County.

Ed Lasater's marriage to Mary Miller in 1902 and the extension of

[11] Nesmith, *The Mexican Texans*, pp. 23–24.

[12] Ignacio Zaragoza Society Documents, Treviño Files, in possession of Florentino Treviño, Falfurrias. There were five prerequisites for membership in the Sociedad Ignacio Zaragoza: the member had to be twenty-one years old, be a Mexican citizen, not be a habitual drunkard, lead a good and honest life, and never have been punished for an obscene crime (Ibid.).

the railroad south from Alice to the Falfurrias Ranch in 1904 were two catalysts that permanently altered the existing way of life in those isolated pasturelands near the Loma Blanca. The railroads provided a cheap and accessible form of public transportation to carry northern settlers, their families, and their possessions into the country south of the Nueces River. Mary Miller's brothers provided much of the personal energy and aggressive effort needed to mobilize a stream of colonists toward the Falfurrias Ranch.

Shortly after 1900, Ed Lasater began actively working to bring rail service into the central part of his property. The logistics involved in shipping cattle off his ranch and in bringing in the fencing and other material necessary to improve his holdings constituted a major problem. The two closest railroad terminals were at Realitos and Alice, thirty to fifty miles away from parts of his property. The northwestern extremity of the Falfurrias Ranch bordered the Texas-Mexican Railway at Realitos. But driving cattle to the shipping point at Alice involved passing through other properties and this often caused friction with neighboring landowners.[13]

The first recorded visit of railroad officials to the vicinity of Lasater's headquarters took place in 1902. Charles Premont drove a hack carrying a railroad official, an attorney, and a contractor south from Alice. James Maupin had to take the group back through Realitos because of heavy rains and flooding that occurred during the tour.[14]

In early 1903, R. J. Kleberg, Robert Driscoll, and Uriah Lott secured a charter to build a railroad from Sinton south to Brownsville, a line that would run through Katherine, a few miles to the east of Lasater's southernmost pastures.[15] A few months later, M. D. Monseratte announced that the San Antonio and Aransas Pass Railroad would build a competing line from their terminus at Alice to Brownsville. Construction of this line toward the Falfurrias Ranch began shortly thereafter, but Lasater's property became the railroad terminus. "Something in their plans appears not to have jelled, for it was not until June 1,

---

[13] Edward H. Caldwell, *Life and Activities of Edward Cunningham Lasater*, p. 11.

[14] *Falfurrias Facts*, undated article, Lasater Files, in possession of Garland M. Lasater, Falfurrias. Premont was founded in 1909 by, and named after, Charles Premont, foreman of the Seeligson Ranch.

[15] Allhands, *Gringo Builders*, p. 12.

1904, that they officially opened their line into Ed C. Lasater's city, Falfurrias, whereupon the extension to Brownsville was abandoned."[16]

When the railroad arrived in 1904, Lasater was ready with plans to subdivide and sell a large block of his land lying near the railroad terminus. The future evolution of this block of pastureland, where herds of sheep and cattle had grazed, was already implicit in the colorful name placed on that original subdivision: "The Falfurrias Farm and Garden Tracts."

The modest opening shot in the publicity campaign that would ultimately draw hundreds of settlers to the Falfurrias Ranch was a short story in the *Alice Echo* in July, 1904, which called its readers' attention to the development to the south. The article stated that the "fine farming and trucking land known as Falfurrias, terminus of the San Antonio and Aransas Pass Railway, and head of the great artesian belt belonging to Ed Lasater, is now for sale; his town property will not be for sale until August 1." Anyone desiring any "further particulars" on the acreage available near Falfurrias was encouraged to write: "Ed C. Lasater, 'Land,' Falfurrias, Texas."[17]

Captain James A. Brooks was one of the first to buy a parcel in the Falfurrias Farm and Garden Tracts. In June of 1904, Brooks purchased eighty acres for $1,200, paying $240 down with the balance due in four equal annual installments at 7 percent interest.[18] This noted Texas Ranger captain had become acquainted with Lasater in the course of his work in the area between Alice and the Rio Grande, and the future state representative and county judge would be closely associated with Lasater in the years following his decision to settle permanently in the Falfurrias area in 1906.[19]

Other early purchasers of land in this subdivision were James Maupin, Frank and Ed Rachal, W. W. Sloan, and Walter and Oliver Caldwell. James J. Allan, Lino Treviño, the Garcías, and the Lozanos were among the first to buy town lots. Most of the acreage sold for $12 to $15 per acre; lots in town brought $100 to $150.[20]

[16] Ibid., p. 41; Edward H. Caldwell, *Life and Activities*, p. 11.

[17] *Alice Echo*, July 7, 1904.

[18] W. L. Dawson, "Abstract of Lands of Ed C. Lasater in Falfurrias Town Tract and Falfurrias Farm and Garden Tracts from June 1, 1904 to May 18, 1906," p. 3.

[19] Dyer, "History of Brooks County," p. 55; interview, John Morgan Brooks, April 4, 1981; Walter Prescott Webb, *The Texas Rangers*, pp. 457–58.

[20] Dawson, "Abstract of Lands," pp. 1–9.

Within a short time after the arrival of the railroad, the quarter-section of land that Lasater set aside for a town began to exhibit the first signs of the community that would develop there. The *Alice Echo* in September, 1904, announced that a local firm was furnishing the lumber for ten homes, a two-story store building, and a hotel in Falfurrias.[21] The hotel was a project owned jointly by Lasater and the railroad company. Frank Rachal owned the first livery stable, and Marcus Phillips installed the first drug store in the little community, where Lino Treviño served as justice of the peace and the Reverend Caldwell's son, Walter, conducted an early Sunday school.[22]

Ed Lasater's formal dedication of the town took place on November 7, 1904.[23] The following month, Birdie Myrick described her arrival in Falfurrias, where she was taken from the depot to the Park Hotel in a two-horse hack for twenty-five cents. The hotel was a two-story frame building with eight bedrooms, a dining room, and a kitchen. "The next morning . . . I glimpsed Falfurrias for the first time by daylight. Falfurrias consisted of several unpainted buildings, the Palace Hotel, the Adams and Garrett Mercantile Store and post office combined, the railroad station and a saloon. . . ." The two large parks were fenced by a whitewashed lumber railing: "Beyond this was brush, spotted here and there by a little jacal. Falfurrias was a barren, desolate, quiet little village, but its inhabitants were a companionable, interdependent people, which took some of the edge off the loneliness."[24]

The railroad company's decision to terminate its southern extension on Lasater's ranch made Falfurrias "the end of the line," a descriptive title which for some captured the character of the new community and the nature of the people who came to populate it: "Falfurrias was the end of the line. The only people who moved here were renegades, derelicts, or individuals who did not fit in anywhere else. And a high percentage of the new residents were alcoholics."[25]

Surrounding the town were thousands of acres of prairie and mesquite brush populated by cattle and horses along with herds of wild

[21] *Alice Echo*, September 1, 1904.

[22] *Falfurrias Facts*, September 29, 1933.

[23] Transcribed Deed Records from Starr County, Brooks County, vol. VII, p. 271.

[24] *Falfurrias Facts*, June 15, 1934.

[25] Interview, Dick McIntyre, July 26, 1981. One early resident disagrees with this characterization of early settlers: "I knew many of these people as church-going Christian ladies and gentlemen" (Florence Schuetz to author, September, 1982).

burros. But through the efforts of the early real estate promoters and later because of its cattle and its products, the fame of the little town at the end of the line would belie its inauspicious beginnings.

One year after he had initiated his subdividing project, Lasater had sold 1,119 acres to fourteen buyers.[26] The low-key approach and the slow pace of the initial land sales, made principally to people who were already residing in the area or who were at least familiar with the region, buyers like García, Maupin, Rachal, and Treviño, represented only the preliminary phase of a new direction. Lasater was occupied with his ranching operation and subsequently with a series of new businesses. The Miller brothers provided the impetus necessary to make real estate promotion and colonization a major enterprise in northern Starr County, permanently transforming life in the Falfurrias country.

Ed Lasater's proposal to Mary Miller brought him more than a second wife. He acquired an entire family, one that unanimously decided that the future looked promising in Falfurrias. Within a short time after the girl from Galveston moved to her husband's home at La Mota, nine other members of her family moved to that quiet village on Palo Blanco Creek. They included her widowed mother, her uncle and his family, and her four brothers. Within the ranks of these relatives, Ed Lasater found a number of partners and associates in his non-ranching enterprises over the following years. And his wife's brothers would play a central role in the real estate development that would populate some forty thousand acres of the Falfurrias Ranch with several hundred farming families from the Midwest.[27]

Whether it was the financial pressure of the heavy additional debt burden Lasater's ranch operation had to support as a result of his loan

---

[26] Dawson, "Abstract of Lands," pp. 19–20.

[27] One brochure stated: "More than 50,000 acres of land from the ranch have been sold for farming purposes" (*Falfurrias Jerseys: Type, Production, Beauty, Utility*, 1919). Another article stated that since 1906 Ed Lasater had sold to some 500 families 60,000 acres of his original ranch (Everett Lloyd, "Ed C. Lasater: The World's Jersey King and His 300,000 Acre Kingdom," *National Magazine*, February, 1920). Garland Lasater is not certain that many acres were ever sold to settlers. After Ed Lasater's death, a sizable tract was turned over to the San Antonio Loan and Trust Company, part of which was in the subdivisions Ed Lasater had separated from his ranch (Interview, Garland M. Lasater, July 29, 1981).

to Edward Cunningham or the presence of the Miller brothers, full of youthful energy and endowed with promotional talents, which caused Ed Lasater to undertake the subdivision of a major portion of his ranch cannot be stated conclusively. Whatever the original motivation behind that project was, however, the Miller brothers provided the active management for the various companies whose imaginative publicity and wide-ranging activity created a new image and ultimately a new vitality in part of the area.

Three of the Miller brothers and Mary Lasater's uncle, William A. Gardner, all moved to Falfurrias in 1904. Like the Millers, Gardner had lived in Galveston, and there he lost his business in the storm of 1900. Gardner became involved in a minor way with the land development activity in Falfurrias in addition to serving as an early justice of the peace and later as postmaster.[28]

Garland and Richard were Mary Lasater's older brothers, and both of them preceded her to the University of Texas. Robert was the fourth child in the Miller family. Laurence, born in 1888, followed his older brothers, moving to Falfurrias when he was eighteen. Garland was a very imaginative individual, a dreamer, according to his youngest brother. Rob Miller was an aggressive young man with an outgoing personality and was a great storyteller. "Rob could walk into a crowd anywhere and immediately become the center of attention."[29]

In addition to their roles in the land development business, the Miller brothers were active in the other Lasater enterprises. Lasater's hiring of his brothers-in-law followed his usual pattern of placing employees whom he liked and trusted in positions of responsibility, which often surpassed their capabilities. Rob knew nothing about farming before moving to Falfurrias, but Lasater installed him as manager of one of the largest farming operations in the state. The young and inexperienced L. D. was put in charge of the office staff that kept the finan-

[28] Interviews, Laurence D. Miller, Sr., September 22, 1971, William B. Gardner, Jr., March 26, 1982. After the devastating Galveston storm, Gardner sent his family to live in Mexico City for several years (Ibid.).

[29] Interview, L. D. Miller, September 22, 1971. The Miller brothers' full names were Garland Burleigh Miller, Jr., Richard Gardner Miller, Robert Gardner Miller (Rob), and Laurence Kleber Dismukes Miller. The name Kleber was added to the youngest son's name as an afterthought during his baptism. Miller later dropped that name and was known to everyone as "L. D."

cial records for this true frontier conglomerate.[30] The report issued by a group of auditors Lasater hired in 1909 left no doubt that the financial records maintained by his office were woefully inadequate.[31]

Garland Miller was the oldest brother and the original driving force behind the Falfurrias real estate promotion. He and B. T. Henry had served as Lasater's assistants on the Cunningham plantation during the period Lasater was charged with managing that operation. When Lasater's involvement there ended, both Miller and Henry moved to Falfurrias.[32] Miller worked on the ranch before gravitating into the more challenging field of real estate development. "At the time the idea of building the town of Falfurrias first occurred to Ed Lasater, Garland Miller . . . was punching cattle on Mr. Lasater's ranch. With ambition and energy to burn, Mr. Miller commenced the building of Falfurrias and the selling of the surrounding land."[33]

At least six different entities were created between 1904 and 1912 to handle the sales of various tracts Lasater cut off of his Falfurrias Ranch. They were the Falfurrias Development Company, the Falfurrias Immigration Company, the Miller Bros. Company, the Lasater-Miller Company, the Cornell-Miller Texas Farms Company, and the Falfurrias Semi-Tropic Homes Company. The Miller brothers played a dominant role in each of these companies, which spearheaded the subdivision and sale of not only a portion of Lasater's ranch but other area properties as well.

[30] Ibid.

[31] Ibid. Ed Lasater had considerable experience hiring relatives prior to marrying Mary Miller. Alex Noble, an uncle of his first wife, Martha Noble Bennett, managed some of Ed Lasater's early Oklahoma grazing operations (Interview, John M. Bennett, February 24, 1967). Two brothers of Edward Caldwell, who married Lasater's sister Ada, worked in various capacities for Ed Lasater. Oliver Caldwell owned a drilling rig and drilled a number of wells on Lasater's ranch. Walter E. Caldwell was an early arrival in the Falfurrias country and was employed by Lasater up until 1909 (Edward H. Caldwell, "An Appreciation of Edward Cunningham Lasater," p. 6; interview, Sarah Cunningham, June 26, 1971). "W. E. Caldwell and family will move to Falfurrias in Starr County where Caldwell will take charge of Ed C. Lasater's cattle and ranch interests on New Year's Day" (*Alice Echo*, December 26, 1901).

[32] Price Waterhouse and Co. to Ed C. Lasater, May 31, 1909, Lasater Files.

[33] *Falfurrias Bulletin.* "Garland B. Miller, the enterprising force behind the progressive movement at Falfurrias, was in Alice Wednesday between the arrival of the SAP from the south and the departure of the Tex-Mex for Corpus Christi" (*Alice Echo*, September 8, 1908).

The Falfurrias Development Company had a brief history. It was created in 1905 as a partnership among Ed Lasater, Garland Miller, and B. T. Henry, who associated themselves "to do any and all business except banking." A year later the agreement was canceled "to the mutual satisfaction of all parties hereto," and its role as real estate developer was taken over by the Falfurrias Immigration Company.[34] This corporation entered into an agreement with Ed Lasater by which it could sell up to 100,000 acres of his ranchland lying between Falfurrias and Realitos. Lasater would pay the corporation a commission of three dollars per acre on all sales, but in no case would Lasater receive less than eight dollars net per acre. The company was required to sell a minimum of 10,000 acres per year between 1907 and 1910; if that sales volume was not maintained, Lasater had the option of canceling the contract.[35]

Lasater was the original president of the Falfurrias Immigration Company, with Garland Miller serving as secretary. W. M. Sims was a vice-president and was in charge of an office the company maintained in the Railway Exchange Building in Chicago. G. R. Spielhagen was the general representative for the state of Texas and was in charge of the company's branch office in San Antonio.[36] Control and ownership of the company subsequently passed into the hands of Spielhagen and the Miller brothers.

A lawsuit filed a few years later by Spielhagen against the Falfurrias Immigration Company provides some insight into the operational approach of that company and the extent of its activities. Spielhagen was the organization's largest individual stockholder, owning thirty-three of one hundred shares. The Miller brothers collectively owned sixty-five shares; W. A. Gardner and B. T. Henry each owned one share. Spielhagen's lawsuit affirmed that the company had created a very profitable operation and alleged that the Millers had conspired to appropriate "the business goodwill, property, contracts, commissions and profits of said company. . . ." This appropriation was accomplished, Spielhagen charged in his suit requesting the appointment of a re-

[34] Falfurrias Development Company partnership agreement, Lasater Files.
[35] Agreement between the Falfurrias Immigration Company, a corporation, and Ed C. Lasater, Lasater Files.
[36] *Falfurrias, Texas Wants You.*

ceiver for the corporation, by shifting the company's business into other competing entities owned by the Millers.[37]

The Falfurrias Immigration Company was "engaged in the promotion of immigration and a general real estate business. . . ." It operated a large and profitable business until the middle of 1907 and had secured a number of lucrative contracts for the purchase and sale of lands on commission. The corporation had one hundred branch offices and agencies scattered throughout the United States and spent $30,000 in a nationwide advertising campaign. This early-day public relations blitz emanating out of the little community in northern Starr County included the printing and distribution of 7,000 maps, 40,000 circular letters, and 250,000 pieces of illustrated literature. The company advertised in 1,800 newspapers and acquired a mailing list of more than 20,000 persons.[38]

After 1907, the Miller Bros. Company became the principal organization involved with the Falfurrias real estate promotion. Branch offices, widespread advertising and distribution of promotional literature, and personal travel through the Midwest put the Millers in contact with prospective buyers. The homeseeker rates available on the railroads made long-distance promotion economically feasible.

Real estate development around Falfurrias and in other parts of the state flourished with the assistance of the inexpensive excursion rates from midwestern cities to Texas. Excursion trains departed on

[37] *Spielhagen v. Falfurrias Immigration Co. et al.*, in 129 *The Southwestern Reporter*, pp. 164–70. Spielhagen's suit was against the Falfurrias Immigration Company, "having its principal office and place of business in the town of Falfurrias, Starr County, Texas, and against Garland B. Miller, Richard G. Miller, Robert G. Miller, Laurence D. Miller and against Garland B. Miller dba Garland B. Miller, Investors' Agent": "On or about May 1, 1907, the said Garland B. Miller, Richard G. Miller, Robert G. Miller and W. A. Gardner entered into a conspiracy among themselves and with Laurence D. Miller, a brother of the said three Millers, to injure the said Spielhagen and the said corporation by appropriating the business goodwill, property, contracts, commissions and profits of the said company and to render valueless the said stock of said company, and in effect to end its existence." On August 1, 1907, Spielhagen was dropped from the Board of Directors at the annual stockholders meeting and W. A. Gardner was elected as director in his stead. "On or about June 15, 1907, the said four Miller brothers organized the firm known as the Miller Bros. Co. and have ever since been engaged at said town of Falfurrias in the same lines and character of business as those of the corporation and in competition, rivalry and conflict therewith" (Ibid.).

[38] Ibid.

the first and third Tuesday of every month. A round-trip ticket from Chicago to Falfurrias cost thirty dollars. One from St. Louis or Kansas City cost twenty-five dollars. The traveler could leave St. Louis at 8:32 P.M. Tuesday and arrive in San Antonio at 7:30 A.M. Thursday. At 9:00 A.M. he would leave on the San Antonio and Aransas Pass Railroad (S.A. & A.P.), arriving in Falfurrias at suppertime that evening.[39] Often an entire trainload from one area would group together to inspect the real estate prospects around Falfurrias or some other part of the state.

The migration of midwestern farmers into southern Texas followed the path of railroad construction, spreading from Houston south toward Kingsville and then into the Rio Grande Valley. In the years following the extension of the S.A & A.P. line from Alice to Falfurrias, other colonization companies in South Texas were selling off parts of the Driscoll Ranch, the King Ranch, and others and were founding communities like Robstown, Bishop, and Riviera.[40]

A 1906 article in a San Antonio newspaper carried the headline: "Big Ranches Rapidly Being Cut Into Farms." The article quoted a resident of Pearsall, a community southwest of San Antonio: "All the vast tracts that have been used for ranches for so many years are being broken into small farms. . . . Companies that own hundreds of thousands of acres are finding that to run cattle on land worth ten dollars an acre is unprofitable and are selling." Once the rangelands were divided and populated, a variety of enterprises were launched to provide the communities with outlets for products produced by the newly arrived farmers: "Several attempts have been made recently to start creameries and canning factories, but most have failed."[41]

South Texas was not the only part of the state where ranchers began cutting up their properties in the early years of the twentieth century. Extensive subdividing occurred in the Texas panhandle during the same period, where the huge XIT Ranch, pressured by capital needs, sold off much of its land. In West Texas the Muleshoe Ranch and the Snyder brothers staked out farms across their grass ranges, and

---

[39] *Falfurrias Bulletin*; interview, L. D. Miller, Sr., September 22, 1971.
[40] L. D. Miller, Sr., to Peggy K. Lasater, August 11, 1964; Allhands, *Gringo Builders*, pp. 81–82.
[41] *San Antonio Express*, January 22, 1906.

S. M. Swenson and Sons and the White Deer Company, a remnant of the gigantic Franklyn Land and Cattle Company, carried out two of the most successful colonization programs.[42]

The promotional literature circulated across the country by the Falfurrias promoters focused on three major selling points: the productive capacity of Falfurrias land, weather that favored crop production and was agreeable year-round, and the general healthfulness of the climate. In the Falfurrias country, cotton was a crop that never failed, corn did well, orange trees were prolific, and the local watermelons were the first to be harvested in the country.

Notarized testimonials provided by area residents were another important part of the literature. John Donohoe, who moved from San Patricio to Falfurrias in 1904, gave one of the enthusiastic early reports: "After one year's residence at Falfurrias and careful observation of the soil and climate, I have come to the conclusion that standard crops such as cotton, corn, sorghum and the like, and truck and fruit can be grown here more profitably than anywhere else in the country." Donohoe stated further: "My experience has been exceedingly profitable to me and I have great faith in the future of the Falfurrias country."[43]

A 1911 Miller Bros. publication quoted Leopoldo García, who lived in Copita. García had grown corn on one field for more than thirty years, and in that time he had never made less than twenty bushels per acre, the average yield being thirty-five bushels. García's field made two crops yearly, with plantings in January and August. The brochure further asserted that local vegetable growers could produce field-grown vegetables early in the spring or late in the fall by irrigating with the warm artesian water "which exists in apparently inexhaustible quantities. . . ."[44]

On a personal level, the agreeable Falfurrias climate offered a uniquely healthful environment for raising a family and for those afflicted with many common ailments: "This section is absolutely free from malaria. . . . The cooling breezes from the Gulf are dry enough by the time they reach here to make this a climate which is good for lung troubles, asthma and catarrh." The publicists were positive but,

[42] Gene M. Gressley, *Bankers and Cattlemen*, p. 270.
[43] *Falfurrias, Texas Wants You*; *Alice Echo*, November 3, 1904.
[44] *About Falfurrias and Copita*.

subtly, with qualification: "In short, there is no healthier section of the United States or of the world, so far as we know."[45]

Successive brochures detailed the pressure of demand on the available acreage and the constantly rising land prices. A 1906 brochure priced land in the Falfurrias Farm and Garden Tracts at fifteen dollars an acre for the "proven artesian territory near town," while more distant parcels could be bought for as low as ten dollars. The offer called for a twenty percent down payment, the balance in four equal annual installments at seven percent interest. The brochure forewarned prospective buyers: "At present prices, we believe these are the cheapest lands, everything considered, in the United States; and we expect quick and rapid advances. For these reasons, we do not guarantee the prices mentioned for any future time."[46]

A brochure published a short time later confirmed the inevitable; land was now selling at fifteen dollars to eighty dollars an acre, depending upon its distance from the railroad. The results realized had surpassed all the expectations of the developers, the publication stated, and inquiries were arriving daily from interested parties all over the Midwest.[47] Even at these inflated prices, the Miller brothers assured their clients, Falfurrias land still represented a solid value for the northern farmer to consider: "He can live in a better climate, have better health, and have three or four acres increasing in value where he now has but one."[48]

Having gotten the attention of midwestern agriculturists, the next step was to get a trainload of home seekers headed for South Texas. Upon arrival in Falfurrias, the group was loaded into buggies (later touring cars) and taken to Loma Bonita (pretty hill), the Miller brothers' farm southeast of Falfurrias. This farm, with extensive citrus groves and vegetables and other crops growing, was maintained as a showplace at considerable expense. At Loma Bonita a widow's walk complete with handrail allowed the prospects to walk around the roof of the main house in order to view the farm in all its productive splendor.[49]

---

[45] *Falfurrias, Texas Wants You.*
[46] Ibid.
[47] *Falfurrias: The Land of Heart's Delight.*
[48] *About Falfurrias and Copita.*
[49] Interview, L. D. Miller, Sr., September 22, 1971; Gardner Miller, July 22, 1981. "Loma Bonita was my mother's home place, and she died there 7-22-1908. . . . Our farm

After touring Loma Bonita, the caravan headed out into the prairie country, which covered a large section of the rangeland to the north and west of Falfurrias before mesquite trees spread over the entire area. A small hotel had been erected for the northern travelers, and it sat on a rise in the middle of an open plain where the Copita Farm and Garden Tracts were located. The rustic hotel and its surroundings had little to offer the weary travelers other than a well-stocked bar. Heavy liquor consumption was an integral part of the land promotion business. Whether Ed Lasater was not aware of the role that unlimited quantities of beer and hard liquor played in his selling effort, or whether he simply looked the other way, recognizing that happy prospects were necessary to close land deals, is not known. A certain understanding must have existed: "Everyone watched out where they drank when Ed Lasater was in town," the youngest of the Miller brothers recalled.[50] But the Miller Brothers' promotional talents and their personal ability to consume alcohol along with the most practiced of their northern prospects offset any negative effect on sales which Ed Lasater's anti-liquor bias might have had.[51]

Despite the extensive publicity and the well-orchestrated tours, only a small percentage of those prospects who journeyed to Falfurrias ever bought land. With the heavy front-end promotional expenditures added to the locally incurred operational expenses, the cost of sales in the land development program was consistently high.[52]

One major obstacle to making sales was a matter of logistics. After the potential buyer read the brochures, talked to the branch office salesmen, and bought a ticket on the home-seeker train, the local sales force could only hope that prospective colonists would be scheduled to arrive on a day when the wind was not blowing. Blowing sand quickly

---

extended one-half mile north of Miller Bros. addition and the entire place was a garden spot. The only trouble was that we never made a dime out of farming" (L. D. Miller, Sr., to Peggy K. Lasater, August 11, 1964).

[50] Interview, L. D. Miller, Sr., September 22, 1971. Brooks County was voted dry shortly after its organization in 1911. Perhaps for that reason the homeseekers were taken to a hotel in Duval County (Florence Schuetz to author, September, 1982).

[51] Garland, Rob, and Richard Miller were all noted for their heavy drinking. L. D. Miller did not drink in later life, and if in early years he had kept up with his heavy-drinking older brothers, "he never owned up to it" (Interviews, Gardner Miller, July 22, 1981; Walter Blumer, July 12, 1981; and Mrs. T. R. Bennett, July 31, 1981).

[52] Interview, L. D. Miller, Sr., September 22, 1971.

dispelled the literary illusions created earlier by the publicists. It was hard enough under the best of circumstances to convince a northern farmer used to heavy black soils that this single "sandy loam" soil was not heavily weighted to the side of sand. With the wind whipping the sand into his face, the sales task was rendered exceedingly difficult.[53]

Few of the reactions of those making the trip to the end of the line were recorded, but one man's remarks expressed in mild language what many others might have stated in more pointed and caustic terms. As one group of home seekers from Missouri was being hauled out to Copita in a buggy, a *paisano* (roadrunner) ran across the road. One of the Missouri farmers asked what it was.

"That's a bird of paradise," answered the land salesman.

"He's a helluva long way from home," responded the prospective buyer.[54]

By 1909, a new business entity appeared on the Falfurrias colonization scene. This one had a longer and more exotic name, which implied that perhaps the sales emphasis had shifted to a different clientele: the Falfurrias Semi-Tropic Homes Company. Now ten-acre tracts were being promoted to northern buyers. These plots could be purchased for twenty dollars down and twenty dollars a month. The promotional material claimed that this small acreage would produce, a $1,500 profit annually: "And best of all, you would be absolutely sure of that amount every year. We know that some land companies claim much greater results for their sections, but we prefer to give you the rule, not the exception."[55]

The promotional mail-outs produced by the latest Miller enterprise included the standard glowing descriptions of the agricultural possibilities awaiting the alert individual in this southernmost land of

[53] Ibid.

[54] Interviews, Marvin Noll, July 4, 1981, and Alonzo Cosby, July 5, 1981.

[55] *Falfurrias Bulletin.* A Miller Bros. Co. brochure published in 1911 stated that the Miller brothers during the past seven years had been involved in selling, either directly or indirectly, a number of properties in addition to Ed Lasater's. This brochure stated that they had sold 10,000 acres out of the Falfurrias Farm and Garden Tracts, 13,000 acres of "La Gloria lands," 44,000 acres of the Galveston Ranch, and 18,000 acres of the Parrita Ranch (*About Falfurrias and Copita*).

In 1909, the Miller brothers acted as agents for Henrietta M. King, the captain's widow, in transacting the sale of a piece of the King Ranch to the real estate partnership of E. O. Burton and A. H. Danforth (Jimmie R. Picquet, "Some Ghost Towns in South Texas" [M.S. thesis, Texas A&I University, 1972], pp. 102–19).

opportunity. And they were filled with testimonials: E. R. Rachal, Sr., credited with planting the first citrus grove in the area, wrote an enthusiastic account of his experience in the Falfurrias country. "I got here October 20, 1904, and in the spring of 1905 I planted beans, watermelons, Irish potatoes, cantaloupes and sweet potatoes. All of these paid well, which was very gratifying. . . ." Rachal stated that he realized one hundred twenty dollars from one-half acre of onions and a profit of eighty-five dollars per acre on string beans, adding that he was confident that a one-hundred-dollar net could be realized twice a year with string beans. "I have lived in Southwest Texas since 1867," Rachal wrote. "Mine is a case of a stockman turning truck-grower and farmer, and a mighty contented one I am."[56]

The Falfurrias Semi-Tropic Homes Company made a special pitch to single women. An article entitled "Falfurrias for Women" went into some detail about how the purchase of land by a woman, whether as an investment or as a home, represented a perfectly safe proposition that would pay a good rate of interest every year. The woman who wanted to move to Falfurrias to manage her investment personally would find that she would be very pleased with the town and its people. If a woman wanted someone else to manage her property, the company would do that for 25 percent of the owner's one-quarter share of the crop: "For the non-resident owner, this three-sixteenths of the crop pays a splendid interest on the money invested, and as the land is increasing in value every year it certainly makes as safe an investment as anyone could ask for."[57]

A number of women responded positively to the alluring propaganda produced by the various companies promoting land sales in Falfurrias and adjacent areas. One of them was Ela Hockaday, who bought a tract of land near Falfurrias and moved there for a short time before moving on to Dallas, where she started a noted girls' secondary

[56] E. R. Rachal, to the editor, *Falfurrias Facts*, July 10, 1906, reprinted in *Falfurrias Bulletin*. The publicists provided extensive detail on what the soil and climatic conditions around Falfurrias could produce. But even on land that was not producing, men were reportedly making good money. The *Falfurrias Bulletin* detailed the history of one ten-acre tract that R. C. Fechner bought for $325. After one year, he sold it to Frank S. Rachal for $650, who in turn sold it for cash a year later at $1,450. "All this time the land hasn't produced one dollar of the money that has been made out of it" (*Falfurrias Bulletin*).

[57] *Falfurrias Bulletin*.

school. Otie York was another single woman who responded to the promoters' invitation. An unmarried school teacher from Kingfisher, Oklahoma, she traveled to Falfurrias and bought a small farm on the Copita prairie. Before she could get out of town, Ed Lasater heard that an unattached educator was in Falfurrias and rushed to find her in order to make her the following proposition: if she would teach school for one year at Copita, he would get her a job in the new Falfurrias school the following year. Miss York accepted the offer. In Falfurrias she met and married A. A. Cosby, who by coincidence had also immigrated from Canadian County, Oklahoma, and together they made that quiet village their permanent home.[58]

Despite the direct appeal to women investors, the Falfurrias area maintained a reputation as a man's country. Men adjusted quickly to the region's particular flavor of frontier living. Many women never adjusted to the rustic environment and the isolation, and even those who adapted and stayed often reacted negatively upon their first contact. Rose Schuetz cried for two weeks after her first glimpse of Flowella, east of Falfurrias, and Marybelle Bennett thought her husband had taken her to "the jumping off place." H. C. Holbrook's wife, Ada Ann, "cried bitter tears" when she first glimpsed the primitive reality. Holbrook's response to his wife's disenchantment may or may not have been typical. He told his wife that if she really wanted to return to their former hometown, he would go into the depot to order a boxcar to transport the family's possessions. But Mrs. Holbrook's momentary relief faded quickly when Holbrook added that she could go back to central Texas if she wished, but he was going to make his home in Falfurrias. Mrs. Holbrook stayed.[59]

Despite the exaggerated claims in the promotional literature and the disenchantment of many of those who ventured south to see this latter-day Garden of Eden firsthand, the land sales progressed, though slowly, and over a period of years several hundred buyers loaded their

[58] Interview, A. Alonzo Cosby, Jr., July 5, 1981. Alvin Alonzo Cosby, Sr. (1869–1945) moved to Falfurrias in 1910 from El Reno, Oklahoma, where he had served as sheriff. He and Chester Wolfe worked for Ed Lasater for a period of time bringing excursion trains to Falfurrias from Oklahoma and Kansas (Ibid.).

[59] Interviews, Miss Florence Schuetz, April 9, 1981; Mrs. T. R. Bennett, July 31, 1981; Mrs. Leslie Holbrook Gammie, July 25, 1981.

families on trains to start a new life in the Falfurrias country. While the Miller brothers were printing enticing copy and traveling around the Midwest promoting sales of South Texas real estate, Ed Lasater's ranch operation was growing and prospering. Even after he made the decision to subdivide and sell a portion of his ranch, Lasater continued to expand his ranch holdings. One of his last major ranchland acquisitions was a sixty-thousand-acre purchase from the neighboring Santa Rosa Ranch in 1906.[60] As the land sales expanded and the population of the Falfurrias country began growing, Lasater responded to the awakening needs of the new community by investing sizable amounts of capital in a variety of new businesses.

The Falfurrias State Bank was chartered and opened for business in September, 1905. This bank had an initial capital stock of ten thousand dollars, with one hundred shares outstanding. The original ownership breakdown was as follows: Ed Lasater, thirty shares; Garland Miller and B. T. Henry, twenty-five shares each; Gus R. Scott, a Corpus Christi attorney, ten shares; and George W. Brackenridge, the San Antonio banker, ten shares. These five men also comprised the original board of directors.[61]

The Falfurrias Mercantile Store, which had operated in Old Falfurrias before moving to the new townsite, was incorporated in early 1906. The charter showed initial capital stock of $40,000 owned by the five shareholders who were also the original directors: R. C. Fechner, B. T. Henry, Ed Lasater, Garland Miller, and Richard Miller.[62]

R. M. Curtis, Lasater, and Richard Miller were the founding stockholders and directors of the Facts Publishing Company in 1906. Organized to publish a local newspaper called *Falfurrias Facts*, the corporation began business with a capital stock of $3,000. Curtis, who moved to Falfurrias from Virginia, had a gift with words and was an important contributor to the promotional materials circulated by the real estate companies.[63]

In 1907, the Falfurrias Power Company was started to construct

[60] Transcribed Deed Records from Hidalgo County, Brooks County, vol. III, p. 19.
[61] Falfurrias State Bank charter, Texas September 8, 1905, Department of Banking, Author's Files; C. R. Wallace, Texas Bank Commissioner to author, March 4, 1982.
[62] Falfurrias Mercantile Company corporate charter, filed February 26, 1906, Texas Secretary of State, Austin.
[63] Facts Publishing Company, corporate charter, filed April 26, 1906, Texas Secretary of State, Austin; L. D. Miller, Sr., to author, September 22, 1971.

and operate mills and gins and to "manufacture and supply to the public by any means ice, gas, light, heat, and electric power. . . ." The three stockholders and directors listed on the original charter were James J. Allan, Ed Lasater, and L. D. Miller. The company had initial stock of $75,000.[64]

Later that same year, Lasater, L. D. Miller, and M. A. Newman chartered the Falfurrias Machine Shops. The purpose of this corporation was "the transaction of any manufacturing business and the purchase and sale of such goods, wares and merchandise used for such business; the erection of windmills, pumps, engines and machinery, repairs of wagons, windmills, well machines, harness, and repair business generally." The company was initiated with $10,000 capital.[65]

Other early stores and businesses were established by Rachal and Mussey, R. E. McBryde, the García brothers, and George Hobbs and sons. Two of the Reverend Caldwell's sons also lived in Falfurrias: Walter was a real estate and insurance agent, and Oliver was an artesian well driller.[66]

As the new community developed, churches and schools were started, W. G. Ray, president of the Falfurrias school board, said that Lasater and the railroad company gave two town blocks for the school and that Lasater bore more than half the expense of getting it launched. He added that Lasater and the railroad company "have given equally to all religious denominations asking for lots upon which to establish their buildings. There are now a Methodist church and parsonage and a Catholic church built and occupied. There are under contract Baptist and Episcopal church buildings."[67]

With rail service, churches, schools, a bank, and a host of other businesses serving a growing population of small farmers and townspeople, Falfurrias was no longer solely the "last stop." In 1906 Ed Lasater commissioned a San Antonio artist to capture his vision of this country: "Ed Lasater is up from Falfurrias and took time on Wednesday

[64] Falfurrias Power Company, corporate charter, filed July 11, 1907, Texas Secretary of State, Austin.

[65] Falfurrias Machine Shops, corporate charter, filed July 11, 1907, Texas Secretary of State, Austin.

[66] Margaret K. Lasater, "Edward Cunningham Lasater: His Development of the Falfurrias County" (Senior thesis, Vassar College, 1965), p. 12.

[67] Ibid., p. 13.

to go down to the bridge on Houston Street and view the work of an artist who, as Mr. Lasater claims, has so faithfully portrayed on canvas the livestock, agricultural and truck growing possibilities of that section." Lasater was pleased with the artist's work but felt that even that man's unique talents could not capture the full impact of the Falfurrias country: "The white-faced cattle, the stalks of cotton . . . and the truck farms are, of course, all taken from nature and while Mr. Lasater is inclined to compliment the artist, he added that the original scenes were even more entrancing than the reproduction."[68]

Two years earlier Lasater and Bob Rice had ridden east from the ranch headquarters, and where they heard a lone coyote barking on a hill, Lasater had selected the site where his town would sit.[69] Lasater gave the town a name that came with one of the first properties he bought in Starr County: Falfurrias. The exact origin and meaning of that name generated considerable discussion over the ensuing years. Different local versions said it meant "the furies," "a hoax," or "a good-for-nothing, a bum," that it represented a corruption of the Spanish word *faldas*, meaning "skirt," or the French word *farfouilleur*, "one who searches aimlessly."[70]

[68] *The San Antonio Express*, January 11, 1906.

[69] Vernon Smylie, *Edward Lasater: A Biographical Portrait*, p. 5.

[70] La Mota de Falfurrias, Falfurrias Ranch, and Rancho de Falfurrias were all terms connected with land Ed Lasater purchased (See fn. 57, chap. 2, and fn. 41, chap. 4. "Maps of early Spanish [and Mexican] land grants designated an oasis marked by huge trees in the center of the sun-drenched South Texas prairie as La Mota de Falfurrias" (Smylie, *Edward C. Lasater*). John M. Bennett said that Falfurrias was a term used by Mexicans to mean a bum or good-for-nothing. (Interview, John M. Bennett, February 24, 1967). Robert Rice, who worked with Lasater in Starr County, said the term referred to an old shepherd who lived near La Mota in the early days. He wore a leather apron, which resembled a skirt—in Spanish, a *falda*—and the shepherd was called a *falduras*, which evolved into Falfurrias (*Falfurrias Facts*, May 11, 1961). Richard King said it meant "mouth of the Furies," while W. E. Caldwell, Falfurrias real estate agent, said it meant "Heart's Delight" (*Alice Echo*, July 7, 1904). A native of Monterrey, Mexico, said Falfurrias was a corruption of *farfouilleur* (French), which means someone who searches for something in a disorderly fashion (Interview, Florence Schuetz, April 9, 1981). Falfurrias might also have evolved from *filfa*, which in colloquial Spanish means hoax or fake and by extension could be used as "eres un filfarrias" (you're a faker). A pioneer Falfurrias resident, Antonio Alaniz, said the name referred to an old Mexican shepherd who lived in a run-down shack in the area. He was referred to as "Don Filfarrias" and people spoke of "Filfarrias Rancho." The name was colorful, and as more people settled in the area, use of the name became widespread (Nícolas González, to the editor, *Falfurrias Facts*, March 19, 1980).

Ed Lasater was not concerned with such academic considerations; he did not indulge in speculation about all the name's possible anteced- ents. For him Falfurrias had only one definition, one meaning: to all who asked, Lasater said the name was a Lipan Indian word, meaning "the Land of Heart's Delight." Once he embellished the story even fur- ther by stating in jest that he was the last descendant of that In- dian tribe, which had once populated the grasslands where his cattle grazed.[71] But Falfurrias was not a subject that Ed Lasater treated lightly. Falfurrias was his creation, his dream. During the last two decades of his life, his concerns and activities were closely linked to his strong and abiding dedication to the ongoing development of the Falfurrias country.

[71] *Falfurrias Facts*, October 8, 1926.

CHAPTER 6

Between Archie and Don Manuel

> I have done all in my power to conciliate, and I shall now
> devote doing all I can to crush, and I am too old a fron-
> tiersman to even think of wounding a snake—kill it or
> leave it alone.
>
> —James B. Wells, ca. 1900

In the dusty courtyard alongside the big stone ranch house at Las
Víboras, north of Rio Grande City, a little girl and her playmates performed a skit on repeated occasions. One of them would act out the
part of Don Eduardo, the Anglo landowner whose property lay north
and east of Las Víboras, while another would play the role of a young
lady. Don Eduardo and the young lady were in love, but theirs was an
impossible love, as the skit portrayed it: Don Eduardo represented Ed
Lasater; the young lady was a Mexican resident of Starr County.[1]

Children's games sometimes reflect their elders' lives and actions
in unusual ways. It is not known what circumstances might have given
rise to that bit of play-acting at Las Víboras, but the principal connection between Rio Grande City and Falfurrias, between northern and
southern Starr County in the first decade of the twentieth century, did
not involve a love affair, even an imagined one. Discord and conflict,
not affection or friendship, characterized the relationship between
those two areas. Men of means who wielded power—men with com-

---

[1] Interview, Jovita González Mireles, March 6, 1982. One of the young children
participating in this skit was Jovita González, who as a young girl lived at Las Víboras,
which was owned by her grandparents. Despite the skit's implication, a number of early
South Texas ranchers had Mexican wives, many of them cultured ladies from wealthy and
educated families. Mifflin Kenedy, whose large ranch lay on the east boundary of Lasater's property, was the most prominent example of this early intermarriage. His wife was
Petra Vela de Vidal from Mier, Mexico (*Nueces County News*, July 14, 1939).

peting financial interests, different backgrounds and motivations—met each other year after year in a political battle.

The men who participated in the political arena in South Texas in the early years of this century played out their roles actively and intensely. In real life it was not a skit, but a drama—one which took place not just in the courtyard of an isolated ranch, but over a large section of the area south of the Nueces. It was a drama that involved malice, graft, and guns; it was rife with innuendo and intrigue, even death.

On January 26, 1907, a lone horseman made the long ride through sand and brush from Roma to Las Víboras. When Manuel Guerra arrived at the ranch house, he dismounted and greeted his cousin's wife, whom he addressed as Tía (aunt). He had come to savor a cup of the coffee for which she was famous, and he would spend the night.

After nightfall, he told Tía that he did not want to sleep in the main part of the house. He preferred to sleep in the *corredor*, an enclosed corridor with bars over the small windows which were set high in the thick walls. He moved the bed from below the window to the center of the wall. "You are frightened by the wind?" Tía asked. "No, I am worried about something else," Guerra replied.

In the early morning dark, those asleep at Las Víboras were awakened by loud knocking on the door. It was a rider who carried an urgent message for Don Manuel. He had come to inform the *jefe* (boss) that Gregorio Duffy had been killed that night in Rio Grande City.

After the horseman had mounted his steed and headed back toward Rio Grande, Tía fixed her gaze on Manuel Guerra: "You shameless scoundrel," she said. "You had something to do with the death of that good man." Don Manuel protested this accusation, which came from his own relative, from one in whose home he had sought peace and refuge for the night: "How could I have, Tía? I was right here, asleep in your home."[2]

Between Las Víboras and San Diego, the landscape changed little as successive gates led from one ranch to the next, from one sandy pas-

---

[2] Interview, González Mireles, March 6, 1982. Mrs. Mireles's grandfather, Francisco Guerra, was a cousin of Manuel Guerra's father.

ture into another one which was also dotted with mesquite trees or distinguished by an occasional oak mott. Only a horseman familiar with the country would have known when he crossed the northern boundary of Starr County, the border of Manuel Guerra's domain, and entered Duval County.

A little more than one hundred miles north of Las Víboras, beyond the Starr County line, John Cleary sat down to eat in San Diego in December of the same year that Gregorio Duffy was slain behind a Rio Grande City saloon. As Cleary sat facing away from the window in a small cafe in the Duval County seat, he was shot in the back and killed by an assailant who fired from the street.[3] The local lawmen failed to take immediate action because of their participation in a fiesta, and the assassin escaped. Cleary's death was apparently politically motivated, but despite a series of investigations and allegations of wrongdoing by both Republicans and Democrats, his murder was never solved.[4]

Regardless of who engineered Cleary's death, one man in Duval County benefited more than anyone else: Archie Parr. With Cleary out of the way, Parr took command of the Democratic machinery and established himself as the boss of Duval County.[5] Parr had been elected to the Duval County Commission in 1896, the same year as John Cleary, and Cleary was his chief political rival. "No one ever tied Archie Parr to Cleary's death, but Cleary was the first on a substantial list of Parr enemies whom fate singled out for violent circumstances and sometimes death."[6]

Falfurrias sat northeast of Guerra's headquarters at Roma and southeast of Parr's headquarters at Benavides. Ed Lasater knew the land well and was confident of its potential for cattle raising. But he probably did not focus his attention initially on the political aspects of life in the area where Ignacio de la Peña and his descendants had pastured their herds. He almost certainly did not realize that he had centered his ambitious plans for a landed empire directly between the political territories being staked out at the time by Manuel Guerra and

[3] "A Death in Duval," *Texas Observer*, April 25, 1975, p. 4.
[4] Evan M. Anders, "Bosses Under Siege: The Politics of South Texas During the Progressive Era" (Ph.D. diss., Univ. of Texas at Austin, 1978), pp. 476–78.
[5] Ibid., p. 479.
[6] "A Death in Duval," p. 4.

Archie Parr, two men whose careers would represent the extreme examples of feudal control, public corruption, and political violence in Texas.

Evan M. Anders, in "Bosses under Siege: The Politics of South Texas during the Progressive Era," provides a fully documented and exhaustive look at Guerra, Parr, and other principal figures in the South Texas political arena between 1890 and 1920. In that work he details fully Ed Lasater's central role in leading the charge against the established political powers in both Starr and Duval counties during the first two decades of the twentieth century.

Anders's work focuses on four men who were the leading Democratic politicians during this period and who wielded the most personal political power in South Texas. They were: James B. Wells, a lawyer, "who consolidated boss rule in Cameron County and emerged as a leading spokesman for the conservative wing of the state Democratic party"; cowman Archer (Archie) Parr, "whose ruthless tactics and misuse of public funds in Duval County established him as one of the notorious corruptionists in the history of the state"; Manuel Guerra, rancher and merchant, "whose authoritarian domination of Starr County was indistinguishable from the practices of his Anglo counterparts in the border counties"; and John Nance Garner, a United States congressman for nearly thirty years before becoming Vice-President in 1932, "who served the interests of these bosses during the formative years of his congressional career."[7]

Soon after Ed Lasater began making his extensive land purchases in 1895, he found himself face-to-face with Guerra, Parr, and the already established Democratic machines in Starr and Duval counties. In the views of Lasater, his relatives, and their associates, the basic issues were simple: both counties were controlled by unscrupulous political bosses, and corruption was rampant. To secure a fair deal for himself and his associates in such matters as land taxation and judicial process, and to achieve a more honest and equitable administration of public funds, Lasater set out immediately to challenge the Democratic powers.[8]

---

[7] Anders, "Bosses Under Siege," p. 5.

[8] Interviews, John M. Bennett, February 24, 1967, and L. D. Miller, Sr., September 22, 1971; Edward H. Caldwell, "The Life and Activities of Edward Cunningham Lasater," p. 17.

Lasater's political activism became a costly and time-consuming activity. Both he and his family were the subjects of repeated assassination and kidnapping threats, and Lasater regularly received letters threatening his life in the event he should make an appearance in Rio Grande City on election day. The financial cost and the personal risk did not deter Lasater.[9] His involvement in Starr County politics met with at least partial success; in Duval County, after more than twenty-five years of personal involvement and considerable expense, Lasater and others who opposed the Parr machine had little to show for their efforts.

The Treaty of Guadalupe Hidalgo in 1848 automatically made American citizens out of thousands of Mexicans who lived in the disputed area between the Nueces and the Rio Grande Rivers. These new Texans were unprepared for United States–style democracy; voting and elections were foreign concepts to them. James B. Wells stated clearly that it was the property owners and the educated elements of society who manipulated the Mexican vote in early South Texas politics.[10] Some observers saw the early bosses not as unscrupulous politicians, but as necessary elements in organizing the political life in a frontier area where the population was largely uneducated, often not fluent in English, and certainly unfamiliar with the American electoral system.[11] Many Mexican Texans continued to be Mexicans, both in their own eyes and in the eyes of their employers and others in the community. They knew little about the state and federal governments to which they had become attached, and voting had little significance to

[9] Interview, Laurence D. Miller, September 22, 1971; Ada Lasater Caldwell, "Recollections," p. 3. Ed Lasater was not new to personal risk and political activism, according to his sister Ada: "Papa and Ed were fearless in the discharge of their duties. Although the Gorman gang had terrorized Goliad for years, no grand jury had ever had the nerve to bring an indictment against Gorman. When Papa was made foreman of the grand jury, Gorman was indicted. This so infuriated Gorman that he threatened Papa's life and came to the store armed to the teeth expecting to find Papa there alone. Fortunately, he had gone home, and on seeing Gorman enter the store, Mr. Simpson leveled his gun on Gorman and said: 'If you harm a hair on Judge Lasater's head, your days will be numbered.' This took Gorman so completely by surprise that he made no further attempt to carry out his threat" (Ibid.).

[10] Jovita González, "Social Life in Cameron, Starr and Zapata Counties" (M.A. thesis, Univ. of Texas, 1930), pp. 84–86.

[11] Ibid.

them other than returning a favor to someone higher up in the system. Politicians, landowners, or other persons of influence typically paid the poll taxes for the Mexican laboring class. On election day, these citizens of Mexican descent would carry their poll tax receipts to a polling place where an election judge would address them in Spanish. The ballots were printed in English; therefore the judge would kindly offer to mark the ballot properly, if indeed he had not already done so to save time.[12]

Manuel Guerra rose to power in Starr County in this late nineteenth-century environment. Guerra was a descendant of a surveyor for the Spanish Crown, who in 1767 received extensive land grants on both sides of the Rio Grande. Guerra was born on the border in the Mexican town of Mier in 1856. As a young man he spent six years in Corpus Christi learning English and gaining business experience before returning to Roma where he began his own business career and married Virginia Cox, the daughter of an Anglo father and a Mexican mother.[13]

Guerra established a mercantile business in Roma in Starr County and was actively involved in his family's ranching enterprises. He also entered the political arena, and by the 1880s he had gained the support of James Wells, the Cameron County political chief.[14] In 1894 Guerra won a seat on the Starr County Commissioner's Court, a position he held until his death in 1915. Guerra was successful in both business and politics: "As a businessman, a banker, a ranchman and a politician, Guerra has been surpassed by no other Mexican on the border." In a short time, Guerra was the recognized leader of the Democratic party in Starr County and the right-hand man of Wells.[15]

Guerra was a tall man with fair skin and black hair. He was a jovial person with an expansive laugh who enjoyed a dual reputation: half-hero and half-villain. His Mexican compatriots considered him *vivo*, shrewd and wily, and they admired him because he was the only man who was capable of putting the gringos in their place.[16]

Lasater's presence in northern Starr County signaled a change:

---

[12] "A Death in Duval," p. 4.
[13] González, "Social Life," p. 88.
[14] Anders, "Bosses Under Siege," p. 115.
[15] González, "Social Life," pp. 88, 89.
[16] Interview, Jovita González Mireles, March 6, 1982.

"Power had always been in the hands of the Mexicans. With the arrival of Lasater, that began to change, and this created conflict and resentment."[17] Lasater soon allied himself with the local Republicans, who had organized not for any political convictions, but to provide a unified manner of opposing the local Democratic machine: "All Don Manuel's enemies, regardless of their political creed, became Republicans."[18]

Due to the widespread illiteracy existing in the border counties of South Texas at the time, the political parties in each county were known by a color, in order to facilitate voter recognition. In Starr County, Guerra's Democrats were the "Reds" and the Republicans were the "Blues." Lasater had several reasons for affiliating himself with the Blues: "Resentful over discriminatory tax policies and his lack of influence at the county seat of Rio Grande City, almost ninety miles from Falfurrias, Ed Lasater threw his financial support behind the local Republican insurgency."[19]

Federal patronage provided one means for the outnumbered Republicans to exert some influence in the border counties. A series of Republican partisans used the Customs House in Brownsville as a political base for recruiting supporters and organizing election campaigns. Lasater cooperated with R. B. Creager and other federal appointees in order to maximize Republican strength.[20]

Within a few years after his arrival in Starr County, Lasater began learning about South Texas–style politics: "With his initiation into Starr County politics in 1900, he received a valuable lesson in Democratic tactics." That year Lasater took the initiative on the Republican side and selected Domingo Garza as candidate for sheriff in an election that degenerated into a series of insulting exchanges and bitter charges. The climax came when the incumbent Democratic sheriff, W. W. Shely, had his opponent jailed just before the election on charges that were later dismissed as groundless.[21]

For additional insurance, Manuel Guerra and his fellow Reds re-

[17] Ibid.

[18] González, "Social Life," p. 89.

[19] Ibid.; Anders, "Bosses Under Siege," p. 119; interview, Laurence D. Miller, Sr., September 22, 1971.

[20] Anders, "Bosses Under Siege," pp. 50, 117.

[21] Ibid., p. 119; González, "Social Life," p. 90.

cruited aliens from Mexico to vote and stationed armed guards at the polling places to intimidate Republican voters: "The Democratic party carried the election by almost 400 ballots, despite the active campaigning of the customs officials and Lasater's generous contributions."[22]

Tom Lasater described another election-day encounter between his father and Manuel Guerra:

As they pulled into Rio Grande City the evening before the election, they noticed that there were many deputy sheriffs standing around practically on every corner of every street. My father and his group went to a local hotel, bathed, and shaved and got cleaned up, put on fresh ranch clothes and stepped out on the plaza to join the festivities. As was customary in the border towns on Saturday night, or on an election eve, everyone put on their very best clothes and went down to the plaza, and the ladies all walked around in one direction while the gentlemen walked around the plaza on the outside of the ladies in the opposite direction.

When any gentleman saw a lady with whom he would like to visit or converse, he would take off his hat, bow, offer her his arm and turn and walk with her for a certain length of time. When the visit was completed, he would again bow and kiss her hand and turn to join the men circling in the opposite direction.

This particular evening my father and Mr. Guerra, who had been long-time political opponents, happened to meet on the plaza and, of course, as was customary Mr. Guerra rushed up, threw his arms around my father, embraced him like a long-lost brother and welcomed him to Rio Grande City. Of course, everyone on the plaza knew these two gentlemen were anything but fond of each other, so they all stopped their conversation to listen to what would be said next.

My father responded by greeting Mr. Guerra and telling him what a pleasure it was to be in his city, then proceeded to remark that as he and his group entered Rio Grande City they saw a tremendous number of deputies all over town and wondered why so many were necessary. Mr. Guerra responded, "But you know how it is, Mr. Lasater, on election day. We want everything to be perfectly peaceful and quiet. We don't want to have any trouble whatsoever, and that is why we thought it advisable to have plenty of deputies in town."

My father responded with the following proposition to Mr. Guerra: "Tomorrow on election day, suppose we de-deputize every deputy sheriff in Starr County, and as the polls open at seven in the morning you will sit in your chair on one side of the entrance to the voting place and I will sit in my chair on the other side. We will each hold a cocked .45-automatic pistol pointed at the other. Should any of my men get out of line in any way whatsoever, you will shoot me; if any of your men get out of line in any way whatsoever, I will shoot you."

---

[22] Anders, "Bosses Under Siege," p. 119.

In other words, this was a challenge, and of course Mr. Guerra could do nothing but accept the challenge, so he responded by saying, "Mr. Lasater, that's a good idea. That's exactly what we will do."

So these gentlemen sat on opposite sides of the polling place for twelve hours, each holding a cocked pistol pointed at the other. Needless to say, Starr County had never been more peaceful and quiet on election day.[23]

A pivotal electoral contest occurred in 1906, and the ultimate result of that bloody confrontation would alter the course of Starr County's history. Factional disputes among the Reds and Democratic electoral setbacks had brought about a truce in 1894. By the terms of that pact, Manuel Guerra and Sheriff W. W. Shely agreed to share patronage and party nominations in Starr County.[24] In 1905 Shely withdrew from politics because of a debilitating nervous disorder. The competition to succeed the Democratic leader split the party. With the support of County Judge John R. Monroe, Guerra moved to consolidate his power in the county by promoting his cousin, Deodoro Guerra for sheriff and his son H. P. Guerra for tax collector. Manuel Guerra was a county commissioner, Guerra's brother Jacobo was the county treasurer, and the prospect of Guerra family members holding four major county offices split the Democrats.[25]

Gregorio Duffy, the deputy sheriff and tax collector, had planned to run for sheriff when Shely retired. When he, tax assessor Miguel Juárez, and former county commissioner Amado de la Garza joined forces to oppose the Guerra takeover, Manuel Guerra expelled them from the Democratic county ring. These three men subsequently defected to the Republican camp, and the Blues nominated Duffy for sheriff.[26]

In the campaign leading up to the 1906 election, Lasater and his Republican cohorts presented themselves as reformers, focusing their attacks on "Manuel Guerra's boss rule, the alleged incompetence of Mexican-American officeholders who could barely speak English, and the use of public schools as a patronage boondoggle, but county finance emerged as the central issue." In his own newspaper, the *Falfurrias*

[23] Interview, Tom Lasater, May 1, 1979.
[24] Anders, "Bosses Under Siege," p. 116.
[25] Ibid., p. 120.
[26] Ibid., pp. 120–21.

Facts, Lasater charged that the Democratic administration discriminated in the assessment of property taxes.[27]

Both sides believed the election of 1906 would have repercussions for the Democratic party all over South Texas, not just in Starr County. The Blues aimed their attacks not only against the Guerra clan, but also against Cameron County's Democratic boss, James B. Wells. Observing the events from Duval County, Archie Parr echoed the alarm when he warned Wells: "If Duffy and his people win, Lasater will run Starr, and from then on Starr will go Republican. Then the county seat will be moved to Falfurrias. . . ." Jacobo Guerra was even more blunt in his assessment of the situation. He said the Democrats needed to "knock the Republican move in the head now and kill it so dead that it [would] not rise to trouble us again."[28]

When the Lasater entourage left Falfurrias for the two-day trip to the river, it had more the appearance of a war party going to the battlefront than a group of citizens preparing to travel to the county seat to vote in one of the world's leading democracies. The convoy included a number of carriages and a large group of men on horseback. All of the men were heavily armed, and L. D. Miller was in charge of a buckboard loaded with Winchester rifles which was camouflaged as a load of grain. Rob Miller, wearing a Stetson hat, resembled Ed Lasater. Someone in the group suggested that Rob be seated in a prominent position in the lead carriage so that if the group were ambushed and an attempt were made on Lasater's life en route to Rio Grande City, they would shoot Rob and the loss would not be as great. Everybody in the group except Rob Miller found this suggestion very humorous.[29]

With the stakes so high, both the Red Club and the Blue Club were ready to resort to almost any tactic. Leaders from both sides paid poll taxes for hundreds of Mexican laborers and both parties recruited Mexican nationals from across the Rio Grande to vote. Each side kept their supporters and henchmen together carousing all night on the eve

---

[27] Ibid., p. 122. Lasater charged that while some landowners faced "double assessments," others escaped taxation altogether because of the absence of their properties from the tax rolls.

[28] Ibid., p. 124.

[29] Interviews, L. D. Miller, September 22, 1971, Tom Lasater, May 1, 1979, and Gardner Miller, July 22, 1981.

of the election, the Democrats within the walls of the courthouse, and the Republicans in a corral belonging to Lino Hinojosa.[30]

The tense, warlike atmosphere erupted in violence on the night before the election when District Judge Stanley Welch, a Democrat, was shot to death while asleep in his bed. Earlier that same night, a gang of thugs had pistol-whipped a local Republican leader and "had left him for dead" outside his house. Welch's murder, not discovered until early on election-day morning, stunned Democratic leaders. During the Democrats' confusion, fifty armed men under Duffy's command took control of the courthouse. In Rio Grande City, Blue Club gunmen outnumbered their opponents, and the telegraph lines to Roma were cut early in the morning to prevent the dispatch of Red reinforcements.[31]

The Republican show of force in Rio Grande City deterred many Democrats from voting, but despite a victory in that town for Lasater and his fellow Republicans, the Democrats carried the election. Deodoro Guerra defeated Gregorio Duffy in the sheriff's race by sixty-three votes.[32]

Several months passed before anyone was charged with Judge Welch's murder. In July, 1907, charges were filed against Alberto Cabrera, a Republican organizer who had worked as a bartender for Duffy's half-brother. Cabrera's trial took place a year later in Cuero. Texas Lieutenant Governor A. B. Davidson served as one of the prosecuting attorneys, while a leading Brownsville Republican, R. B. Creager, headed the defense team. Ed Lasater and a fellow Republican, customs collector John Vann, attended the proceedings and provided Cabrera with moral support. The trial reached a climax when Lasater interrupted the lieutenant governor's closing argument: "As the two men

[30] González, "Social Life," p. 92; Anders, "Bosses Under Siege," p. 124.

[31] Ibid., pp. 126–27.

[32] Ibid., p. 129. By 1906, nearly 300 residents of the Falfurrias area had registered to vote. The margin of victory for the Democratic party had not fallen below 400 ballots in any Starr County election since 1892 (Ibid., p. 123). The Democratic party profited from a landslide vote at Roma and an unexpected victory at Falfurrias in 1906. News of Judge Welch's murder produced a backlash among the newcomers to the northern section of Starr County. On the day of the election, Falfurrias residents organized a mass meeting to pay tribute to Welch and to demand the apprehension of his assassin. This local Democratic breakthrough was short-lived however, and Falfurrias re-emerged as the mainstay of the GOP insurgency in subsequent elections (Ibid., p. 129).

engaged in a heated argument and verged on an exchange of blows, Collector Vann and his customs agent reached for their pistols. Although the Rangers and the local lawmen were able to prevent the outbreak of violence, many spectators fled from the building in panic." The jury found Cabrera guilty and sentenced him to life imprisonment. The judge jailed Lasater briefly for interrupting the trial.[33]

The violence engendered by the 1906 Starr County election did not end with the Red Club victory. After his narrow loss in the sheriff's race, Gregorio Duffy secured an appointment as the customs inspector at Roma. One night in late January, 1907, Sheriff Deodoro Guerra and two deputies followed Duffy as he made his rounds of the Rio Grande City bars. When Duffy stepped out behind one saloon to relieve himself, Guerra accompanied him. The two deputies were waiting outside, and after shooting erupted a few minutes later, Duffy fell, mortally wounded.[34]

Conflicting eyewitness testimony and ambiguous physical evidence hampered the investigation of Duffy's killing. Manuel Guerra was linked to the crime by two individuals who claimed that Guerra had earlier approached them with propositions to kill Duffy. The Starr County grand jury for the State District Court, consisting of Guerra loyalists, charged the deputy sheriff with murder, but refused to implicate either Deodoro or Manuel Guerra.[35]

The partisan politics which protected Manuel Guerra in Starr County worked against him outside his own fiefdom. An aggressive Republican partisan, assistant U.S. district attorney Noah Allen, and his superior won support from the administration in Washington for federal intervention in the case. Eventually, even President Theodore Roosevelt expressed an interest in the prosecution of the "cowardly as-

---

[33] Ibid., pp. 131–32; interview, L. D. Miller, September 22, 1971. Miller related how Mary Lasater picked up a paper the following morning and saw the headline which read: "Ed Lasater Jailed" (Ibid.). In 1912, Cabrera escaped from prison and fled to Mexico, where he joined Venustiano Carranza's Constitutionalist army and eventually advanced to the rank of lieutenant. The Mexican authorities refused to arrange Cabrera's extradition to Texas (Anders, "Bosses Under Siege," p. 133).

[34] Anders, "Bosses Under Siege," pp. 133–34. In his position as customs inspector at Roma, Duffy "posed a threat not only to Manuel Guerra's hegemony over Roma politics, but also to the smuggling operations from which Guerra and other merchants profited" (Ibid.).

[35] Ibid., pp. 134–37.

sassins of poor Duffy." Six months after he had successfully rebuffed the serious Republican electoral challenge in 1906, a federal grand jury in Brownsville indicted Manuel Guerra for conspiracy to commit murder.[36]

Duval County was sheep country when Edward Caldwell moved to the Borjas Ranch to enter the ranching business in 1875. But the days of glory for the sheep industry in that part of Texas were nearing their end, and the transition to cattle was already underway when a young cowboy named Archie Parr moved to Benavides to work on a ranch in 1882. The county was named for a Goliad martyr, B. H. Duval, but a century after its creation its notoriety was inseparably linked to another man's career. Duval County had become synonymous with the name of Parr, who became a landowner and cattleman, taking his place alongside Manuel Guerra as one of the dominant political figures in South Texas during the first years of the twentieth century. A 1954 magazine article stated: "For forty years . . . a man named Parr has ruled Duval County in South Texas with the power of a monarch and the aid of a gun-toting private army."[37]

The future brush-country potentate's arrival in Duval County was inauspicious. Parr went to work on a ranch near Benavides, where one of his neighbors described the young cowboy as "free from so many vices general and common here. He has the picture of a country boy— red face with an Irish look about him. . . ."[38]

Archie Parr was born in Calhoun County on Christmas Day, 1860, only a few weeks after Ed Lasater's birth near Goliad. Archie's father died when he was a young boy, and he quit school after the third grade to go to work. At age eleven he was wrangling horses; three years later he went to work for the famous Coleman-Fulton Pasture Company as a drover, and at seventeen he served as a trail boss on a cattle drive up the Chisholm Trail.[39]

[36] Ibid., pp. 135–38. In May, 1907, U.S. Attorney McDaniel persuaded the federal grand jury at Brownsville to return murder and conspiracy indictments against Manuel and Deodoro Guerra, Juan and Gabriel Morales, and a fifth man, Desiderio Pérez (Ibid.).

[37] Harold H. Martin, "Tyrant in Texas," *Saturday Evening Post*, June 26, 1954, p. 20.

[38] Dudley Lynch, *The Duke of Duval: The Life and Times of George B. Parr*, p. 11.

[39] Ibid.

In 1882 Parr moved to Duval County to take a job on the Sweden Ranch near Benavides, a little village consisting of "a clustering of stores, depot, market, fandango hall, saloon, restaurant, post office and some houses, all plopped down in the middle of the prairie." [40]

Duval was not a border county, but its population and character were still predominantly Mexican, despite a sizeable mixture of immigrants from European countries. San Diego, the county seat, was sixteen miles north of Benavides near the eastern county line. It was a typical Mexican town built around a plaza some three hundred feet square. The principal business establishments, the *cantina* (saloon), several gambling joints, and the residences of its most prosperous inhabitants were grouped around the four sides of the square. [41]

Archie Parr learned to speak Spanish fluently. He befriended the Mexican Americans who worked for him, and in time they came to regard him not as an Anglo, but as one of them. [42] After he acquired land and cattle of his own, Parr became involved in county politics. Many of the Anglo ranchers had a low opinion of their Mexican employees and neighbors, but Archie "virtually became a Texas-Mexican and thus became their leader and protector." [43]

Parr developed a close political relationship with attorney James Wells. Wells consulted with Parr on patronage matters as early as the 1890s, but Parr did not establish his dominance over county politics until after John Cleary's murder in 1907. [44]

In the months following Cleary's assassination in San Diego, only suspicions existed concerning Parr's involvement with that unsolved murder. They were not diminished by Parr's aggressive moves to take advantage of his former rival's absence. By 1908, Parr had consolidated the dominant position in El Guarache: "To hear Parr backers talk, it

---

[40] Ibid.

[41] Priscilla L. Buckley and William F. Buckley, Jr., eds., *W.F.B.—An Appreciation,* p. 9. A major local celebration occurred on September 16, the anniversary of Mexican independence from Spain. On that occasion, the plaza with its bandstand became a center of entertainment and merrymaking. A uniformed brass band was imported from Laredo for this gala affair, which lasted two weeks, "just long enough to drain the townsfolk of their meager savings" (Ibid.).

[42] Robert E. Baskin, "Archie Founded Dynasty in 1882," *Dallas Morning News,* August 19, 1974.

[43] "A Death in Duval," p. 4.

[44] Anders, "Bosses Under Siege," p. 53.

was El Guarache, the sandal, against La Bota, the boot; the poor against the rich, the Democrats—as it turned out—against the Republicans."[45]

Parr perfected the practices used by his fellow political bosses along the border. He, and later his son, cared for his constituents, often using money drained illegally from the county treasury, and when largesse did not accomplish their ends, armed gunmen masquerading as special deputy sheriffs used force and terror to keep the electorate in line.[46] The Parrs' approach was similar to Guerra's: "Paternalistic oversight of his Mexican constituents, voter manipulation, rampant corruption and political violence all contributed to Parr's ascent."[47]

The aftermath of the violent 1906 election in Starr County and the legal action growing out of the Welch and Duffy killings dragged on for several years. In the meantime, relations between Manuel Guerra and Ed Lasater alternated between a conciliatory and a bitterly hostile state. The culmination of this ongoing personal feud, which characterized relations between northern and southern Starr County, came in 1911 when a new county was formed with Falfurrias as the county seat.

The financial corruption in Rio Grande City alleged by Lasater was difficult to prove because the Commissioners Court, in defiance of state law, had failed to publish any comprehensive reports on county finances for several years. In the 1908 election, Republicans got one seat on the County Commissioners Court with the election of a Lasater employee from Falfurrias. The new GOP county commissioner, B. T. Henry, was able to observe Democratic fiscal management firsthand.[48]

During 1909, Ed Lasater and his allies inundated Governor Thomas M. Campbell with complaints about political abuses in Starr County. Lasater's petitions described Guerra in the following terms: "The defendant is a man of dominating character, inordinate ambition and soulless purpose. He is surrounded by an incompetent, and yielding set of men. . . ."[49]

Lasater's complaints to Governor Campbell included a description of how the Starr County Commissioners Court created an all-purpose

[45] Lynch, *The Duke of Duval*, p. 13.
[46] Martin, "Tyrant in Texas," p. 21.
[47] Anders, "Bosses Under Siege," p. 53.
[48] Ibid. p. 144.
[49] Ibid., p. 145.

"County Salary and Expense Fund" and transferred appropriations from duly constituted accounts to this contrived fund: "Manuel Guerra and his associates regularly drew money from the fund, far exceeding their official county salaries, to cover political and personal expenses."[50] In the spring of 1909, Governor Campbell sent his personal representative, Monta J. Moore, to Starr County to investigate Lasater's allegations. In a memorandum addressed to the governor on May 9, 1909, Moore confirmed Lasater's charges of bossism, graft, and the absence of an impartial system of justice in Starr County.[51]

The court battles resulting from the indictment of Manuel Guerra in the Duffy murder case continued for three years. In 1909 a jury acquitted Manuel and Deodoro Guerra of all charges, and in 1910 a judge dismissed the case against their co-conspirators: "After two grand jury investigations, extradition hearings, three trials and repeated continuances and changes of venue, the state and federal authorities failed to win any convictions for the killing of customs inspector Duffy."[52] The investigation and legal proceedings resulting from Duffy's death "revealed both the influence of the Democratic bosses over the local grand juries and state courts and the tenacity of Republican federal officials in challenging the power of the South Texas machines."[53]

By late 1909 both Guerra and Lasater saw an advantage in establishing a political truce, and they drafted a political agreement under which the opposing sides would each control a share of the elected county offices. Together the two parties would nominate a single slate of candidates for all county offices to be presented to the electorate on an Independent ticket. Under the terms of this pact, the Red Club would choose the sheriff, tax collector, district clerk, and county superintendent of schools. The Blue Club would select the county judge, tax assessor, county clerk, and treasurer. In addition, each group would choose two county commissioners, one-half of the justices of the peace, and one-half of the constables in the county. The agreement was signed on November 16, 1909, by Ed Lasater and R. B. Creager for the Blues

[50] Ibid., p. 146.
[51] Monta J. Moore to Governor T. M. Campbell, May 9, 1909, quoted in Margaret K. Lasater, "Edward Cunningham Lasater: His Development of the Falfurrias Country" (Senior thesis, Vassar College, 1965), pp. 41–42.
[52] Anders, "Bosses Under Siege," p. 141.
[53] Ibid., p. 133.

and on behalf of the Reds by Manuel Guerra, Deodoro Guerra, and Jesús María Ramírez.[54]

This bipartisan approach to county government and the prospect of cooperation between Falfurrias and Rio Grande City lasted a mere six months. Each side accused the other of bad faith and of reneging on various aspects of the joint agreement. As the political climate and personal tempers heated up during the summer of 1910, Manuel Guerra and Ed Lasater had a public exchange of letters in which they attacked each other in vindictive and slanderous language. The letters were run as ads in the *Falfurrias Facts* or were printed as circulars for public distribution.

On July 13 Guerra wrote the first of two letters replying to a *Facts* article of July 2 in which Ramírez and Lasater announced that Guerra had ended the political agreement signed the previous November 16. On July 18 Guerra produced a second circular in which he accused his opponent from Falfurrias of deceit and racism and held him indirectly responsible for the deaths of two Mexicans.

Guerra wrote that he was forced to terminate the agreement due to Lasater's "Machiavellian conduct" and said that this action was seen as necessary by "all Mexicans of honor who do not sell their opinions and who do not humble themselves or fall on their knees like wretched pariahs before one who intends to trample on the dignity and good name of our race."[55]

Guerra's letter dwelled at length on the deaths of Severo López and Baltazar García. Guerra accused Lasater of taking López to Rio Grande City with a group of armed men with whom he planned to take possession of the public offices at the county seat. López was killed there late one night while resisting arrest. García's death took place in Falfurrias, where he was "miserably and in cowardly fashioned mur-

[54] Edward H. Caldwell, "Life and Activities of Edward Cunningham Lasater," p. 17; Agreement, November 16, 1909, Lasater files. On one of the few occasions that James B. Wells and Lasater found themselves on the same side of the fence, the Cameron County Democratic boss stepped in to quell opposition to the Blue Club leader from Falfurrias: "Just two weeks before the November election, several Falfurrias Democrats threatened to sabotage the agreement by challenging Lasater's hand-picked candidates at the precinct level, but James B. Wells intervened to block the move." (Anders, "Bosses Under Siege," p. 143).

[55] Manuel Guerra to Ed C. Lasater, July 18, 1910, Lasater Files, in possession of Garland M. Lasater, Falfurrias.

dered in broad daylight . . . after leaving a passenger train, unarmed, in full use of his mental faculties, . . . believing . . . that he was protected by the law."[56]

According to Guerra, Lasater's mistake in the first case was to have taken a man with López's reputation for alcohol abuse and impulsive action to Rio Grande City. When López was killed, Lasater was "obliged to take his side for, because of [Lasater's] mistake, a family became orphaned. . . ." Guerra saw only self-interest in Lasater's attitude: "He has appeared as a protector of one of our people, as happened in the matter of Cabrera whom he defended. . . . In the prosecution of the killer of López, he has acted out of necessity . . . and not because of affection for the Mexican element. . . ."[57]

By contrast, at the time of García's death, Guerra stated that Lasater left Falfurrias when his presence could have averted a conflict between Anglos and Mexicans. Afterward, "with a shamelessness that excites indignation," Guerra said, Lasater referred to García's death as an "act of justice." Guerra stated that he had to protest such an assertion, "for as a Mexican I felt offended and hurt that the life of an honest Mexican and a member of a good family gets so little consideration from Mr. Lasater."[58]

Guerra's circular portrayed Lasater as a poor loser who did not play by the rules: "How can one believe in your political honesty when after the election you do not cooperate with elected officials . . . to improve the condition of the country, but on the contrary you are hostile to them, motivated by the spite of having been defeated?" Lasater had called the county commissioner from Roma a nonentity. Guerra asked: "If I am a nonentity, why do you propose agreements with me? . . . Do you label as a nonentity the person who as head of the Democrats in this county has defeated you in campaign after campaign? Well, you are a funny man."[59]

In his reply a few days later, Lasater called Guerra's circular "a

---

[56] Ibid. When Severo López was killed, Guerra was in Victoria, "defending myself against the slanderous accusations presented to the federal court by my treacherous enemies, among whom I count Mr. Lasater, having been able to demonstrate to them in a court in which they exercise so much influence my correct conduct, thanks to which I obtained from the jury a verdict absolving me of guilt. . . ." (Ibid.).

[57] Guerra to Lasater, July 18, 1910.

[58] Ibid.

[59] Ibid.

tissue of misrepresentations and lies, tied together by some hundreds of words." Lasater wrote that he did not take López to Rio Grande City and that he was not even aware of López's presence in that town until after he was killed. In response to Guerra's accusation that Lasater left Falfurrias to avoid any connection or responsibility with the incident that left Baltazar García dead, Lasater stated: "I left town before any clash between the races was expected to keep an engagement entered into practically one year before this occurrence, the same being to attend a meeting of the Executive Committee of the Texas Cattle Raisers Association held at Fort Worth, Texas."[60]

Lasater said that Guerra's letter illustrated how easy it is for a man who does not regard his pledged word to become a common liar: "Were it not for the harm your unrefuted lies might do to our unfortunate community, I would ignore them and you." Lasater ended his reply by stating his belief that even Guerra's compatriots would not continue to support him: "Knowing the Mexican race from years of business and social contact, I do not think they as a people will maintain as their leader one who has been shown to be without shame and without truth. I know they can command from their own men leaders who possess both honor and truth."[61]

By late 1910, Manuel Guerra was growing weary of the running battle with Ed Lasater. What had begun as a minor irritant after Lasater moved into northern Starr County in 1895 had developed over the years into a continual confrontation. The political division between the northern and southern parts of Starr County had produced discord and violence and had proved costly and time-consuming for both sides.

Only a few months after the first truce had ended with the bitter exchange of letters, Guerra reopened negotiations with Lasater and Creager to form a fusion ticket for the county elections in 1910. Guerra's allies, including County Judge John Monroe, thought such an approach was dangerous and constituted a threat to the Democratic organization of Starr County: "We must never let that Lasater faction get power in this county. What could our friends have meant? . . . They know that Lasater will do anything to divide the county as he pleases. . . . Give him part now, and the next time he will take all."[62]

<hr />

[60] Ed C. Lasater to Manuel Guerra, July, 1910, Lasater Files, in possession of Garland M. Lasater, Falfurrias.

[61] Ibid.

[62] Anders, "Bosses Under Siege," p. 149.

But Guerra did not agree with Monroe, and he saw his Blue Club adversaries in northern Starr County as determined foes: "So long as antagonisms within the Democratic Party endanger party unity, Ed Lasater and his constituents pose a real threat to take control of the county." For the sake of his own political security, Manuel Guerra in 1911 withdrew his opposition to the campaign to organize a new county.[63]

Lasater had made his first attempt to create Falfurrias County in 1907, but he had met defeat in Austin at the hands of South Texas Democrats. James Brooks, the former Texas Ranger captain and the Democratic candidate for the Texas House of Representatives, had participated in the negotiations between Lasater and Guerra in 1908 and had agreed to support Lasater's plan to organize a new county centered at Falfurrias: "In making this commitment to the formation of Falfurrias County, Brooks acted on his own initiative and misrepresented the intentions of his fellow Democrats."[64]

A second attempt to separate the Falfurrias country from Starr County was made in 1909 when Representative Brooks introduced a bill for the creation of the County of Falfurrias from parts of Hidalgo, Starr, Duval, and Nueces counties. Along with Guerra and other South Texas politicians, one of Lasater's main opponents that year in the passage of this bill was his neighbor to the west, Bill Jones. Jones charged that those pushing for this new county were attempting to create "an outright Republican county" due to the large number of northern settlers in the Falfurrias area. The *San Antonio Express* reported that one exchange in Austin between Lasater and his fellow rancher "waxed exceedingly warm." The article added that a substitute bill would be introduced to alter the territory to be included in the new county and to change its name to Bryan. However, opponents of the proposed county were able to stall any positive action in that session of the Texas legislature.[65]

Local support for a new county continued to grow in Falfurrias, where a mass meeting was held on February 4, 1911. At that gathering the attending citizens approved a document entitled "Resolutions Pertaining to the Creation of the County of Falfurrias," which included the statement: "The people of Falfurrias are vitally interested in the

[63] Ibid., p. 151.
[64] Ibid., p. 143.
[65] *San Antonio Express*, February 4, 1909.

formation of a new county in order to secure relief from the almost intolerable conditions which they now suffer." This resolution was signed by more than sixty local men, including Dr. H. M. Bennett, A. A. Cosby, B. T. Henry, H. C. Holbrook, R. J. McIntyre, Richard Miller, E. R. Rachal, and R. H. Rice.[66]

With Manuel Guerra now supporting the new county, an act to create the County of Falfurrias was once again placed before the Texas legislature in 1911. The county was to be formed out of parts of Starr, Hidalgo, and Zapata counties. One proposed amendment to the bill would have changed the county name to Ross in honor of former governor L. S. Ross, but the legislature passed a subsequent amendment that changed the county name from Falfurrias to Brooks.[67]

The "Act to Create and Establish the County of Brooks" was passed in March, 1911. It included the naming of five men as commissioners to organize the county: Amado de la Garza, Ed C. Lasater, E. R. Rachal, Frank S. Rachal, and H. D. Thomas. These men met in Lasater's office on March 17, 1911, to begin the business of organizing the new county.[68]

With the creation of the new county, Lasater's lands were removed from the control of the political bosses on the border: "The separation of the Falfurrias region restored the homogeneous character of Starr County with its overwhelming Mexican majority and its economy

[66] Resolution in the files of the Brooks County Historical Committee. No Falfurrias residents of Mexican descent signed the resolution.

[67] *Journal of the House of Representatives of the Regular Session of the Thirty-Second Legislature of Texas*, pp. 435–37. The bill creating Brooks County repeated language similar to that which appeared in the resolution passed at the mass meeting at Falfurrias the prior month: "The great inconvenience to which the people are subjected living in the territory from which said new county is created by being compelled to travel extraordinary distances to attend to their private and public business at the county seats. . . ." (Ibid., p. 435). The former Ranger captain for whom the county was named stated succinctly the view of at least part of the local citizenry. Brooks wrote that the creation of this county served to segregate the Mexican population of southern Starr County from the Anglo residents in the north: "placing the control of their own affairs in their own hands instead of being dominated by the corrupt bosses of the Mexican element. . . ." (James A. Brooks, printed letter to the members of the Thirty-Third Legislature, 1913).

[68] *Journal of the House of Representatives of the Regular Session of the Thirty-Second Legislature of Texas*, p. 434. "Minutes of the Proceedings of the Commissioners Appointed to Organize the County of Brooks, Texas," County Commissioners Minutes, Brooks County, March 17, 1911. The first five were named in the original House Bill No. 94. Bill Jones's son, A. C. Jones, and Ralph McCampbell, were apparently added to the organizing committee at a later date (Ibid.).

geared almost exclusively to ranching and commerce."[69] Lasater continued to be actively involved in local politics, but in the years ahead his main target would be Archie Parr.

One year after Ed Lasater's running battle with the Guerra machine in Starr County was resolved, a dramatic event occurred in Duval County which produced very different long-term results for Lasater and his allies. Archie Parr had consolidated his power within the local Democratic party after John Cleary's death in 1907, but his real political breakthrough came in 1912 when the increasing strains between the Mexican and Anglo residents of Duval County reached a bloody climax. On May 18, during a special election, a group of Anglos shot and killed three Mexican-American county officials during a confrontation at the courthouse in San Diego.

Parr sided with the Mexicans in the bitter racial feud which followed, and he counseled them not to retaliate with bloodshed: "He knew the answer to their problem: it was through the vote. From that time on, he was master of Duval County."[70] There were no more close elections between Democrats and Republicans in Duval County. After 1912, with Parr in complete control of the Mexican vote and despite frequent charges of election fraud, Parr's Democratic candidates were swept into office with lopsided victories.[71]

Parr's approach was feudal, and his method of looking out for his constituents was paternalistic. Parr ran a one-man welfare department. He treated the Duval County budget as his own personal bank account, but some of the funds trickled back to his Mexican supporters: "When they were hungry, he fed them; when they were jobless, he

[69] Anders, "Bosses Under Siege," p. 152. "Within the traditional social-economic environment of the western-most valley county, Manuel Guerra reasserted his supreme authority. He even managed to force J. R. Monroe from office in 1914. When the Starr County boss died in 1915, his sons inherited his political power, and the Guerra family continued to rule until the post–World War II era" (Ibid., p. 151).

[70] Baskin, "Archie Founded Dynasty"; interview, Huston Jenkins, July 13, 1981.

[71] Interview, Huston Jenkins, July 13, 1981; "A Death in Duval," p. 4. After the shooting of the three Mexicans in front of the Duval County courthouse, messengers rode to the Parr ranch to give the news to the political boss. "Archie received them grimly, and the knot of men talked at length out on the narrow porch to the makeshift ranch house where in less troubled times and under a dying sun the head man liked to sit and rock, a bucket of pecans at his side. He would take one of the pecans from the pile, snip its ends away with his knife and peel the hull back from the meat like it was a mere appleskin" (Lynch, *The Duke of Duval*, p. 3).

found them work; and when their wives and babies fell sick, he paid the doctors' bills. It was only natural, therefore, that they should vote en bloc for his candidates for public office."[72]

In the decade after 1912, Parr's political control of Duval County was unchallenged. The partisan struggle continued on two other fronts, in the Texas legislature and in the courts: "As the legal and legislative battles raged, Ed Lasater . . . emerged as Parr's leading antagonist."[73]

The legislative skirmishes in the 1913 and 1915 sessions of the Texas legislature were dominated by a series of bills to divide Duval County, to annex parts of its territory to other counties, and finally to dissolve the county altogether. These varied moves, none of which passed the legislature, were promoted by Parr to extend his authority and by his opponents to escape Parr's domination: "To the relief of the rest of the legislature, the question of eliminating or splitting Duval County did not resurface after 1915."[74]

The lengthy legal battles in Duval County opened on January 14, 1914, when Ed Lasater and a group of dissident ranchers and businessmen filed petitions in district court that charged county officials with misappropriation of funds and called for an audit of county finances. Later that same month, Lasater's accountant, George Kidd of Houston, began an independent survey of the county books. Within a short time, Kidd had discovered numerous financial irregularities, only to have the Duval County commissioners refuse him further access to the records.[75]

In the litigation surrounding the effort to audit the Duval County

---

[72] Martin, "Tyrant in Texas," p. 20; "A Death in Duval," p. 5; interview, Walter Blumer, July 12, 1981.

[73] Anders, "Bosses Under Siege," p. 486.

[74] Ibid., p. 494. Anders's thesis provides a very detailed look at the "charade of moves and counter-moves" regarding proposed county reorganization on pages 485–95. The separation of the Falfurrias country from Starr County did not solve all of Ed Lasater's local political problems. During the 1913 legislative session, Lasater suffered a setback when Bill Jones lobbied successfully for the creation of Jim Hogg County by cutting off a large portion of western Brooks County: "Ironically, Jones' power play benefitted from the protests of a group of Brooks County residents who charged that Lasater dominated the politics of his county through management of the Mexican-American vote. According to these dissidents, the Falfurrias promoter had purchased hundreds of poll taxes for his Mexican constituents. Both Parr and Lasater proved adept at adopting each other's tactics, but Lasater's experiments in boss rule resulted in the division of his county" (Ibid., p. 489).

[75] Ibid., pp. 495–96.

books, an attorney asked Parr if he was going to let the plaintiffs look at the records.

"No, we are not going to let you see them," Parr answered.

"We will have some difficulty in obtaining proof, probably, Mr. Parr, won't we?"

"It sorta looks like it," he said.[76]

In June, 1914, Lasater and his associates filed another action seeking to restore the accountant's access to the county records. After four days of hearings, Judge W. B. Hopkins issued an injunction against any interference with a citizen-sponsored audit. In explaining his ruling, the judge cited fourteen types of illegal activities that George Kidd had already uncovered. But even with the court's favorable ruling, the Lasater group's task was not a simple one: "Hopkins' order upholding the citizens' right to conduct a private audit did not force the surrender of Archie Parr and his colleagues, but only encouraged them to resort to more unorthodox tactics of circumvention."[77]

On the same day that a new group of auditors arrived in San Diego in August, 1914, "there occurred one of those fortuitous incidents which distinguished the Parr career." In a spectacular late-night blaze, the Duval County courthouse burned to the ground, destroying all the financial records. Most other county records, housed in a fireproof vault, were not even singed. Archie Parr was pragmatic about the fire: "The county needed a new courthouse, anyway."[78]

The providential blaze in the Duval County courthouse did not bother Archie Parr. Neither did an indictment for paying other people's poll taxes. In the midst of all the legal activity which commenced in 1914, Parr won a seat in the Texas senate. Parr served in that body for twenty years "while retaining virtually dictatorial control over Duval County and expanding his dominion over adjacent South Texas counties."[79]

---

[76] "A Death in Duval," p. 4.

[77] Anders, "Bosses Under Siege," pp. 496–97.

[78] "A Death in Duval," p. 5; Lynch, *The Duke of Duval,* p. 17; *Falfurrias Facts,* August 20, 1914.

[79] "A Death in Duval," p. 5. The indictment against Parr for paying poll taxes was subsequently dropped. Garland Lasater described his father's involvement in this poll tax question: "In one election, Dad was incensed about Archie Parr buying poll taxes. He employed a lawyer from Fort Worth to hire detectives and get some evidence. Later the attorney stood up in the senate and read the charges and stated that he had proof Mr.

Parr's election to the state senate and the destruction of the county records did not deter Lasater and other Parr opponents. In January, 1915, a grand jury returned twenty-six indictments against Archie Parr and ten Duval County officials, including the county judge, the treasurer, and the clerk.[80] Ed Lasater was an active opponent. In addition to the constant barrage of state cases he and his allies filed against the Parr group, Lasater's chief lawyer, Chester Terrell of San Antonio, wrote letters and filed numerous memorandums and briefs with the Justice Department in Washington. The slow pace of the state cases prompted Lasater to take further action. He traveled to Washington, D.C., in 1915 to make a personal appeal to Woodrow Wilson's attorney general for federal intervention in Duval County.[81]

As the state cases dragged on through months of legal maneuvering and postponements, Lasater grew impatient and proposed a change of venue to San Antonio or Amarillo. Instead, the district attorney transferred the trials to Hidalgo County in South Texas, "where John Closner's political domination and Wells' influence undermined the prospects for convictions." Neither the Lasater attorneys nor the prosecution witnesses, except for George Kidd, attended the scheduled trial, and the district attorney persuaded the judge to dismiss all the charges against the Duval County officeholders.[82]

Lasater and his group continued to challenge Parr in the courts in the following years, with little success: "Not only did Archie Parr and his henchmen survive the state indictments, but federal investigations and the continuing barrage of civil suits, but they showed no inclination to reform their management of county government."[83] The Parr abuses continued unabated, and the Parr power was undiminished. Archie Parr was only the beginning. He was "the first Duke of Duval, the founder of a dynasty that has held vast political power in South Texas for more than sixty years."[84]

Parr had paid the poll taxes. Parr was asked if he had anything to say. Parr said, 'yes,' and when he got to the podium, he said, 'I have been accused of buying poll taxes. I have 200 right here in my pocket. We all buy them,' and he swept his hand around the room. Everyone just whooped and hollered and that was the end of the whole investigation" (interview, Garland M. Lasater, February 21, 1981).

[80] Anders, "Bosses Under Siege," p. 499.
[81] Ibid., pp. 504, 516–21.
[82] Ibid., p. 503.
[83] Ibid., p. 508.
[84] Baskin, "Archie Founded Dynasty," p. 1.

Ed Lasater's decade-long struggle with the Democratic powers in Starr County had a successful conclusion in 1911. His election-day opposition, expenditures of time and money, and protracted legal assault on the Parrs in Duval County did not meet with similar success. Archie Parr and his successors established themselves as one of the most durable political machines in the United States. The repeated attempts by Lasater and others to restrain Parr or to modify his methods produced few positive results. The governor of Texas and four former governors attended Archie Parr's funeral, underscoring his local power and regional influence three decades after the San Diego shoot-out which had served to solidify his political control of the county. But another Texas governor summed up one common view of Parr and his methods: "For many years, the Parr regime has been a cancer. The light of freedom has been snuffed out in Duval County. There was no law there, no liberty, no free elections."[85]

The Parr saga did not end with Archie's death. The lives and actions of the Parr family continued to provide a bizarre sideshow in South Texas. "It's a case of life imitating melodrama," one article commented: "If Hollywood made the Parr story into a movie, the critics would say they were unbelievably violent and corrupt. . . ."[86] George Parr fine-tuned his father's approach to brush-country despotism and carried on the family traditions for several decades after both Ed Lasater and Archie Parr had passed from the scene. But the younger Parr continued to face political and legal opponents who tenaciously fought the Parr machine as Lasater had.

After a particularly eventful year involving local power plays, political crises, and federal grand juries, George Parr drove to Los Horcones, an old family ranch south of Benavides, and put a .45-caliber pistol to his head. "George was quite a guy," a nephew commented. "He wrote his own skit. . . . He called the shots until the end."[87] But Manuel Guerra, Archie and George Parr, Ed Lasater, and other political activists in Starr and Duval counties in the early decades of the twentieth century did not appear in a skit. They were serious actors in a real-life drama that involved malice, graft, and guns; it was rife with innuendo and intrigue, even death.

[85] Martin, "Tyrant in Texas," p. 21, quoting Texas Governor Allen Shivers; "A Death in Duval," p. 3.

[86] "A Death in Duval," p. 1.

[87] Ibid., p. 3.

CHAPTER 7

Jersey Cows at Heart's Delight

The land is as fertile as that of the wonderful valley of the
Nile, and the climate is that of which the poets have
sung in California and Italy.

—R. M. Curtis

QUITE a sensation was caused at the 1928 National Dairy Show when three gentlemen appeared together on the podium. They were Eugene C. Perredes, the largest breeder of Jersey cattle on the Isle of Jersey, D. O. Bull, the largest Jersey breeder in the British Empire, and Ed C. Lasater from Falfurrias, Texas, owner of the largest Jersey herd in the world.[1]

Twenty-one years earlier Lasater had plunged into the dairy business with customary speed and determination.[2] H. W. Giddens, a farmer from the north who had come to the Falfurrias area as a result of the Miller-Lasater land promotion, asked Ed Lasater if he would finance the purchase of a few dairy cows. Lasater replied that he would, and that he would accompany Giddens when he went to buy them.[3]

1907 was a dry year in parts of northeastern Texas. A number of stock farmers reduced their herd numbers that year and many dairymen were shipping their stock into the Fort Worth Auction.[4] Giddens found the cows he was looking for. Lasater, who was not inclined to be a

---

[1] R. M. Gow, "Ed C. Lasater," *Jersey Bulletin*, March 26, 1930, p. 558.

[2] An early Falfurrias Creamery butter carton states: "The Falfurrias jersey herd and the Falfurrias Creamery were founded by Mr. Ed C. Lasater in 1907." Other articles and references place the date of Lasater's entry into the dairy business in other years between 1906 and 1909.

[3] Interview, Florence Schuetz, April 9, 1981.

[4] "Climatic Summary of the United States, Section 32, Northeast Texas"; interview, L. D. Miller, Sr., September 22, 1971.

passive observer in any transaction, also developed an interest along the way. He returned to Falfurrias with a trainload of Jersey cattle.[5]

Until he was almost fifty years old, Lasater's entire experience had been with horses and beef cattle. Whether Giddens's desire to buy some dairy cows and the drought in northern Texas were the catalysts in a new direction in Lasater's thinking, or if those events simply coincided with an idea that had already begun taking shape in his mind, is not known. But that first purchase of dairy cows marked the beginning of a business venture that would develop into a consuming interest and would have a major impact on Lasater's business fortunes in the last two decades of his life.

Lasater and the Miller brothers had put out brochures with extravagant claims about the productive potential of the land they were selling to settlers from the north and the east, at prices ten to twenty times its established value only a few years earlier. Developers in other parts of Texas were populating the state with settlers attracted by similar promotions. Lasater was not a land developer and real estate promoter by profession or by nature, however. He had come to the Falfurrias country to stay; he was not the smooth-talking salesman who was ready to move to the next promising area when the project was sold out. He was not a man to stand by idly and watch the farmers he had enticed to the area go broke and move back to where they had come from. "Had I not supplied them with the dairy cow and developed a market for their products, their holdings would have inevitably reverted back to me for ranch purposes."[6]

Lasater studied and observed the development of other western areas and concluded that in most instances it took three generations of settlers to develop a region and to establish a permanent foothold. He was convinced that the time necessary to successfully convert a grazing country into a farming community with a stable population could be shortened. The dairy cow was a major factor in his search for the proper

[5] Interview, L. D. Miller, Sr., September 22, 1971. Giddens and Lasater apparently had a partnership arrangement, which was dissolved in 1909 (Deed Records transcribed from Starr County, Brooks County, vol. X, p. 322).

[6] Ed C. Lasater to Gilbert N. Haugen, March 7, 1920, quoted in Lasater, "Meat Packer Legislation," statement before the Committee on Agriculture, U.S. House of Representatives, March 1, 2, 3, and 6, 1920, p. 210, in Edward C. Lasater Collection, Eugene C. Barker Texas History Center, University of Texas, Austin.

mix of activities that would allow the first generation of agriculturists to succeed. "I knew that one dairy cow had an earning capacity equal to five or six beef cows. If I could create a market for the product of the dairy cow, the first farmers who came would be able to hold on. . . ."[7]

As Lasater became increasingly involved in the dairy business, his rancher friends joked about the big cattleman trading in his spurs for a milk pail.[8] Dairying was a new venture for Ed Lasater, but dairy cattle and Jerseys were not new to Texas, despite the state's reputation as the home of the big ranches where vast herds of Longhorns, Herefords, and other beef breeds, roamed over unbroken prairies. A report on the Texas State Fair in 1890 stated that the cattle "were pretty evenly divided between Holsteins, Herefords and Jerseys, with Jerseys a little in the lead in numbers."[9] The Texas Jersey Cattle Club held their annual meeting in 1892 in the Menger Hotel in San Antonio. Two years later J. O. Terrell, the secretary of that organization, reported that the club had more than 250 members.[10]

Ed Lasater was not the only major cattleman in Texas to become interested in Jersey cattle. Robert J. Kleberg of Santa Gertrudis was also actively involved: "His purchase of Combination Premiere and the Cid with the great brood cow herd of T. S. Cooper in 1916 firmly established southwest Texas as a national center of Jersey activities."[11] Nor was Lasater the only person to see dairying as a positive, even necessary, factor in rural Texas' development.

In the years prior to the first World War, a number of Texas leaders, and in fact many prominent persons throughout the South, were active and vocal advocates of diversification on the farm. Many farmers in Texas and in the South were heavily dependent on income from one crop: cotton. In dry years or in periods of low cotton prices, that reliance on one revenue source was often disastrous. K. K. Legett, a prominent lawyer and judge in Abilene, worked tirelessly to convince the farmers in Taylor County that they would be wise to decrease their

[7] Ed C. Lasater, "What I Did When I Lost $130,000 Farming," *Farm and Fireside*, March, 1919, quoted in ibid., p. 204.

[8] R. Clyde Allen, "Single-Handed He Conquered 380,000 Acres of Texas Prairie," *Manufacturers Record*, April 7, 1927, p. 94.

[9] Arthur Dieterich, "Jerseys in Texas Date Back to '73," *Jersey Journal*, May, 1961, p. 41.

[10] Ibid.

[11] Ibid., p. 42.

cotton acreages and increase their production of livestock. That change would free the agriculturist from "two of the most unpredictable forces on earth—cotton market and rainfall."[12]

In 1914 Judge Legett invited Governor Edmond F. Noel of Mississippi, a consistent foe of King Cotton, to come to the Abilene Fair to describe to West Texas farmers the evils of a one-crop agricultural system. Legett himself, speaking at a Chamber of Commerce banquet, "put every person in the audience on record that whenever in the future he was called on to make a speech, he would talk about dairying and diversification."[13]

That same year an article on Ed Lasater's operation at Falfurrias discussed his much-repeated conviction that the farmer's financial destiny would be improved if he would plant only one-third as much cotton. Lasater believed the remaining acreage should be put into general crops and used to support cows and hogs. "This doctrine has been preached for a long time by agricultural improvers. I have demonstrated it to my own satisfaction on this Texas land, and it must convince those who see it," Lasater said.[14] In other conversations, Lasater was even more emphatic. He stated that he was "willing to pay any price" to demonstrate the importance of diversification to the farmers of South Texas.[15]

Lasater's ideas, which developed into a master plan for the development of the Falfurrias country, did not meet with unanimous support or approval. George Brackenridge gave Lasater a strong negative reaction, although he had backed the rancher for more than two decades before the subject of dairy cattle arose. After listening to Lasater detail his plans to establish a large-scale dairying enterprise, Brackenridge responded firmly, "It's not worth a damn."[16] Brackenridge did not think dairying would be a viable proposition in the Falfurrias area. He had observed Lasater's progress over the years, however, and he had confidence in Lasater's abilities as a businessman and as a cattleman. Instead

[12] Vernon G. Spence, *Judge Legett of Abilene*, p. 182.
[13] Ibid., pp. 188–89.
[14] Charles A. Gapen, "Cows in Cactus Land," *Country Gentleman*, January 31, 1914.
[15] Interview, L. D. Miller, Sr., September 22, 1971.
[16] Hugh G. Van Pelt, "The Man from Falfurrias," *Field Illustrated*, March, 1924, p. 13.

of providing the backing Lasater sought, Brackenridge offered him "control of two of the largest banks in San Antonio and enough financing to go as far as he might like in straight ranching. . . ."[17] Lasater was determined to implement his own ideas, though, and the attractive offer from his banking mentor did not tempt him. "There are hundreds to run banks, but if I do not develop my plans, no one will," Lasater stated.[18]

Lasater did not secure major bank financing for his dairy operation until 1911. In the meantime, he proceeded headlong into the project which he considered of vital importance to the economic future of the Falfurrias community. He had entered the business with only a trainload of Jersey cows, but his plan soon assumed characteristic proportions, and he moved rapidly to implement it. In 1907 he set aside 40,000 acres of his ranch to be developed into a series of dairy farms, each containing between 100 and 125 milk cows. By the following year, the first barns and croplands were ready.[19] Within a few years, more than fifty silos were constructed to handle feedstuffs grown on Lasater's farms.[20] Lasater set up eight separate and completely equipped dairies. Three were located south of Falfurrias, one at his ranch headquarters at La Mota, two south of there, and two northwest of La Mota.

After an intensive study of dairying and dairy breeds, Lasater concluded that the Jersey cow was the one that best fit the program. This breed was noted particularly for its milk's high butterfat content, a critical factor at that time since butter would provide the means for marketing this new industry's production.[21] In the course of his investigation, Lasater found others who like Brackenridge doubted the wisdom of his plan: "The experts said it couldn't be done, that the climate was against me." But he remembered the rich milk and good butter on his mother's table as he grew up in Goliad County, and he could not accept the doubts expressed by others: "I believed our native Texas grasses were better than the far-famed blue grass of Kentucky. Believing this myself, I set about to prove it to others."[22]

[17] Ibid.
[18] Ibid.
[19] Ibid.
[20] *Falfurrias Jerseys: Type, Production, Beauty, Utility.*
[21] Interview, Garland M. Lasater, February 21, 1981.
[22] Lasater, "Meat Packer Legislation," p. 208.

Lasater's first dairy cows were of commercial quality. His purchase of J. O. Terrell's herd in 1909 provided the initial basis for Lasater's later fame as a leading breeder of quality Jersey seedstock. Terrell's St. Cloud herd was noted as one of the best-bred herds of high-producing Jersey cattle in Texas. Lasater purchased his entire herd and moved it by train to Falfurrias.[23]

The St. Cloud purchase was only the beginning. Lasater traveled over the entire country seeking out the highest producing bloodlines available. He bought cattle as far east as the Ayre Farm in Maine and the Hood Farm in Lowell, Massachusetts. Lasater developed a strong admiration for Mr. Hood, a pioneer in the selection of cattle based on their productive merits. Lasater bought heavily of Hood's Tormentor strain; these cattle were not noted for their beauty, but were long, rangy cows with the capacity to take on large quantities of roughage and to produce record quantities of milk. Among the sires purchased from Hood was Sophie 19th Tormentor, a son of the cow who held the world's championship for cumulative butterfat production of all breeds.[24]

Ed Lasater became a familiar figure at the major Jersey sales around the country. When Lasater started to bid, he was the last one to stop, and he started often: "Many a man has traveled hundreds of miles to a Jersey sale and gone home with an empty halter or bullring because Lasater outbid him . . . and I never saw him start bidding on a common one. Secondly, his determination to get good sires is almost a mania."[25] One of the bulls in Lasater's herd in 1911, Nobleman, was bought at an auction for $15,000 and was considered the most valuable bull in the world.[26]

Cattle from many parts of the country were put on the train to

[23] *San Antonio Light*, October 4, 1909; interviews, L. D. Miller, Sr., September 22, 1971, and G. M. Lasater, February 21, 1981. The article in the *San Antonio Light* says that Terrell sold 351 head to Lasater and the Miller Brothers for $53,000, or $150 per head.

[24] *Falfurrias Jerseys: Type, Production, Beauty, Utility*; interview, G. M. Lasater, February 21, 1981. Garland Lasater remembers visiting the Hood Farm with his father. Many of the large eastern dairies were underwritten by families whose large incomes from manufacturing allowed them to indulge their fancies in cattle breeding. Hood was unique in this respect. He was a working dairyman, a practical farmer.

[25] Van Pelt, "The Man from Falfurrias," p. 13.

[26] Edward H. Caldwell, "The Life and Activities of Edward Cunningham Lasater," p. 21.

that little town at the end of the line. In 1912 bloodlines from the Isle
of Jersey were added to the mix: "I sought the best Jersey herds in the
country, buying only American-bred cattle at first. Then it became my
ambition to give my community the benefit of one of the best Jersey
herds in the world. I secured a herd of select Island-bred Jerseys, 100
cows, costing an average of $600 each."[27] That was a substantial price
in 1912. Lasater's own balance sheets that year valued his beef cows,
which he had been improving and selecting for more than a decade, at
$30 per head.

Within a short time after his first purchase of high-quality Jersey
seedstock, Lasater began exhibiting his cattle around the country. In
1911 he returned to Falfurrias with Grand Champion prizes from state
fairs in Louisiana, Ohio, Illinois, and Kentucky.[28] Cattle of Lasater's
own raising were making a strong showing within a few years; in 1916
they won the coveted Breeder's Diploma for Lasater at the National
Dairy Show at Springfield, Massachusetts, and the Dairy Cattle Congress at Waterloo, Iowa. A year later he won top prizes with his show
herd of twenty-seven Jerseys, twenty-two of which had been bred on
the ranch. When one of his bulls took the Grand Champion prize at
the National Dairy Show in 1918, it was only the second time in the
history of the show that a bull of the exhibitor's own breeding had won
the top prize.[29] The ability of his cattle to capture top honors in these
national competitions reaffirmed Lasater's faith in the sandy land surrounding the Loma Blanca: "That seems to me conclusive proof that
our native Texas grasses are equal to Kentucky blue grass or any other
grass. If the country had not been as I had sized it up, I could not possibly have gotten these results."[30]

Lasater's first dairy was a primitive setup. One picture shows a
group of milk cows tied in a semicircle to a net wire fence shaded by
mesquite trees in a sandy pen. Milk cans labeled "Falfurrias Jersey
Dairy Company" sit in the middle of the pen in front of the tarp
stretched over a frame made of posts. But he soon went beyond that.
As his vision of a diversified community of stock farmers became a re-

[27] Lasater, "Meat Packer Legislation," p. 208.
[28] *About Falfurrias and Copita*, p. 5.
[29] *Falfurrias Jerseys: Type, Production, Beauty, Utility*.
[30] Lasater, "Meat Packer Legislation," p. 208.

La Mota ranch house, southeast elevation. Lasater constructed this home by hauling four frame houses to La Mota from various locations on the ranch. The houses were joined together by a rambling network of porches. Courtesy G. M. Lasater

The living room of the La Mota ranch house. Courtesy G. M. Lasater

Tom and Lois Lasater in front of their father's office in Falfurrias, circa 1914. San Isidro Church is in the background, left. Courtesy Tom Lasater

Garland and Tom riding ponies near "the Playhouse," circa 1915. Ed Lasater built this as a schoolhouse and recreation center for his children. Courtesy G. M. Lasater

Left to right: Albert, Garland, Tom, Mary, and Ed Lasater, circa 1915. Courtesy G. M. Lasater

Left to right: Albert, Lois, Tom, Ed, and Garland Lasater, circa 1915. Courtesy G. M. Lasater

Tom Lasater with his shetland pony, circa 1915. Courtesy Tom Lasater

Albert (*left*), Garland, and Lois Lasater in their pony cart, circa 1916. Courtesy
G. M. Lasater

The cousins, 1929. *Back row, from left:* Richard Miller, Burleigh Gardner, Garland Lasater. *Front row:* Kleber Miller, L. D. Miller, Jr., Brad Miller, Tom Lasater. *Seated:* Helen Mary Miller holding John Miller. Courtesy Tom Lasater

Left: Ed Lasater with his daughter, Lois, circa 1917. Courtesy Tom Lasater. *Right:* Ed C. Lasater, 1929. Courtesy Tom Lasater

La Loma Blanca, a principal landmark of the Falfurrias country, 1912. Courtesy Falfurrias Heritage Museum

Picnic group on the Loma Blanca, overlooking Salt Lake, circa 1912. Courtesy Edena Clere Noll

Falfurrias, circa 1910. This is the north side of East Miller Street, looking west, at the corner of South Lasater Street. The two-story building on the far left is the Palace Hotel. Courtesy Falfurrias Heritage Museum

Falfurrias Mercantile Company, circa 1910. This was its second location in Falfurrias, on the north side of East Rice west of the railroad depot. Courtesy Brooks County Historical Commission

The original Falfurrias Creamery, circa 1907. This building faced west on the
northeast corner of St. Mary's and Rice streets. Courtesy G. M. Lasater

The second Falfurrias Creamery, built in 1925. Courtesy G. M. Lasater

ality and as financing became available, Lasater equipped each of the
eight dairies fully, almost elaborately. Large barns with steel stanchions
and troughs, silos, and houses for the workers were built at each
location. Juana González married Agapito Treviño in 1912 and moved to Las
Conchas Dairy. Treviño had come to Falfurrias from Mexico as a young
boy and he worked for many years at Las Conchas and then at the Alto
Colorado Dairy. At Las Conchas there were a foreman and eight workers. Six were milkers, one handled the feeding, and one handled the
separation of the cream from the milk. Each of the men had families
and they lived in nine houses which sat in two rows facing each other
along a road. The houses typically had one or two rooms and were
wood-frame construction.[31] Milking was done twice a day, at 3:00 A.M.
and 3:00 P.M. It usually took about three hours to complete a milking.
Each milker was in charge of between fifteen and twenty cows.

The main reason for establishing the different dairies was to have
sufficient pastureland for each herd in close proximity to the dairy. In
addition to native and improved pastures, the cows were fed silage a
large part of the year along with a supplement containing cottonseed
cake. The cultivated land in Lasater's operation totaled between six
thousand and eight thousand acres.[32] The silage, principally redtop
cane and milo, was packed in silos, originally built upright, but later
constructed underground after the early ones were destroyed by
hurricanes.[33]

Ed Lasater's plan was not simply to have a large dairy with the
highest-producing bloodlines that money could buy. Soon after his
dairy enterprise was underway, he involved the colonists who had
bought land in the area. These farmers bought Jersey cows from Lasater on credit and sold their cream to the Falfurrias creamery. They paid
off the cows with one-third of the cream check they received each

[31] Interviews, Juana González Treviño, July 7, 1981, and G. M. Lasater, July 29,
1981. Otto Feenstra, a Norwegian, for many years had charge of the show herd. He lived
at La Fruta where the show herd was kept (Ibid.) At La Fruta, the houses were built
along the south side of a green area. In the middle of that area was a building that was
raised off the ground. There a beef, butchered every week or two, was hung in chunks,
and each family would slice off its share (Interview, Tom Lasater, July 22, 1981).

[32] W. D. Hornaday, "Dairying on a Large Scale," *Hoard's Dairyman*, June 12, 1916,
p. 773.

[33] Interview, C. J. McBride, March 7, 1982.

month. The remainder of the cream sales provided the colonists with a monthly source of revenue and removed them from complete dependence on the success or failure of a single crop.[34]

By 1916 about one-quarter of the five hundred families brought in by Lasater were raising Jersey cattle. At the peak of this operation, three hundred area farms sold cream to the Falfurrias creamery. Among those were the descendants of Sabas Pérez who hauled their cream into town each day from their property on the south side of the Laguna de Loma Blanca.[35]

With Lasater's large herd in place and with many small dairy farmers in production, the daily output of butter from the Falfurrias creamery prior to the First World War ranged from twelve hundred to fifteen hundred pounds, depending on the season. The butter reached all the major markets of Texas, and Falfurrias butter commanded a premium price, usually three to eight cents above the Elgin quotation.[36]

Lasater spent considerable time and money taking his Jerseys to shows around the country. All his show animals were working cattle from the dairies, however. He felt strongly that producing qualities were of utmost importance in placing dairy cattle in the show ring. Lasater did not concentrate his selection on any one of the several bloodlines incorporated into his herd. Rather, he attempted to select and mate those individuals which most nearly represented the ideal Jersey.[37]

Careful production records were kept on each dairy cow, and once a month the cow's milk was tested for its butterfat content. Every cow that did not show a profit went to the butcher. Lasater sold to

[34] Interview, G. M. Lasater, February 21, 1981. H. E. Sanders was one of the earliest dairymen. He came from Ohio in 1909 and began farming on twenty acres. Later he rented additional land and bought Jerseys from Lasater on the "pay for it out of the cream check plan" ("Falfurrias, the Dairyland of South Texas," *Acco Press*, vol. 12, no. 8 [August, 1934]: 5).

[35] Hornaday, "Dairying"; interviews, G. M. Lasater, February 21, 1981; and Petra Pérez, March 24, 1982.

[36] Hornaday, "Dairying."

[37] *Falfurrias Jerseys: Type, Production, Beauty, Utility.* Lasater maintained a number of cows on Register of Merit tests. This was done under rules established by the American Jersey Cattle Club and was carried out with supervisors from the Texas Agricultural and Industrial College at Kingsville. He had more than 150 cows on those tests in 1919 (Ibid.).

area farmers only those cows whose milk and butterfat output paid their way.[38]

Lasater was convinced that the highest-producing cow was the cheapest cow, regardless of any first cost within reason. That was the guiding factor in all his breeding programs. If any female on the ranch did not give sufficient milk for her offspring, she was disposed of. This included the family's cats and dogs.[39]

Ed Lasater became convinced of dairying's role in the future of Falfurrias, and he cut off a large section of his cattle ranch to put this project into motion when he was almost fifty years old. He invested very substantial sums of capital to improve the land, to build and equip the facilities and to purchase the best breeding stock available. Ed Lasater would naturally speak positively about this project in which he invested so much time and money. His enthusiasm, magnified by his energy and conviction, was evidently contagious.

One man whose statements surpassed even Lasater's optimistic forecast was J. O. Terrell, the longtime Jersey breeder and respected president of the Central Trust Company in San Antonio. In October, 1911, Terrell made an inspection tour of the Falfurrias Jersey Dairy Company in his role as a prospective lender. Terrell was an experienced cattleman, and as a banker he certainly knew the necessity of profits to sustain a business proposition and to service debt. He must have been in Falfurrias on a day when the wind was not blowing. Perhaps a recent rain had greened the sandy pastures. And he and Ed Lasater must have spent more time looking at pretty Jersey cows grazing contentedly as they toured around between the dairies at Uña de Gato, Cabeza Blanca, and Charco Salado than they did looking at the books.

Terrell's report was reminiscent of the promotional brochures distributed earlier by the Miller brothers in their land-selling campaign. His language seemed more that of a real estate promoter than of a banker: "I feel justified in saying that this is one of the more productive portions of the state . . . and winter there is even more delightful

[38] Caldwell, "Life and Activities of Lasater," p. 21.

[39] Mary Whatley Clarke, "Ed C. Lasater, Ninth President of the Association, was a Creative Thinker and Doer," *Cattleman*, January, 1952, p. 20.

than summer, although summer is moderated by the constant Gulf breeze." The condition of the forage crops which he saw growing "surpassed anything in that line that I had ever seen."[40]

Terrell wrote that the Falfurrias Jersey Dairy Company's forty thousand acres were laid off in the form of a parallelogram divided into pastures and fields ranging from one hundred to two thousand acres. The whole property was well watered by several flowing artesian wells and by others fitted with steel windmills varying in depth from three hundred to one thousand feet. Terrell reported the farm was stocked with 1,315 head of commercial Jersey cattle, 565 head of registered Jerseys, 356 horses and mules, and 710 hogs.[41]

Terrell estimated that this dairy and farming enterprise had an earning capacity of $70,000 annually. His bank evidently accepted his report's positive conclusions. One month after Terrell's inspection trip, the Central Trust Company loaned Ed Lasater $300,000. As security, the bank took a mortgage on the 40,000 acres Lasater had separated from his ranch holdings to form the Falfurrias Jersey Dairy Company.[42]

Lasater saw his vision transformed into a reality. The colonists he and the Miller brothers had brought in would not all lose their farms and return to their northern homes. With the example of his eight dairy farms and the credit and the market he provided, these settlers would be able to succeed financially in that area south of the Nueces River. In time, Falfurrias butter found its way onto grocery shelves all over Texas and as far south as Mexico City. The area's reputation as a leading dairy center and the home of one of the country's largest and finest Jersey herds brought fame to the little town that sat near the center of Ignacio de la Peña's Los Olmos y Loma Blanca grant.

Fame did not translate into profitability, however. Despite Terrell's projections and Lasater's own confidence in the project's viability, the dairy farms became a burden his ranch had to support. Lasater had said

---

[40] J. O. Terrell "To Whom It May Concern," October 23, 1911, Lasater Files, in possession of Garland M. Lasater, Falfurrias. Terrell's letter states that Lasater was farming 6,000 acres—4,000 in cotton and 2,000 in forage crops. The farming was done by Mexican tenant farmers who were supplied with houses, teams, and equipment and who received one-half the crop as their share. The average yield was one-third of a bale of cotton per acre.

[41] Ibid.

[42] Trust Deed Records, Brooks County, Book 1, page 89.

he was willing to pay any price to make his plan a reality, to show the area farmers the value and necessity of diversification. The first results appeared to justify the early optimism, but the problems mounted up faster than he anticipated, and he could not have foreseen how high that price would ultimately be.[43]

[43] Interview, L. D. Miller, Sr., September 22, 1971.

CHAPTER 8

The Bottom Line

I made me great works; I builded me houses; I planted
me vineyards; I made me gardens and orchards, and I
planted trees in them of all kinds of fruits.

—Ecclesiastes 2:4, 5

AT the turn of the century, most of Ed Lasater's beef cattle were
Herefords or Shorthorns (then called Durhams) and crosses between
those two breeds. Lasater was counted among the renowned Hereford
breeders in Texas at that time, along with B. N. Aycock and John M.
Gist, Midland; Elgin O. Kothmann, Mason; J. S. Bridwell, Wichita
Falls; R. P. Lucas, Berclair; and a number of others.[1]

Lasater bred all his Herefords with a ring of red pigmentation
around their eyes in order to reduce the risk of cancer eye. Using the
base he had secured when he purchased the Kenedy Ranch cows in
1895, Lasater worked continuously to upgrade his breeding herd. H. P.
Drought, in a 1901 letter to William Mackenzie in Scotland, was enthusiastic about his borrower's cattle: "His cattle, as we told you previously, are as good a herd as can be found in southwest Texas; probably
as good as can be found on any range anywhere."[2]

Lasater had good cattle, but he was always open to new suggestions and ready to change. Even as he advanced in years, he never
hesitated to strike out in a new direction, once he concluded that an
idea had merit. He shocked many of his rancher colleagues by his enthusiasm for the Jersey cow. About the same time he startled many of
them when he became convinced that the sacred cattle recently imported from India were the salvation of the South Texas stockmen.

[1] Mary Whatley Clarke, A Century of Cow Business, pp. 238–39.
[2] H. P. Drought to William Mackenzie, March 21, 1901, Drought Files, in possession of Thomas Drought, San Antonio.

Several small importations of Brahman or Zebu (*Bos indicus*) cattle were made to the United States from India in the last half of the nineteenth century.[3] In 1904, the U.S. Secretary of Agriculture visited the Pierce Ranch on the Texas Gulf Coast to view some of the descendants of those early animals. After seeing the cattle firsthand, and after listening to the reports regarding their immunity to tick fever and their thriftiness on coastal pastures, the secretary issued a special permit to the Pierce Ranch to import a herd of purebred Brahmans from India. A. P. Borden, the Pierce Ranch's manager, went to India in 1906 and returned to the United States with the first major importation of Brahman cattle.[4]

That group of Brahmans were divided between the Pierce Ranch and the O'Connor Ranch at Victoria. Two years later, Ed Lasater, whose friend Al McFaddin from Victoria·was another early Brahman enthusiast, decided to try some of the cattle himself. Borden had become discouraged with his efforts to crossbreed the Brahmans, but when Lasater arrived at the Pierce Ranch, he liked what he saw and acted in characteristic fashion: "Mr. Borden told me that Lasater cut out so many and was going into his herd so deep that he had to call on Lasater to stop. The publicity from that sale started the Brahman cross in Texas."[5]

Lasater initiated a longrange crossbreeding program with the stock purchased from Borden in 1908. He crossed Ghir bulls on his Durham cows and bred Nelore and Krishna Valley bulls to a herd of Hereford cows. Both crosses produced a marked improvement over his straight-

---

[3] Clarke, *Century of Cow Business*, pp. 241–42.

[4] "Sacred Bull of India Popular in South Texas," *Cattleman*, March, 1920, p. 117. When Borden arrived with his Brahman herd on the East Coast, officials took the cattle's temperature and determined that they had a fever. The herd was immediately quarantined, and health authorities began to shoot those animals with the highest fevers. Desperate, Borden got the slaughter halted temporarily until he could go to Washington to see President Theodore Roosevelt. Roosevelt was very much interested in the matter and wired the authorities in New York to stop everything, that he would take personal responsibility for the herd. On further investigation, it was learned that the Brahman cattle's normal temperature is higher than that of the European breeds. Unfortunately, nearly half of Borden's herd had already been disposed of. After a lengthy quarantine, Borden was allowed to proceed to Texas with the survivors (Interview, John M. Bennett, February 24, 1967; "Brahma Cattle Increasing," *Cattleman*, July, 1919, p. 23; William States Jacobs, "The Romance of the Brahma," *Cattleman*, December, 1923, p. 25).

[5] Interview, John M. Bennett, February 24, 1967; Jacobs, "Romance of the Brahma," pp. 25–27.

bred English cows: "I think the results have been satisfactory in every way. If I were in a position to choose between these breeds of Indian cattle from the data at hand, I would take the Ghirs."[6]

Lasater stated that the Brahman cows were more nervous than the English breeds, but when handled quietly they were responsive and manageable. "I personally much prefer to handle the Brahma cattle under range conditions than any breed I have ever handled," Lasater wrote in an article for the *Cattleman*. "While difficult to force them to do anything, they are wonderfully intelligent cattle and can be trained so as to make the handling of them a pleasure. You want to avoid all noise and excitement in handling the Brahmas. They seem to handle more like range horses than cattle."[7]

Lasater was not merely impressed by the intelligence and responsiveness of his Brahman and Brahman-cross cattle, however. He saw them as better able to utilize both native pastures and grain rations, and he saw that a higher percentage calf crop resulted from his use of Brahman bulls. Those facts translated directly into ranch profitability: "My judgment is that a ranch stocked with these crossbred cows will return in net five to ten percent more than the best management can get out of the same ranch stocked with Durham cows." And he was equally positive about the results produced by mating Brahman bulls with his Hereford cow herd.[8]

Lasater's young brother-in-law observed the early reaction to the rancher's purchase: "When Ed Lasater started bringing in Brahman bulls, many of his colleagues said that he had ruined a damned good herd of cattle."[9] But Lasater grew steadily more positive about the cattle from India. The hump-backed Brahman was not a passing fancy, but instead took its place alongside the Jersey milk cow as a major factor in Lasater's livestock operation. Fifteen years after making his first purchase of Brahman cattle, Ed Lasater wrote: "I recommend both the Brahman and Durham cross and the Brahman and Hereford cross. After once using the Brahman cattle, I am satisfied you will not return to the use of any other."[10]

[6] Ed C. Lasater, "Brahma Cattle," *Cattleman*, March, 1923, p. 61.
[7] Ibid.
[8] Ibid.
[9] Interview, L. D. Miller, Sr., September 22, 1971.
[10] Lasater, "Brahma Cattle," p. 61.

In early 1911, a move to elect the Falfurrias cattleman head of the Texas Cattle Raisers Association began among a group of North and West Texas cattlemen. S. B. Burnett, George T. Reynolds, Arthur Godair, Marion Sansom, and others signed a document promoting Lasater's candidacy, which was circulated prior to the convention that year. The cattlemen called Lasater a "staunch advocate of the principles and purposes of our Association" and described him as "essentially a livestock man and progressive farmer, having one of the best graded up herds of Hereford cattle in Texas, perhaps the best brand of Thoroughbred Kentucky horses in Texas, and enough purebred swine and sheep to make him a formidable competitor. . . ." The document added that Lasater: "has won his way in the world by his own exertions, and is deserving of all honor at the hands of the livestock interests of Texas." [11] Lasater's colleagues elected him president of the association at its annual convention held in San Antonio in March, 1911. [12]

While serving as president of the cattle raisers' organization, Ed Lasater became increasingly involved in Republican party politics. He had first assumed a prominent role when he was named to the Republican State Executive Committee in 1906. [13] Working on that committee, Lasater became a close associate of Cecil A. Lyon of Sherman, the Republican leader in Texas. Lyon, who became GOP state chairman in 1900 and national committeeman in 1904, was the recognized dispenser of Republican patronage in the state and was an ally and hunting partner of Theodore Roosevelt. [14]

The bitter contest between Roosevelt and William Howard Taft for the presidential nomination in 1912 split the Republican party. The two Republican factions in Texas held separate conventions in 1912, and each elected a slate of delegates to go to the national convention in Chicago the following month. Lyon, Lasater, and H. L. Borden, a Houston attorney, headed the Roosevelt delegation. After extended

---

[11] *San Antonio Express*, undated 1911 clipping, Lasater Files, in possession of Garland M. Lasater, Falfurrias.

[12] Clarke, *Century of Cow Business*, pp. 48, 100. The Cattle Raisers Association of Texas became the Texas and Southwestern Cattle Raisers Association in 1921 (Ibid., pp. 131–32).

[13] Paul Casdorph, *A History of the Republican Party in Texas, 1865–1965*, p. 105.

[14] Lewis Gould, "Theodore Roosevelt, William Howard Taft, and the Disputed Delegates in 1912: Texas as a Test Case," *Southwestern Historical Quarterly* 80 (July, 1976): 35.

debate to decide which of the disputed delegations should be recognized, the Credentials Committee seated the Taft delegation from Texas at the national convention, which ultimately gave the incumbent president the Republican presidential nomination.[15]

In early August, Roosevelt's backers held a convention in Chicago to nominate their candidate. The party supporting Roosevelt was officially named the National Progressive Party. Of subsequent importance to the Texas party, blacks were barred from participation in the convention and in the new party. The Texas Progressives, meeting a week later in Dallas, endorsed Roosevelt's Texas Republican organization and the Chicago Bull Moose platform.[16]

The Texas Bull Moose Party nominated Lasater as its gubernatorial candidate; W. H. Featherstone, a banker from Henrietta, received the nomination for lieutenant governor.[17] Lasater told the convention: "The opposition party to the Democrats was born here today, and the dominating party of Texas is in need of a strong opposition."[18]

John Bennett observed Lasater on the stump and remembered Lasater's creating a positive impression, despite the odds against his candidacy: "He was articulate. He made a good appearance on the platform as a speaker."[19] But the Republican candidates in Texas in the early years of the twentieth century did little more than preserve the semblance of a competitive system of politics. Lasater's hometown newspaper lamented his campaign prospects: "It is a great pity that there is

[15] Casdorph, *History of the Republican Party*, pp. 99–103.

[16] Ibid., p. 105. At their state convention in August, 1912, the Texas Progressives approved the national convention stand that read the blacks out of the party. A. J. Winters of Fort Worth declared at that convention that "no party can be built in Texas to accomplish anything that will permit Negro affiliations" (Paul D. Casdorph, *Republicans, Negroes, and Progressives in the South, 1912–1916*, p. 145). "[Cecil] Lyon's policy of excluding Texas blacks from the party had alienated black Republicans, the GOP's principal electoral resource" (Lewis Gould, "Theodore Roosevelt," p. 36). The party's stance with regard to blacks did little to further the national ambitions, either: "Neither Texas nor national progressives were able to fulfill their earliest hopes and provide for as much progressive change as was needed. This failure was in part due to the total disregard for the Negro in Texas and an evident lack of concern for the Negro and his rights as shown by such northern progressives as Theodore Roosevelt and Woodrow Wilson" (James A. Tinsley, "The Progressive Movement in Texas" [Ph.D. diss., Univ. of Wisconsin, 1953], p. 321).

[17] *San Antonio Express*, August 13, 1912.

[18] Casdorph, *Republicans, Negroes, and Progressives*, p. 145.

[19] Interview, John M. Bennett, February 25, 1967.

no prospect of his being elected. Texas, like most other states and the national administration, is lawyer-ridden." The article affirmed that in order to clean up the "present condition of political corruption" it was necessary for businessmen to enter politics and to be elected.[20]

On October 24, 1912, the *Dallas Morning News* commented on the Lasater candidacy: "Ed C. Lasater of Falfurrias probably will not have a chance of serving the State of Texas as its Bull Moose governor, but he is already rendering it a great service in the promotion of better stock growing. . . ." The article continued: "We do not mean to suggest that Mr. Lasater is incapable of serving the state politically, but instead . . . that there is no doubt about his industrial service to the Commonwealth."[21]

All the bitter feeling and complicated maneuvering between the two Republican factions in Texas was largely academic: "It was a foregone conclusion that once [Woodrow] Wilson was nominated, he would carry Texas. Democratic candidates had enjoyed that security in Texas since Reconstruction days."[22] In the state gubernatorial race, Governor O. B. Colquitt was easily elected to a second term. The total vote was: Colquitt (Democrat), 234,352; Redding Andrews (Socialist), 25,258; C. W. Johnson (Republican), 23,089; Lasater (Progressive), 15,794, and A. J. Houston (Prohibition), 2,356.[23]

Ed Lasater's move into the dairy business, his decision to introduce Brahman blood into his beef cattle herd, his leadership role in the cattle raisers association, and his active participation in state politics all coincided with the years in which his cattle operation and other enterprises reached their maximum extension. His last major land acquisition, made more than a decade after his Starr County purchase from Ignacio de la Peña's granddaughter, was a 60,000-acre portion of the Santa Rosa Ranch. Lasater bought this tract in 1906 for a little less than three dollars an acre from Colonel Dillard Fant, one of the young men who grew up in Goliad and went on to become a major factor in the Texas livestock industry.[24]

[20] *Falfurrias Facts*, undated article [August, 1912], Lasater Files.
[21] *Dallas Morning News*, October 24, 1912.
[22] Tinsley, "The Progressive Movement," p. 302.
[23] Casdorph, *History of the Republican Party*, p. 107.
[24] Transcribed Deeds from Hidalgo County, Brooks County, vol. III, p. 19.

Fant started his career driving cattle up the northern trails. By the time he went to Francis Smith and H. P. Drought for a loan in 1891, the former colonel was "probably the richest stockman in this section of the country."[25] Drought and Smith made many loans to Fant, "an old-fashioned cowman" and, based on years of experience, considered him a good credit risk. In one communication Drought, describing Fant to his Scottish lenders, said that the rancher "has gone through all the ups and downs of the stockman and at different times has been worth all the way from nothing up to a million dollars."[26]

Dillard Fant was a big operator at a time when it took extensive holdings to qualify in that category. At one time he owned and operated the 225,000-acre Santa Rosa Ranch in Hidalgo County, a 60,000-acre "pasture" in Live Oak County, and other ranch properties around the state, which altogether totaled some 700,000 acres.[27] But Fant's holdings began disintegrating a decade before his death. He had followed the pattern of many other livestock men who operated on a grand scale and bet heavily on turns in the cattle market and on the weather. When the bets went sour, the results were often devastating for those early cattle speculators who typically used large amounts of borrowed capital. Several of Fant's ranches were sold in foreclosure proceedings in 1904, and he and his wife were subsequently involved in a lengthy and bitter series of lawsuits with D. Sullivan and Co., the San Antonio lending agency.[28]

When he bought part of the Santa Rosa Ranch from his aging and financially troubled neighbor to the east, Lasater was reaching the peak of his career. Even the heavy financial burden that had been added to Lasater's total indebtedness as a result of his loan to his uncle, Edward Cunningham, did not slow him down, and he was confident his

[25] Francis Smith to William Mackenzie, May 25, 1981, Alliance Trust Letterbook, no. 1, Drought Files.

[26] H. P. Drought to William Mackenzie, May 30, 1905, Alliance Trust Letterbook, no. 7, Drought Files.

[27] J. Marvin Hunter, *The Trail Drivers of Texas*, p. 518.

[28] *Alice Echo*, January 23, 1908; "Sullivan v. Fant," 110 *The Southwestern Reporter*, pp. 509–23, and 160 *The Southwestern Reporter*, pp. 614–23. This suit and others clouded Ed Lasater's title to the Santa Rosa tract for a number of years. In their suit, Fant and his wife accused D. Sullivan and Co. of inducing them to enter into an agreement whose ultimate intent was to take possession of the Fants' property fraudulently.

large operation could service that debt in addition to a host of other mortgages and operating loans.

Personal energy, optimism, and confidence had propelled the young trader into a position of national prominence in an important industry. His devastating losses in 1893 and 1894 notwithstanding, he remained optimistic as he considered the prospects for a future in Starr County: "I still had faith in the country. . . . I knew the range was there; I felt sure the opportunity was there." He set out immediately to recover his losses, and he capitalized on the depressed state of the livestock business: "I was confident I could do it. . . . Faith in myself has helped me to do a lot of seemingly impossible things."

It was not until eleven years after his entry into the ranching business in Starr County that Lasater began recording the details of his business transactions on paper. During those intervening years, he bought and sold between 10,000 and 26,000 head of grazing cattle each year, started a major breeding herd, and bought more than 350,000 acres of ranchland without the benefit of written records. In 1906, the year he purchased the Santa Rosa tract, he hired an accountant to begin recording the details of the business.

Three years later, Lasater retained Price, Waterhouse and Co. of Saint Louis to perform an audit on the books of his diverse operations. That firm's letter at the conclusion of its audit summarized the accounting history of Lasater's enterprises: "Our examination covered the period of two and one-half years from July 1, 1906, to December 31, 1908, for although your first purchase of ranchlands dates back, we understand, to 1895, it was not until July 1, 1906, that any regular books of account were opened." [29]

When the Saint Louis accountants arrived in Falfurrias, they found everything out of order. Entries, "in cases where such had been recorded," were charged or credited to such accounts as "loan payments," or "suspense." The books did not distinguish between capital and expense items. The voucher system was "so defective that the risk of errors was multiplied rather than eliminated," and the ledger accounts were not in agreement with the bank statements. [30] The accoun-

---

[29] Price, Waterhouse and Co. to Ed C. Lasater, May 31, 1909, Lasater Files.
[30] Ibid.

tants were astounded that Ed Lasater could carry all the details of a
business of that magnitude in his head.[31] But they were not complimentary about the bookkeeping function that he had initiated in 1906.
"Briefly stated," Price, Waterhouse wrote, "the records submitted to
us gave no indication whatever of the condition of the business. . . ."[32]

The financial statements which Price, Waterhouse prepared in 1909
and which Lasater's office staff prepared in the following four years,
provided the earliest financial details on Lasater's business undertakings.[33] By implication, those statements also provide some insight into
the man behind that operation. Lasater could see that the accounting
records were useful and that his bankers liked them. But figures told
only part of the story. The accountants' columns did not reflect fully
the current market price for land and livestock, and the yearly figures
did not predict the future. Lasater was always looking ahead and antici-
pating the next development, and the books reflect both his youthful
optimism of 1887 and his confident vision of the future.

Price, Waterhouse completed its audit of Lasater's records and
prepared a balance sheet as of June 30, 1909. That balance sheet, as
well as profit and loss summaries for the years 1910–13, and a balance
sheet for June 30, 1913, prepared by Ed Lasater's office, are repro-
duced in appendix B. In addition, Lasater's cattle inventories from 1910
to 1914 are copied from the Lasater files.

As of June 30, 1909, Ed Lasater's net worth was approximately
$1,500,000. His assets included mercantile stores in Falfurrias and Rea-
litos, a growing herd of Jersey cattle, and a number of other business
investments. By far, the two largest assets listed on the balance sheet
Price, Waterhouse prepared were 276,632 acres of land and 24,126
head of beef cattle. Cost figures do not exist on portions of the land,
and the acreage could be compiled only from the county clerks' records
in Starr, Duval, and Hidalgo counties. The accountants wrote that

[31] Interview, Laurence D. Miller, Sr., September 22, 1971.

[32] Price, Waterhouse and Co. to Ed C. Lasater, May 31, 1909, Lasater Files.

[33] The financial statements from Ed Lasater's operation between 1909 and 1913 and
the cattle inventories for those years exist today because they were removed from
Lasater's business files by Margaret (Peggy) Lasater Clark when she wrote her senior thesis in history at Vassar in 1964. Subsequently, those statements and inventories were kept
separate from the main body of Lasater's records, which were largely destroyed in the
flooding in Falfurrias following Hurricane Beulah in 1967.

since the various properties were purchased, considerable sums had been spent on improvements such as wells, fences, and grubbing, and "we understand that the lands are now watered to an average extent of one well to each three miles of land."[34]

The auditors wrote that it was impossible to value the land based on cost plus improvements because the records did not exist to do that: "Under the circumstances, we have set up the lands on your books at the valuation of $5.00 per acre. . . . We understand that recent sales of ranch lands of poorer quality and not nearly so well watered have been made at prices exceeding this figure."[35]

Between 1909 and 1914, the total beef cattle herd on Lasater's property ranged from 24,126 in 1909 to 15,659 in 1913. Annual variations in total head count of between 2,000 and 4,000 animals were typical. The size of Lasater's cow herd, including yearling heifers, averaged 10,443 in the years 1910–14, ranging from 9,761 in 1911 to 12,039 in 1914. In addition to brood cows and their calves, Lasater's operation for several of those years involved keeping male calves on the ranch and grazing them until they were two- to four-year-old steers ready to ship to northern pastures or to the Fort Worth, Kansas City, and Chicago markets.

The increase of Lasater's brood cow herd to peak figures in 1914 followed the total liquidation of his inventory of steers in 1912 and 1913. Calf numbers listed on the inventories average a little less than fifty percent of the total number of cows and yearling heifers. If the 1910 breakdown between cows and heifers (75 percent cows, 25 percent heifers) remained constant, then the calf count was equal to between sixty and sixty-five percent of the total number of mother cows.

Lasater, by his own calculation, made $800,000 by buying and selling thousands of head each year in the period of rising cattle markets between 1895 and 1900, the years during which he bought most of

[34] Price, Waterhouse and Co. to Ed C. Lasater, May 31, 1909.

[35] The acreage included in the Falfurrias Ranch at its peak is referred to in various places as 380,000 acres (For example, R. Clyde Allen, "Single-Handed He Conquered 380,000 Acres of Texas Prairie," *Manufacturers' Record*, April 7, 1927, pp. 94–95). Lasater's June 30, 1911, balance sheet lists 323,000 acres, including the 40,000 acres which had been transferred to Lasater's Falfurrias Jersey Dairy Company. Some 50,000 acres were sold in the Lasater-Miller land promotions, which would put the total extension close to the 380,000 figure. However, some of the farms were sold before Lasater's last large purchase, the 60,000 acres bought from Colonel Dillard R. Fant.

the land comprising the Falfurrias Ranch and laid the foundation for the agricultural enterprises that would occupy the last half of his life. The Saint Louis accountants recorded total earnings of $230,123 for the three years prior to 1909, and at the end of their audit they calculated Lasater's net capital at $1,513,674.01.

The statements prepared by Lasater's office for the following four years reported spectacular profits. [36] By June, 1913, Lasater's net equity had increased by almost $1,000,000 to $2,494,176.02. The yearly profit and net worth figures shown on his financial statement are listed below:

Year Ending June 30	Annual Profit	Net Worth
1909	—	$1,513,674.01
1910	$129,246.00	1,666,229.59
1911	636,261.00	2,272,005.33
1912	106,523.25	2,342,753.18
1913	149,695.09	2,494,176.02

Certainly the years of dedicated effort had paid off for Lasater. The profitability and potential of his operation, combined with his energy and the force of his personality, allowed Lasater to achieve a major breakthrough in financing in 1913. In the course of the prior two decades, as he had put together his holdings, Lasater had borrowed from anyone willing to lend him money, and a number of people and institutions over the years had obligingly supplied the sizable amounts of capital that he had put to work. He had borrowed from his first father-in-law, John M. Bennett, Sr., and from his neighbor, Henrietta M. King. He had borrowed from H. P. Drought and Co., D. Sullivan and Co., American Exchange National Bank of Dallas, The Aetna Life Insurance Co., the National Stockyards National Bank in Illinois, the Central Trust Company in San Antonio, the Bankers Trust Company in Houston, and the George Bares Livestock Commission Company. [37]

---

[36] The annual profit shown on Lasater's financial statements when added to the prior year's net worth, does not equal the current year's net worth. No explanation was given for the adjustments that were made in 1910, 1911, and 1913. The 1912 change results from an acreage discrepancy on land purchased in the Marcelo Hinojosa Grant.

[37] Starr County Deed Records, Book F, p. 557, Book P, p. 353, vol. XXXIV, p. 401; Brooks County Deed Records, vol. I, page 184, vol. III, p. 491; Deed Trust Records, Brooks County, vol. I, p. 340, vol. II, pp. 59, 586; Transcribed Deed Trust Records from

By early 1913, Lasater had a debt of $1,271,685.00 on eleven different notes from six lending companies and four individuals. The notes ranged in size from $7,180.80 to $330,000.00. Several of these notes matured in four or five years, including some vendors' liens on property he had purchased. Other loans, which placed chattel mortgages on his livestock, were for six-month and one-year durations.

In the middle of 1913, Lasater negotiated a major loan with the San Antonio Loan and Trust Company, which permitted him to consolidate all his financing into two long-term loans. Colonel George Brackenridge had recently sold his interest in the San Antonio National Bank and San Antonio Loan and Trust Company to Judge Leroy G. Denman in exchange for Denman's notes. The colonel was eighty years old and had never married, and he had chosen Denman, a prominent attorney, as his business heir.[38]

The trust company Brackenridge founded provided Lasater in 1913 with the largest single loan of his business career. This loan also provided Lasater with a favorable rate of interest and a far longer-term maturity than average.

The bond issue which Lasater transacted with the San Antonio Loan and Trust Company on July 1, 1913, was for $1,250,000. At that time, this transaction reportedly represented the largest loan ever made on an individual Texas ranch.[39] The loan carried an 8 percent interest rate with payment spread over ten years. The debt was issued as 380 bonds, with interest coupons due every six months, starting on July 1, 1914. As security for the note, Lasater put up 290,000 acres in Brooks, Duval, and Willacy counties, 10,000 female cattle, 500 bulls and their increase, $300,000 in life insurance policies, and vendor's lien notes from 136 farmers who had purchased land from Lasater in the Copita Farm and Garden tracts and in the Realitos Subdivision. The note was payable at the offices of the San Antonio Loan and Trust Com-

---

Starr County, Brooks County, vol. II, pp. 195, 241. After selling Lasater his interest in the land purchases that he and Lasater had made jointly starting in 1895, John M. Bennett, Sr., continued to loan Lasater money. One promissory note for $130,000 was dated July 1, 1902. That note was paid off in 1904 (Transcribed Deed Trust Records from Starr County, Brooks County, vol. II, p. 127; Transcribed Deed Records from Starr County, Brooks County, vol. VI, p. 494).

[38] Marilyn McAdams Sibley, *George W. Brackenridge: Maverick Philanthropist*, pp. 204, 214.

[39] Interview, Garland M. Lasater, February 21, 1981.

pany "in United States gold coin of the present standard of weight and fineness."[40]

This loan refinanced ten of Lasater's existing loans totaling $971,685 and provided him with additional working capital. Lasater's other remaining note was one he had secured from the Central Trust Company in San Antonio in 1911 to finance his dairy project. That note also provided Lasater with very favorable terms: it carried a 6 percent interest rate with principal payments due six to ten years after the loan was made. It was secured by the 40,000 acres Lasater had separated from his ranch to form the Falfurrias Jersey Dairy Company.[41] With two sources of financing at favorable interest rates and with long-term maturities, Lasater was indeed in an enviable position.

Lasater's cattle sales for the period 1910 to 1914 averaged over $200,000 annually, with sales in 1913 totaling more than $350,000. On a cash basis, Lasater lost money on his cattle operation in 1910 and 1911 and made money in 1912 and 1913. He averged approximately $40,000 annual cash profit for the four years.

In addition to beef cattle results, Lasater's statements report other income, which included revenue derived from farming both in the Falfurrias and the Realitos areas, land development and colonization, and miscellaneous rents and sales. Gross sales from areas other than beef cattle varied from $10,000 in 1911 to $67,000 in 1913. But interest costs and general overhead expenses incurred by these other businesses were consistently high and caused these varied enterprises to contribute a loss to Lasater's operation. The annual net loss from all these other businesses averaged $62,000 during this four-year period. That was a heavy loss and represented a substantial cash drain, considering the fact that his cash profit from his beef cattle operation averaged some $40,000 during the same period.

The Jersey dairy business is mentioned only twice in the financial statements for the years 1910–13. In 1911, under "Other Income," a loss of $6,290.84 is reported under the heading "Jersey Operation." No figures were given on the profit and loss statements for the next two years. On Lasater's 1913 balance sheet, one asset listed is a receivable

[40] Deed Trust Records, Brooks County, vol. II, pp. 115–45.
[41] Deed Trust Records, Brooks County, vol. I, p. 89.

from the Falfurrias Jersey Dairy Company, labeled "Loan Account," for $19,932.87. Based on these two entries, it may be surmised that the dairy operation was losing money.

The Falfurrias Mercantile Company was another substantial business at this time. Sales and income figures for that business do not appear in the statements under consideration here. Only one entry on the profit and loss statement prepared on June 30, 1913, provides any insight into that enterprise. Under the heading "Income from Stocks and Bonds" is the following entry: "Profit on Issuance of Stock of Falfurrias Mercantile Company increased capital, 732 shares: $73,200.00." That item would seem to imply that the mercantile store was operating at a profit, although the exact meaning of the entry is uncertain.

If all of Lasater's other varied enterprises produced a cash loss 50 percent greater than the cash profit generated by his beef cattle, how did Lasater's operation generate a net gain of nearly $1,000,000 in four years? A major share of the net earnings reported on the 1910–13 financial statements was derived from sources which would not qualify as profits under standard accounting procedures. These items included the profit from sales of land to other Lasater companies, a variety of book adjustments, and increased valuations of unsold livestock inventories.

The book adjustments amounted to almost $200,000. Several of these adjustments were made to increase the value of purchases made during the year to the level of values given to similar assets on prior balance sheets. This in effect valued land and livestock inventories at the higher of cost or current market value. These upward inventory adjustments were booked as profit in the annual profit and loss statements.

Profits resulting from transfers of land to companies owned by Lasater accounted for a large share of the total profit reported on his financial statements during this four-year period. One minor transfer occurred in 1912, but the year before, Lasater transferred 40,000 acres of land into the Falfurrias Jersey Dairy Company. The transfer figure of $1,255,749.12 represented a $737,170.50 increase in value over the cost of that land. This transfer of land which Lasater made from his beef cattle operation into a wholly owned corporation did not represent a commercial transaction. The land would be used more intensively than his other grazing lands and its value certainly enhanced, but the transfer did not produce any revenue. However, that arbitrary increase in value became part of the profit reported on Lasater's 1911 financial statement.

Lasater's view regarding the value of that 40,000 acres was supported by his own land sales to farmers in the small tracts he had subdivided and sold. His values were also supported by outsiders. One of those was J. O. Terrell, president of the Central Trust Company in San Antonio. Terrell was a banker, but also a man with years of direct experience in agriculture, and in particular with dairy herds. He claimed to have sold more Jersey cattle annually between 1886 and 1911 than any other person or firm in the world.

In the fall of 1911, following a visit to the Lasater operation in Falfurrias, Terrell wrote a report containing a glowing assessment of the Falfurrias country.[42] Terrell stated that the productive capacity of the Falfurrias area made it an excellent locale for farmers, and he predicted that the area would move largely into cultivation over the ensuing ten years. Terrell wrote that he had been acquainted with the Falfurrias country since it was first cultivated some four or five years earlier, and he felt justified in calling it one of the most productive portions of the state. With regard to the block of land Lasater had decided to dedicate to his Jersey operation, Terrell's assessment was similar to Lasater's: "It is my judgment that the 40,000 acres of land belonging to the Falfurrias Jersey Dairy Company is reasonably worth the sum of $25 per acre, and I believe it can be sold in small farms or pastures at an even greater price. . . . I know many persons would place the value of the real estate and personal property far above my figures, but I am merely giving my judgment along safe and conservative lines."[43]

Even though Lasater and one of his bankers were in agreement as to the current market value of that 40,000 acres, the transfer of that land out of his beef cattle operation into the dairy project did not generate a profit. Yet the gain booked by Lasater's accountants as a result of that transfer offset operating losses and provided Lasater's operation with a reported profit for 1911 of $636,261.00.

If the total book adjustments, $198,812.17, and the profits recorded from land transfers to other Lasater companies, $747,170.50, were deducted, the $1,000,000 profit shown on Lasater's books be-

[42] J. O. Terrell, "To Whom it May Concern," October 23, 1911, Lasater Files.
[43] Ibid.

tween 1910 and 1913 would drop to a mere $50,000. In addition to these two items, cattle inventory valuation changes further distorted the true earnings picture of the Lasater enterprises, because his office staff included changes in per head values in its annual earnings calculations.

Lasater's financial statements valued his cows at $28.50 per head in 1910, and by 1913 that value was raised to almost $43.50. Calves valued at $12.50 per head in 1910 were included at $15.00 in 1913. The net increase in the total value of Lasater's livestock inventory between 1910 and 1913 resulting from raised per-head valuations was $179,714.07. That figure was included in Lasater's profit and loss statement and became part of his net capital, even though it represented a market-value estimate, not a realized profit on inventory sold. If that figure had been eliminated from Lasater's earnings, along with the book adjustment and the profit on land sales to relegated companies, Lasater's statements for the period 1910–13 would have recorded a substantial loss instead of a $1,000,000 profit.

But the profit and loss statements that Ed Lasater proudly carried to his bankers showed no losses. And the bankers who looked at those statements and who studied this man and the assets he controlled supported Ed Lasater's own self-confidence and his positive assessment of his business enterprises.

One such banker was Leroy Denman, an experienced businessman. The two Texas banking institutions that he headed loaned Ed Lasater money for many years. In a 1914 letter, Denman echoed the positive sentiments expressed earlier by his mentor, George Brackenridge: "The San Antonio National Bank and the San Antonio Loan and Trust Company, with whom I have been connected for a number of years, have had various and large transactions with Mr. Ed C. Lasater, and as a result of such experience I consider him one of the most capable and responsible men in this section." [44] Judge Denman's letter did not merely contain idle words of praise. One year earlier the trust company he headed had loaned Ed Lasater as much money as any institution had ever loaned a Texas cattleman in a single transaction.

Colonel Dillard Fant ranked with the biggest of the Texas empire builders in 1890, but his holdings disintegrated in the early years of the

---

[44] Leroy G. Denman, Sr., "To Whom It May Concern," May 21, 1914, Lasater Files.

twentieth century.[45] The colonel died in Goliad in 1908, and as he and his operating glories began a precipitous descent, Ed Lasater was moving full-steam ahead. In directing his office staff and in reviewing the numbers which his bookkeepers put together, Lasater could see more than the concrete details of what was actually taking place. He had no trouble looking beyond the heavy interest burden and the high overhead cost which his operation incurred. He could see land prices rising steadily in the years ahead, and he could see an unbroken period of prosperity stretching into the future.

Not everyone involved in his operation shared Lasater's optimistic view. His young brother-in-law, L. D. Miller, worked in Lasater's office during these years. "He had a tremendous debt load. All of us who knew the shape he was in were terrified," Miller recalled many years later.[46]

One year after consolidating his borrowings into two long-term notes with favorable interest rates, Lasater was again exploring new sources of financing. He was not entirely satisfied with his established lines of credit. In 1914, he made contact with W. A. Smith, the representative of a Houston loan company. Lasater explained his situation as follows: "A change of base of supply of funds is prompted only by a desire to secure cheaper money. My relations with the bankers and persons who are furnishing me with funds are most cordial and satisfactory. The benefits have been mutual. I have paid high rates, and the soundness and earning ability of the enterprises are proven by the ease with which it has carried this burden."[47]

Lasater's loan application included his financial statements, a letter of recommendation written by George Brackenridge, along with letters from bankers in Kansas City, Saint Louis, and Galveston. In a "Review and Analysis" of his ranching enterprise prepared by his office to accompany the application, earnings from ranch operations available for interest were stated to be an average of $114,000 for the previous five years. The report asserted with confidence that earnings "will show an average for the years 1912, 1913 and 1914 of about $139,000 . . . and it is safe to predict that the conditions surrounding the beef

[45] *Alice Echo*, January 23, 1908; Walter Prescott Webb and H. Bailey Carroll, eds., *The Handbook of Texas*, I, 583.

[46] Interview, Laurence D. Miller, Sr., September 22, 1971.

[47] Ed C. Lasater to W. A. Smith, July 16, 1914, Lasater Files.

cattle industry of the world and the local conditions affecting this particular enterprise will make possible as good, if not better, a showing in the years to come."[48]

Lasater made other reassuring statements time and again. "The security offered is of the soundest character fundamentally, land of proven earning capacity supplying common necessities to readily available markets."[49] And elsewhere: "I will state that in 1894, I planned the acquisition of and the development of the Falfurrias Ranch. The acquisition and initial development were accomplished altogether by the use of borrowed capital. During the twenty intervening years, I have created the large equity shown in the attached statements in what has become one of the greatest ranching and farming properties in Texas."[50]

Ed Lasater was proud of his accomplishments. He was not a colonel like his uncle, his neighbor, and his banker, and the Texas electorate had rejected his bid to claim the office of governor. But even without those titles, Lasater was a man to be reckoned with. A later Texas governor wrote of his compatriot from Falfurrias: "He is a man who attained success in his business. He is esteemed by all who know him as a man of character, integrity and ability."[51]

Two decades after settling near Los Olmos Creek, Lasater had one of the biggest beef cattle ranches in Texas. He farmed as many acres as anyone in the state. He had brought a new industry into the area with his creamery business, and the community he had founded was prosperous. His bankers thought enough of his abilities and of the assets he owned to loan him whatever capital he requested. His colleagues in the cattle business had elected him president of the country's most powerful regional cattle association, and he served on the executive committee of the national cattlemen's organization. He was a son of the frontier who had recognized opportunity and had actively pursued his dreams: "In every sense of the word, he was a cattle king."[52]

In 1914, the "man from Falfurrias" summarized the transforma-

[48] "Review and Analysis," July 15, 1914, Lasater Files.
[49] Ed C. Lasater to W. A. Smith, July 16, 1914, Lasater Files.
[50] Ibid.
[51] Governor Dan Moody, "To Whom It May Concern," August 12, 1929, Lasater Files.
[52] William Warren Sterling, *Trails and Trials of a Texas Ranger*, p. 16.

tion that had taken place in the sandy country surrounding the Loma Blanca: "I commenced with an undeveloped, nonproductive wilderness. I have put on the map a community that is furnishing to the world annually food supplies and raw materials whose value runs into the millions." The past had provided pleasure and profit; the years ahead looked even more promising: "The foundation has been laid that will sustain a constantly expanding production of agricultural products for many generations to come."[53]

[53] Ed C. Lasater to W. A. Smith, July 16, 1914, Lasater Files.

PART 2
Loma Blanca: Sentinel of Passage

CHAPTER 9

Mr. Swift and Mr. Hoover

If we admit that it is right for those who sell to the farmer
to fix the prices at which they sell . . . we must also admit that it is right for the farmer to fix the prices at which
others shall buy from him. But really it is not a question
of right at all—it is a question of power.

—J. A. Everitt, 1903

THE witness testifying in the U.S. House of Representatives Committee on Agriculture in 1920 had been on the stand only briefly when
he warmed to his subject and got the attention of all those present. The
matter under consideration involved a fight, the witness said, a fight
between the home-builders of America and the Chicago meat-packing
industry. In order to avoid any misunderstanding, the witness stated
his views more directly: "I think that every male adult of the houses of
Armour, Swift, Morris, Wilson and Cudahy, with their personal attorneys, could be put in the penitentiary without seriously disturbing the
economic slaughter and distribution of livestock and livestock products
for more than ninety days. . . ."[1]

Ed Lasater's testimony was interrupted after that statement, but
following a brief exchange between Chairman Gilbert N. Haugen and
another committee member, he was allowed to continue. Lasater explained that he meant to say that these particular packers were not essential to the nation's well-being. In fact, he asserted, they represented
an evil element that was "preying upon the country."

Lasater was in Washington testifying once again about the meat-
packing industry, a role that had become a familiar one during the pre-

[1] Ed C. Lasater, "Meat Packer Legislation," statement before the Committee on
Agriculture, U.S. House of Representatives, March 1, 2, 3, and 6, 1920, pp. 1–2, in Ed-
ward C. Lasater Collection, Eugene C. Barker Texas History Center, University of
Texas, Austin.

ceding years. By 1920, Lasater was more certain than ever that his own problems and those of the livestock industry in general were in large part due to the business tactics and the pervasive control exercised by the packers in the areas of financing, shipping, selling, processing, and distribution of cattle and meat products. He was certain that the situation demanded government intervention at the national level: "I am absolutely convinced that some of the inequities of the packing business should be corrected by legislation. I think they will have to be corrected if we are to feed our people."[2]

Ed Lasater's longstanding duel with the packing industry had been in full swing for many years by the time he appeared before Chairman Haugen's Agriculture Committee in Washington. As an active leader in the southwestern cattle industry a decade earlier, Lasater had helped spark the fire which burned all the way to Washington where, after years of inquiries, hearings, and investigations by a variety of committees and agencies, the Justice Department and the U.S. Congress took action which permanently altered the meat-packing industry in the United States.

Lasater first demonstrated his deep concern with the marketing phase of the livestock industry when he organized a special meeting while serving as president of the Cattle Raisers Association of Texas in 1911. A gathering held in Fort Worth in September was motivated principally by the low returns realized by livestock producers and the wide gap between live cattle prices and the retail price of beef. In his letter inviting interested parties to participate, Lasater stated: "The crop of beef and mutton marketed the past six months has been taken from the producers at the market centers of the country at much less than the cost of production. The consumers . . . have paid higher prices than ever for these staples." Lasater invited all interested livestock producers, representatives of labor unions and consumer groups, the Texas congressmen and senators, and the governor, O. B. Colquitt, to the meeting: "Certainly there is no economic question before the country of more vital importance than this one, affecting, as it does, the very life of our agriculture and the well-being of every wageearner."[3]

[2] Ibid., p. 3.
[3] Ed C. Lasater to Governor O. B. Colquitt, August 5, 1911, Scrapbook No. 4, Lasater Files, in possession of Garland M. Lasater, Falfurrias.

Lasater organized the meeting for two reasons: 1) to find some means of marketing livestock that would allow the producer a fair rate of return over the cost of production, and 2) to see if the margin between what the producer is paid and what the consumer is charged cannot be narrowed. Lasater was convinced that the issue was a critical one and that the situation demanded cooperation between producers and consumers: "A continuation of present practice must mean that meat will have to be largely eliminated from the bill of fare of our wage-earners."[4]

The Fort Worth meeting undoubtedly yielded few concrete results. But for Lasater and for a number of his colleagues, it was a beginning. The profit that Ed Lasater's books and records reflected for the fifteen years prior to 1911 was substantial. The operating loss realized in 1911, although not known at the time, marked a turning point in Lasater's financial affairs. It was, in fact, the first in an extended string of unprofitable years for many cattlemen. As Lasater and his colleagues contemplated the deteriorating state of their business fortunes in the decade following 1911, the focus of their ire frequently settled on the smaller and smaller group of very prosperous meat-packing companies that purchased the produce from their ranches on the stockyards of Fort Worth, Kansas City, Saint Louis, and Chicago.

The meeting Lasater organized in Fort Worth was the first leg of a long quest, one which followed a trail to Denver, Chicago, Phoenix, and, over and over for nearly ten years, Washington, D.C. It involved meetings, hearings, debates, and testimony. It took place before various committees of the U.S. Senate and the House of Representatives, the Interstate Commerce Commission and the Federal Trade Commission. Ed Lasater, along with a few of his ranching comrades, covered almost every mile of that trail.

The quest carried Lasater far away and for extended periods of time from the sandy pastures along Baluarte Creek. An exact log of the trains ridden, the miles covered, the time and the dollars spent on this

---

[4] Ibid. Seventy years after Lasater invited Governor Colquitt to the Fort Worth meeting, exactly the same concerns continued to be topics at every cattlemen's convention and meeting. Lasater's letter was considered of sufficient current interest seven decades after being written to warrant being reprinted in the monthly newsletter of one of the country's largest and most powerful livestock organizations (*Newsletter*, Texas Cattle Feeders Association, April 10, 1981).

quest would make interesting, perhaps startling, reading were it available. The end of the trail brought perhaps some degree of satisfaction to those who fought this long and often lonely battle. But it brought no permanent answer to the recurring question of prosperity on the range, which by tradition was an unpredictable and highly erratic matter. And it provided no easy solutions for the serious problems that plagued the Falfurrias Ranch and many others like it in the years following the First World War.

The fifteenth annual convention of the American National Livestock Association was held in Denver in December, 1911. The executive committee of the national association included Texans John Landergin, Vega; Lasater; J. H. Parramore, Abilene; Ike T. Pryor, San Antonio; and W. D. Reynolds, Fort Worth. In addition, Lasater served as chairman of the committee on stockyards and livestock exchanges.[5]

Murdo MacKenzie was the association's president in 1911. MacKenzie, born in Scotland in 1850, had moved to Trinidad, Colorado, in 1885 to serve as assistant manager for the Prairie Cattle Company, owned by Scottish investors. In 1891 he had become manager of the Denver-based Matador Land and Cattle Company, with holdings of five million acres in several states.[6]

Prior to the Denver meeting, MacKenzie and Lasater, as presidents respectively of the American National Livestock Association and the Cattle Raisers Association of Texas, sent to the president and to all members of Congress a resolution regarding the Canadian Reciprocity Treaty, which included a proposal to place meats from that country on the free list. The cattlemen protested the unequal treatment: "For whose benefit is this proposal made? Can the wage-earner of the manufacturing cities who demands a tariff on manufacturers demand that we feed him on a free trade basis for our business?"[7]

Canadian meats were not actually the primary concern. The cat-

---

[5] "Proceedings of the Fifteenth Annual Convention of the American National Livestock Association," reprinted in Lasater, *Some Printed Addresses and Statements in Public Service, 1900–1930*, pp. 5–6, copy in Lasater Files.

[6] *Texas and Southwestern Cattle Raisers Association Presidents.*

[7] "Plea of the American National Livestock Association and of the Cattle Raisers Association of Texas in Opposition to Placing Livestock and Meats on the Free List," reprinted in Lasater, *Some Printed Addresses*, p. 1.

tlemen were worried that if import duties were removed from Canadian products, the next step would be to put Mexican and South American cattle on the free list, which, according to the ranchers, would ruin the U.S. cattle business. And behind all this was a growing concern with the worldwide concentration and the increasing power of the meat-packing industry. The cattle associations argued that if South American meat was received on the East Coast, then shipments from the western markets to the East would cease: "competitive buying at the glutted markets of the West will be curtailed and the cattle producer will be demoralized . . . , while the big packers will ship in the beef from their packing houses in the Argentine."[8]

Tariff charges were only one of many possible threats to cattlemen and their financial well-being. MacKenzie, on the eve of departing for Brazil, where he would manage the largest livestock undertaking in the world, exhorted the cattlemen of the United States not only to support their state and regional associations, but to maintain and strengthen the national association so that the combined voice and strength of all cattlemen could secure the necessary results: "All other interests are organized for their mutual protection, and the livestock men ought not to be laggards in looking after their own welfare."[9]

Following his own address as president, MacKenzie presented a number of other speakers to the assembled cattlemen. Among those was Ed Lasater, whom MacKenzie introduced as "a gentleman whose name is a household word in the part of the country from which he comes. . . . He is one of the most progressive men in the state of Texas—a breeder and feeder and an all-around good fellow."[10]

Lasater expanded on MacKenzie's tariff remarks, underlining that it was a major concern to cattlemen that year. Prior to the 1911 convention, Sam H. Cowan, the association's attorney from Fort Worth, E. L. Burke, a Nebraska cattleman, Lasater, and others had been in Washington testifying before the Senate Finance Committee on monetary and tariff questions. Lasater viewed the tariff as a subject closely connected with the matter of the nation's soil fertility, an expendable asset that had been central to the rise and fall of great nations since the days of the Roman Empire. "Let us as a nation realize that the one national

[8] Ibid., p. 3.
[9] "Proceedings of the Fifteenth Annual Convention," p. 29.
[10] Ibid., p. 57.

resource that demands conservation above all others is our soil fertility," Lasater stated. He urged his fellow cattlemen to "demand from our legislators tariff legislation that will not encourage or make necessary still further soil depletion."[11] Agricultural production provided the basis for the nation's greatness, he said, in his call for legislation that would be constructive and would "back up the great cities we have built with fertile farms and happy, contented husbandmen who will pass on to future generations an ever-advancing civilization."[12]

The meat-packing industry was another dominant theme of Lasater's 1911 address to the national convention. "I do not care to be considered antagonistic to the packers. I am not. The packers' brains, enterprise and energy entitle them to the possession of a fortune." Lasater's conciliatory opening remarks were substantially modified as he further expanded his views on the subject. The Texan told his colleagues that the packers' power "has become so vast that it staggers one to contemplate it. Not only do they dominate the food supply of the nation, but they are a power in banking and transportation. Coping with them is far beyond the power of the individual."[13]

Lasater presented to the assembly a description of an organization outlined in a prospectus recently drawn up by the executive committee of the Cattle Raisers Association of Texas. The entity would be called the Texas Cattle Raisers' Sales-Directing Agency. If the idea received the necessary backing from cattlemen, its primary function would be to direct the marketing of all cattle, sheep, and hogs in Texas and Oklahoma.[14] It would provide central control and management for all livestock marketing in Texas and Oklahoma. It would coordinate all shipments of livestock for sale, enabling the producer to consign his product to the most advantageous market. The isolated and uninformed status of most agricultural producers was a problem with severe financial consequences: "The fact that the buying interests largely act in concert and that there is no directing mind controlling the selling interests places a heavy handicap upon the selling interests in favor of the buying interests." The proposed agency was designed to correct that unequal posture: "It would substitute plan and methodical procedure

[11] Ibid., pp. 24, 57–60.
[12] Ibid., p. 60.
[13] Ibid., p. 64.
[14] Ibid., p. 65.

for what is now absolute chance, and would teach the producers of livestock the value and benefit to be derived from cooperation."[15]

Lasater went on to say that he did not believe it was practical for livestock producers to unite in one mammoth national marketing organization. However, he thought it was both feasible and necessary that cattlemen in the various producing regions should unite in a cooperative marketing effort: "In many things I think we can imitate our packer friends. We can imitate his enterprise, his thoroughness and his practice of cooperation."[16]

Responding to Lasater's propoasl, Murdo MacKenzie said that he did not see the proposed marketing organization as the final answer because he had already participated in a similar undertaking some years before: "Supported by some of you, a company started out on practically the same plan Mr. Lasater speaks of. It did not go into the packing business; it did go into the commission business, hoping you would give us your support in our cooperative work." MacKenzie had experienced firsthand the difficulty of keeping cattlemen organized in a collective marketing program: "You dropped off one by one until we had nothing left."[17]

The concerns about the meat-packing industry and about the entire marketing phase of the cattle business, which loomed so prominently at that Denver meeting, were not new ones. And as MacKenzie's response to Lasater's proposal implied, cattlemen had made a variety of attempts over the years to change the structure of the cattle marketing system. Almost always, the concerns peaked and were crystallized into action during periods of falling markets and financial losses, but over time one or more years of rising prices would give cattlemen encouragement and they would return to business as usual.

The precipitous decline in cattle prices and the heavy losses realized by cattlemen in the decade after 1883 had earlier convinced many

---

[15] Ibid.

[16] Ibid., p. 66. Another resolution passed in 1911 by Lasater and his fellow members of the Executive Committee of the Cattle Raisers Association of Texas called for the proper federal agency in Washington to begin publicizing on a regular basis market prices at different terminals for live cattle, a breakdown of meat-packing expenses, and dressed beef and retail beef prices. Lasater and his Texas colleagues saw dissemination of this market information as a remedy for "exorbitant and unfair charges and practices perpetuated on cattle raisers by the meat-packing industry" (Ibid., p. 63).

[17] Ibid., p. 67.

cattlemen that their fortunes were controlled by the railroads and by the combination of meat packers and commission men in Chicago. Producers during that era also noted that as prices continued to drop, there was no corresponding decline in the price of beef to the consumers.[18]

This situation produced a growing antagonism between cattlemen and meat packers, and resulted in one of the earliest congressional investigations of the livestock industry. The testimony taken by the Select Committee of the U.S. Senate on the Transportation and Sale of Meat Products in 1888 became known as the Vest Report.[19] This congressional inquiry did not improve the livestock producers' situation, which deteriorated steadily from the height of the boom years in 1883 until 1894. But during that same period, a group of cattlemen united in an attempt to get control of their own destiny and to improve the profitability and stability of their large and fragmented industry.

After months of rumors regarding the formation of a gigantic cattle trust, cattlemen received their first concrete information about the trust in early 1887, when Edward M. McGillin, a heavy investor in the western range cattle industry, addressed the International Range Association in Colorado. "His acid speech was directed at the meat packers of the East who he maintained controlled the cattle market. By this monopoly, they were bankrupting the cattle grower with ruinous prices."[20]

Ed Lasater's call to action in 1911 echoed the dire warnings contained in Edward McGillin's cattle trust proposal in 1887. McGillin stated that the only sensible answer to the cattlemen's predicament was to fight monopoly with monopoly, and he presented a plan for a trust capitalized at one hundred million dollars. The proposed corporation would ultimately control the raising, management, and marketing of every beef animal in the country from the time a calf was born until it reached the consumer's basket as beef. McGillin and others were convinced that this cattle trust was not only a pressing necessity, but a matter of life and death: "Fail to organize the company I propose, and inside of ten, more likely five, years, there will be no such thing in this

---

[18] E. S. Osgood, *The Day of the Cattleman*, p. 106.
[19] Ibid., pp. 94, 106.
[20] Gene M. Gressley, *Bankers and Cattlemen*, p. 259.

country as a ranchman, and not one-third of even the present depressed prices for ranch property will be realized."[21]

The *New York Times* of May 3, 1887, reported the organization of the American Cattle Trust. The organization was modeled after the Standard Oil Trust and included the participation of one of the country's leading meat packers, Nelson Morris. The cattle industry was represented on the trust's initial board of directors by John L. Routt, governor of Colorado, R. G. Head of New Mexico, C. C. Slaughter and John T. Lytle of Texas, Thomas Sturgis of Wyoming, and others. The impressive roster included a number of prominent eastern financial figures as well.[22]

Widespread dissent existed within the cattle business on the advisability of organizing such an enormous undertaking. In addition, basic questions such as how to appraise ranch properties put into the trust and how much credit to extend to the affiliated producer until the cattle were in the stockyards proved difficult to resolve satisfactorily. Continuing dissension and financial problems which plagued the trust almost from its inception doomed the organization that some had hailed as the salvation of the ranching business. After a tumultuous three-year history, the trust was dissolved in 1890.[23]

In financial terms, the trust was an unmitigated failure. As a protest movement, it was a significant barometer of the attitudes and the approach of cattlemen in the late nineteenth century. The demise of the American Cattle Trust signaled an important turning point: "With a couple of notable exceptions . . . cattleman and investor now switched from economic to political means as a proper weapon to relieve their plight."[24]

Gustavus Franklin Swift started the company that bore his name in 1855, two years before Albert Lasater moved from Arkansas to Texas. Several years later, after moving his operation from the East Coast to Chicago, Swift had a dramatic idea: instead of shipping live cattle east for slaughter, he would slaughter in Chicago and ship dressed car-

---

[21] Ibid., p. 260.
[22] Ibid., pp. 261–62.
[23] Ibid., pp. 260–66.
[24] Ibid., p. 266.

casses, thereby drastically reducing shipping costs. Over the following decades, that innovation propelled Swift's company into the ranks of the nation's corporate elite. By 1916, the company was so prosperous that Swift paid a total of $31 million in dividends, including an extra one of $33.50 a share.[25]

Armour was another name that became synonymous with the meat-packing business in the last decade of the nineteenth century. Philip D. Armour started a produce and commission business in Minneapolis in 1859, moving in 1867 to Chicago, where he founded Armour and Company with two brothers.[26] Swift, Armour, and three other men headed meat-packing companies that grew to rival anything in industrial America: "Near the turn of the century, Philip Danforth Armour and G. F. Swift had become darlings for the pages of Scribners and Harper's. . . . By the time Upton Sinclair's *The Jungle* appeared, McCoy's 35,000 red meat animals of 1867 had mushroomed into 10,000,000 cattle and as many hogs for Chicago each year. The Big Four had become more powerful than public opinion."[27]

The road to riches and power was not without a few rough spots and minor adversities for the nation's meat packers. The Vest Report of 1888 was followed fourteen years later by another major investigation of the meat-packing industry which was initiated by Congressman S. W. Martin of South Dakota. "The Martin Resolution was a culmination of two years of public and legislative flagellation of the dressed beef industry."[28] When he was interviewed by magazine editor B. C. Forbes in 1916, J. Ogden Armour reminisced about the stormy public controversies that surrounded his business: "I inherited a huge business and a good name, but it was not long before I changed my views, for I had nothing but trouble, especially when the United States government brought all sorts of grave charges against me and other packers." Armour affirmed that he had tried to run his company honestly and fairly: "The indictments, nevertheless, caused me terrible humilia-

---

[25] Paul Ingrassia, "Corporations: A Perilous Life at the Top," *Wall Street Journal*, February 5, 1981.

[26] B. C. Forbes, *Men Who Made America Great*, p. 8.

[27] Charles Walters, Jr., *Angry Testament*, pp. 143–45. The Big Four were formerly the Big Five—Armour, Swift, Wilson, Cudahy, and Morris—with the latter being absorbed by Armour. Joseph G. McCoy shipped 35,000 longhorns from Abilene, Kansas to Chicago in 1867 (Ibid.).

[28] Gressley, *Bankers and Cattlemen*, p. 267.

tion and unhappiness. I have been proud of my father's name and record, and have tried sincerely to maintain both unsullied."[29]

Despite these inconveniences, the growth of the meat-packing business and the fortunes of its principal founders were indeed spectacular. Philip D. Armour was born in New York in 1832. When he died in 1901, his company was doing $100 million in sales annually. By 1917, under the direction of the founder's son, total revenues had risen to $500 million. As Armour grew, the company, like those of the other leading meat packers, had expanded its business into many related fields. In 1917 Armour's auxiliary enterprises were doing more business in the aggregate than the meat-packing company: "Armour Grain Company handles more grain than any other concern . . . ; Armour has the second largest leather business in the world; he ranks among the foremost manufacturers of fertilizer; he controls more refrigerator and other special cars than any railroad system in the country."[30] Senator Vest and Congressman Martin spearheaded two of the earlier investigations into the meat-packing industry. The Grosscup injunction of 1903 restrained the meat packers from violating the Sherman Antitrust Act. But the continual concentration and expansion of the meatpacking industry brought on repeated investigations and trials in the first two decades of the twentieth century. In 1916, Representative Borland spearheaded another congressional initiative seeking an investigation by the Federal Trade Commission to determine whether or not there was a combination among the five largest meat packers to control the price of livestock and meats. The Borland resolution never got off the ground, but over the ensuing five years a further series of inquiries, decrees, and bills would substantially alter the structure of the country's meat-packing businesses.[31]

An internal memorandum prepared by Swift and Company lawyers in 1916 provides some insight into the packing industry's perspective as it saw discontent building in the ranks of the cattlemen who were carrying their story to Washington. At the time the Borland Resolution was being considered in congress, Swift's legal department expressed grave concern with the new round of proposed inquiries and investigations: "If we are to avoid indictments, we must immediately

[29] Forbes, *Men Who Made America Great*, p. 8.
[30] Ibid., p. 3.
[31] "Meat Packer Legislation," pp. 27, 43, 216.

decide upon such steps as will first bring better feeling by showing a disposition to cooperate." One remedy suggested was to get the packers' friends and allies in the livestock organizations to lead a campaign to discredit and undermine the cattlemen favoring an investigation of the meat-packing industry. Another was to "get something cooperative started that cannot be finished for some time."[32]

Not all cattlemen saw eye to eye on the matter of packer control and domination of the livestock markets. The memorandum prepared for Louis F. Swift by his company's legal department analyzed a series of ranchers and livestock producers with regard to their attitudes about the congressional investigations. The memo summarized the situation as follows: "There are many cattlemen who believe the packers are in a combination and have destroyed competition. Some of them are bitter and want revenge, believing in indictments and prison sentences. On the other hand, there are many conservative cattlemen who are satisfied."[33] The Swift lawyers stated that the conservative members were not organized and that the "radicals" had taken control of the American National Livestock Association and of the Cattle Raisers Association of Texas.

Charles Clayton, of Denver, and W. D. Reynolds and Jim Nail, both of Fort Worth, were three of the conservative ranchers discussed in the Swift memorandum. These cattlemen were all opposed to the Borland Resolution. Reynolds was described as a cattle grower who owned an oil mill in the vicinity of mills operated by Swift in Texas: "He raises calves and makes big money every year ($20 a head)." The memo stated that Reynolds believes that "agitation hurts every branch of the business and that there is nothing in the business requiring legislative assistance."[34]

A subsequent Swift memorandum dated April 21, 1916, discussed further the idea that the packing companies needed to assist the conservative elements within the livestock associations to get control. This was to be accomplished by "making suggestions to the conservative members of the associations through proper channels and endeavoring to get them to take action."[35]

[32] Law Department to Louis F. Swift, April 3, 1916, in "Meat Packer Legislation," p. 25.
[33] Ibid., p. 24.
[34] Ibid., p. 22.
[35] Ibid., p. 28.

Ed Lasater was not one of those ranchers who was "satisfied." Nor was he one of the cattlemen whom the packers could depend on to promote their case. A picture of him in a magazine article had the following caption: "A look at this picture will make the Chicago packers swear and kick the furniture. It is the likeness of Ed C. Lasater of Texas, ready to start to Chicago or Washington at a moment's notice."[36]

By 1916 Lasater had already spent parts of five years giving speeches around the country and testifying in Washington about the meat-packing industry and its broad control over the livestock producers' economic destiny. Lasater continually preached the necessity of cooperation among agriculturists. The farmer and rancher in producing and marketing his product came into contact with three major businesses—banking, transportation, and meat packing—Lasater asserted in a 1912 speech: "These three businesses are handled largely by men in whom the predatory instincts are more developed than in any other business, except that part of the legal fraternity that is engaged in the damage suit business and politics."[37]

The meat packer was continually on Lasater's mind. "We cannot do without the packer; we do not want to eliminate him," Lasater affirmed, adding: "We want to show our ability to handle our end of the deal and to put ourselves in a position where the packer will have to treat with us for our commodities instead of naming the price on them."[38]

Four years later in a speech in Chicago in 1916, Lasater stated that the question of whether or not the stockyards should continue to be controlled by the meat-packing interests was of more vital importance to the nation than the question of whether shipyards and munitions factories should be controlled by the private sector or by the government: "The one has to do with the cost of the defense of our national honor and our rights; the other has to do with whether or not there is anything worth defending."[39]

Lasater painted a stark picture of the basic confrontation existing

[36] Unidentified magazine article, Lasater Files.

[37] Ed C. Lasater, "Address Delivered at the Annual Convention of the Texas Cattle Raisers Association," Fort Worth, Texas, March 23, 1912, in Edward C. Lasater Collection, Barker Texas History Center, University of Texas, Austin.

[38] Ibid.

[39] Ed C. Lasater, "Address to the National Conference on Marketing and Farm Credits," Chicago, 1916, Edward C. Lasater Collection.

in the livestock industry, where the opposing sides were unequal and ill-matched: "The Chicago packer has been an intelligence as cold, pitiless and penetrating as the north wind fresh from its frozen wastes. Before it stands a nation of farmers bewildered, dreading, questioning." As a solution to this state of affairs, Lasater called for all those representing cattle producers to give their full support to a governmental inquiry "into the cost of production of livestock and the marketing of all products therefrom so that this industry so vital to our welfare can be saved while there is yet time."[40]

Herbert Hoover was born into a Quaker family in 1874 in West Branch, Iowa. Those who could recall him later remembered little about his earlier youth other than his inordinate shyness. Hoover was orphaned at age nine, and his subsequent itinerant life in the homes of a series of Quaker relatives and friends hardened his natural shyness into a defensive shell and developed his reputation as a loner. As a teenager he was sent to live with relatives on the Pacific Coast, "armed with his Quakerism, his defensive diffidence and an ingrained sense of Jeffersonian agrarian idealism. . . ." Later, at Stanford University, Hoover walked around the campus with his eyes riveted on the ground, seldom speaking unless addressed first: "Affection for Hoover [was] not a sudden, dazzling discovery, but a gradual dawning. . . . The crown of his personality was his shyness."[41]

After Stanford, Hoover began a spectacularly successful career as a mining engineer, holding a series of posts in Australia, Burma, China, Egypt, and finally London. The son of a small-town blacksmith, Hoover epitomized the self-made man and became enormously wealthy. In 1914 he had a dozen major undertakings in progress and he was "in an ideal position to make himself one of the world's richest men if he chose."[42] But his presence in London at the outbreak of World War I was fateful.

In October, 1914, Hoover was summoned to the U.S. Embassy in London. There he met the Belgian ambassador, the head of the leading Belgian financial house, the British Baron Lambert, and others. The group recounted to Hoover a gruesome story of collapsed industry,

[40] Ibid.
[41] Joan H. Wilson, *Herbert Hoover, Forgotten Progressive*, pp. 3, 9, 11.
[42] Eugene Lyons, *Herbert Hoover: A Biography*, p. 80.

spreading starvation, and eminent epidemics in Belgium and northern France, areas that had been overrun by German armies on land and were cut off by Allied blockades at sea. The Belgian financier summarized the situation: "We in Belgium and northern France are faced with life and death for millions of our people. You alone have the setting for the job." The financier further argued that a massive relief effort must be headed by an American and that Hoover, with his worldwide experience and extensive knowledge of transportation, was the man.[43]

Hoover asked for two days to think it over and decided that he would undertake the task: "It was a decision that would affect the lives of literally hundreds of millions of human beings—since Belgium was only the first act in a long-term drama of benevolence. . . . Never had a great business career been so sharply renounced for a greater career of service."[44]

The United States Congress declared war in April, 1917. In early May, Hoover returned to the United States at President Wilson's request, and on May 9 the United States Food Administration was launched. Since his undertaking the Belgian relief effort, Hoover's reputation had flourished, and the Great Engineer had emerged as the Great Humanitarian. Everyone recognized that food mobilization would be America's primary obligation when it joined the war, and the press headlined Hoover as the "Food Czar."[45]

Hoover issued a press release explaining his approach to the new task he had been handed. "The whole foundation of democracy lies in the individual initiative of its people and their willingness to serve the interests of the nation with complete self-effacement in the time of emergency." He added, "I hold that democracy can yield to discipline and that we can solve this food problem for our own people and for our allies by voluntary action."[46]

The same month the Food Administration was created, Hoover telegraphed Lasater and other cattlemen requesting a summary of livestock conditions as well as recommendations for any government action which would serve to stimulate the agricultural production needed to

[43] Ibid., p. 79–80.
[44] Ibid., pp. 81–82. This phase of Hoover's career is a truly remarkable and moving story. For further details, see ibid., pp. 56–97.
[45] Ibid., p. 100.
[46] Ibid., p. 101.

meet wartime demands. The overview of the livestock industry which Lasater wrote for Hoover clearly spelled out one of the ranchers' principal concerns: the relationship of the meat packer with the producer. In the opening paragraph of his memorandum, Lasater pinpointed the necessity of carrying out the program outlined at the American National Livestock Association meetings in 1916 and 1917. What was required was "to have a thorough investigation of the production and marketing of livestock and the manufacturing, distribution and sale of the products therefrom by some governmental agency whose report would command the confidence and respect of both consumer and producer."[47]

Lasater asserted that no informed producer would make any effort to increase production with market conditions left unchanged: "Unless the producing world can be assured of fair treatment, the increase of meat supply will continue to fall short of the increase in population." Lasater wrote Hoover that assurance of fair market conditions was all that was needed to stimulate meat production, adding: "I hope you will serve our nation by assisting in getting the facts of this game of livestock production and distribution before the public in a way that no one can question their exactness."[48]

Evidently Hoover was impressed by Lasater's presentation and asked the Texan to work with him. On July 25, 1917, Lasater moved to Washington to assume his volunteer duties as Chief of the Department of Livestock and Food Production in the U.S. Food Administration.[49]

When Lasater moved to Washington, "Food Will Win the War" was a popular slogan. Some twenty million citizens ultimately signed a pledge making them members of the Food Administration. Meatless and wheatless days, new dietary habits to release the grain and fats needed for the armies and for export, and many other tactics depended upon the average American for their success. Volunteerism was not the approach elsewhere: "The prevailing system of food management in the warring European countries was on a strictly regimented basis. One man controlled crops, rations, prices, everything, and enforced his orders by police methods." Hoover's approach was different: "The

[47] Ed C. Lasater to Herbert Hoover, May 4, 1917, Lasater Files.
[48] Ibid.
[49] Ed C. Lasater to Herbert Hoover, November 12, 1917, Edward C. Lasater Collection.

whole complex of raising, processing and distributing food remained less controlled and closer to normal in the United States than in any other warring country."[50]

Hoover and Lasater were both sons of the American West, although Lasater's earlier life was on the Texas frontier, while Hoover's was in a series of small Quaker communities in the Middle West. Hoover's personality must have been a mystery to the direct and outspoken man from Falfurrias. Hoover's reticence and difficulty in personal communication must have mystified the unabashedly frank Lasater. One historian wrote that during personal interviews, Hoover's "answers are given in a rapid, terse manner, and when he is finished he simply stops. Other men would look up, smile or round out a phrase. Hoover is like a machine that has run down. . . . He stares at his shoes or at the desk in front of him as he speaks.. . . ."[51]

Through conversations with Hoover and from communications sent by Hoover to various individuals in the livestock sector, Lasater got the distinct impression that increased beef supplies were needed and that the producers could expect a reasonable return for their efforts. In a letter written on September 24, 1917, to W. T. Creasy, chairman of the Federal Board of Farm Organizations, Hoover underlined the importance of increased food production: "While the government guarantee on wheat assures this production, stimulation of the production of feeding stuffs and animal food products is of no less, or even more, importance."[52] Hoover went on to say that the Food Administration intended to the fullest extent of its power and through its influence in export buying to maintain a price for animal products that would give a reasonable return to the producer. He wrote: "This in-

---

[50] Lyons, *Herbert Hoover: A Biography*, pp. 101–103.

[51] Wilson, *Herbert Hoover, Forgotten Progressive*, pp. 28–29. Despite their differences of background and personality, Hoover and Lasater actually had much in common. Both rose from modest backgrounds to become independently wealthy through their own efforts at an early age. Politically, Lasater ran for governor as the Progressive candidate in 1912, the same year Hoover financially supported Theodore Roosevelt, the country's leading Progressive. Hoover wrote extensively on the American character and the American system, and he believed that only through "cooperative individualism" could the United States succeed in the twentieth century as a modern technological nation and still preserve some of its best nineteenth-century rural values (Ibid.).

[52] Herbert Hoover to W. T. Creasy, September 24, 1917, in Ed C. Lasater, "Policies and Practices of Mr. Hoover as Food Administrator Are Harmful to the Common Welfare," March 7, 1918, p. 3, in Edward C. Lasater Collection.

crease in animal production must be to the farmers' own interests, for a market not only exists today for such increase at highly profitable levels, but must continue long after peace is declared, for Europe is being steadily denuded of its animals." Hoover went even further, stating that the Food Administration was supplied with the necessary power "to prevent any unjust, unreasonable, discriminatory and unfair charge, profit or practice affecting the welfare of the producer."[53]

Lasater took Hoover at his word and entered into his duties in Washington full of patriotic zeal and enthusiasm. But he had little time to gain an appreciation of Hoover's organizational and executive skills or of his unusual humanitarian approach. When Lasater found that his old foes from Chicago were his new bedfellows in the Food Administration, he immediately suspected the worst. Before long he found the telltale signs indicating new attempts by the meat packers to manipulate prices and dominate the American agriculturalist. This time, however, it was not just the Big Five conspiring amongst themselves to the detriment of the untutored, isolated, and unorganized entrepreneurs of American agriculture. Now Lasater thought he could see signs that the federal government, embodied in Hoover, was conspiring with his old nemesis under the cloak of a national emergency.

Only one week after Hoover wrote to W. T. Creasy, Lasater learned from an allied beef buyer that Hoover had advised him to stay out of the market for several days because Hoover "thought the beef market would go cheaper."[54] A few days after the allied buyers' statement, E. Dana Durand, a high-ranking Food Administration official, made headlines in Chicago when he declared it was the government's intention to stabilize hog prices at ten dollars per hundredweight and corn at one dollar per bushel. This statement appeared at a time when it was costing farmers eighteen dollars per hundredweight to produce hogs, and a deluge of immature hogs and cattle were dumped on the market as a result.[55]

Later testimony brought to light other Food Administration activities behind the scenes. A few weeks after making the statement that alarmed hog producers, Durand called Edward F. Swift and Charles H. Swift, along with representatives of Armour, Morris, Wilson, and

---

[53] Ibid.
[54] Lasater, "Policies and Practices of Mr. Hoover," pp. 5–6.
[55] Ibid.

Cudahy to his Chicago office. F. E. Wilhelm of Cudahy described the session as "quite a meeting. . . . Dr. Durand said that this thing would have to be handled in some way to avoid advancing the cattle market; that that was the thing that absolutely could not come about and if it did, he would take drastic measures to prevent it. . . ." According to Wilhelm, the representatives from the five packing companies assured the Food Administration official that they would not pay any more for livestock.[56]

Whether due to Hoover's statement to the allied buyer, other Food Administration initiatives, or natural market causes, the cattle market declined sharply during the fall of 1917. Losses to cattlemen selling stock during that period were severe. Lasater had observed more than one period of violent market fluctuation in his career, but in this instance he had no doubt as to the source of the downdraft in beef prices: "The Food Administration cooperating with the packers did succeed in breaking the market for beef cattle from September 1 to December 1 about $4 per hundredweight."[57]

The cattle market was experiencing its precipitous nosedive just at a time when more production was needed and when the increased demand for U.S. beef by allied countries might reasonably have signaled higher prices. The spirit of patriotism and cooperation with which Lasater and his colleague, Gifford Pinchot, had undertaken their unsalaried roles in the Food Administration began diminishing rapidly. Their worst suspicions were realized when an official articulated Food Administration policy in a Chicago speech: "The consumer must be considered; the producers must remember that we are at war, and patriotically prepare themselves to practice self-denial."[58]

The rapid transition in stated policy was alarming to Lasater and confirmed the conclusions he had drawn as soon as he had become aware of the prominent role that meat-packing company employees were playing in Hoover's organization. The same official who talked about "self-denial" for the producer stated that it continued to be the Food Administration's policy to allow packers a profit ranging from 9 percent to 15 percent on their different industries. The official added that these liberal returns were necessary "in order that the packers'

[56] Ibid.
[57] Ibid., p. 7.
[58] Ibid.

credit might be protected."[59] In only a few weeks, the official statements regarding the agricultural producers' reward for increasing production had changed markedly. From the early assurance that the Food Administration would use its influence and power to maintain prices at levels that provided a "reasonable return" to the producer, an official of that same administration was now publicly urging producers to "prepare themselves to practice self-denial."

With his personal financial losses and those of his colleagues mounting, Lasater's patience very rapidly wore thin. On October 20, less than ninety days after moving to Washington, Lasater submitted his resignation from the Food Administration. But during an interview with Hoover, Lasater decided perhaps Hoover was acquiring a clearer understanding of meat production and in particular the relationship between the meat-packing industry and the livestock producer. Hoover made several remarks to Lasater that made the Texan believe that Hoover's attitude toward the packers was changing. Hoover said that in the beginning he had expected to accomplish a lot through the packers' patriotic cooperation, but that the U.S. Food Administrator for Illinois had just left his office after stating that any further "temporizing with the Chicago packer would be foolish, that nothing but the strong arm would get results." Hoover added that one of his assistants had wired similar opinions from Chicago and that Food Administration policies would be set accordingly. Lasater turned optimistic about collaboration with Hoover, and when the latter expressed appreciation for the rancher's assistance and his conviction that Lasater could be of further service, Lasater withdrew his resignation, commenting that he did not want to "rock the boat."[60]

That conciliatory gesture was only a brief interlude. After spending two weeks in central and west Texas assessing industry conditions, Lasater returned to Washington and once again became convinced that Food Administration policies were damaging the livestock industry and that he was being used as a "camouflage" to deceive cattle producers into thinking that they had representation in the Food Administration. Confusion and misunderstanding related to the proposed

[59] Ibid.
[60] Ed C. Lasater to Herbert Hoover, November 12, 1917.

government seizure of cottonseed cake for distribution to Texas cattlemen, hard hit by the most severe drought of recent years, proved to be
the final straw for Lasater. On November 9, he resigned from the Food
Administration.[61]

Mark L. Requa, a California oilman serving as Hoover's assistant,
wrote Lasater after his resignation, criticizing Lasater's suggestion that
the government should take over and operate the packing plants. "Your
antagonism to the packer was not a surprise to me; it was simply a repe-
tition in another form of the old struggle that I had recognized as existing for many years—the oil producer vs the oil refiner; the water
owner and the land owner; the smelter and the miner." Requa added:
"I did not believe, nor do I now believe, that it is the function of the
Food Administration to solve this problem."[62]

Henry C. Wallace, Lasater's colleague on the Marketing Committee of the American National Livestock Association and the future secretary of agriculture in the Harding administration, read the correspondence between Lasater and Requa in 1917 with dismay. In a letter
to Gifford Pinchot, a member of the Food Administration who resigned
in protest at the same time Lasater did, Wallace stated that he had
found in Requa's response to Lasater's letters an attitude "very antagonistic toward meat producers." Wallace felt that if this attitude became
generally known, it would "tend to shake still further the confidence of
both meat producers and grain farmers in the Food Administration and

---

[61] Ibid. Gifford Pinchot and Lasater both resigned in protest about the same time.
Pinchot had been chief forester in the Taft administration and would later be governor of
Pennsylvania. Pinchot stated that he was resigning because of the failure of the Food
Administration to take effective action for increasing the production of meat. He hoped
that his resignation might force Hoover to see the question of agricultural production
more clearly (Gifford Pinchot to Henry C. Wallace, October 26, 1917, Scrapbook #3,
Lasater Files). Lasater stated in subsequent testimony: "The distrust of Mr. Hoover's intentions to be fair has now become so pronounced by the producing interests of the
country that normal supplies of foods and feeds cannot be expected under his administration. A combination of ignorance, duplicity and misrepresentation cannot lead to the
production of the 'food that will win the war'" ("Texan Says Hoover Not Efficient," unidentified 1918 newspaper article, Edward C. Lasater Collection).

[62] M. L. Requa to Ed C. Lasater, November 22, 1917, quoted in Lasater, "Reply to
Statement Filed by United States Food Administrator, Herbert Hoover, on May 1, 1918
with Hon. Thomas P. Gore," p. 27, in Edward C. Lasater Collection; David Burner,
Herbert Hoover, A Public Life, p. 108.

will therefore result in decreased production to the serious jeopardy of our national and international interests."[63]

Requa accused Lasater of failing to grasp the magnitude of the Food Administration's undertaking and the complexity of the problems involved. Wallace disputed Requa's charge: "From the letters I have seen and from long experience, I fear that if the Food Administration fails, it will be because of the unwillingness of those high in authority to give consideration to the judgment of practical men who are thoroughly familiar with actual conditions."[64]

Wallace wrote that he understood Pinchot's and Lasater's feelings with regard to the "ungracious reception which your sincere and patriotic efforts have met," adding: "I wish to express my very great admiration for the spirit in which both of you have acted. You displayed at Chicago a charity and patriotism which might well be emulated by some of those with whom you have tried to work."[65]

Lasater's volunteer role in an official capacity as a member of the wartime organization created to oversee and promote food production had ended only three months after he moved to the nation's capital. But Lasater's inability to work within the structure of the Food Administration did not imply lack of determination or perseverance. He remained in Washington as a resident and then as a frequent visitor during the next two years as he and others carried the agriculturalists' campaign against the meat-packing industry to its conclusion.

In 1920, the Justice Department forced Swift—along with Armour, Wilson, Cudahy, and Morris—into a landmark consent decree

---

[63] Henry C. Wallace to Gifford Pinchot, December 11, 1917, quoted in Lasater, "Reply to Statement Filed by United States Food Administrator," p. 35.

[64] Ibid. Lasater's colleagues in the American National Cattlemen's Association also came to his defense. Ike T. Pryor, the association's president, in a letter to Hoover on December 12, 1917, stated that Requa's letter to Lasater contained the insinuation that Lasater was motivated by "a selfish purpose and was seeking to gain an unfair advantage either for himself or for our industry." Pryor called this unjust, adding that his colleagues admired Lasater for his "intense patriotism, for his unselfish devotion, and for the personal sacrifices he made to help our country in its struggle to maintain our idea of civilization. . . ." Pryor added, "His departure from your force is a matter of keen regret to us, for we recognize his especial fitness to aid in the solution of the many livestock and agricultural problems confronting the Food Administration" (Ike T. Pryor to Herbert Hoover, December 12, 1917, Edward C. Lasater Collection).

[65] Henry C. Wallace to Gifford Pinchot, December 11, 1917.

that kept them out of one hundred different product lines. The major meat-packing companies were told to abandon grocery retailing; to sell their interest in public stockyards, stockyard railroads and terminals, and livestock market publications; and to avoid various forms of vertical integration forward and backward.[66]

The following year, the U.S. Congress passed legislation that brought to a conclusion the decades-long effort to modify and control the power exercised by meat-packing companies over the livestock industry's producing sector. The Packers and Stockyards Act of 1921 was a watered-down version of various congressional bills that had been debated in previous sessions. The passage of this act "was full recognition that the cattlemen were cognizant of what the Grangers had realized three decades before; a successful attack on a monopoly depended on a political, not an economic vehicle."[67]

The events of 1920 and 1921 brought to a head more than three decades of investigations, agitation, charges, and court cases. It was the culmination of the Vest report, the Grosscup injunction, Congressman Martin's public hearings, the National Packing Company court case, the Borland resolution, the House and Senate hearings, and the Federal Trade Commission's investigation. Through the last ten of those years Ed Lasater and a handful of his colleagues were continually at the center of the action.

Along the way there had been setbacks and disagreements in many quarters. Not just the packers and their highly paid legal counsels opposed Lasater and others in agriculture who shared his opinions. Many cattlemen, including some of the most prominent and respected, op-

---

[66] James Shideler, *Farm Crisis, 1919–1923*, p. 27; Charles Walters, *Angry Testament*, p. 145; "Government Compromises Suits against Packers—Packers Will Give Up Stock Yards—Also Groceries and Other Side Lines," *Cattleman*, December, 1919, pp. 11–13; Ingrassia, "Corporations."

[67] Gressley, *Cattlemen and Bankers*, p. 268; "Kendrick-Kenyon Bills Revised," *Cattleman*, January, 1920, pp. 11–13; *New York Times*, January 27, 1918. The 1920 Consent Decree and the Packers and Stockyards Act of 1921 were not major factors in Swift's later financial woes. Instead, it was the competition provided by a late-arriving upstart, Iowa Beef Processors. IBP began operations more than a century after Swift, building plants in the plains area close to large cattle feeding facilities. Instead of shipping dressed carcases, IBP began carving the beef into chunks and shipping it in boxes, leaving only the final slicing to the supermarkets. This "boxed beef" innovation saved both shipping and labor costs, and undercut the strength of Swift and the other old-time packing companies (Ingrassia, "Corporations").

posed the initiatives Lasater supported. Among them was his neighbor to the east, Robert J. Kleberg, Henrietta King's son-in-law. Kleberg was an eloquent and powerful voice opposing the idea of government investigation or intervention in the meat-packing industry.

In a letter written in August, 1919, to Texas congressman John Nance Garner, Kleberg detailed his views on why the various bills then pending before Congress which were related to the packing industry should not be passed. Kleberg stated that the packers had gotten into various auxiliary businesses such as stockyards, cold storage plants, and refrigerator cars because they were "absolutely essential to the economical and efficient handling and marketing of all the packers' products. . . ." Kleberg expressed the view that if these various businesses were placed under government control, the result would be ruinous not only to the packers, but also to the meat producers and consumers. Kleberg concluded his letter by saying: "I am not writing this letter for the purpose of taking up the fight for the packers, but out of a sense of duty to protest against legislation that will lead to a bureaucracy in this country."[68]

But another large contingent of powerful cattlemen in Texas and elsewhere were convinced that some form of governmental action with regard to the meat-packing industry was vitally necessary. Ike Pryor was a Texas rancher and frontier empire-builder whose credentials could stand up against those of any of his colleagues, who elected him head of the American National Livestock Association. In testimony during the Senate hearings, Pryor described the seven men he had appointed to serve on the association's marketing committee, one of the groups responsible for persuading Congress to appropriate the funds for a formal investigation of the meat-packing industry. Although packing-company memorandums and testimony labeled these men as "radicals," they were, according to Pryor, all large operators and seasoned businessmen fully familiar with all aspects of the cattle industry. The seven members of the committee were: Henry A. Jastro, one of the largest cattle owners in California, who also farmed 200,000 acres;

---

[68] Robert J. Kleberg to John Nance Garner, August 7, 1919, in Lasater, "Meat Packer Legislation," pp. 52–53. Unlike Lasater and most other ranchers, who shipped their cattle to the stockyards and then sold them through a commission firm, the King Ranch had a deal by which they sent their market cattle directly to Swift and Co. (Interview, Garland M. Lasater, February 21, 1981).

E. L. Burke, longtime Nebraska cattle feeder; Joseph M. Carey, Wyoming cattleman and former governor; Dwight B. Heard, large Arizona rancher; Lasater; W. R. Stubbs, Kansas cattleman and former governor; and Henry C. Wallace, Iowa cattleman and publisher of a farm periodical.[69]

Wyoming cattleman John B. Kendrick, U.S. senator and two-time president of the American National Livestock Association, was another leader in this campaign and was one of the most vigorous and tenacious backers in the congressional drive for legislation between 1918 and 1921. Senator Kendrick summarized three of the reasons he had concluded that legislation was necessary: "the Big Five packers do from 60–80% of all interstate commerce in meat and meat products. . . . Through ownership of the stockyards of the country . . . they exert an undue influence on the producing market. . . . Through ownership of the refrigerator cars they control the distributing system."[70]

After Ed Lasater resigned from the Food Administration in November, 1917, he remained in Washington to testify in the U.S. Senate hearings on the meat-packing industry, which were almost continuous through the winter and early spring of 1918. Lasater felt that the hearings themselves performed a useful service to the industry. Lasater said that the exposé of how the packers and the Food Administration had worked together to hold the price of finished cattle below the cost of production "was so complete that those agencies deemed it advisable to permit these grades of cattle to advance to a point that would return costs plus a reasonable profit. I think it is safe to conclude that if this exposé had not been made, the markets would not have advanced."[71]

By March, 1918, Hoover and his colleagues in the Food Administration had evidently had some second thoughts about the government's policy with regard to the livestock industry. In a letter to President Wilson, Hoover stated: "I feel that we have reached a position

---

[69] Ike T. Pryor testimony, in Lasater, "Meat Packer Legislation," pp. 45–46; "Regulation of Packing Companies and Stock Yards Again Urged by National Association," *Cattleman*, February, 1920, pp. 11–12.

[70] John B. Kendrick, "Why Uncle Sam Should Supervise the Meat Business," *Cattleman*, June, 1919, p. 23.

[71] Ed C. Lasater to the American National Livestock Association, January 16, 1919, in Lasater, "Meat Packer Legislation," p. 64.

with regard to the whole meat industry of the country that requires a reconsideration of policy." Hoover termed the meat industry situation "one of the most complex with which the government has to deal. . . ." Hoover's new views were no doubt music to Lasater's ears: "This change of policy may take the form of more definite and systematic direction of the large packers . . . or may even take the form of operation of the packinghouse establishments by the government." [72] The Food Administration report issued several months later by Hoover fell short of advocating the policies favored by Lasater and some of his cattlemen colleagues. But the Federal Trade Commission report published in July, 1918, was sharply critical of the meat-packing industry's methods and practices, which it described in detail. The Big Five packing companies controlled nearly 95 percent of the livestock slaughtered at the twelve major packing centers, and together they had a controlling interest, in 574 different companies. In addition to cattle slaughter, the report said that the meat packers "are backers in cattle loan companies making the necessary loans to growers and feeders of livestock . . . are interested in railways and private car lines transporting livestock and manufactured animal products; in most of the important stockyard companies . . . and in livestock trade papers on which growers and feeders rely for market news." The FTC report concluded: "A fair consideration of the course the five packers have followed and the position they have already reached must lead to the conclusion that they threaten the freedom of the market of the country's food industries and of the by-product industries linked therewith." [73]

On August 9, 1918, Lasater wrote Al M. McFaddin, John Landergin, and Henry Wallace, enclosing a copy of the FTC report. The report summarized the real threat posed by the industry's structure: "After reading this report, I am satisfied you will realize that there is no issue before the American people as important to the nation as the production and distribution of the nation's food supply." Lasater stated, "None can know the facts herein disclosed without realizing that the production of the food supply is imperiled." [74]

Five months later, in January, 1919, Lasater wrote the president of

[72] Herbert Hoover to Woodrow Wilson, March 26, 1918, Scrapbook #4, Lasater Files.
[73] "Facts about the 'Big Five' Packers," *Cattleman*, July, 1919, p. 11.
[74] Ed C. Lasater to Al M. McFaddin, August 9, 1918, Scrapbook #4, Lasater Files.

the American Livestock Association to give a report on his activities during the previous year and to submit his resignation from the associ- ation's Market Committee. Lasater, writing from Washington, stated that he regreted being unable to leave the capital to attend the annual convention and to give his report in person, but he felt that he needed to be present at various legislative sessions scheduled concurrently with that meeting. Since the last annual meeting, Lasater had spent the entire year in Washington except for "brief intervals when I made hur- ried trips to my ranch." He had testified in Interstate Commerce Com- mission hearings and in House and Senate hearings and had worked closely with the Federal Trade Commission's investigation. He felt that to leave Washington at that time "would lessen the possibility of the passage of any effective legislation or control of the packers at this ses- sion of Congress."[75]

Lasater's close cooperation with the FTC had won him a number of friends and supporters in that agency. One FTC official wrote Lasa- ter that "several of your friends here are praising your wonderful testi- mony before the House committee. We certainly will not let them 'hang you with J. Ogden Armour' after that great service." He added: "You have several friends and admirers in the Commission. We all ap- preciate what you are doing."[76]

While he was content that the Washington effort was yielding re- sults, Lasater was very dissatisfied with his own trade organization and with the attitude and actions of his ranching colleagues. After passing a series of convention resolutions and approving a variety of initiatives with regard to the activities of the Market Committee, the association had failed to appropriate adequate funds or to provide sufficient per- sonnel to get the job done. Lasater, at his own expense and at times single-handedly, had stayed in Washington to ramrod the activities with which the Market Committee had been charged.[77]

Lasater approached this task as he approached any activity in which he was involved, with energy, money, and determination. He viewed his placement on the Market Committee and the resolutions

---

[75] Ed C. Lasater to the American National Livestock Association, January 16, 1918; *New York Times*, November 18, 1917, January 27, 1918, and March 31, 1918.

[76] Earl S. Haines to Ed C. Lasater, March 27, 1919, Edward C. Lasater Collection.

[77] Ed C. Lasater to the American National Livestock Association, January 16, 1919, "Meat Packer Legislation," pp. 72–74.

passed by the 1918 convention as a call to action. When other members of the committee and the association were not available for the series of meetings and hearings, Lasater devoted increasing amounts of his own time. When the American National Livestock Association's funds proved inadequate to carry out the task, he simply used his own money.

By early 1919, Lasater, still busy in Washington, D.C., had concluded that his ranching colleagues were moving too slowly and were not willing to allocate the necessary resources and time to get the job done. On January 8, P. H. Landergin, of Landergin Brothers in Amarillo, wrote Lasater: "I also want you to know that we believe in your good work. . . . But we agree with you that if we can get relief, it will have to be through some other means than the American National."[78]

Other farm organizations with which Lasater cooperated in Washington had responded more readily and more rapidly to his call for endorsement of the Federal Trade Commission's report issued in July, 1918. Those organizations represented more than a million members, and Lasater was convinced that strength of numbers was a powerful tool in Washington: "It takes votes to put punch into a demand for legislation here." Lasater's experience convinced him that many of his ranching colleagues were not aware of the magnitude of the problem. "I wish to express the opinion that as long as you are content to represent the livestock interests by occasionally appearing before some legislative committee in advocacy of measures desired and then vanish from Washington, nothing will be accomplished for the interests of our people." Lasater expressed the hope that the American National Livestock Association would become in fact a national organization and that the association would learn from the example provided by other trade groups: "It takes continuity of effort to accomplish anything here. Both the packer and the labor organizations furnish you an example of how to do it. . . ."[79]

Lasater was convinced of the necessity of the effort in Washington and dedicated himself to seeing it through. In 1916, when another round of inquiries into the meat-packing business was getting under way, Lasater had declared that he had started out to get an investigation and legislative action and that he intended to continue working

[78] P. H. Landergin to Ed C. Lasater, January 8, 1919, Scrapbook #4, Lasater Files.
[79] Ed C. Lasater to the American National Livestock Association, January 16, 1919.

toward that end. Lasater underscored the seriousness of his views when he stated: "If some change could not be brought about in the situation . . . I would be perfectly willing to turn my holdings over to anybody that would pay my indebtedness. . . . I did not care to pass down to my sons a business where they could not be assured of returns, regardless of how efficiently it might be managed. . . . "[80]

A year after resigning from the association's Market Committee, and having affiliated himself more closely with other farm organizations, Lasater was again in Washington testifying about the meat-packing industry. When he appeared before Congressman Haugen's House Agriculture Committee in early 1920, Lasater was not introduced as a representative of the Texas or National Livestock Association. Instead, he appeared as the chairman of the Committee on Packing Plant Legislation of the National Board of Farm Organizations.[81] Lasater spent hour after hour proceeding through two hundred pages of testimony and exhibits.

Toward the end of his testimony, Lasater discussed with the congressmen on the committee his own time constraints. After two days on the stand, Lasater requested that the packer witnesses be given their turn so that he could subsequently submit to further questions before departing for Texas. This was to be his final statement, and he did not plan to return soon to Washington. The pressure of events on the ranch, in addition to his oft-repeated views about Mr. Swift and Mr. Hoover, were giving an added bite to his words and further shortening his Irish temper. "I cannot come back for several months. That is impossible,"

[80] "Meat Packer Legislation," p. 195. Aside from legislation on the meat-packing industry, another principal concern of Lasater's, on which he spent a considerable amount of time between 1911 and 1921, was the establishment of a better means of providing agriculturalists with long-term financing. A. C. Williams, the first editor of *Cattleman* magazine, and later president of the Farm Credit Administration of Houston, said in a speech in the 1930s: "I recall just a year or two after I went to work for the [Texas Cattle Raisers] Association . . . Ed C. Lasater started a crusade for a better system of credit for the ranchmen in this state, and a better marketing system. I remember with pleasure having had the opportunity to discuss with Mr. Lasater the question of livestock credits, and having served as stenographer and having him dictate to me the plan which he formulated . . . practically the system we now have. At that time, Mr. Lasater was some years ahead of the procession, and people thought he was visionary—that he expected too much. One of my sincere regrets is that Mr. Lasater did not live to see the realization of his dreams" (A. C. Williams speech, Lasater Files).

[81] "Meat Packer Legislation," p. 1.

Lasater told the members of the Agriculture Committee. "My spring
work is on and I must give my attention to it."[82]

Ed Lasater had more than spring work on his mind. The treaty
signed at Versailles in 1919 restored peace to the world, at least for a
few years. But the war's end spelled trouble for agriculture and marked
the beginning of an extended crisis affecting cattlemen and farmers all
across the country. As he approached sixty, Ed Lasater felt a pressing
need to return to his ranch, where diverse problems that would re-
quire all his personal and monetary resources were growing rapidly.

The consent decree and subsequent legislation related to the
meat-packing industry represented a victory of sorts, a modest justi-
fication for the years of effort and expense. But the legal and legislative
landmarks did not alter the harsh financial realities of life on the range,
nor did they end the periodically violent fluctuations in the cattle market. The post–World War I slump in agricultural prices was just getting
started when Lasater left Washington. Before the downturn was over
Lasater and many of his colleagues in the livestock business would be
fighting for their economic survival.

[82] Ibid., p. 189. More than six decades after Lasater, Pryor, and others testified in
Washington, that city was once again the center of an investigation and controversy regarding another aspect of pricing and marketing beef cattle. This time it was the live
cattle futures market, a mechanism that allows a producer, a user, or a speculator to buy
or sell a given quantity of various classes of livestock for delivery at a future date. On this
occasion, the fight was spearheaded by Congressman Neal Smith of Iowa, chairman of
the House Small Business Committee. Smith and others charged that the futures markets were subject to manipulation by speculators who were responsible for at least part
of the drastic cattle market fluctuation. Along with the futures market, Iowa Beef Processors, an upstart which in a very few years had become the nation's largest meat-
packing company, was another principal target of Smith's investigation. Ironically, that
company, by combining new methods of handling beef with aggressive business tactics,
had added to the financial woes of Swift, Armour, Wilson, and Cudahy, which had all
been taken over by conglomerates and had experienced years of marginal economic results (James Cook, "Nothing but the Best," p. 155–59; "Washington Wire," *Beef Business Bulletin*, October 31, 1980, p. 1, and September 25, 1981, p. 2; "Low Price Reasons
Analyzed," *Record Stockman*, April 30, 1981, pp. 1–2; "Plant Closings Put Wilson Figures in Red," *Record Stockman*, September 17, 1981, p. 1).

CHAPTER 10

After Versailles: Peace and Panic

> Although the rest of the economy also suffered depression, agriculture's collapse was a special adversity, going deeper and lasting longer than the general post-war deflation.
>
> —James Shideler

MINNIE Alice Priour McBride sat silently looking through the window as the miles of flat land rolled by. She saw the coastal plain and grassy savannahs broken by sections of newly developed farmland as she contemplated the life that awaited her family in Duval County. The Texas-Mexican Railway, which ran from Corpus to Alice, San Diego, and Realitos en route to the Rio Grande River at Laredo, carried Minnie McBride west, away from her home near Corpus Christi. In 1890 she had boarded this train for another trip, a honeymoon excursion to the border as the pretty young wife of Peter McBride. That had been a happy trip, a brief introduction to a new and exciting chapter in her life. But this time she did not board the train with joy and expectation; she was making the trip reluctantly and with serious reservations.[1]

Peter McBride, after experiencing reverses in the cattle business, decided in 1913 to move a few miles west to make a fresh start. McBride was the son of an Irish sea captain who settled near Corpus in 1849. As a young boy, McBride had herded wild horses on the wide open prairie between Corpus and Robstown. He had spent his life with livestock and had farmed and operated a dairy near Corpus. In 1913, McBride leased Los Melones, a ranch located near the Borjas Ranch

---

[1] Interview, Bird McBride Victor, March 5, 1982; *Corpus Christi Caller-Times*, August 21, 1955.

that Edward H. Caldwell had leased, and moved his family inland to their new home.[2]

Behind the car in which Minnie McBride sat with her family was a boxcar with furniture and household belongings, and behind that a second one loaded with plants. She had not wanted to make this move, and she had agreed to it on two conditions: she would not live in Realitos, which surely was the end of the world, but in San Diego, thirty miles to the northeast, where there was at least some evidence of civilization. And she would go only if she could take all of her plants. That meant securing another boxcar, which was loaded with ferns, geraniums, begonias, and the other plants and flowers that she loved to grow and care for.[3]

The McBrides settled in to a home on the main plaza in San Diego. But Minnie McBride changed her mind and consented to live in Realitos only a few months later. In the midst of the excitement and celebrating of the annual San Diego fiesta, a stray bullet entered the McBride home and lodged in a wall just above the bed where young C. J. was sleeping. The relative tranquility and isolation of Realitos looked more appealing after that incident, and the family moved to that town, which was closer to Los Melones.[4]

Realitos was a small settlement located on the northwestern extremity of Ed Lasater's property. The town's most noteworthy structure was Lasater's large mercantile store, which supplied area residents with food, clothing, lumber, ranch equipment, farm machinery, and caskets. A year after moving there, McBride took on the job of foreman for Lasater's Realitos division, while continuing his personal cattle business.[5] McBride's territory included La Golona, a small pasture used to

---

[2] *Corpus Christi Caller-Times*, August 21, 1955. Peter McBride's father left his home near Dublin when he was fourteen. James McBride became one of Corpus Christi's early settlers when he arrived there about 1849 (*Corpus Christi Caller-Times*, May 25, 1952).

[3] Interview, Bird McBride Victor, March 5, 1982.

[4] Ibid.

[5] Interview C. J. McBride, March 7, 1982. McBride first moved his family into a rented two-story house, then later into Lasater's foreman's house. The previous foreman, a heavy drinker, was fired by Lasater after he got mad at a horse and beat the animal to death. Though McBride did not drink, he did have an eggnog at Christmas, and whenever he caught a cold he would make a hot toddy with lemon juice, sugar, and whiskey: "He would drink that, get in bed under a heavy quilt, and we would not see him again until the next day when he would reappear free of the cold" (Interview, Bird McBride Victor, March 5, 1982).

assemble cattle to be shipped out of Realitos, La India, Buena Suerte, Cadena, and Palo Blanco, where Lasater kept a herd of Shorthorn cows that were big, wide-framed, and blood-red. McBride also oversaw Lasater's extensive farming operations at Sejita and Copita, where he kept his registered Herefords.[6]

When McBride went to work for Ed Lasater, some of his friends were skeptical: "They told me that I wouldn't last a month with Mr. Lasater, that he was too particular to work for. But I worked for him almost fifteen years, and we got along just fine."[7] One reason for their compatibility was that neither McBride nor Lasater wanted anyone around who drank. Throughout the years of their close working relationship, they addressed each other as "Mr. McBride" and "Mr. Lasater." But to his men and his friends, McBride was known as "Don Pedro." Curiously, Lasater and McBride were two of the few ranchmen in the area who wore high-topped laced boots with a low heel instead of the customary cowboy boots.[8]

While McBride ran the Realitos end of the ranch, Jesse Coward was one of the foremen on Lasater's Encino division, which covered the southeastern part of his ranch. Coward had worked for Lasater around Realitos before moving south to take charge at Encino after the previous foreman there, Lloyd Gorbid, was struck by lightning and killed. As he recalled his days as a Lasater ranch foreman more than six decades later, Coward was unclear about certain names and dates. But a few months after his one-hundredth birthday, Coward could remember two things clearly: Ed Lasater always had plenty of good horses, and he was particularly fond of Brahman bulls.[9] In 1914 Lasater purchased 162 Brahman bulls to use on his beef cow herd.[10] By 1918 he could say, "Brahman cattle raise the value of South Texas rangeland $2.00 an acre."[11]

[6] Interview, C. J. McBride, March 7, 1982.

[7] *Corpus Christi Caller-Times*, August 21, 1955.

[8] Interviews, C. J. McBride, March 7, 1982, and Dennis McBride, July 27, 1981. Peter McBride and Lasater were once riding through a pasture in a two-wheeled cart. A mesquite branch hit Lasater in the eye, and he leaned forward with his hand over his eye repeating, "God, oh God." That was the closest Lasater ever came to uttering a profanity in McBride's presence (Interview, Bird McBride Victor, March 5, 1982).

[9] Interview, Jesse Coward, February 24, 1981. Both Gorbid and his horse were killed by the lightning bolt, which left a large hole in the ground (Ibid.).

[10] According to his 1914 Balance Sheet, Lasater that year purchased 162 Brahman bulls for $16,669.00.

[11] Tom Lea, *The King Ranch*, II, 649.

In July, 1919, the *Cattleman* ran an article entitled "Brahma Cattle Increasing," which gave a report on a meeting hosted in Victoria by Al McFaddin for the officers and members of the Executive Committee of the Cattle Raisers Association of Texas. During an evening dinner, short talks on the merits of Brahman cattle were given by McFaddin, Ike Pryor, Lasater, Tom East, and Cyrus Lucas. The article described early Texas ranchers' prejudice against the cattle because of their "grotesque appearance" but added that "the ease with which cattle showing Brahma breeding took on flesh on short range, their apparent immunity to ticks and fever, and the rapidity with which they multiplied proved beyond doubt that the quality of cattle of that section could be improved by crossing with the Brahmas. . . ."[12]

Al McFaddin stated that Brahman cattle in South Texas withstood the heat better than any other breed, were not bothered by ticks, flies or mosquitoes, and seldom had to be treated for screwworms. He said that his Brahman cattle fattened more rapidly on the range than any other cattle and that buyer acceptance was good: "Packers have found that they dress well at all ages and they pay good prices for them."[13]

Tom East added to the accolades heard at McFaddin's "Brahma Banquet" celebrating the beef-producing qualities of the sacred cattle of India. He said that he had recently conducted an experiment with Hereford and Brahman calves on feed: "Both lots were fed the same ration and the Brahmas showed the largest gain in weight and sold for the highest price."[14]

Each of the testimonials described the positive qualities of Brahman cattle and the contribution that the breed was making to their operations' profitability. Lasater told the assembled cattlemen: "After many years' observation, I decided to try breeding Brahma bulls to some of my high-bred Hereford and Shorthorn cows. The experiment has proved highly satisfactory, and I am now breeding them to several hundred Hereford and Shorthorn cows." He continued: "During the drought when Shorthorn and Hereford yearlings were not in condition to sell, I sold my Brahma yearling steers for an average of $41 net. . . . My records show that I get more profitable results from cattle crossed with the Brahmas."[15]

[12] "Brahma Cattle Industry," *Cattleman*, July, 1919, p. 21.
[13] Ibid., p. 23.
[14] Ibid., p. 39.
[15] Ibid., p. 38.

The convivial atmosphere of camaraderie at Victoria and the testimonial speeches about the cattle that could produce higher profits for Texas stockmen were not marred by any doubts related to the effect that events taking place across the world would have on the livestock industry. But at almost the same time that these ranchers gathered together in response to Al McFaddin's invitation, a somber group of men sat around a table in a palace outside Paris. Their actions would have a more profound influence on Texas ranches in the following decade than the crossbreeding program which had been started with the Brahman breed would.

The shot fired at Sarajevo launched Europe into an extended period of hostility which left behind a legacy of human tragedy on a massive scale. The treaty that was signed nearly five years later restored peace to many strife-torn nations. But the turmoil in the economic sphere which occurred during the First World War did not end at Versailles. Hoover's "food will win the war" campaign, which symbolized agriculture's role and its importance in the Allied war effort, had no follow-up in the postwar years. The wartime agricultural expansion dumped mounting surpluses on shrinking markets after the war was over: "Although the rest of the economy also suffered depression, agriculture's collapse was a special adversity, going deeper and lasting much longer than the general post-war deflation."[16]

Between the Civil War and the First World War, agriculturalists had experienced a series of severe price jolts as the nation moved from a rural-agrarian society to an urban-industrial one. World War I delayed and ultimately intensified the adjustments that were taking place in agriculture, and the war years separated the individualistic and exploitative agricultural methods of the prior years from the modern industry that agriculture would become later: "It was a gulf between two worlds of American agriculture, an old world of soaring ambition resting upon expansion and land value increment and a new world of uncertainty distinguished by diversity, inequality, and contraction."[17]

The years prior to World War I had been some of the best ever known in the rural sector. In those years agriculture in general enjoyed a favorable relationship with commerce and manufacturing: "There were problems to worry about . . . but they were for the most part

[16] James Shideler, *Farm Crisis, 1919–1923*, p. 1.
[17] Ibid., pp. 1–2.

problems of prosperity, not of adversity."[18] Prices for farm commodities between 1899 and 1910 rose more than 89 percent. Those years coincided closely with the years during which Ed Lasater made more than one million dollars' net profit from a rising cattle market (exclusive of any land transactions or valuations) and assembled the bulk of his Falfurrias Ranch. Between 1910 and the outbreak of the war, the rise in prices for farm products slowed but kept pace with most other price levels.[19]

As Lasater wrote in the letter which accompanied his loan application in 1914: "The security offered is of the soundest character fundamentally—land of proven earning capacity supplying common necessities to readily available markets." He continued: "The foundation has been laid that will sustain a constantly expanding production of agricultural markets for many generations to come."[20] Lasater was not alone in his optimistic view of agriculture's future: "The picture was nearly one of stability, balance, satisfaction and economic justice, as farmers understood it." He was only one of many who had taken risks, worked hard, and been rewarded: "The affairs of agriculture were outwardly more satisfactory than they had been for generations. A buoyant faith and progress pervaded the country and opportunities in agriculture assured young men a respectable calling as well as the accumulation of a competence."[21]

The dislocation caused by increased wartime production followed by a slackening demand brought an end to the two decades of comparative prosperity that agriculture had enjoyed. Expansion of farm production did not end suddenly with the end of the war in November of 1918; "instead, forces set in motion by the war emergency and the sustained high demand from export markets together with a persisting high price level continued to swell agricultural production."[22] The U.S. Department of Agriculture predicted strong markets for agricultural

[18] John D. Hicks, "The Western Middle West, 1900–1914," *Agricultural History* 20 (April, 1946): 77.

[19] Shideler, *Farm Crisis*, p. 5.

[20] Lasater's optimism in 1914 appears, with hindsight, to have been well founded. That year was the peak year in terms of the purchasing power represented by the average price paid for beef animals in the United States as reported in the *USDA Yearbook* ("Range of Prices for Beef Cattle," *Cattleman*, May, 1922, p. 19).

[21] Shideler, *Farm Crisis*, pp. 4–6.

[22] Ibid., p. 18.

products after the war's end: "No cause for alarm as to the ability of American agriculture to maintain its position in world trade during the period of readjustment is foreseen by the Department, which declares that a considerable demand from European countries is assured for a year or more."[23]

But that favorable environment was short-lived: "Export demand had remained effective until 1920, when Europe's ability to buy American goods was exhausted." Agriculturalists had increased their borrowings to expand production and meet high production costs, and as postwar prices began to decline a credit crunch added to their woes: "Price declines forced local banks loaded with agricultural paper to seek shelter by calling their loans, an action that in turn forced farmers to dump their products on a demoralized market, adding greatly to the price panic."[24]

In the beginning the panic was not unlike other periodic panics that farmers and cattlemen had come to expect in their business. This time, however, it was an ominous portent of conditions that would persist during much of the coming decade: "Agriculture was poorly coordinated in the national life and moved painfully along from crisis to chronic depression, a dangerously sick industry in an otherwise thriving decade. Farmers and planners for agriculture could not thenceforth be indifferent to the historical record of 1919–1923."[25]

In 1913 L. D. Miller left Falfurrias for Saint Louis, to join his brother Rob in managing the various real estate companies organized to merchandise parts of their brother-in-law's ranchlands. Sales were slow, but a small and growing group of people did respond to the promotional efforts. Some could not resist the attractions of life in the Falfurrias country: "How would you like to have a business of your own . . . a business that never feels panics and bank failures . . . a business that would keep you out in the open where you could breathe fresh air and live next to nature?"[26]

[23] "A Review of Timely Topics," *Cattleman*, February, 1919, p. 9.
[24] Shideler, *Farm Crisis*, p. 47.
[25] Ibid., p. 4.
[26] Interview, L. D. Miller, Sr., September 22, 1971; *Falfurrias Bulletin*, 1909. One incident with the Miller brothers before they left Falfurrias characterized the times. Rob and L. D. were walking down a wooden sidewalk, both wearing gunbelts, when they got

Garland Miller, the oldest Miller brother and the original driving force behind the early Falfurrias colonization, dropped out of sight around the time L. D. moved to Saint Louis. Garland was a heavy drinker and died in New York in 1918, when he was about forty years old. The fourth Miller brother, Richard, had found a satisfying role as president of the Falfurrias State Bank. That left Rob and L. D. to ramrod the ongoing real estate promotion.[27]

L. D. Miller recalled that Lasater frequently passed through Saint Louis en route to Chicago or Washington and that he continually pushed his associates to generate more land sales: "He was very impatient with us. . . . He was under a financial strain, and he wanted us to make a greater effort to sell parcels of his land." The Miller brothers worked through agents scattered throughout the Midwest. "Those were the unhappiest years of my life," Miller recalled. "We were taking people out of good farming areas and putting them into a situation where they couldn't make it."[28]

Robert Ferdinand von Blumer, a Chicago doctor, and Wilbert Jenkins, a blacksmith from Paris, Illinois, were two men whose lives changed after meeting the Miller brothers. In addition to his medical practice, Blumer owned the Lincoln Chemical Works, a firm that manufactured patent medicines, ointments, pills, and tonics. Blumer first met the Millers in 1909, and several years later on a trip to Mexico in search of medicinal herbs, he stopped in Falfurrias to inquire further about South Texas real estate. The doctor bought land from the Millers in the Copita Farm and Garden Tracts and also several thousand acres of La Parrita Ranch, a tract that the Miller brothers had originally sold for Henrietta King.[29]

---

into a heated discussion with a passerby. The other man called L. D. a son-of-a-bitch, which in those days was a forbidden word. L. D. immediately drew his pistol and fired. He was prevented from hitting the man by his brother Rob, who reacted just as quickly and knocked L. D.'s arm upwards (Interview, Gardner B. Miller, July 22, 1981).

[27] Interview, L. D. Miller, Sr., September 22, 1971; "Affidavit," Deed Records, Brooks County, vol. X, p. 386.

[28] Interview, L. D. Miller, Sr., September 22, 1971.

[29] Interviews, Walter Blumer, July 12, 1981, and Huston Jenkins, July 13, 1981; Jimmie A. Picquet, "Some Ghost Towns in South Texas" (M.S. thesis, Texas A&I Univ., 1972), p. 121. William F. Noll was another man who met the Millers in Chicago, bought land at Parrita, and moved to the Falfurrias area in 1918. Noll suffered from asthma, and doctors recommended a change of climate (Interview, Marvin Noll, July 10, 1981).

Jenkins, along with a number of his neighbors in central Illinois, attended a 1916 meeting at which Rob Miller held forth eloquently on the many attractive features of land ownership in the Falfurrias area. He described the region's agricultural potential, the pleasant life, the agreeable climate, and the good schools awaiting the settlers' children. Rob Miller "stretched the truth," Jenkins's son stated. "He convinced the midwesterners that they could make a good living on 160 acres. The homeseekers thought they would find a veritable garden spot." Jenkins and his neighbors, the Woodbridge family, bought farms in the Realitos Subdivision. The Woodbridges lasted less than two years before returning to Illinois, but Jenkins and his family stayed.[30]

About the time Robert Blumer made his purchase at La Parrita, Rob Miller bought the land he had originally sold to the developers Burton and Danforth, founders of Flowella. In early 1917, Miller contracted with Blumer to handle the promotion and sales of tracts in La Parrita. Blumer moved his young son, Walter, into the old Parrita headquarters house to manage the project and to act as sales agent. Dr. Blumer's plan was to clear the land, plant orchards, and subdivide it. Walter Blumer had as many as one hundred Mexican laborers working on the project, receiving five dollars per acre for land clearing. He also installed nineteen water wells and hired the Cantu brothers from Encino to build earthen tanks to hold water for irrigation.[31]

Blumer's association with the Miller brothers occurred at a time when South Texas real estate sales were drying up. A critical blow to the land promotion projects took place after the United States' entrance into World War I, when the railroads discontinued the excursion trains and the special homeseeker rates, which had been a major inducement in getting northern buyers to South Texas. The devastation and loss of lives in Texas from hurricanes in 1916 and 1919 and recurring incidents along the Rio Grande River were other factors which also hurt the selling campaign: "National publicity given to the border clashes with Mexican insurrectionists and to the Mexican bandit raids into Texas inhibited all but the most adventurous. . . . South Texas was for several years synonymous with outlawry."[32]

[30] Interview, Huston Jenkins, July 13, 1981.
[31] Interview, Walter Blumer, July 12, 1981; Picquet, "Some Ghost Towns," pp. 120–21.
[32] Ibid., p. 122.

In 1920, Ed Lasater summarized the added productivity and the increased population supported by the Falfurrias Country a quarter-century after he had made his first purchase: "At the time of my acquiring this territory, there were less than 100 people being afforded a means of livelihood on it. Now there are more than 5,000 people occupying this same territory. They have been brought here by my efforts, and the system of farming and marketing of dairy products has enabled the first generation to stick."[33] Ed Lasater was optimistic as he approached sixty. He was confident that both his own large-scale agricultural operation and the small farm units now covering parts of his former ranch holdings would prove successful in the end. In fact, by 1920 a number of the people who had moved into the Copita, Sejita, and Realitos areas had already packed up their belongings and returned to their native states, convinced they could not make a go of it.[34]

Others, on further investigation, decided they had been misled and that the land was not as it had been represented. George Spark and his wife, residents of South Dakota, filed suit in November, 1919, against Rob Miller and Ed Lasater to rescind their land purchase agreement and to recover damages. In 1918, Spark had entered into a contract with Miller Brothers, Rob Miller, agent, to purchase 1,329 acres owned by Lasater in Jim Hogg and Duval counties at forty dollars an acre. Spark's suit alleged that he was: "induced to enter into the purchase of the land by reason of the fraudulent representation of Robert G. Miller as to the location, quality and topography of the land."[35]

Spark had made four trips to Falfurrias in the course of completing the transaction. On the second trip, he and Miller toured the property together: "In this trip of inspection, the land coming under his observation was brushy, more so in some places than others, and particularly so in the center where the brush was so thick they could not drive their buggies through it. He saw at least one interior 'lagoon' and Miller told him of another near the center of the tract." Spark testified that Miller

[33] Ed C. Lasater to Gilbert N. Haugen, March 7, 1920, in Lasater, "Meat Packer Legislation," statement before the Committee on Agriculture, U.S. House of Representatives, March 1, 2, 3, and 6, 1920, p. 209, in Edward C. Lasater Collection, Eugene C. Barker Texas History Center, University of Texas, Austin.

[34] Interviews, L. D. Miller, Sr., September 22, 1971, Huston Jenkins, July 13, 1981, and C. J. McBride, March 7, 1982.

[35] "Spark et ux v. Lasater et al.," 234 *Southwestern Reporter*, p. 717.

represented the land as being the "very best proposition he had in an agricultural line," and added, "I think I asked Miller what the land was worth, and I think he said it was worth $40.00; he said the land would grow anything. I don't think he specified any special thing that would grow on it. He said that you could make corn, and that from the well to the road would make a fine orange orchard."[36]

The jury found in favor of the defendant, and the Court of Civil Appeals affirmed that judgment. "Miller could not have meant, nor could Spark have been deceived into believing . . . that the land was all free from brush, since brush was everywhere apparent . . . ," the Court wrote, "nor that there were no lagoons or low places on the land when samples of both were lying there before the eyes of both men, nor that the soil was all dark and rich when they both saw that it was 'chalky and gray' all around the lagoons. . . ."[37]

The land promoters were correct when they told potential buyers that they could grow almost anything on the Falfurrias area farms, Walter Blumer later recalled. What they did not point out was that this assumed a rainfall that was less dependable around Falfurrias than it was in many of the areas where the homeseekers originated. "They oversold the country; they overestimated this region in comparison with the farming areas of the middle west," Blumer affirmed.[38]

The productivity of the virgin soils was also partly responsible for the overselling. L. D. Miller explained how everyone was fooled by the land's potential: "The first crops were excellent, and everyone was enthusiastic. From what I saw myself, that confidence seemed to be well-founded. But the land just didn't hold up." L. D. Miller married a Saint Louis girl in 1915, and he took her to Falfurrias for a visit. Lasater took Miller and his bride around the ranch in a buggy. At La Fruta they saw Duroc hogs and Jersey cows grazing on lush pastures. "It was one of the prettiest sights I have ever seen," Miller recalled later.[39]

When the Falfurrias area's long growing season and sunny climate happened to coincide with a year of abundant moisture, the results could be spectacular, but that did not happen often. Albert Dale, son

---

[36] Ibid., p. 718.
[37] Ibid., pp. 719, 1108.
[38] Interview, Walter Blumer, July 12, 1981.
[39] Interview, L. D. Miller, Sr., September 22, 1971.

of an early dairy farmer, summed up one view of the Falfurrias country
this way: "No land promises more and delivers less year after year after
year."[40]

Some residents of the Falfurrias country were drawn there by the
enticing literature distributed by the Miller brothers and their associates. Others came to work in Ed Lasater's various enterprises or to start
new businesses of their own in the small community that served the
growing rural population. Still others appeared in the area by chance,
or had simply boarded a train somewhere to the north or to the east
and had ridden it to the end of the line.

R. J. McIntyre came looking for a better life and new opportunities. McIntyre had been in the lumber business in Van Buren, Arkansas. When chain lumberyards moved in, his business deteriorated, and
he decided to seek new horizons elsewhere. He boarded a train and
rode it to the last stop, Falfurrias. There in the little village that sat at a
sandy crossroads in the middle of mesquite brush country, he organized the Starr Lumber Company in 1908.[41]

The long trip for northern Starr-County residents to Rio Grande
City ended when Falfurrias became the seat of a new county in 1911.
Former Texas Ranger Captain James Brooks became the first judge in
the county bearing his name. The other original county officeholders
included: Amado de la Garza, sheriff and tax collector; E. R. Rachal,
Sr., tax assessor; Rufino García, Sr., county and district clerk; and
Lázaro López, descendant of an early-day rancher, county treasurer.[42]

The county got a new courthouse in 1913, designed by Alfred
Giles, an English architect who moved to San Antonio in 1873. But the
year before the courthouse was constructed, Brooks County lost a
large part of its territory with the creation of Jim Hogg County. Lasater's ranching neighbor to the west, Bill Jones, having failed in opposing
Lasater's drive to split off his territory from Starr County in 1911, succeeded in cutting the new county in half only two years later.[43] Captain

---

[40] Interview, Albert Dale, August 25, 1971.

[41] Interview, Dick McIntyre, July 26, 1981; *Southwest Texans*, p. 456.

[42] Brooks County Historical Commission, "Brooks County Elected Officials, 1911–
1978," 1979. Other original county officials were J. F. Clarkson, county attorney, and
F. C. Rahlmann, county surveyor (Ibid.).

[43] Lloyd N. Dyer, "The History of Brooks County" (M.S. thesis, Texas College of

Brooks was one of many county residents who made known their opposition to the creation of Jim Hogg County: "The proposed new
county . . . would be absolutely dominated by men who are wholly
concerned in holding it as mere ranch properties and in perpetuating
intolerable conditions which have existed and now exist in Zapata and
Starr Counties."[44]

Local politics in the first decade after the county's formation gave
rise periodically to heated campaigns, but on the whole few issues of
real substance were involved. Personalities and ties of friendship were
the principal concerns, and an area resident was either a "Lasater man"
or a member of the opposition. H. W. Oberwetter, manager of the Sullivan ranch, and Lasater were chronic foes. "If one of them was in favor
of something, the other was automatically opposed. It made no difference what the issue was," Neil Rupp, an early citrus grower, recalled.[45]

Frank Rachal joined Oberwetter in the opposition camp of local
politics. Rachal, a one-time Lasater employee, had developed a sizable
cattle operation of his own by the end of the World War. After a dispute
with Lasater, possibly over a land deal, Rachal decided to carry his political opposition into the business field. In 1920 he was the principal
founder of the First National Bank of Falfurrias, which provided new
competition for the Falfurrias State Bank, controlled by Richard Miller
and other members of the Lasater faction. Rachal had been a minority
stockholder in the State Bank; J. R. Scott, Jr., a former employee of
Miller's bank, and Roy Bennett, one of Lasater's former bookkeepers,
joined Rachal in the new enterprise.[46]

Arts and Industries, 1938, p. 19); *Corpus Christi Caller-Times*, July 19, 1942; "Brooks
County Courthouse," undated article in the files of Florence Schuetz, chairman, Brooks
County Historical Commission; Florence Schuetz to author, February 20, 1983, Author's
Files.

[44] James A. Brooks, printed letter to the Thirty-Third Legislature, 1913, Lasater
Files, in possession of Garland M. Lasater, Falfurrias.

[45] Interviews, Neil Rupp, July 28, 1981; Leslie Holbrook Gammie and Martine
Holbrook, July 25, 1981.

[46] Interviews, L. D. Miller, Sr., September 22, 1971; Edena Clere Scott Noll, July
20, 1981; Mrs. T. R. (Marybelle) Bennett, September 22, 1971. The capital stock of
Falfurrias State Bank was increased from $10,000 to $25,000 in September, 1911. The 100
shares issued prior to the increase were owned as follows: Mary M. Lasater, 11; B. T.
Henry, 23; George W. Brackenridge, 10; G. R. Scott, 10; L. D. Miller, 11; Robert G. Miller, 10; Garland B. Miller, 10; Richard G. Miller, 10; and Ed C. Lasater, 5. The additional
150 shares issued in September were subscribed by: Richard G. Miller, 110; Ed Rachal,

Amado de la Garza resigned the sheriff's post under fire in 1913 and was succeeded by James Maupin, who had moved to Falfurrias as Lasater's first ranch foreman in 1895.[47] In 1918, Lake Newell Porter was elected sheriff, marking the first time a Lasater candidate for major county office had been defeated. Porter was raised in Goliad and was a one-time trail driver. His grandson later gave one reason for Porter's election: "Even though Lasater did not misuse his position, many residents feared the concentration of power in his hands."[48]

Falfurrias voters were listed by name as they entered the polls, and ballots were numbered, thereby allowing county officials to match up each citizen with his voting record. Lasater expected the numerous employees of his various businesses to vote as he directed, and at election time he passed out handbills identifying the candidates and the issues. Florence Schuetz, who began her teaching career on the Loma Blanca Ranch of Sabas Pérez's heirs, subsequently taught school at Number Five, the community at Lasater's farming headquarters west of town. In 1918, Schuetz's father voted against the Lasater ticket, and the following Monday morning Lasater sent Captain Brooks to advise her that she had lost her job. Voting could be risky, whether you were for or against the Lasater ticket. In 1922, Florence Schuetz, a Catholic, voted against the slate supported by the Ku Klux Klan, which Lasater also vigorously opposed. On that occasion, since the school board was dominated by Klan members, she was temporarily dismissed from her teaching job in Falfurrias.[49]

Lasater's merantile business in 1920 had developed into a sizable

---

10; Frank S. Rachal, 10; George W. Brackenridge, 15; and Ed Lasater, 5 ("Amendment to the Charter of the Falfurrias State Bank," Texas Secretary of State, November 10, 1911). The Falfurrias State Bank subsequently increased its capital stock from $25,000 to $75,000 on July 17, 1920, the same year the First National Bank of Falfurrias was founded (J. C. Chidsey to C. D. Mims, July 17, 1920, Texas Department of Insurance and Banking files).

[47] Brooks County Commissioners Court Minutes, vol. I, p. 243. Interviews, Mildred Maupin Smith, July 14, 1981, and Florence Schuetz, April 9, 1981. I have been unable to pinpoint the circumstances that led to Amado de la Garza's resignation. Nearly seven decades after the event, a number of old-timers refused to discuss that situation.

[48] Interview, Matthew Gouger, March 20, 1982.

[49] Interviews, Florence Schuetz, April 9, 1981; Leslie Holbrook Gammie and Martine Holbrook, July 25, 1981, and Neil Rupp, July 28, 1981. After being dismissed from her post at Number 5, Schuetz taught at Flowella for one year. The following year Lasater had her invited back to her post at Number Five (Ibid.).

enterprise and provided a substantial payroll in the community. Florentino Treviño, son of one of Los Olmos' early settlers, was employed there as a young man and worked in the store for fourteen years. Albert Dale was another early employee; his father purchased a small dairy farm and a herd of Jersey cows from Lasater on the "pay-for-it-out-of-the-cream-check plan." Dale recalled that he had worked in Lasater's store for two years before he met him. And he remembered hearing Lasater's rapid and distinctive footsteps as the rancher walked along the raised wood platform outside the Falfurrias Mercantile Company.[50]

Lasater's creamery had grown steadily as a result of his continued expansion of his own Jersey herd and his sales of dairy cows to local farmers. By 1919 Lasater's Jersey herd numbered more than 2,000 cows. "These were the foundation and the nucleus for herds that now—within a radius of forty miles of Falfurrias—numbered well over 6,000. . . ." The sweet cream butter produced by the creamery was sold at all the major Texas markets and commanded the top price.[51]

The Pérez family hauled their cream in early each morning to the Falfurrias Creamery Company from their property on the south side of the Laguna de Loma Blanca. But most of the cream from the three hundred farms which supplied the creamery at its peak was brought in daily on wagons and later on trucks. Bill Gardner, Mary Lasater's cousin, established a trucking business on one of the four cream routes operating during World War I. His route started at Realitos and ran through Concepcion on the way to Falfurrias.[52]

T. S. Proctor was one of the colorful personalities connected with Lasater's creamery business during its peak years. Lasater hired Proctor, a Kentucky native who had run creameries in Colorado, Nebraska, and Waco, Texas, to manage the Falfurrias Creamery in 1916. Proctor's standard outfit was khaki pants, a white shirt, and a black tie. He was well-known for his practical jokes and for his heavy drinking: "He would stack the furniture in a restaurant every once in a while." Despite his fondness for alcoholic beverages, Proctor enjoyed a wide

[50] Interviews, Albert Dale, August 25, 1971, and Florentino Treviño, July 1, 1981.

[51] *Falfurrias Jerseys: Type, Production, Beauty, Utility*; Edward H. Caldwell, "Life and Activities of Edward Cunningham Lasater," p. 22; interview, Garland M. Lasater, February 21, 1981.

[52] *Falfurrias Facts*, November 19, 1981; interviews, Petra Pérez, March 2, 1982, and William B. Gardner, Jr., March 26, 1982.

reputation for his ability to produce a superior butter product, and he was the only known case of Lasater's tolerating a habitual drinker in his employ. On one occasion, another employee came to Lasater to complain about Proctor's being under the influence. Lasater fixed his eyes on the man and stated, "Proctor can make better butter than any man I know of, even when he is drinking."[53]

Proctor was famous for his exacting ways, and he held firmly to a 7:30 A.M. deadline for the delivery trucks in order to ensure the freshness of the cream, which soon after that time would turn sour rapidly in the South Texas heat. The cream trucks would start toward Falfurrias from various locations at 4:00 A.M., and at 7:25 A.M. Proctor would step out onto the creamery platform with a stopwatch in hand: "Those little old trucks would come zooming in there, and at 7:30 he would drop his fist down. . . . If a truck was coming down the driveway and hadn't unloaded by 7:30, he would just motion them to go on home. . . . He wouldn't accept the cream. He stuck to it. He was brutal."[54]

Proctor and Lasater worked out an accommodation of sorts, but others were unable to coexist with Proctor's autocratic ways. Wilbert Jenkins's family carried their cream two miles east of their farm in the Realitos subdivision to meet the cream truck before dawn until Proctor cut them off: "Proctor wouldn't accept our cream; when he was against you, there wasn't anything you could do," Huston Jenkins said. "Mr. Proctor was another cross that Mr. Lasater had to bear. He was always cantankerous and hard to get along with." Proctor turned down cream from Lasater's own dairies, as well as from other farmers. George Frank, a Lasater dairy foreman, and Proctor on more than one occasion tried to settle their differences with a fist fight.[55]

One early-morning phone conversation with the driver on the Realitos route exemplified Proctor's approach and the basis for his hardboiled reputation. A torrential cloudburst had covered the region. Large areas were inundated with water, and all the small creeks were running high. The driver called Proctor at 4:00 A.M. to tell him that he

[53] Interviews, Louella Proctor Hauser and Lawrence Hauser, April 7, 1981, and Garland M. Lasater, July 29, 1981.

[54] Interview, Tom Lasater, January 12, 1980. Lasater's creamery was the first in Texas to make butter from "sweet" cream. This sweet cream butter could last for months without refrigeration (Ibid.).

[55] Interview, Huston Jenkins, July 13, 1981.

did not believe it would be possible to make the cream run from Realitos due to road conditions. Proctor responded immediately: "You get stuck heading toward Falfurrias. Then it will be my responsibility."[56]

Several years after Ed Lasater boarded a train in 1920 to return to Falfurrias, he confided to his oldest son that during the war he had received an offer to purchase his holdings that would have allowed him to pay all his indebtedness and retire with a substantial capital. Lasater told his son that he had not accepted the proposal because he could see a difficult period ahead for the livestock industry: "The buyer would not have been able to make the payments on his note," he asserted. Lasater also felt honor-bound to stand by the farmers and dairymen he had brought into the area, and despite his own forecast of a crisis for agriculture after the war, he had decided simply to "ride it out."[57]

Two months before Lasater left Washington, the official statistician of the Chicago Union Stock Yards predicted high beef prices "for a long time to come." The analyst cited the excellent demand for beef during recent years and the fact that slaughter levels had exceeded production for the previous five years as reasons. "Packers have been forced to turn to lighter and cheaper steers . . . causing a scarcity of feeding cattle and raising the cost of fat cattle."[58]

Livestock producers did not have long to enjoy the optimistic prognostications contained in that detailed study of beef production and marketing. Near the end of 1920, a livestock analyst writing in the *Cattleman* stated: "Deflation of a disorderly character is the regular program at the stockyards. Every market on the map has shared in the demoralization, and it has been a veritable orgy of depreciation. Occasional reactions have revived hope at intervals that the worst was over, but such reactions merely heralded renewal of the slump."[59]

Declining livestock markets were not the only complication in Lasater's life when he lived in Washington and in the postwar years. Drought and tick fever were two other factors which added substantially to his operating costs during those years. In the middle of 1916,

[56] Interview, Tom Lasater, January 12, 1980.
[57] Interviews, Garland M. Lasater, July 29, 1981, and Tom Lasater, May 6, 1969.
[58] "Predicts Seven Year Shortage of Cattle and High Beef Prices," *Cattleman*, January, 1920, p. 33.
[59] James E. Poole, "Livestock Market Review," *Cattleman*, December, 1920, p. 11.

Lasater shipped one hundred cars of cattle to pastures near Houston due to drought. After some relief in the fall of that year, the country lapsed into a prolonged drought that lasted through all of 1917 and early 1918, when precipitation was 30 percent of normal. "The whole country was a powder keg of dust. There was no grass anywhere. Dad stuck it out for a long time, then decided in order to save his breeding herd he would have to ship his cattle to Oklahoma," Garland Lasater recalled "I remember him shipping carload after carload of cows, calves and bulls. The irony was that no sooner than he had gotten them all loaded, it began to rain."[60]

Sickness and mortality caused by the fever tick had long been a scourge of Texas cattle. Colonel Ike Pryor summarized the situation: "Ask any cattle dealer from Colorado, Kansas, Oklahoma, or the Northwest why South Texas cattle are not desired in those states. If the tick is the only objection, and it is, why not do away with it?" Texas cattlemen were deeply divided over the tick eradication issue, and the cattle raisers association was bitterly criticized for its stand. When laws were passed requiring all cattle to be dipped, many cattlemen refused to comply and rebelled by blowing up the government dipping vats.[61]

Before dipping became mandatory, Ed Lasater decided to clean his ranch of fever ticks. In 1917, he ran an ad in the *Falfurrias Facts* stating: "Experience has proven to me that I cannot under present conditions make money out of a bunch of mother cows infested with ticks, so I have decided to free my country of the tick. This is to advise the public that all traffic through my country will be confined to the public

[60] Interviews, Garland M. Lasater, February 21, 1981; Dennis McBride, July 27, 1981; "Drought Conditions," *Cattleman*, August, 1916, p. 40.

[61] Mary Whatley Clarke, *A Century of Cow Business*, pp. 65–66; Dayton Moses, Jr., "Tick Eradication in Texas," *Cattleman*, March, 1921, pp. 223–25; Dayton Moses, Jr., "Texas Begins Last Fever Tick Drive," *Cattleman*, February, 1922, pp. 15–19. "Texas Fever" was one of the many names applied to the "strange malady" that began plaguing the western livestock industry in the middle of the nineteenth century. "While there were a number of theories, nobody knew what caused the disease or how it spread. The disease seemed to vary at different times of year. . . . Cattle that became infected in the hot summer would develop a high fever, become depressed, lie down or stand off by themselves with ears drooped and back arched; their muzzle would be dry; they had no appetite; constipation at first, followed by diarrhea; rapid respiration and pulse; and bloody urine. . . . Death would usually occur in three to seven days" (Dr. John L. Wilbur, "Historical Data, Texas Animal Health Commission," May, 1978, *Cattleman* files).

roads. . . ."[62] To accomplish this, Ed Lasater double-fenced much of his large ranch, leaving a space which the tick could not cross over from neighboring properties, and then he proceeded to set up a dipping routine for his entire cow herd. Lasater had three cow outfits working full-time while he cleaned up his ranch—one near Realitos, one at Vargas, and one at Encino. All the pastures were paired up, and every eighteen days the cattle from one pasture would be rounded up, dipped, and moved to the other pasture, with the process repeated over and over at eighteen-day intervals. It was a long, time-consuming, and very expensive undertaking.[63]

Lasater's colleague, Ike Pryor, had been involved in the cattle business as long and as heavily as almost any cattleman operating at the end of the First World War. He had weathered the drastic market slump and drought in the decade starting in 1884 and other shorter but still severe price declines. And he knew well that his rancher associates typically operated with an excessive amount of short-term debt. Pryor said that cattlemen were "the greatest borrowers on earth—no men can borrow more, and I have known them to borrow $30 on a $20 steer. You cannot get that much out of a $20 gold piece."[64]

Although Pryor was not speaking specifically of Lasater, Lasater had certainly positioned himself as a leader among his peers in terms of his ability and willingness to use large amounts of borrowed capital. But Lasater never had enough credit to be satisfied, and he was continually looking for new sources of capital.

The firm which became H. P. Drought and Company first loaned Ed Lasater money in 1891. Twenty-eight years later Lasater was back in Drought's office in San Antonio to visit about a new loan. H. P. Drought, whose lavish praise for Lasater covered a six-page memorandum to William Mackenzie in 1901, was still very positive about the South Texas rancher when he wrote Henry James in Scotland about Lasater's new loan application in March, 1919. Drought wrote that

---

[62] *Falfurrias Facts*, July 23, 1917.

[63] Interview, Tom Lasater, January 12, 1980. It took Texas thirty years to clean up the ticks. The most active year was 1919, when the Livestock Sanitary Commission of Texas and the U.S. Bureau of Animal Industry supervised the inspection and dipping of 1,617,267 head of cattle. A total of 4,649 vats were used (Clarke, *A Century of Cow Business*, p. 70).

[64] Ed C. Lasater, "Meat Packer Legislation," p. 47.

Lasater "has very decided opinions of his own, and that you cannot force him to do anything which he does not wish to do, so there is not any use of our trying to argue him into making this loan." Drought was anxious to transact the deal with Lasater and tried to convey to his Scottish associates the necessity of making their best offer in the first proposal to Lasater: "In answering us, please bear in mind that there will be no comeback from Mr. Lasater, so we wish to get before him our best proposition."[65]

As Lasater approached his sixtieth birthday, Drought recognized Lasater's mortality: "In addition, we believe that the energy of Mr. Lasater is necessary for the carrying out of the proposition as outlined by him; that we cannot expect without Mr. Lasater that these lands will sell at the prices placed on them by him." But Drought was confident nevertheless that the Lasater loan was a good one: "We think, however, that we can assume in the event of a mishap to Mr. Lasater that this proposition will continue as a growing concern."[66]

The banker who had written so effusively about Lasater several decades earlier remained extravagant in his description. After the new loan to Lasater was transacted in May, 1919, Drought wrote in a memorandum: "Mr. Lasater, aside from his ability of handling successfully the farm and improvements above mentioned, is one of the best informed stockmen in Texas. In fact, we believe he is about the only stockman in Texas who can tell the cost per head of producing, maturing and delivering cattle to market. He is an enterprising, energetic man and withal he is a man of good judgment."[67]

A year after concluding the new loan with H. P. Drought, Lasater was off to Saint Louis to discuss a new credit line with that city's National Bank of Commerce. He carried along letters from two San Antonio bankers and from one in Illinois with whom he had dealt for twelve years. Wirt Wright, of the National Stockyards National Bank, wrote: "His name in the livestock industry in that state is a synonym for efficiency and successful operation."[68] J. O. Terrell, who had written so enthusiastically about the Falfurrias Jersey Dairy Company in 1911,

[65] H. P. Drought to Henry James, Alliance Trust Co., Ltd., Loan Records, March 8, 1919, Drought Files, in possession of Thomas Drought, San Antonio.

[66] Ibid.

[67] H. P. Drought, memo to the Alliance Trust, May 7, 1919, Drought Files.

[68] Wirt Wright, To Whom It May Concern, May 16, 1921, Lasater Files.

called Lasater: "one of the most successful and best known business-men in Texas," adding, "A recent audit of his books shows a net worth of about $3,000,000, but his lands were entered therein so far below their valuation, in my judgment, that I consider $4,000,000 a reasonable estimate."[69]

Although he turned down the purchase offer he received during the war, within a short time after the war Lasater had evidently initiated a plan to sell part of his ranchland and to reduce his debt. O. M. Corwin, vice-president of the Wells-Dickey Company of Minneapolis, wrote to Lasater in April, 1919, "You are still carrying a heavy load in the way of indebtedness, but if your plan is consummated of disposing of that part of your ranch which you wish to and converting part of the cattle into cash, your indebteness should be reduced to a point where from this time on you should have no trouble in actually decreasing it."[70]

Corwin added that Lasater was at a turning point and that it appeared that as he sold property he could begin to pay down his debts and to commence "the more intensive development of the proposition which you hope to keep intact."[71] Lasater made the first concrete move along these lines when he sold twenty thousand acres out of the south-eastern part of his ranch to John Ball in June, 1919.[72]

Corwin applauded Lasater's new direction, not only because of financial considerations, but because of his opinion of the South Texas rancher: "I consider you one of the real men of the country; a man with a vision and a purpose in life beyond the accumulation of money for selfish purposes."[73] Corwin later expanded on this statement: "You are the type of man who . . . could devote his time to a public service, which I believe would be even more valuable than for you to leave a heritage to the State of Texas of the best herd of beef or dairy cattle."[74]

In August, 1921, Corwin wrote Lasater again, after Lasater had secured some additional interim financing. Once more he expressed approval of Lasater's partial liquidation and debt-reduction program: "I

[69] J. O. Terrell, To Whom It May Concern, May 17, 1920, Lasater Files.

[70] O. M. Corwin to Ed C. Lasater, April 15, 1919, Scrapbook #4, Lasater Files.

[71] Ibid.

[72] Deed Records, Brooks County, vol. VII, p. 598.

[73] O. M. Corwin to Ed C. Lasater, April 15, 1919, Lasater Files.

[74] O. M. Corwin to Ed C. Lasater, August 6, 1921, Scrapbook #4, Lasater Files.

hope you will not permit anything to interfere with your program of selling out. This financing will assist you in tiding over a time which would be greatly to your disadvantage if you had to sell . . . but during the next year or two there ought to be possibilities which would permit you to liquidate and save a good, comfortable fortune for yourself and your family."[75]

Corwin's hopeful words in 1921 represented wishful thinking. Corwin's company was Lasater's largest single creditor, and Corwin was well aware of conditions in the livestock industry. Cattlemen had experienced a price crisis in the fall of 1919 and then a partial recovery in 1920. In September, 1920, new price declines contributed to a panic that forced prices down nearly 33 percent by the end of the year. All prior records for receipts at the Chicago Stock Yards were broken in November: "As livestock prices fell, it became unprofitable for cattle feeders in the Corn Belt to continue operations, and the market for feeder cattle from western ranges disappeared, so that immature stock and even breeding stock found outlet only in the packing houses at distressed prices."[76] Lasater's colleague, Ike Pryor, described the situation that confronted western cattlemen: "In 1920, cattle began to decline in price, and by 1921 they had lost as much or more in value than they had gained in the previous eight or ten years. . . ."[77]

At the end of 1922, Lasater's ranching and farming lands totaled approximately 280,000 acres. Lasater's balance sheet showed over 10,000 head of cattle, including 8,700 brood cows. In addition to his beef cattle ranch, Lasater operated three other major businesses and was involved in a number of minor ones.[78] The 1920 sales of his four largest enterprises were: Falfurrias Mercantile Company, $627,293; ranch (sale of livestock), $521,455; Falfurrias Creamery Company, $373,785; farm (cotton and cottonseed), $101,300.[79]

[75] Ibid.

[76] Shideler, *Farm Crisis*, pp. 47–48.

[77] Ike T. Pryor, "The Past, Present, and Future of the Cattle Industry of the United States," *Cattleman*, December, 1924, p. 15.

[78] Ernst and Ernst, "Audit Report," pp. 5, 19. The livestock inventory also included 761 horses and 565 mules (Ibid.).

[79] Everett Lloyd, "Ed C. Lasater: The World's Jersey King and His 300,000 Acre Kingdom," *National Magazine*, February, 1920. Ed Lasater had a number of small businesses that were a drain on his time and resources. One example was the Falfurrias Power Company, which operated the town's electric plant, ice plant, water plant, and a

Although these were distinct undertakings, all of them either directly or indirectly were subject to the market movement of agricultural commodities, which all experienced sharp declines in the postwar years. As the agricultural economy worsened between 1919 and 1923, Lasater's various operations produced heavy losses. His net operating loss for 1921 was $205,000. The loss the following year was $165,000.[80]

Lasater's real estate mortgages on December 30, 1922, totaled $1,277,000, payable to the Wells-Dickey Co. ($487,000), the San Antonio Loan and Trust Co. ($443,000), the Commerce Trust Company of Kansas City ($247,000), and H. P. Drought and Co. ($100,000). In addition, he had short-term notes payable to the Central Trust Co. ($255,000) and the National Cattle Loan Company ($210,000) and lesser sums owed to the Gross National Bank, the Federal Land Bank of Houston, and the Austin National Bank.[81]

That debt load would have constituted an enormous burden for an agricultural enterprise to carry in a favorable economic environment. During the extended postwar decline, it compounded Lasater's difficulties. He paid nearly $200,000 in interest charges in 1922, and at year's end his financial statements showed an additional balance of $93,000 in accrued interest payable.[82]

Lasater's bankers just after the war had still been willing to write enthusiastic letters related to their client's character, and the earning capacity of his holdings. But by late 1922, Lasater's operating losses combined with his enormous debt load had undoubtedly sown an element of doubt and concern in the minds of those bankers who had only recently been willing to grant him new credit as well as extensions on old lines. O. M. Corwin's 1921 letter contained some of the highest praise and most flattering comments ever written about Lasater. But by

---

cotton gin. Lasater sold the business in 1911 to G. W. Smith from Brownsville. Smith ran into financial difficulties and could not make his payments. This caused Lasater to take the business back over in 1911 and to be involved in an expensive and time-consuming series of lawsuits which stretched over five years. Finally, in 1921, Lasater sold the business to William B. Gardner and Carl F. Wagenschein. Wagenschein, a native of DeWitt County, had gone to work for the power company in 1913 (Ed C. Lasater v. Magnolia Petroleum Company et al., pp. 1–3, 58, 527–29; interview, Dr. Miriam Wagenschein, March 3, 1982).

[80] Ernst and Ernst, "Audit Report," pp. 7, 12.
[81] Ibid., pp. 4, 25, 26, 30.
[82] Ibid., p. 30.

the end of the following year, Corwin had joined the ranks of his worried colleagues whose portfolios were bulging with large and delinquent loans to ranchers and farmers. The Minneapolis banker was no longer writing letters of praise, but was spending an increasing amount of time scrutinizing the deteriorating value of his firm's collateral located many miles away between the Nueces and the Rio Grande.

CHAPTER 11

Ranch Brats and Shetland Ponies

He told Mama: "You just wait until I have a house of my own. I will have twelve rooms in the house and twelve dogs in each room."

—Ada Lasater Caldwell

THE end of the railroad's homeseeker rates combined with publicity about Texas hurricanes and bandit raids on the border dealt a lethal blow to the Falfurrias land promotion business, from the beginning a slow-moving and marginally profitable operation. As activity in the real estate area came to a halt, Lasater's erstwhile partners, Rob and L. D. Miller, began casting about for another business to enter.

The Millers had earlier made a loan to a man who put up some Oklahoma real estate as collateral. When the loan went sour and the Millers went to Oklahoma to foreclose on the property, they became interested in the oil business. Their first forays yielded few results, but the Miller brothers "played it right down to their last dime."[1] Living in Saint Louis, the brothers maintained an apartment in Okmulgee, Oklahoma, equipped with all the amenities, including a butler. Older brother Rob was a flamboyant plunger, a high liver, and a big party giver, and the Miller apartment in Okmulgee was a center of activity. Just as the Millers exhausted their capital completely, their luck changed: they hit a strike on a forty-acre oil lease they held on the edge of what became a major field. In a short time in the early 1920s that lease produced some $300,000 in income for the brothers. By the standards of the day, L. D. Miller in his early thirties and his brother Rob were wealthy men.[2]

---

[1] Interviews, John C. Miller, June 30, 1981, L. D. Miller, Jr., July 2, 1981, and Gardner Miller, July 22, 1981.

[2] Interview, Gardner Miller, July 22, 1981.

Two decades earlier, Ed Lasater had executed the first oil lease on his ranch, the same year that Spindletop had burst onto the nation's consciousness. Drilling at Spindletop near Beaumont in 1901 produced a gusher that flowed thousands of barrels of oil before the well could be capped. That find, the first salt-dome oil discovery, created a world-wide sensation and inaugurated an era that would radically alter Texas' heretofore pastoral and agricultural economy and life-style.[3]

Sixty days after Spindletop, Lasater signed an oil and gas lease with the J. M. Guffey Co. of Pittsburgh. The Pennsylvania company leased from Lasater for the sole purpose of mining and operating for oil and gas "all the lands owned by him in Hidalgo, Starr, Nueces and Du-val Counties, known as Falfurrias Ranch, containing about 220,000 acres extending from Realitos, a station on the Texas-Mexican Railroad, to a pasture called 'Finados' in Hidalgo County belonging to the Kenedy Pasture Company."[4]

In June of 1901, J. J. Allen, a Lasater foreman, was reported to be in Alice "looking as hearty as ever . . . but showing signs of succumbing to oil fever." Allen, as well as his boss, may have been touched by that exotic disease, but they subsequently had plenty of time to recover from its initial effects. The first lease produced nothing, and subsequent drilling in 1908 and 1913 to the south and southeast of Falfurrias yielded no commercial mineral finds, notwithstanding the local presence of such firms as the Starr Petroleum Company and the Texas Geyser Oil Company. In 1915, Lasater leased the forty-four thousand acres of his dairy lands to another Pennsylvania company, but once again the exploration produced no results.[5]

In the two decades after Lasater negotiated his first oil lease, several of his ranching colleagues learned that their grazing lands sat atop giant pools of oil. A water-well drilling outfit on the Waggoner ranch hit oil and brought in a major field in 1903, and the Waggoner refinery was built in 1911. Another big find was on the Burkburnett property in

[3] *Texas Almanac and State Industrial Guide*, 1970–71, p. 426.

[4] Transcribed Deed Records from Starr County, Brooks County, vol. V, p. 661; Mildred Seaton, "Abstract of Land Owned by Ed C. Lasater in Grant of Los Olmos y Loma Blanca," Corpus Christi, 1904, p. 15.

[5] *Alice Echo*, June 27, 1901; Lloyd N. Dyer, "The History of Brooks County" (M.S. thesis, Texas College of Arts and Industries, 1938, p. 33); Deed Records, Brooks County, vol. III, p. 571; "The Land of Heart's Delight," *The Inch*, p. 5.

Wichita County in 1919. Al McFaddin, Lasater's fellow Brahman enthusiast, left his Victoria County ranch long enough to make a fortune as
an early operator in the Beaumont oil field.[6]

At the time the Miller brothers made their Oklahoma strike and
moved to Okmulgee to pursue their oil interests full time, oil firms
were still searching for their first discovery on the Falfurrias Ranch.
After years of anticipation, a drilling supervisor sent word that the
prospects for a Lasater ranch well looked particularly good and the
company expected a major find. Lasater took his son Garland out west
of the headquarters to watch the activity and to savor the exciting moment. As Lasater and his teenage son sat in the shade of a mesquite
tree waiting for the well to come in, Lasater was making plans for the
future and he assured his son: "This will take care of my indebtedness."[7] But he was jumping to conclusions. No such easy and simple
solution materialized, and the dry hole drilled that day in a sandy pasture west of La Mota provided him no relief from the growing weight
of his financial obligations.

The oldest Miller brother, Garland, died in 1918. The second
brother, Richard, was the only one to settle permanently in Falfurrias.
He went to work as a young man in the Falfurrias State Bank, which Ed
Lasater founded in 1905. With the increase in capital stock in 1911,
Richard Miller became the largest individual stockholder, and with his
brothers he had a controlling interest in the bank.[8] "Richard Miller was
an aggressive banker and a good businessman," one early associate recalled. Richard Miller was a ladies' man with an eye for the new school
teachers who would periodically alight from the train at the end of the
line, and, like his brothers Garland and Rob, he was a heavy drinker.[9]

To all the Miller brothers, Mary Lasater was "Sister." L. D. Miller
said: "She was our only sister, and we all worshipped her. We were all

---

[6] *Texas Almanac*, p. 426; Mary Whatley Clarke, *A Century of Cow Business*, Mary
Whatley Clarke, "Ed C. Lasater, Ninth President of Association, Was a Creative Thinker
and Doer," p. 81; *Cattleman*, February, 1952, p. 20.

[7] Interview, Garland M. Lasater, February 21, 1981.

[8] "Amendment to the charter of the Falfurrias State Bank," Texas Secretary of
State, November 10, 1911.

[9] Interviews, Walter Blumer, July 12, 1981, Leslie Holbrook Gammie and Martine
Holbrook, July 25, 1981, and Mrs. T. R. Bennett, July 31, 1981.

extremely devoted to her." The youngest Miller brother was grateful to Sister for her effort to help Richard deal with his alcohol problem. For a period of time, Richard rode horseback every day from the Miller Farm, Loma Bonita, to La Mota for an early morning meditation session with Sister before going to the bank. L. D. Miller credited his sister with extending their brother's life.[10]

Mary Miller had little involvement with the life of the town her husband founded two years after their marriage. She lived on the ranch and was fully occupied there, maintaining an attractive home for Ed Lasater and raising the five children she bore him in his second family: Albert (b. 1903), Mary (b. 1904), Garland (b. 1907), Lois (b. 1908), and Tom (b. 1911).

Mary Lasater was a reserved person and highly structured in her personal relationships. Some of the townspeople who saw her only occasionally when Hilario García drove her to town in an enclosed black carriage thought she "put on airs." But others saw through her stiff formality and appreciated her warmth and concern. One early Falfurrias resident commented, "I will always remember with so much joy Mary Lasater's nice courtesies and attentions to me, a scared little bride." Mary Lasater would send a ranch hand into town with a leg of lamb or some venison, and when she came into her husband's office she would frequently bring his accountant's wife a book. "I remember one beautifully bound volume, *The Flight of the Swan*, the autobiography of a dancer which I thoroughly enjoyed."[11]

Mary Lasater loved music and the cultural activities of the urban setting where she had grown up. During Ed Lasater's long workdays and during his frequent absences from the ranch, she kept herself occupied with books and music. She was particularly fond of Beethoven, Mozart, and Chopin: "She had everything Beethoven ever composed." She read poetry and novels and was continually ordering new books. John Bennett, the brother of Lasater's first wife, said that his sister Patti, who lived most of her married life in Corpus Christi, and Mary Lasater, had they known each other, would have been friends. "They

[10] Interviews, L. D. Miller, Sr., September 22, 1971, and Gardner Miller, July 22, 1981.

[11] Interviews, Mrs. T. R. Bennett, July 31, 1981, and Florence Schuetz, April 9, 1981.

had a similar way of thinking. Both of them were cultured women. Mary Miller really loved the ranch more than Patti did. Mary maintained a very complete home on the ranch. She developed it and made it attractive. She loved La Mota."[12]

Mary Lasater enjoyed life on the Falfurrias Ranch, but her closest friends were in San Antonio, where she, her university friend, Jamie Armstrong, who married John Bennett, and Amanda Cartwright Taylor formed an inseparable trio and maintained a close lifelong friendship. With them she enjoyed attending recitals and reading club meetings whenever she was in San Antonio, and through "Mant" Taylor she met Emily Edwards, a young artist and teacher.[13] Mary Lasater and Emily Edwards quickly became good friends, and soon after they met in 1922 Emily made the first of many extended visits to La Mota. She found Mary Lasater to be a highly spiritual person, despite the fact that she did not attend church: "Her spiritual nature was apparent in her daily life. Although I grew up in a convent where the sisters were praying openly all day long, I have never known anyone who more truly prayed in each act of her life." For Mary Lasater, religion was open and living, and she could not place it within the confines of a particular denomination or church congregation.[14]

Meditation was a daily practice for Mary Lasater. When visiting, Emily Edwards would join her on the long porch of the ranch house, where they would sit in silence, holding in common some spoken thought such as "Divine love is here." At times they were joined by others, like Willie Best, the black cook who became a valued family friend. Emily remembered that "the experience was a very powerful one. It was a time of openness and receptivity, with a strong current running through us."[15]

Mary Gardner Miller had been a spiritualist, and Mary Lasater carried on the tradition after her mother's death. In addition to her regular meditation, Mary Lasater held seances with different people

---

[12] Interviews, John M. Bennett, February 26, 1967, Tom Lasater, July 17, 1969, and Carolyn Kampmann Lasater, March 29, 1982.

[13] Interviews, John M. Bennett, Jr., July 24, 1981, and Emily Edwards, February 25, 1967.

[14] Interview, Emily Edwards February 25, 1967.

[15] Ibid.

on a number of occasions. T. S. Proctor's oldest daughter died at an early age several years after a fall down the stairs in the Falfurrias schoolhouse. Sarah Proctor and her younger daughter went to La Mota for sessions with Mary Lasater in an attempt to make contact with the deceased daughter.[16]

Emily Edwards recalled being with Mary Lasater at La Mota after a mutual friend's death, when they experienced the friend's presence: "I can't say exactly that we saw her, but we felt very strongly that she was with us. I remember Mary Lasater's radiance at the time. The same radiance I have seen about her when she found something she felt to be true and beautiful." On another occasion, Emily was at Falfurrias when she received word of a relative's death. While sitting with Mary Lasater, she thought the relative seemed to be present: "Then to my amazement, Mary Lasater's hand was in violent action. Out of control. She asked me for paper and pencil. I brought these. The hand movement became very violent and wild, and I substituted larger sheets, at her request. The motion involving the whole arm was meaningless. This may have lasted for a minute or more. She felt perfectly exhausted when it was over."[17]

To some of the local townspeople, Mary Lasater was excessively reserved, even standoffish. But Emily Edwards saw the rancher's wife in a different light: "I never felt closer to any person or had a better or truer friend. She had a real sense of the value of each day and of each personal contact. Her tolerance was great, and she was slow to condemn. She was a true mystic. A person who had a concern for others and who had an extra sense about what was happening." On numerous occasions, Mary Lasater wrote or made contact with friends who she knew—without being told—were ill or in need of help.[18]

Mary Lasater did not have neutral relationships with people: "All her friends were more interesting and more spiritually alive as a result of their contact with her. She brought each of them something important. There was an intensity of living about her that was contagious." Music and ideas were essential to her, and sharing her interest was equally important. She was always eager to bring culture to Falfurrias;

[16] Ibid.; interview, Louella Proctor Hauser, April 7, 1981.

[17] Interview, Emily Edwards, February 25, 1967.

[18] Ibid.; Interviews, Mary Casey Lasater, August 17, 1976, and Carolyn Kampmann Lasater, March 24, 1982.

on a number of occasions, she organized recitals and talks by out-of-town guests to which she invited her local friends.[19]

Despite Mary Lasater's unusual sensitivity in other areas, it took Emily Edwards to help her appreciate some of the things which surrounded her on the Falfurrias Ranch. Emily and Mary joined Ed Lasater for a buggy ride out across the ranch. Lasater stopped in a pasture with a herd of Brahman cattle: "We walked right out among these huge and stately animals. They were so impressive, and they seemed so unaware of us that I could hardly believe it. When we got back to the house, she told me that I had made her see them as beautiful, as if she hadn't seen them that way before."[20]

John Bennett, the San Antonio banker, viewed the lady from La Mota from a different angle. "We were of the opinion that Mary was an idealist. She was a very high-minded person . . . dreaming about the perfect life, the perfect existence for everybody," Bennett recalled. "She was altruistic, a great believer in justice. She was slightly socialistic in her point of view. She believed that the greatest good would come by developing people and by giving advantages to people who were submerged."[21]

Mary Lasater's views of society were not entirely out of keeping with the mood of the times even in the frontier environment of Texas. For George Brackenridge, Bennett's banking colleague who for many years was also Ed Lasater's financial mentor, "business was a side issue . . . apart from the world in which he really lived." During the years in which the former Union colonel accumulated his large fortune, he "read thoughtfully the communistic philosophers of his era, especially Henry George, and found stimulation in the company of Dr. Ferdinand Herff and Gustave Schleicher, who had migrated to Texas with the unsuccessful communistic colony of Bettina."[22]

Mary Miller and Ed Lasater formed a close relationship, despite very different personalities. She was more detail-conscious and more of a manager, more systematic in her approach to life. Ed Lasater was a hard-driving plunger, an energetic son of the South Texas frontier.

[19] Interviews, Emily Edwards, February 25, 1967, and A. Alonzo Cosby, Jr., July 5, 1981.

[20] Interview, Emily Edwards, February 25, 1967.

[21] Interview, John M. Bennett, February 26, 1967.

[22] Marilyn McAdams Sibley, *George W. Brackenridge: Maverick Philanthropist*, p. 8.

Mary Miller's nature and outlook were shaped by culture and refinement, to the extent those terms could be applied to Texas towns and cities at the turn of the century.[23]

Ed Lasater did not share his wife's love of music, and as he pursued his varied activities he did not have time to read the books she enjoyed or to meditate with her. "He was extremely dynamic. He was in constant motion. He never sat down except to eat. Riding around the ranch with him could be terrifying. He didn't use the roads at all. He went directly to what he wanted to see," Emily Edwards said. John Bennett's son recalled that Ed Lasater approached many activities and subjects with energy and gusto: "Whether he was talking about pure-bred cattle, a new cross that would produce a better variety of mule, or any other topic, he was intensely enthusiastic. His commanding blue eyes sparkled and crackled when he spoke of a subject that interested him." One subject he expounded on eloquently on more than one occasion while carving at the head of the table was the rare eating qualities of the Dorsett lambs that he raised specifically for the mealtime enjoyment of his family and friends.[24]

Mary Lasater's religious beliefs, her spiritual nature, her music, and her books sustained her during long periods when she was alone except for her children on an isolated ranch. But physically she was frail, and she suffered from a variety of ailments, especially from frequent severe headaches and from stomach problems. In 1916 when her condition became acute, her Texas doctor advised an operation. At the suggestion of her brothers, she went to Saint Louis to consult a noted surgeon, Dr. George Gellhorn.[25]

Because of her delicate state of health, the contemplated operation was considered risky. One day while she was at the clinic, Dr. Gellhorn returned from a consultation with other doctors. He looked distraught. Suddenly he grabbed a book and opened it to a certain page, saying: "You don't need an operation. This is what you need." The

[23] Interviews, Emily Edwards, February 25, 1967, Tom Lasater, July 17, 1969, and G. M. Lasater, February 21, 1981.

[24] Interviews, G. M. Lasater, February 21, 1981, and John M. Bennett, Jr., July 24, 1981.

[25] Interviews, Sarah Caldwell, June 26, 1971, Tom Lasater, March 10, 1978, and G. M. Lasater, July 29, 1981.

book was a translation of Euripides, and he read her the concluding lines from a chorus: "To stand from fear set free/to breathe and wait/to hold a hand uplifted over hate/and shall not loveliness be love forever." Dr. Gellhorn's diagnosis proved to be correct, and she recovered without an operation.[26]

Growing up on a large ranch in a relatively unsettled part of Texas in the early years of the twentieth century meant ponies, Great Danes, cart races, picnics to the bottomless pit (a favorite swimming spot in the Laguna de Loma Blanca, by then called Salt Lake), and brush country round-ups followed by evenings of storytelling in cow camp. On the Falfurrias Ranch, it also meant tutors, violin lessons, and donning white shirts and black shoes to have tea with Mary Miller.

Ed Lasater was busy managing his far-flung affairs, arranging his financing, and participating in livestock-industry matters around the country during the years when the children from his second family were growing up. He was fifty years old when his youngest son was born in early 1911, the same year that he succeeded in separating his ranchlands and the surrounding territory from Manuel Guerra's fiefdom in Starr County. That was also the year his colleagues elected him president of the Cattle Raisers Association of Texas, which later became the Texas and Southwestern Cattle Raisers Association. He had little time to spend with his children, but when he did his offspring remember him as a generous and loving father, who romped with them on the lawn when they were small and kept them supplied with dozens of Shetland ponies as well as with a wide assortment of dogs. "I wouldn't say he was an indulgent father, exactly, but he tried to show his concern and interest."[27] Lasater took his children along on outings whenever he could. That meant periodic trips to Realitos when he went to check his cattle or work with Peter McBride. There the Lasater children, whose ages corresponded to those of Peter McBride's five youngest offspring, would play ball with their contemporaries. John Bennett remembered that Lasater had an easy, relaxed communication with his children, but he was a serious man and a busy one. "In those days, a father was a parent at all times; they were not pals." Son Gar-

[26] Interview, Emily Edwards, February 25, 1967.
[27] Interview, G. M. Lasater, February 21, 1981.

land remembers that they were included in trips when possible: "He'd take us to cow camp and when we were small he would detail a cowboy to lead us around. He didn't neglect us."[28]

But Ed Lasater's diverse affairs and many commitments kept him frequently out of town; when he was at home, he left La Mota before daylight and returned late in the evening. As a result, Lasater almost always deferred to his wife as chief of staff in all matters related to the children. And although Mary Lasater was very mild and gentle in the directions she gave to her children and their visiting friends, she also had very strong and specific ideas related to their overall upbringing and experience.[29]

John and Jamie Bennett's children were frequent visitors at the ranch during the 1920s, and the close friendship of the parents continued on to the next generation. John Bennett, Jr., remembered Mary Lasater as remarkable in her willingness to let this large group of young children roam around the ranch with very little interference: "These frontier women were different. They did not worry about the trivial things. They assumed everyone knew what a rattlesnake was."[30]

Mary Lasater gave only "mild instructions." As the youngsters would depart for some point on the ranch, she would caution them and bid them good-bye with an understated "hope you make it." Ed Lasater equipped all his children with Shetland ponies, which the children rode and also used as teams. "We hooked up teams of four ponies to old wagons and buggies and would go flying out across the countryside. Bridles would break and harnesses would come apart. We had frequent runaways. Why none of us got killed, we will never know." A riding accident on the neighboring ranch—when a horse fell in a hole and rolled over John Armstrong, killing him—led to more specific cautions to the children: "Whenever we were thrown from a horse, we would keep rolling after hitting the ground."[31]

His young companions admired Garland Lasater's navigational ability as they rode around through mile after mile of mesquite brush and live oak groves, across prairies and sand dunes. Garland was also

[28] Ibid., Interviews, John M. Bennett, Jr., July 24, 1981, and Bird McBride Victor, March 5, 1982.

[29] Interview, John M. Bennett, February 25, 1967.

[30] Interview, John M. Bennett, Jr., July 24, 1981.

[31] Ibid.

the daredevil and led the team of willing participants through a series of escapades, horse and buggy races, and home-grown rodeos. A windmill, a water tower, and a dirt holding pond sat behind the house at La Mota. The older children would entice the younger ones up the ladder to a high tower, which included a second shorter ladder that protruded out around a narrow platform with no railing. Once on top, the older members of the group would sneak around the tower in an effort to surprise their young cohorts with a sudden "Boo!"

After that ritual, it was time for a swim. A wire ran from the windmill across the large earthen tank to the other side. Garland rigged up a pulley and crossbar on the wire so that the youngsters could climb up and descend at high speeds from the top of the mill into the cool water below: "We later marveled at Mrs. Lasater, who either didn't see us, didn't hear us or looked the other way."[32]

Richard Miller's son, whose mother died when he was an infant, spent a lot of time on the ranch with the Bennetts and the Lasaters and often served as foil in the activities and pranks of that robust and rowdy crowd. In one race, John Bennett and Tom Lasater were mounted on fast horses, with cousin Richard on a fat, slow pony. Lois Lasater and Mollie and Josephine Bennett were in a cart at the finish line to start the race and to name the winner. As the race began, John and Tom spurred their horses, which started pitching and ran off in opposite directions. Richard's pony galloped slowly to the finish line, an easy winner. But in the commotion caused by the girls' yelling and cheering, the pony would not cross the line, and Richard had to dismount and push his steed across to victory.[33]

On another occasion, John Bennett, the Lasater boys, and Richard Miller piled into a cart drawn by four ponies and started out across a brushy pasture. Somehow the reins were dropped and the horses took off, out of control. As the ponies bolted off through the brush, all but cousin Richard jumped to safety. Richard crouched down between the seats, holding on tightly to the seat back in front of him. The cart careened off through the mesquite trees, and by the time the team got hung up in brush "all the hide had been peeled off Richard's knuckles and the back of his hand."[34]

[32] Ibid.
[33] Ibid.
[34] Ibid.; interview, G. M. Lasater, July 24, 1981.

One of the most enjoyable experiences for the boys when they were old enough was to join the cow outfit at Vargas, where Jim Mc-Bride, a son of Peter McBride, was foreman. McBride's youngest son Dennis was the same age as Tom Lasater, and together they would take their bedrolls and stay out in the cow camp for a week or two at a time. Jim McBride, who later ran Lasater's Encino division, was a young and very capable cowman. Like Lasater he was a serious man, not a story-teller or pal, but he was very tolerant of the boys and their friends, who liked nothing better than to join his outfit.[35]

John Bennett joined the Lasater boys on several outings to Vargas. He remembered Ed Lasater's going there to participate in some partic-ular work or to go over plans with Jim McBride. Lasater always showed up in a two-wheel cart drawn by a team, which with its wide, steel-rimmed wheels could negotiate the sand much more successfully than the early cars. "This was his standard means of transportation, and he used it to the fullest," the young Bennett recalled. "I can still picture Mr. Lasater moving rapidly across those pastures, usually with an aide-de-camp in the form of a young Mexican boy who opened the gates and took care of the horses."[36]

Twice a year the whole family would spend a week or ten days camped at Lucero, one of the main headquarters of Lasater's Encino division, which covered the southeastern part of his ranch. There were several small houses where the family, friends, and a Mexican cook would bed down at some distance from the mill and pens where the chuckwagon was parked and the cow camp was set up. For the family, these were great adventures and fun outings. For the cow outfit, the seasonal work represented only another series of long workdays during which they were pushed to the limit by the hectic pace Ed Lasater set.

When the cowboys spent all day working with a herd, they would take turns going to the chuckwagon at lunchtime: "The Mexican cow-boys were great at sign language. One of them could look across a huge herd of bellowing cattle with dust flying and catch another one's eye, make a quick signal, and that man would know that he was supposed to cut out a particular cow or bull or to go to the cow camp to have some lunch.[37]

[35] Interview, G. M. Lasater, July 24, 1981.
[36] Interview, John M. Bennett, Jr., July 24, 1981.
[37] Interview, Tom Lasater, January 12, 1980.

Despite years of working with Mexican cowboys, Ed Lasater never mastered their ability to communicate with signs. He was very excitable during the heat of the action, but in the noise and confusion of a large herd, even his powerful voice was often inaudible: "He was brutal. When he wanted a particular animal cut out of the herd, he would scream and holler and wave his hat. If a cowboy started to cut out the wrong animal, he would start shouting again." Lasater always had a clear idea of what he wanted accomplished, but trying to follow his instructions was often a matter of trial and error. Two herds might be approaching a corner where two or more gates led into different pastures. Lasater would begin waving his hat and yelling. The only audible word might be *puerta* (gate). The man on the spot would not know which gate or whether it was supposed to be open or shut: "The only solution was to try one thing, and if the yelling continued to try another." [38]

Despite his momentary outbursts, Lasater's temper subsided quickly, and he never belabored any mistakes or indulged in further recriminations. But his eighteen-hour days exhausted all those who worked with him. At the end of one particularly long day, young Tom Lasater was riding with Ray Oberwetter, a Lasater foreman, as they headed back toward the cow camp. Tom bounced along on his Shetland pony alongside the tall and lanky Oberwetter, who rode hunched forward with the brim of his hat pulled down over his forehead. Tom was reliving the highlights of the day's activities and jabbering happily about how much fun it all was. Finally, Oberwetter cocked his head just enough to be able to see Tom out of the corner of his eye and said: "Son, one of these days you may realize that working for the other fellow ain't such fun." [39]

Mary Lasater was content to let her children learn to ride and work, to play their pranks and have their fun as they roamed around the Falfurrias Ranch. But her attitude was not entirely laissez faire in terms of raising her children. And since the ranch with its horses and cattle and its cowboys were what surrounded them day in and day out, she worked constantly to educate them about other aspects of life, to give them an appreciation of literature and music, and she was determined to make her offspring aware of the world that lay beyond the sandy pastures surrounding the Loma Blanca.

[38] Ibid.; interview, John M. Bennett, Jr., July 24, 1981.
[39] Interview, Tom Lasater, January 12, 1980.

Ed Lasater responded to his wife's views on raising children by building the "playhouse," which was designed by the same English architect who had drawn the plans for the county courthouse. It was similar to an English thatched cottage and had a study room, a kitchen, a music room equipped with a player piano, a record player, and a fine collection of classical music. The playhouse was a schoolroom during the several years when tutors taught the children on the ranch, and there Mary Lasater had tea with her children individually. At the appointed hour, each child would appear in a white shirt, black shorts, black socks, and black shoes to join their mother, who instructed them how to hold a teacup and how to enunciate properly as they carried on polite conversation.[40]

Mary Lasater did not want her children to be "South Texas ranch brats." She wanted them to have broad experience outside their rural environment. To accomplish this, she took her children to Saint Louis, Washington, New York, and San Antonio for extended stays, and she was instrumental in sending her offspring east to summer camps and then later to prep schools and colleges. Mary Lasater had once expressed an interest in having a home in San Antonio, and Ed Lasater recognized his wife's need for more contact with her city friends and with the social and cultural life which she missed on the ranch. He located a residence at 118 East Summit Avenue in San Antonio, and on their next trip to the city, Lasater took his wife to the house near the head of Main Avenue and said simply, "Here it is."[41]

One of the earliest outings away from the ranch was to Saint Louis during the summer of 1916, when Mary Lasater spent several weeks in that city consulting with doctors about her health problems. She considered it essential that her children be exposed to city life and the summer spent in the Buckingham Hotel in Saint Louis was the first of several attempts to give them the needed urban exposure. The Lasater children returned to the ranch from Saint Louis with two visions of city life that had made a lasting impression. The fire station sat directly across the street from their apartment. Each time the fire bell rang, the enormous Clydesdale teams drawing the fire trucks would emerge: "They would come out running wide open. As they turned to the right

---

[40] Ibid.; Interview, Carolyn Lasater, March 24, 1982.

[41] Interviews, Tom Lasater, July 17, 1967, and Emily Edwards, February 25, 1967.

or left, the horses would claw the pavement with their huge rubber shoes. They would come out going a million miles an hour. Every time we would hear the bell, we would run to the window to watch. We were fascinated. It was just terrific."[42]

The other memorable Saint Louis experience involved the hotel elevator. Albert and Garland, the oldest sons, would open the door after the elevator had descended and would crawl around to the opposite side of the wire cage inside the elevator shaft. Then it was a contest to see which one would stay there the longest after the elevator started back up. Lois and Tom stood by watching this oft-repeated stunt with horrified delight: "As the elevator would start up to our floor, Albert and Garland would begin scrambling around the cage toward the door. Lois and I would stand there screaming, crying, hollering. It was wild."[43]

When Ed Lasater went to the capital to join the Food Administration in 1917, his wife and children went, too, moving into a rented house at 1616 Twenty-Second Street N.W. The Lasater children got their first taste of big-city private schools during that year spent in Washington. They also discovered a sword inside a cane which had belonged to an old sea captain whose wife owned the house they rented, met President Taft's widow, and had occasion to see their father in an uncomfortable and uncommon posture.

The family had gone for a Sunday drive to see the sights around Washington. On one particular road they met a large contingent of troops and were forced to pull over to wait. Ed Lasater grew impatient while the troops were marching by, and spying railroad tracks alongside the highway, he instructed the chauffeur to pull onto the tracks and drive around the marching troops. When they had gotten about halfway past the company, a train came speeding toward them. The chauffeur pulled abruptly off the tracks into the middle of the formation, with soldiers bouncing off the hood and fenders in all directions. The commanding officer halted his men and walked over to the Lasater car: "He gave my father hell, called him all sorts of unsightly names. My father sat quietly looking at the floor, which amazed us, because he was always so outspoken, always giving everybody hell himself. When the

[42] Interview, Tom Lasater, November 9, 1980.
[43] Ibid.

officer finished, he said, 'All right, now. Get out of here.' Away we went."[44]

Two years after the Washington experience, Mary Lasater moved her brood east again, this time to the LaSalle Hotel at 33 East 60th Street in New York. There she enrolled her children in the Lincoln School, an experimental institution connected with Columbia University, where a variety of new teaching theories were tried out on the children of prominent New York families.[45] While in New York, Mary Lasater located a violin teacher, a Mr. Simon, and the following year she brought him to Falfurrias, where he spent the winter giving her children violin lessons. Tom proved to be the least musically promising of her offspring. After a winter of instruction, he had mastered only parts of "Old Black Joe" and "Cielito Lindo."[46]

Hilario García was driving a carriage that stopped at a gate in the heavy sand along the road between La Mota and Falfurrias. Mary Lasater, Lois, and Tom sat inside the shining black conveyance. After the carriage had passed through the gate, Hilario spoke to the horses and popped the reins. As the carriage lurched forward, Hilario out of the corner of his eye saw Tom lean out the door, lose his balance, and fall between the high wheels. Knowing that he could not stop the team in time, Hilario jumped from his seat, grabbed the extended axle on the back wheel, and with a burst of strength lifted the wheel high enough that the steel rim left only the faintest imprint as it crossed Tom's shirt.

Mary Lasater jumped out and ran to comfort her youngest son. Frightened by the commotion, the horses bolted and took off toward town at a dead run, with the terrified Lois alone in the carriage. Hilario immediately started out running in pursuit, and in a second display of physical power and stamina, he overtook the carriage, climbed over the top and out onto the tongue between the team, where he retrieved the fallen reins and brought the horses under control.[47]

Hilario García's quick-thinking response and his super-human feats in averting two dangerous accidents endeared him permanently to the Lasater family. But Ed Lasater's life had its share of sad events,

[44] Ibid.
[45] Ibid.
[46] Ibid.; interview, John M. Bennett, Jr., July 24, 1981.
[47] Interviews, Tom Lasater, January 13, 1980, and Julian García, July 25, 1981.

and personal calamity stalked him until he was well past middle age. Not only did he lose his first wife and their three children; on two other occasions tragic events rudely interrupted those endless days of swimming and cart races, of cow camps and Shetland ponies, that filled the blissful years of childhood in the Land of Heart's Delight.

Mary, the Lasater's oldest daughter, got sick in 1908, when she was four years old, and died very suddenly. Her mother later confided to a friend that she blamed herself for her daughter's death because it had happened so quickly that she did not even realize that Mary was seriously ill. The loss of Mary, "a pretty girl with a laugh like the tinkle of a bell," was a severe shock. Ed and Mary Lasater suffered yet again when they lost their oldest son, a bright youngster with a sunny personality, who had reached young manhood before he met his untimely end.[48]

During the fall and winter of 1918–19, between the two years the family spent in Washington and New York, Albert and Garland attended school in Falfurrias. The boys, fifteen and eleven years old, drove to school each day in a Model T Ford with a canvas top. On the way home one afternoon in February, they had reached the entrance gate to the horse pasture at the ranch when the heavy sand caught the front wheels, pulled the car sharply to the right, and flipped it. Garland was thrown clear, but Albert was pinned in the sand beneath the back of the seat. Gasping for breath, he implored his younger brother to get the car off of him. Garland pushed and shoved, but could not budge the automobile. Finally, in desperation, he took off in a run for La Mota, about a mile from the scene of the accident. At the house, Garland collapsed on the front porch after calling for help. Mary Lasater and several others jumped in a car and sped to the gate to assist Albert, but when they arrived, he was already dead.[49]

Ed Lasater was out of town, most likely in Washington, the day the oldest son of his second family was killed. With Albert's passing, Lasater had lost his first five children, born between 1893 and 1904.

Ed Lasater was struggling with increasingly difficult financial problems in the years immediately following Albert's death, but he always looked to the future with confidence. His three youngest offspring sur-

[48] Interview, Emily Edwards, February 25, 1967.

[49] Ibid.; interviews, Sarah Caldwell, June 26, 1971, and G. M. Lasater, April 9, 1981.

vived the perils of childhood in that remote and relatively primitive section of Texas, and Ed Lasater could see the future clearly in his remaining children: a beautiful blond daughter and two energetic sons.

Tom was the youngest son, outgoing, lively, and uninhibited. As a small child he was pampered by his elders, by a series of governesses and tutors, by the employees in the house and around the headquarters, and by his brothers and sister. At an early age he ventured out to watch and to imitate the daring feats of his older brothers. He followed them to the cistern behind the house, where they helped him up the ladder to the rickety platform high above the dirt tank. He watched in awe as they slid down the wire into the cool water below. Tom went with his brothers and sister Lois to the big La Mota dairy barn, where they climbed up into the loft, peered out toward the farm ground at Number Five, or into the verdant foliage of the live oak trees which surrounded the collection of frame houses connected by a rambling series of porches and passageways.

Tom's special pets were a family of bulldogs, a pig which came running when he blew a whistle, and a growing flock of exotic chickens. He giggled with delight the day he made his first ride on a Shetland pony. At first Albert and Garland led his pony in circles around the house, the tank, and the barn. But soon Tom was not happy riding with a lead rope in the hands of his older brothers; he wanted to ride his pony on his own. Later he rode a little mare into Falfurrias every morning to attend school. It took him exactly thirty minutes to travel the four miles from La Mota to the pens behind Ed Lasater's Falfurrias office, where the teams and chuckwagons parked when they came into town for supplies. He left his mare there and ran across South St. Mary's Street to the limestone schoolhouse. At noon he walked back across St. Mary's to have lunch at the Park Hotel.

On Emily Edwards's first visit to Falfurrias, eleven-year-old Tom was waiting on Rice Street with a cart and horse to meet her and escort her to the ranch. As Emily and her towheaded driver headed west across the flat pastureland, she saw an apparition rise up on the northern horizon. It was bluish, and it shimmered like a mirage. She asked Tom excitedly what it was. "Oh, that's just the eucalyptus," Tom replied, disdainful of the artist's enthusiasm and her ignorance of such a prominent landmark.[50]

---

[50] Interview, Emily Edwards, February 25, 1967.

Tom attended first grade at the Potomac School in Washington. The following year he stayed out of school and spent his time roaming around the ranch. As Tom explained it, he was "giving the others a chance to catch up." That early sabbatical may have set a difficult precedent. A few years later, Ed Lasater, in Falfurrias for an evening meeting, confided his concern to his fellow schoolboard member, Neil Rupp: "I've tried everything, but I can't get Tom interested in a darned thing but a Brahman cow."[51]

Tom liked the little mare, which could maintain a smooth gallop for mile after mile, and he enjoyed driving the carts and buggies pulled by teams of ponies. He also learned to drive a car, but after Albert's accident his parents did not encourage his driving. Willie Best, wife of Nathaniel Best, Lasater's chauffeur, who later worked in the Falfurrias Creamery Company, had moved to Falfurrias to work in the Park Hotel before going to work in the Lasater home. Every time she went into town for groceries, Tom went with her, and as soon as they were out of sight of the headquarters, Tom did the driving. Mary Lasater sensed something and one day confronted her cook and asked her why Tom was always so enthusiastic about accompanying her to town. "I don't know," Willie replied. "You ask Tom." No one inquired further about the secret pact between Tom and Willie Best.[52]

Not long afterwards, however, Tom began driving his father on his tours around the ranch. Ed Lasater never learned to drive a car, his one attempt to master the art having resulted in a comic but potentially dangerous incident. Lasater got in a large automobile in front of his office opposite the Baptist church. After his instructor explained everything about the car, Lasater stepped on the accelerator and roared across the street, ramming the side of the church and causing considerable damage to his car and to the Baptists' place of worship.

As Tom drove his father around the ranch, they would start off slowly, but before long Ed Lasater would be moving his hand back and forth saying, "Let it move along, son, let it move along." Then, traveling at a higher speed, they would hit a hole or some other obstacle and Lasater would shout, "Slow this darned thing down!" But before they had gone very much farther, he would again be waving his hand, saying, "Let it move along, son, let it move along."[53]

[51] Interview, Neil Rupp, July 28, 1981.
[52] Interview, Willie Best, April 18, 1981.
[53] Interview, Tom Lasater, November 9, 1980.

On May 6, 1921, Ed Lasater signed a document conveying ownership of fifty Shetland mares, one black paint Shetland stallion, and a black saddlebred stallion named Rex to his son Tom. That sheet of paper symbolized anticipation and optimism.[54] Tom's childish exuberance, his fondness for the big red Brahman-cross cows in the Muertos pasture, and the joy he found riding horseback to Cabeza Blanca, to Katherine (which by then had become Armstrong), and to Copita were not clouded by thoughts of declining markets, massive interest payments, and nervous creditors. Tom saw only the expert horsemanship of the Mexican cowboys and the new green of South Texas prairies after a rain. He heard only the enthusiastic *gritos* echoing through the brush on a roundup and the stories of prowess that were savored time and again in the cow camps af Vargas and Lucero.

Ed Lasater was still strong and confident the year that he signed that bill of sale. The rancher knew the rope was getting short in his financial affairs, but he was still hopeful that industry conditions would improve rapidly enough to alleviate the growing pressure on his business enterprises. Only the Loma Blanca knew that Lasater would soon be signing other instruments, ones that would not represent youth and expectation. Those documents would reflect the relentless march of life; they would track the transition and change produced by the passage of time.

[54] "Bill of Sale," Ed C. Lasater to Tom Lasater, May 6, 1921, Lasater Files, in possession of Garland M. Lasater, Falfurrias.

CHAPTER 12

By the Order of the Judge

Credit supports agriculture like a rope supports a hanged man.

—Louis XIV

In late July, 1923, Ed Lasater boarded a train in San Antonio to return to his ranch. Memories of his earlier life were only fleeting thoughts as the train crossed the rivers and creeks and traversed the South Texas country that he had traveled over so many times during the course of more than six decades. As the train continued south toward Skidmore, he could not get his mind off the events of the last few days.

He had lost his temper in a meeting in Marshall Terrell's office, and he had jumped up, pounding on the table. They could do it, he had shouted at the room full of men. They could go ahead and do it, but they would see for themselves that this was a paying proposition, that these properties would service all the debt and would make a good profit as well. As he reflected on that meeting, the rancher momentarily felt the weight of his years, and he leaned back against the high seat. No, it was just being in San Antonio with all those lawyers and bankers that had worn him down. After a little rest he would feel better.

Later Lasater boarded a second train, which carried him across the Nueces River, through Alice, and on to the end of the line. He thought of his wife Mary; he knew that she would listen quietly while he related these events and that she would be displeased to hear him tell of this outburst. She would tell him that he should have maintained his composure and that he could have persuaded the group to go along with his plans on an amicable basis. Mary Miller was right; he knew that already. But this had happened, and now the die was cast. He would simply have to make the best of the situation. It would all work out. They would see.[1]

A little more than ninety days after Ed Lasater rode that train south, the phone rang in Okmulgee, Oklahoma. L. D. Miller answered it, and as soon as he heard Helen's voice he knew that the bank was in trouble. He listened while his brother Richard's widow related the events that had transpired recently and as she described the series of problems that had reached a climax in the last few days. His sister-in-law needed his help. She asked if he could come at once to Falfurrias.

L. D. Miller was thirty-five in 1923. His brother Garland was dead, Richard had died a year earlier, and Rob had divorced his wife and had moved to Colorado, where his health was failing rapidly. Sister and her husband were embroiled in a financial debacle that had left her distraught. Only a few weeks earlier, L. D. Miller had made a hurried trip to Falfurrias to counsel and console her. When he got there, Mary Lasater told him that she had been in bed crying for two weeks. L. D. and his wife Harriet advanced a substantial amount of money to save some of Sister's property. But the situation was growing more complicated every day, and he knew that he would be called on for further assistance.

Richard Miller died in 1922, and his widow Helen Devine Miller, the largest stockholder in the Falfurrias State Bank, stepped in to run it with John C. Thomas, who had joined the firm in 1908. Whether because of the overall agricultural decline and the rising number of delinquent loans, because of specific errors of management, or because of competitive factors resulting from the founding of a second bank in Falfurrias three years earlier, the Falfurrias State Bank's condition deteriorated steadily during 1923. In the last few weeks the meetings had been nothing more than ongoing discussions about the growing number of delinquencies and about the repeated calls from the bank examiner who made clear his increasing concern with the bank's financial status. On the phone in mid-November, 1923, L. D. Miller listened to his sister-in-law's story. Then he assured her that he would leave immediately.

Falfurrias was dark and quiet when Miller stepped off the train

[1] Interview, Garland M. Lasater, February 21, 1981.

and walked quickly down Rice Street from the depot to the Falfurrias State Bank. There he worked through the night, going over the books and assessing the bank's condition. He concluded a few hours later that the bank was in fact in very serious shape and that something needed to be done immediately. At 3:00 A.M. he called J. R. Scott, Jr., of the First National Bank and asked him to come to the bank for a meeting. Miller told Scott that the state bank had a serious liquidity problem but that its assets were sufficient to cover its liabilities. Miller went over all the details with Scott and explained to him that it was necessary for all concerned to conclude a deal that very night. The only thing Miller did not disclose was the fact that the bank examiners were due to arrive the following morning and that they were expected to close the bank.

For nearly two hours Scott reviewed the books with Miller, and then the two of them agreed on a deal by which the First National Bank would take over the Falfurrias State Bank. Scott assembled his employees to begin the transfer of his bank's records into the imposing structure on East Rice Street that housed the state bank. L. D. Miller walked back to the depot at 5:00 A.M., where he reboarded the same train that had carried him south for the return trip to Skidmore.

No one in Falfurrias except for the bank employees had seen L. D. Miller. When the populace began circulating around town later that morning, the Falfurrias State Bank's sign had been replaced by its former competitor's. When the bank examiners arrived for a final review of the bank's condition, they entered the new offices of the First National Bank. Miller and the Falfurrias State Bank—the bank whose ads proclaimed that it had "grown up with the country"—had vanished in the night.[2]

A Senate Committee report issued in April, 1923, stated: "The condition of agriculture has been steadily growing worse since 1920. At first the situation was regarded as a local and temporary one, curable

---

[2] Interview, Gardner B. Miller, July 18 and July 22, 1981; "Lot Eleven, Block Eleven, Falfurrias Farm and Garden Tracts," Brooks County Abstract Company, August 8, 1931, p. 73; interviews, John C. Miller, June 30, 1981, Marvin Noll, July 10, 1981, and Edena Clere Scott Noll, July 20, 1981; Bradford F. Miller to author, November 3, 1981, Author's Files; C. R. Wallace to author, March 4, 1982, Author's Files; *Southwest Texans*, p. 458.

by readjustment to postwar conditions. . . . Despite the efforts and sacrifices which were almost universally made, the situation has gradually become more critical, until today the entire agricultural structure is threatened."[3]

The postwar period marked a turning point for Ed Lasater's financial affairs, and for many others in the livestock industry: "When we consider that the cattle loan business had grown to a point where hundreds of millions of dollars were loaned on cattle each year, the extent of the disaster brought about by this enormous shrinkage in values must be apparent. . . . Financial depression set in, and there came a great shrinkage in the deposits of most western banks, forcing them to collect loans when possible to do so."[4]

Many large and prominent Texas cattle operators were caught in the middle of this crisis. Ike Pryor and George West survived the downturn, but their extensive operations were greatly reduced. Tom Coleman and Cyrus Lucas had overexpanded and were badly hurt financially. James Dobie operated a large ranch spread over several South Texas counties and was one of the area's biggest operators. At the end of the war, he was reportedly worth one million dollars; by 1925 he was bankrupt.[5]

Henrietta King and her son-in-law, Robert J. Kleberg, headed one of the few livestock operations positioned solidly enough to take advantage of the periodic slumps that hit the cattle business. The captain's widow and her family continually expanded their holdings in the years following his death. In 1922 the ranch properties were enlarged again when her son-in-law, Tom East, transferred title to the 76,870 acres of his San Antonio Viejo Ranch to her in full payment of the indebtedness he had contracted during the ruinous years of drought and failing markets.[6]

Price declines were not a new phenomenon to livestock operators, but the postwar period was extreme in the severity of the drought and the duration of the crisis. "By 1923 every branch of the business was in

[3] James H. Shideler, *Farm Crisis, 1919–1923*, p. 282.

[4] Edward Everett Dale, *The Range Cattle Industry: Ranching on the Great Plains from 1885–1925*, p. 167.

[5] Interviews, Leroy G. Denman, Jr., October 15, 1981, and John M. Bennett, February 25, 1967; J. Marvin Hunter, ed., *The Trail Drivers of Texas*, p. 842; J. Frank Dobie, *Cow People*, p. 54.

[6] Tom Lea, *The King Ranch*, II, 576.

the depths of depression. Feeders had lost money. Ranch men were nearly all in distress."[7] Extensive credit and maximum leverage had proved useful and highly profitable for Ed Lasater between 1895 and 1914. After the war, as operating losses mounted and cattle and land prices declined, the perils of a heavy debt load became glaringly apparent. Lasater had passed up the opportunity to sell out. He had not proceeded rapidly enough on his plan to liquidate part of his ranch holdings and to pay down his debt to manageable proportions. And now the optimism, confidence, hard work, and ability that had kept his bankers satisfied during three decades of heavy borrowing were no longer sufficient.

By 1923 Lasater was having increasing difficulties making the interest payments on his notes, and on some of them he had fallen as much as two years behind. On July 10, 1923, H. P. Drought wrote Lasater that if he was not able to make his delinquent interest payments by September 1, Drought and Co. would have to initiate foreclosure proceedings. Drought explained that he no longer had any flexibility in the matter and that he absolutely had to conform to the instructions he had received. Drought added, "We hope that your cotton crop and cattle sales will make it unnecessary for us to follow out these instructions by enabling you to liquidate your interest. . . ."[8]

Two weeks later Marshall Terrell, a lawyer and son of J. O. Terrell, the longtime Jersey breeder and owner of the noted St. Cloud herd Lasater had purchased in 1909, wrote a four-page typewritten letter to the Falfurrias rancher. Terrell told Lasater that it was time for some plain talk "so that there can be no possible misunderstanding." Terrell said that he was writing as a friend and that although he was speaking perhaps more frankly than he should, he hoped Lasater would take his advice to heart: "If you will take this letter in the spirit in which it is written, I feel sure you will be grateful instead of offended by it."[9]

Terrell explained that despite his best efforts, the two loan companies he represented, both major Lasater creditors, were on the verge of having him begin foreclosure proceedings on a large portion of Lasater's property. Terrell urged Lasater to sell part of his property and

[7] Dale, *The Range Cattle Industry*, p. 169.

[8] H. P. Drought to Ed C. Lasater, July 10, 1923, Drought Files, in possession of Thomas Drought, San Antonio.

[9] Marshall W. Terrell to Ed C. Lasater, July 23, 1923, Denman Files.

cattle immediately to pay his past-due interest and to reduce his debts in order to protect the balance of his assets: "There is no more reason for you to hold your land at former prices than to hold your cattle, horses or mules at former prices, or for a farmer to refuse to sell his wheat because the price has fallen. . . . With this inevitable action facing you, I am going to urge a course of action for you to pursue and which I think you should have pursued long ago."[10]

Terrell knew that Lasater would argue that under current conditions he would not be able to get what the land was worth, but Terrell wrote that if Lasater could get a reasonable price, he "would have left more than most men can hope to earn in a lifetime, and if death should call you, your family could work out your estate." Terrell continued, "It is all right for you to contend that you have the best herd of beef cattle and the best herd of Jersey cattle in the world, but as Mr. Corwin once wrote you, it will not profit you much to make such a reputation if in the end you cannot pay your indebtedness, and instead of doing the good you have intended to do and encouraging others, it may deter others from trying to better equip their places and breed better cattle."[11]

Ed Lasater had made his first purchase of high-quality Jersey breeding stock from Marshall Terrell's father. Terrell's deceased brother Chester had been Lasater's lawyer during the years when he filed numerous lawsuits against the Parr machine in Duval County and made his appeals to the U.S. attorney general in Washington. In 1923 Terrell was a partner in the law firm of Terrell, Davis, Huff and McMillan.

Marshall Terrell had a mixed reputation around San Antonio. He was an early-day wheeler-dealer, a promoter and financier who arranged financing for people, sold the bonds, and on numerous occasions later represented the bondholders in suits against the borrowers when the loans went bad. Loaning money in those days was unfettered by the governmental regulations passed a few years later. Many people around San Antonio thought Terrell had taken advantage of them. The son of one of Terrell's legal colleagues stated: "The type of activity he carried out today would come under the label 'conflict of interest,' and many of the things that went on then were made illegal by the SEC Act. My father and uncle respected Marshall Terrell's abilities, but they

[10] Ibid.
[11] Ibid.

always felt they had to watch him closely when they were involved with him." [12]

L. D. Miller had little respect for Terrell: "We had the highest regard for Chester Terrell. We considered him a very honorable man. We didn't think Marshall was of the same caliber. He was out for Marshall first, last and always." John Bennett, brother of Lasater's first wife, knew Terrell at close range in San Antonio: "The kindest thing that can be said about Marshall Terrell is that he was peculiar and unbalanced. Others referred to him in terms more harsh." The negative view of Terrell was not strictly a family affair. Several years later his own partners united to eject Terrell from the law firm his father had founded. [13]

Terrell himself claimed to be a friend and admirer of Lasater's, and if Terrell could be taken at his word, he was indeed interested in the rancher's welfare and was attempting in his July 23, 1923, letter to offer his best advice and counsel. Terrell wrote: "After thinking about you and your affairs for months, and for almost every waking moment since my return from Falfurrias, I have decided to write you one more letter of advice, although I am afraid that I am going to say some things that may offend you." [14]

Before Terrell wrote Lasater, the rancher had visited with the King Ranch owners about purchasing some of his property. He had told Terrell that the Klebergs had expressed an interest in only the 108,000 acres east of the Edinburg Road, but that if they had offered him five dollars an acre for it Lasater would have refused it. Terrell advised Lasater to pursue immediately the conversation with Robert Kleberg and in addition to sell some farm ground as well as a portion of his beef and dairy herd. Terrell's proposal was for Lasater to reduce his indebtedness by a million dollars while still maintaining very extensive holdings. "I am not going to argue with you about the value of the land," Terrell wrote. "But should litigation begin and the land be sold by a trustee, a sheriff or a receiver, I doubt that it would bring that amount, and even though it did the attorneys' fees and costs would amount to so

[12] Interviews, Gilbert Denman, October 14, 1981, and Leroy G. Denman, October 15, 1981.

[13] Interviews, L. D. Miller, Sr., September 22, 1971, John M. Bennett, March 17, 1967; and John M. Bennett, Jr., July 28, 1981; "Historical Memorandum," Law Firm of Terrell, Davis, McMillan and Hall, 1930–76.

[14] Terrell to Lasater, July 23, 1923.

much that it would be better to sell the land now at $5.00 an acre than to sell it at $7.00 an acre through a foreclosure."

If Lasater followed this advice, Terrell thought he could forestall any immediate action on the part of Lasater's creditors. "I hope that you will wire me that you will see Mr. Kleberg Wednesday morning and wire me on that date if he will take the land, and if you will I will wire for permission to delay foreclosure and request giving you a reasonable time to close the deal."

Terrell reminded Lasater that he had backed the rancher with more than words on several recent occasions. Terrell stated that he had himself paid past-due interest and some principal on personal loans made to Lasater by several individuals in San Antonio, including Alexander Joske: "The $20,000 note that Mr. Joske holds has been renewed with my endorsement, and in order to protect Mr. Joske, although he did not ask it, I pledged to him $25,000 of my life insurance. And in view of the above and in view of the further fact that the interest due my mother is also past due, I was willing to stand by and see the Wells-Dickey Company and the Commerce Trust Company take a chattel mortgage on the cotton crop."

Terrell reaffirmed his friendship and his high opinion of Lasater: "Now I can say without any spirit of flattery that you are in many respects one of the biggest men that I have ever known, and I think you are generally so regarded. . . ." But Terrell felt Lasater was not focusing properly on the pressing issues of the moment: "You owe it to your family, to your creditors who upon the faith of your integrity, ability and judgment, have loaned you more than they have loaned any other man in Southwest Texas in whose upbuilding you have been one of the greatest factors, to your friends . . . and to yourself to keep out of litigation and receivership. . . ." Terrell appeared to be writing both frankly and sincerely when he said: "It is easy to start a foreclosure or a receivership, and it may be all right for you to think that it will wind up satisfactorily to you, but let me, as one of the best friends you have in the world, impress upon you that if you go into a receivership it may be a long time before you see the end of it, and what it will leave you no one knows."[15]

[15] Ibid.

Lasater's response to Terrell, if he responded at all, is not known. It was not Lasater's nature to take the conservative approach, to cut back, to consolidate. He would have voted to push ahead, to work harder and to move faster, if indeed he had any choice at all in July, 1923. This time, however, events were closing in on him. On July 30, 1923, District Judge Duval West in "Commerce Trust Company et al v. Ed C. Lasater" appointed Marshall Terrell "receiver of the said Ed C. Lasater, defendant, and of all his properties, real, personal or mixed, of every kind or character, owned, held, possessed or controlled by the said Ed C. Lasater."[16]

The suit to establish a receivership was filed on behalf of the Commerce Trust Company of Kansas City and the Wells-Dickey Company of Minneapolis, holders of mortgages totaling more than $800,000 against parts of Lasater's holdings. The *San Antonio Express* article's headline called it a "friendly suit." Attorneys for the two companies bringing the suit affirmed that Lasater's assets far exceeded his liabilities and that the suit was filed "to preserve his equity in his properties." In addition to appointing Terrell, the court named Leroy G. Denman attorney for the receiver.[17]

Judge West's decree stated: "And the said Ed C. Lasater is hereby required forthwith upon demand from said receiver to turn over and deliver to him all of the books, papers, monies, deeds, leaseholds, properties, vouchers, stocks, bonds, choses in action and every other evidence of property right or of debt, real, personal or mixed . . . which was in his possession on the 30th day of July, 1923, or which may come into his possession in the future. . . ."[18]

The complications involved in running a large and diversified

[16] "Appointment of Receiver," July 30, 1923, Deed Records, Brooks County, vol. VII, p. 509.

[17] *San Antonio Express*, August 2, 1923; Lea, *The King Ranch*, p. 637; "Appointment of Receiver," July 30, 1923, Deed Records, Brooks County, vol. VII, p. 509. Denman was a son of Judge Leroy G. Denman, George Brackenridge's talented young lawyer and protégé who bought the colonel's interest in the San Antonio National Bank and the San Antonio Loan and Trust Company in 1912. Judge Denman died suddenly four years later; his family believed his life was shortened by Brackenridge's misrepresentation regarding the risky nature of some of the notes held by the two financial institutions (Marilyn McAdams Sibley, *George W. Brackenridge: Maverick Philanthropist*, pp. 214–16).

[18] "Appointment of Receiver," VII, 509.

business with a court-appointed receiver and four sets of attorneys reviewing and passing on every move and each decision, regardless of how minor, was quickly apparent. L. A. Dickey, Lasater's office manager, was soon kept busy nearly full-time complying with request after request from Terrell and Denman regarding details of land and cattle ownership and inventories, alphabetical lists of employees and salaries, itemized statements of every expenditure made, tax data from each of the several counties in which Lasater's holdings were situated, and details of the operating histories of the various businesses. Denman was shocked by Lasater's operating expenses and by other items such as the cost of carrying the Jersey show herd around the country to livestock fairs and exhibits. [19]

Lasater attended two meetings with the receiver, the lawyers and the creditors on October 20 and October 22. Terrell wrote after the meeting that "everybody agreed that the only way the matter can be worked out is by drastic liquidation. . . . Mr. Lasater was here today and stated that he would go to see Mr. Robert J. Kleberg today or tomorrow. I hope within thirty days to make you some definite and favorable report." [20]

Lasater's large herd, numbering more than twelve thousand head, was mortgaged to two lending institutions, San Antonio Loan and Trust Company and the National Cattle Loan Company of National Stockyards, Illinois. That split collateral would cause considerable confusion in the following months as the creditors oversaw the liquidation of a substantial portion of the herd. On November 23 Wirt Wright, president of the latter company, wrote Marshall Terrell, "It is rather clear to us that Lasater had been moving his cattle around to suit his own convenience and his own ideas without particular reference to the divided liens existing, and that has created a problem as to division of the proceeds of the cattle. . . ." [21]

The marketing of Lasater's cattle was the first major disagreement between Lasater, the attorneys, and the creditors. Lasater was holding out for a major shipment of livestock in the spring, when he was

[19] Leroy G. Denman to Marshall W. Terrell, October 13, 1923, Denman Files.

[20] Marshall W. Terrell to Commerce Trust Co. and Wells-Dickey Company, November 1, 1923, Denman Files.

[21] Wirt Wright to Marshall W. Terrell, November 23, 1923, Denman Files.

convinced the cattle market would be much improved. He found it difficult to conform his ideas about cattle marketing to the group decision-making routine put into effect when his assets were placed in receivership. Wright wrote Denman on November 28: "We agree with you that an effort should be made to market these cattle out steadily so as to get the best average of what the market will be. It is much better, in our judgment, than gambling on shipment of a large number of cattle within a short period next spring."[22]

On January 15, 1924, Lasater wrote Terrell that he planned to ship his calves as soon as they were old enough and to ship the cows as they got fat. He added that certain of the cows should be sold at private treaty: "I do not intend to ship from the Muertos, Mota Negra, Tule, Baluarte, Tajos, Víboras or Lindero pastures which contain my Ghir-Brahman and Durham crosses and my purebred Herefords and other best cows, as these should not be sold on the market."[23] F. T. Silliman, sent to Falfurrias by the National Cattle Loan Company, wrote Wright three days later that Lasater "doesn't want the cattle shipped or sold on the present market when there is a chance for a much better market this spring which would enable him to pay his cattle paper and have a good-sized herd left."[24]

Wright was upset at receiving this news and immediately wrote Leroy Denman: "We did expect that these shipments would start promptly after the first of January and continue without intermission right along, and certainly it was my understanding that Mr. McCormack and Mr. Silliman should between them be in absolute control of the shipping program and that Lasater was to have nothing to say about it."[25] Writing to Silliman in Falfurrias, Wright further expressed his displeasure with Lasater's attitude and approach to the cattle shipments: "It looks to me as though Mr. Lasater has as usual overridden all opposition and put his own schemes across. . . . We not only expected that these shipments were going to come out and the work actually be done under the supervision of yourself and Mr. McCormack, but also that Lasater fully understood that." Wright sent a copy of his letter to Denman and to

[22] Wirt Wright to Leroy G. Denman, November 28, 1923, Denman Files.
[23] Ed C. Lasater to Marshall W. Terrell, January 15, 1924, Denman Files.
[24] F. T. Silliman to Wirt Wright, January 18, 1924, Denman Files.
[25] Wirt Wright to Leroy Denman, January 19, 1924, Denman Files.

Holman Cartwright, the loan company's agent in San Antonio, "in the hopes that immediate measures will be taken to get out everything that is fat just as rapidly as they can be put on the cars."[26]

A few weeks later, the receiver secured a court order mandating a foreclosure sale of all lands mortgaged to the Wells-Dickey Company on July 1, 1924. All the cattle covering that portion of the ranch, some 164,000 acres, would need to be liquidated prior to that date. Denman wrote Lasater on March 25: "Will you please inform the men in charge of the cattle that the handling of them has been turned over to us, and that they will be paid by Mr. Silliman and Mr. McCormack, and that we have complete charge?"[27]

Shipments of cattle continued steadily through April and May, and by the end of that month, in addition to the calves and yearlings, about twenty-five hundred head of Lasater's brood cows had been loaded on trains and shipped to terminal markets. Wright wrote Denman on June 2 that Lasater had been in the banker's office in Illinois the day before and had been very anxious to stop the shipment of forty cars of cattle the following week. Wright had written only a few years earlier that Lasater's name in Texas was a synonym for efficiency and success. The Illinois banker admitted that it was unfortunate to be selling an outstanding breeding herd at slaughter prices, but he felt obligated to proceed with the liquidation of his company's collateral: "I realize that it seems somewhat of a tragedy to have to market this fine herd of breeding cattle which probably cannot be replaced, but . . . from our standpoint I cannot see any other recourse except to sell the security out."[28]

As Lasater's cattle were being gathered and shipped, sale of other assets moved steadily ahead as well. Lasater's creamery was about to be sold for a fraction of its value when John Bennett stepped in to buy it from the receiver, later selling it back to Lasater in exchange for his notes. A substantial herd of Jersey cows was sold, and two large land sales as well as a number of smaller ones were finalized. The Wells-Dickey mortgage was paid in part out of cash received from other sales, and in satisfaction of their remaining loan balance that company took title to eighty-five thousand acres of land on the west side of the

[26] Wirt Wright to F. T. Silliman, January 21, 1924, Denman Files.

[27] Leroy G. Denman to Ed C. Lasater, March 25, 1924, Denman Files.

[28] Wirt Wright to Leroy G. Denman, June 2, 1924, Denman Files.

Falfurrias-Edinburg Road. Lasater leased the land back and had a one-year option to repurchase it.[29]

Leroy Denman and Ed Lasater held a number of discussions over the course of several months with Robert Kleberg regarding a possible land sale. Kleberg in one conversation stated emphatically that he would not purchase any of the property unless Ed Lasater wished for him to. Lasater responded that if he could not own the land himself, he could think of no one he would rather have own it than the Klebergs.[30]

The largest individual sale during the receivership occurred when the receiver sold Lasater's Encino Division to Kleberg for $456,045. That transaction covered 108,000 acres, all of Lasater's lands lying south of the north line of the Tío Ayala grant and east of the road leading from Falfurrias into the Rio Grande Valley.[31] Prior to the sale, Lasater had moved Jim McBride from Vargas to become foreman at Encino. When the property was sold, McBride, who with his son would oversee that large tract for many years to come, stated, "Ed Lasater sold me along with the Encino Division."[32] The warranty deed, executed on June 30, 1924, completed the Encino sale except for a brief postscript.

Two young boys rode along together through the live oaks and mesquite in the Víboras pasture. It had been a long day and a hot one. Now the sun was getting low, and the air was cooling slightly. Tom was the ranch owner's youngest son; Julián was the grandson of Hilario García, the man who had earlier saved Tom's life. Their closeness of age and the shared joy of days together out in the brush and in cow camp had established a firm bond between the two. A year earlier they had camped together at Vargas while working with the cow outfit. They both liked the feel of a good horse and the sound of the bellowing herd on a roundup. They enjoyed the stories around the fire in the evening.

---

[29] Ernst and Ernst, "Audit Report," December 31, 1924; "Order Discharging Receiver," Deed Records, Brooks County, vol. VIII, pp. 38–40; Marshall W. Terrell to John M. Bennett, April 18, 1924, Denman Files; interview, Garland M. Lasater, February 21, 1981.

[30] Leroy G. Denman to Wirt Wright, April 22, 1924, Marshall W. Terrell to Leroy G. Denman, May 13, 1924, and Edward A. Kleberg to Leroy G. Denman, May 16, 1924, all in Denman Files; interviews, L. D. Miller, Sr., September 22, 1971, and Tom Lasater, July 23, 1981; Lea, *The King Ranch*, p. 637.

[31] Deed Records, Brooks County, vol. VII, pp. 597–601, vol. VIII, p. 147.

[32] Interview, Tom Lasater, January 12, 1980.

Tom and Julián had spent many days riding together, joking and laughing. They were friends.

Today the bounce of their horses was different, and so was the boys' conversation. The work of the past few days had not been the exciting game it had been on other occasions. The land had been sold, and the boys had helped gather the cattle to complete the transaction. That was the last time they would work the Víboras pasture together. Other tracts from the Falfurrias Ranch had already been sold. Now the Encino Division was gone.

When they reached the gate, Tom got off his horse to open it. Suddenly he grabbed his hat and hurled it into the sand. He threw his arms around the post and leaned his head against the mesquite wood.

"They're going to take it all, Julián. They'll take all, and then what will we do?" the young cowboy asked his companion.

Julián dismounted and walked to the gate. He stood quietly by his friend with his hand on his shoulder. Later they rode on together silently to the camp at Lucero.[33]

The next day the thirteen-year-old Tom saddled his horse early and started off from Lucero to the southeast, making a big swing through the Quitéria pasture, where he had recently helped gather eight hundred cows. He rode north past the Pinole Lake, where Dr. Ellis had once found an eastern banker sitting as if frozen in an unattended carriage on the South Texas prairie. He stopped at the San Tomás pens, where brother Garland had made a spectacular leap over a high wooden fence only seconds before an outlaw Brahman bull had hurled his full weight with deadly force into the corner where Garland had been standing.

He rode through the Sacahuistal pasture and past the Leoncitas windmill. Then he turned his horse back west to ride across the Muertos pasture. A few days earlier he and Julián had helped round up the cattle there, nearly nine hundred head of big red cows, a red Brahman-Shorthorn cross. Some had said it was the best set of brood cows in South Texas, and they had been loaded on trains and sold as beef.[34]

[33] Interview, Alfredo García, July 6, 1981.

[34] When Ed Lasater sold the Encino Division to the King Ranch, he priced the cows at $40 per head. This was an outstanding herd of red Brahman–Shorthorn-cross cattle, known as the Muertos herd. The King Ranch offered $35 per head. Lasater said he would not take that and shipped them to a terminal market, where they sold for slaughter at $44 a head (Interview, Garland M. Lasater, February 21, 1981).

By then it was late, and Tom's horse was tired. As he rode out of the Muertos and headed toward the Bordo Trozado, a cut through the abandoned railroad grade of the line which had reached only as far as Falfurrias, tears were streaming down his face. Behind him lay a large section of his father's ranch, his favorite part, and one that he would not ride over again.

Alice Gertrudis King Kleberg, the captain's daughter who had stayed on the ranch with her parents and had married her father's lawyer and counselor in 1886, heard about Tom's farewell ride around the Encino Division. Mrs. Kleberg knew Tom well, and as in most friendships, a shared interest had served to create a special feeling between them. In this case it was their common attraction to poultry, an unlikely bond between an aging matriarch and a young boy whose destinies were so closely linked to ranches and cattle.

Alice Kleberg and Tom Lasater were both fascinated by chickens, and on more than one occasion when Tom and his family had gone to visit she had taken him on a personal tour of her poultry menagerie. She had Rhode Island Reds, Plymouth Rocks, several kinds of guineas and turkeys, and a host of other species of fowl. Tom and his friend compared notes about their respective flocks, and Mrs. Kleberg told him about her various crosses and experiments as they admired her large collection of exotic birds. And then they went inside the big house where men and women alike talked of rain or drought, of the green grass that was or that would be, and of cattle.

A few days after Tom's solo ride, a Pierce-Arrow pulled up in front of the white frame house at La Mota. Several large boxes were strapped to the car's running boards. The boxes were filled with blue-gray guineas, the cross which was Mrs. Kleberg's pride and joy. She sent her son Bob with those guineas to console the young cowboy from Falfurrias. In the midst of the big deals and the dramatic changes there was still time for friendship, even with a little boy who did not understand why things happened as they did.[35]

Sufficient assets were sold and enough creditors were satisfied during the late spring and early summer that the sheriff's auction scheduled for July 1 was canceled, and a month later the receivership was terminated. Judge West filed an order on August 8, 1924, directing

[35] Interview, Tom Lasater, January 12, 1980.

Marshall Terrell to return Lasater's remaining property to him.[36] Ed Lasater was once against the captain of his own ship, the driving force and sole decision maker in a still sizable group of business enterprises.

Eighteen months after the receivership ended, an exchange of letters between O. M. Corwin and Leroy Denman summarized the effect of that experience on Lasater's business career. Corwin, a vice-president of the Wells-Dickey Company, had written letters filled with extravagant praise for Lasater in 1921, less than two years before his company filed the suit that threw Lasaater's properties into a receivership. In a January, 1926, letter asking for Denman's assistance with regard to various details related to Lasater's option contract and interest payments, Corwin made reference to the "fair" and "generous" treatment he felt Lasater had received from the Wells-Dickey Company.[37]

Denman differed with Corwin's analysis. "I agree with you that they have granted him many favors, but I think that Mr. Lasater has also done a great deal more than most debtors in similar situations and I think I am able to appreciate that the more fully because my attitude towards him is also that of a creditor," Denman wrote. "He waived service of citation and practically everything was done by agreement and no judge of values will deny that the property sold by the receivership was sold at a great sacrifice."[38]

The Minneapolis banker was concerned with an interest charge of $635 that he felt his bondholders were due. In his response Denman wanted Corwin to understand the overall situation from Lasater's vantage point: "His herd of breeding cows, one of the most famous in the country, was shipped to market and sold as beef. The bulk of his ranch was sold to the Kings at a sacrifice which I think will be demonstrated by the fact that the Kings will today, I am sure, refuse twice the price they paid for it."

Denman tried to put Corwin's trivial concern in perspective: "When we all made our loans to Mr. Lasater, any of us would have agreed that he had an equity of not less than two and a half million dollars. Today we believe he has little, if any equity left. After he had held his properties for a lifetime, the creditors forced him to liquidate

[36] Deed Records, Brooks County, vol. VIII, pp. 38–40.
[37] O. M. Corwin to Leroy G. Denman, January 25, 1926, Denman Files.
[38] Leroy G. Denman to O. M. Corwin, February 6, 1926, Denman Files.

them on the most unfavorable market for lands, with one exception, that our country has known since the Civil War." [39]

Lasater's career was not finished when the receivership ended. As he approached his sixty-fourth birthday, Lasater still controlled nearly ninety thousand acres of land, stocked with a sizable beef cattle operation and the largest Jersey herd in the world. He operated a renowned creamery and a large mercantile store. But his empire had been sharply reduced and greatly weakened by the extensive sales of both land and cattle at sacrifice prices, and those assets that remained in his hands were still burdened by an exceedingly heavy debt load.

After all those years of intense and varied activity, of planning and building, Lasater's affairs had passed a difficult and trying stage, one characterized by losses and painful reduction. Certainly the overall agricultural picture between 1919 and 1923 was an important contributor to the evolution of Lasater's business just before and during the receivership. Lasater was not alone in having to face the consequences of the severely depressed prices available for the products produced on his pastures and farms in the years after the First World War.

As previously noted, Lasater's extensive use of borrowed money was another major factor in the rancher's problems, which came to a head in the 1920s. W. W. Turney, who also served as president of the Texas and Southwestern Cattle Raisers Association, could have been speaking of Lasater's career when he described the two-edged sword that debt so frequently proved to be for those livestock entrepreneurs that Ike Pryor had called the greatest borrowers in the world. "Speaking as a banker as well as a cattleman, let me tell you that you are only safe when you have such investment in your own business that no other institution or man's loans to you can destroy you," Turney said in his speech, adding: "When you have reached that situation, you can battle against drought; you can battle against money panics; you can say, regardless of these failures that come, they cannot, like they did in 1920 and 1921, take and destroy the accumulation of a lifetime." [40]

Ed Lasater had become convinced a number of years earlier that diversification was a vital necessity for the farmers of the Falfurrias area. He saw farm income from crops supplemented by dairy cows and

[39] Ibid.
[40] Mary Whatley Clarke, *A Century of Cow Business*, p. 191.

hogs as providing a better and more stable economic base than a complete dependence on cotton, and he set out to prove this by his own example. Lasater's large-scale farming operation and his dairy herd lost money from the start. In good years, supporting those enterprises was a costly burden for his range cattle operation. In the years when his beef cattle lost money, the farms and dairy herds added to the already heavy annual operating losses. But Lasater had determined that crops could be grown and that dairy cows could be raised profitably in the Falfurrias country, and he had said on repeated occasions that he was willing to pay any price to demonstrate that.[41]

Those who knew Lasater, who dealt with him or observed him, would point to other traits and circumstances that determined his career. Some saw him as a plunger whose tendency was always to move too fast, a man with a consuming weakness to own all the land that adjoined his ranch. He was viewed as a farsighted businessman, but also as a bad manager with little concern for day-to-day operational details. Others pointed to his tendency to spread himself too thin, to undertake too many diverse activities at once. Some who knew Lasater felt he was a poor judge of men, that he tried to run large and involved businesses with inadequate help. He was remembered as a man with a cavalier disregard for money and little concern for the careful and conservative husbanding of his assets. He was too trusting of human nature; some of those closest to him as well as his neighbors repeatedly stole from him and availed themselves of his resources to line their own pockets.[42]

He was called a driven man, a compulsive worker who never stopped long enough to enjoy the fruits of his own efforts. He was seen as a visionary, a man who could see into the future and who would commence a course of action and then would stick with it despite subsequent difficulties, convinced that the merits of his long-term plan would carry him through. Over the years his supporters and detractors would

[41] Interviews, L. D. Miller, Sr., September 22, 1971, and Garland M. Lasater, February 21, and July 29, 1981.

[42] Interviews, John M. Bennett, February 24, 1967, Emily Edwards, February 25, 1967, Tom Lasater, May 6, and July 17, 1969, and January 12, 1980, Garland M. Lasater, February 21, 1981, J. M. Brooks, April 8, 1981, Huston Jenkins, July 13, 1981, Neil Rupp, July 28, 1981, Dr. Miriam Wagenschein, March 3, 1982, William B. Gardner, March 8, 1982, Bird McBride Victor, March 5, 1982, C. J. McBride, March 7, 1982, and Matthew Gouger, March 20, 1982.

continue to discuss and debate his aspirations and achievements, the reasons and the remedies, the successes and the failures of the man who had ridden his horse south across the Nueces many years before with nothing more than his good name, energy, confidence, and a substantial line of credit.[43]

John Bennett, the San Antonio banker, was a man who knew Lasater as well as anyone over a period of forty years. Several decades after Lasater's death, Bennett pointed to another important fact, a situation that was unknown to most of Lasater's local contemporaries and that was only sketchily known to his own family. Bennett singled out the Cunningham affair, the $300,000 which Lasater loaned to Colonel Edward Cunningham at the turn of the century and never recovered, as a major cause of the financial crisis that overtook Lasater two decades after he had been named receiver of his uncle's Sugarland Plantation. Bennett stated: "Ed Lasater would probably have ridden through the droughts and depressions except for an act of loyalty to his uncle, Ed Cunningham. . . . I don't know how a man could sacrifice himself in a greater way than when he took on that big debt. This was a grand gesture, an important part of Ed Lasater's story."[44]

Lasater was a controversial figure. He was opinionated, demanding, impatient, and strong-willed. In the course of his career he had accumulated an array of enemies around Falfurrias, within the cattleman's organization, and in the political arena. But along with an impressive company of detractors, he had numerous friends and supporters. One public statement, which echoed the positive sentiments of some of his contemporaries, appeared in a 1924 newspaper article in Hebbronville, seat of the county that his ranching neighbor and political foe, Bill Jones, had split off from Lasater's newly formed county in 1913.

The article was headlined "He Comes Back" and reported the end of the Lasater receivership: "His comeback was a great thing, not only for Brooks County, the home of most of his big operations, but for all of South Texas which has benefitted by his great development work and which felt the blow which came when financial trouble overtook him.

[43] Ibid.
[44] Interview, John M. Bennett, February 24, 1967.

The News knows of no individual who has done greater development work in South Texas than Mr. Lasater."[45]

The *News* said that Lasater had established the greatest dairy in the United States, perhaps in the world. "He has brought in farmers to develop his broad acres of prairie lands; has seen them establish farms and build homes . . . has helped them to stock their farms with fine milk cows and has paid them good prices for their products; has done everything to encourage them and largely through his good offices has seen his county become one of the state's most prosperous farming sections." The article concluded: "Mr. Lasater can truly be classed as an empire builder, and more developers of his kind would be a great thing for South Texas."[46]

[45] *Hebbronville News*, 1924, no date, Lasater Files, in possession of Garland M. Lasater, Falfurrias.
[46] Ibid.

CHAPTER 13

The Ninety-Eighth Year

The thing that hath been, it is that which shall be; and
that which is done is that which shall be done; and there
is no new thing under the sun.

—Ecclesiastes 1:9

THE year 1929 is infamous. "Some years," writes economist John Kenneth Galbraith, "like some poets and politicians and some lovely women, are singled out for fame far beyond the common lot, and 1929 was clearly such a year. Like 1066, 1776 and 1914, it is a year that everyone remembers."[1]

Nineteen twenty-nine is significant principally for economic reasons. In October of that year several momentous days on Wall Street suddenly and devastatingly ended the high-flying illusions of the roaring twenties and heralded a different decade, a difficult one. "As a year, 1929 has always been peculiarly the property of the economists. It was a year of notable economic events; indeed, in that year began the most momentous economic occurrence in the history of the United States, the ordeal of the Great Depression."[2]

In many communities with agricultural bases, 1929 did not mark the abrupt turning point that it did in other places. For those in agriculture, the change had come earlier and even before the crash they could not join in the general euphoria signaled by President Coolidge's last State of the Union address in December, 1928: "In the domestic field, there is tranquility and contentment . . . and the highest record of years of prosperity." Those reassuring and satisfied words did not apply to rural America, where agriculturalists "were unhappy and had

[1] John Kenneth Galbraith, *The Great Crash: 1929*, p. 1.
[2] Ibid., p. 2.

been ever since the depression of 1920–21 had cut farm prices sharply, but left costs high."[3]

In Falfurrias, 1929 is not remembered with any special clarity, and the year was not marked by any noteworthy local event. There, perhaps, 1926 was a more memorable year. A January headline in the *Falfurrias Facts* read: "Veni, Eureka, Falfurrias," and in the article which followed, editor E. W. Dickey further elaborated on the local tradition that had produced a bountiful collection of colorful and optimistic prose in the course of more than two decades: "Whoever the discoverer of the Falfurrias country may have been, he has handed down to humanity a section which needs only man's touch to cause it to blossom. . . . You may sing of the magic valley of the Nile, the golden fields of Alaska and the mines of the Orient, but in the final analysis, the Falfurrias section crowns them all." The article described in glowing terms the area's fertile soil and inexhaustible water supply and the development of the dairy and citrus industries in the region. The Falfurrias country offered a good living for prospective residents and would reward any citizen willing to work: "There is no reason why any juggling of figures is necessary to convince even the most skeptical that this is a real land of promise."[4]

Dickey's article continued, "The young year 1926 is filled with the promise of wonderful achievement in many lines, and there is no telling what a day or a month will bring forth." Like a prophecy fulfilled, a banner headline in the *Falfurrias Facts* only ten months later announced that the Southern Pacific Railroad had been granted permission by the ICC to extend its service south from Falfurrias. This would connect Falfurrias, which had been the end of the line since railroad construction halted there in 1904, with the Rio Grande Valley. The paper was ecstatic about the prospects: "A new day is breaking for all the Falfurrias land. Mark well this prediction: few people living in this section realize the great changes that will take place within the next few years."[5] Not even Garland Miller and R. W. Curtis at the height of the first Falfurrias land boom had been more euphoric. The prose in the *Facts* was second to none in its glowing assessment: "This extension will open up for settlement and development an empire greater than all

---

[3] Ibid., pp. 6–7.
[4] *Falfurrias Facts*, January 21, 1926.
[5] Ibid.; *Falfurrias Facts*, November 23, 1926.

New England; richer than the plains of Mesopotamia; more pleasant to dwell in than France's famous Riviera."[6]

Despite the local enthusiasm and the optimistic words of Falfurrias area boosters in the late 1920s, for Ed Lasater the years following his receivership were difficult ones, each marking another chapter in his ongoing effort to protect some of his property from the oppressive weight of his still extensive indebtedness. Lasater sold forty thousand acres in 1925 to J. D. Cage, a large and successful operator described as "one of the most vivid and colorful characters the cow-kingdom has produced."[7] The tracts sold to Cage that year were part of the land repossessed by the Wells-Dickey Company which Lasater had an option to repurchase. Lasater was not in a position to reclaim the land for his own ranching operation, but he made a small profit on the sale.[8]

Real estate sales in the Falfurrias area to northern farmers and investors had practically come to a halt during the First World War. A month after the railroad extension was approved, the *Falfurrias Facts* announced that Ed Lasater was preparing to subdivide a new tract. The article stated that much of the land in this proposed subdivision consisted of red sandy soil "which many experts predict will prove to be some of the best berry and tomato lands in the United States." Lasater opened a real estate office in his creamery building for handling the local work of the sales campaign. L. A. Dickey was in charge of that project in addition to serving as general manager of the Falfurrias Mercantile Company.[9]

An ad describing the new subdivision that Lasater proposed offered eighty-acre tracts at fifty dollars an acre with a one-third cash down payment and the balance carried at 7 percent for ten years. The ad asserted that the average income for area farmers in 1926 was $4,500, double the state average: "Diversification is an established practice here. The result is a profit to farmers and dairymen year after year."[10]

In May, 1929, the Texas Jersey Cattle Club met in Falfurrias. Two months earlier, a Falfurrias Jersey Dairy cow, May Blossom Fond Pet,

---

[6] *Falfurrias Facts*, November 23, 1926.

[7] Bryan Wildenthal, "Jim Cage, Cowman," *Cattleman*, February, 1942, p. 20.

[8] Deed Records, Brooks County, vol. VIII, pp. 349–55, 524–27.

[9] *Falfurrias Facts*, December 10, 1926.

[10] Undated newspaper clipping, Lasater Files, in possession of Garland M. Lasater, Falfurrias.

won the Grand Champion prize at the Fort Worth Fat Stock Show. Lasater's herd in the winter and spring of 1929 also appeared at the state fairs in Missouri, Indiana, and Kansas and at the National Dairy Show in Memphis, where they continued to bring renown to his Jersey operation, which had made its mark in seventy-three national, regional, and state shows starting in 1912. In the late 1920s, Lasater had some two thousand dairy cows, and his creamery produced more than two thousand pounds of butter daily with the cream from his own cows as well as that purchased from 150 local farmers.[11]

The cream outlet and the premium paid by the creamery offered a boon to many of the area's stock farmers, but a number of them were nevertheless losing the battle to stay afloat financially. Wilbert Jenkins had heard Rob Miller extolling the advantages of life on a South Texas farm at a meeting near Paris, Illinois, in 1916. He responded to Miller's suggestion and purchased a farm that year in the Realitos subdivision of the Copita Farm and Garden Tracts. Jenkins adapted well to the new environment, but his wife never adjusted to life in rural Duval County. In 1928, when Federal Land Bank financing that would have permitted them to save the property became available, Jenkins's wife refused to sign the papers, assuming that when they lost the farm they would at last return to their former home in Illinois.[12]

The San Antonio Loan and Trust Company repossessed Jenkins's farm, but Jenkins did not leave his adopted country. Instead, he leased the farm from his former creditors, paying the firm a one-quarter share of the crops, and five years later he bought the farm back for half the price he had originally paid in 1916.[13] Jenkins's case typified what had been occurring all across rural America: "The decline in farmland prices from the 1920 peak, some nine years before 1929's stock market debacle, was triggered by a traumatic move to deflation in 1921, with prices of agricultural products pacing the decline. . . . From the peak of the farm boom in 1920 to the depths of the Depression, the price of land shrank by 60%."[14]

[11] *Brooks County Texan*, March 22, 1929, April 5, 1929, and April 12, 1929; W. C. Barnes, "Falfurrias and Ed Lasater," *Hoard's Dairyman*, January 25, 1929, p. 64; O. C. Haworth, *The Land of Heart's Delight*; R. M. Gow, "Ed C. Lasater," *Jersey Bulletin*, March 26, 1930, p. 558.

[12] Interview, Huston Jenkins, July 13, 1981.

[13] Ibid.

[14] Steven Leuthold, "Grim Reapers: The Great Bull Market in Farmland is Ending," *Barron's*, August 9, 1982, pp. 5–7, 16.

Jenkins was not the only farmer in Duval County unable to make his land payments. Leroy Denman's law office was kept busy filing foreclosure papers against the farmers who had purchased land around Realitos and Copita. The repossessed land caused an adverse chain reaction in Lasater's financial affairs. He had used the buyers' notes as collateral for loans, but when the land was repossessed it had a current market value far less than the face value of the notes. This situation added to Lasater's woes in the late 1920s, as he struggled to keep his remaining land holdings intact. [15]

H. P. Drought's firm first loaned Ed Lasater money in 1891. In 1895, Drought's former partner, in arranging financing for Lasater to purchase land in the Falfurrias area, called Lasater a "first-class cowman" who had "made and lost a great deal of money in the business, but is understood to be quite a considerable sum ahead." Drought himself in a 1901 letter to his Scottish associates wrote effusively about the South Texas rancher: "Of Mr. Lasater we cannot speak too highly; he is hard-working, industrious, frugal, thoroughly well versed in his business, and in every respect a man worthy of confidence and credit." In 1919, H. P. Drought again wrote his colleagues in Scotland a memorandum to accompany a new loan application from Lasater. He continued to express very positive views about the rancher: "Mr. Lasater, aside from his ability of handling successfully the farm and improvements above mentioned, is one of the best informed stockmen in Texas. . . . He is an enterprising, energetic man and withal he is a man of good judgment."

But thirty-five years after that first loan, Drought's communications assumed a different tone. Lasater had fallen behind in his interest payments on a loan secured by eleven thousand acres in Duval County. In July, 1926, Drought cabled Scotland: "Lasater in conference last week stated he expected to be able to obtain money to pay interest on new loans when due if we could give extension on balance for year or less. . . . Matter receiving attention. Will cable developments." In a subsequent letter, Drought discussed the Lasater loan: "We sought to impress on Lasater that he escaped foreclosure by us this time by a very narrow margin, and that should another year elapse and find him in the condition he is in now, he cannot hope for any forebearance be-

[15] Letters and memorandums, February 21, 1927, to February 4, 1928, Denman Files.

cause, we explained to him, your directors are inclined to the opinion that he is merely struggling on without making any headway toward improving his condition." He continued, "We insisted on the payment of all the funded interest, not because we thought he could pay it now, but because we wanted to force him to offer as much as he possibly could pay, and this we think he did."[16]

By early 1927, Drought once again expressed his opinion about the man behind the loan which had become a concern to his Scottish colleagues: "Such recent information as we have regarding this borrower leads us to believe that he is making a little progress toward bettering his financial condition, but he is still afflicted with his boundless optimism and it is the opinion of some of his creditors that this leads him to overlook opportunities which would appeal to others in his condition."[17]

In July, when Lasater's interest payments came due, Drought cabled more bad news to his associates: "Serious insect damage Lasater cotton. No payments before September. Writing." About twelve hundred acres of Drought's security was planted in cotton, and both Lasater and Drought had been hopeful that the crop would more than suffice to cover Lasater's overdue interest balance. "However, much to our disappointment and chagrin, insect pests, particularly the boll weevil, have damaged all of Lasater's cotton to a great extent. . . ."[18]

The early dry spell and the late rains which set the stage for the insect damages to Lasater's crops had one positive aspect: "The late rains and these showers have put Lasater's lands in a favorable condition for prospective purchasers and he is giving attention to several sales which he has in prospect, but which are not sufficiently far along to justify us in placing any reliance whatever in them."[19] By September, Lasater's situation showed no sign of improvement, and Drought advised the mortgage holders that he had decided it was time to initiate foreclosure proceedings: "Whether or not Lasater can make such payments as to protect himself against these proceedings being carried on to their conclusion, we do not know at present, but we are inclined

[16] H. P. Drought to J. Kenneth Greenhill, July 26, 1926, Alliance Trust Company Correspondence, Drought Files, in possession of Thomas Drought, San Antonio.

[17] Ibid.

[18] Ibid., July 21, 1927.

[19] Ibid.

to believe he will not be able to do this, although he is actively trying to obtain funds from other sources as well as to make some sales of real estate."[20]

In December, 1927, Drought secured a judgment of foreclosure on Lasater's property. The judgment provided for an order of sale the following spring: "Of course, we may be surprised by Lasater's arranging a sale of our security, which would result in our obtaining our money, but this is an event which we do not foresee. . . ."[21]

On June 19, 1928, Drought wrote Kenneth Greenhill in Dundee, Scotland, that the Lasater situation had finally been resolved. Thirty-seven years after Drought's company first extended financing to the young South Texas cowman, the last Lasater loan on Drought's books was liquidated by a foreclosure sale presided over by the sheriff of Duval County.[22]

Lasater's profit and loss statement for 1928 included a $67,790 loss caused by the Drought sale. That figure represented the difference between the valuation given the property on Lasater's books and the actual sum received in the sheriff's auction.[23] Drought's correspondence at the time his company took possession of the Duval County tract referred to the broader problems Lasater faced: "As none of Lasater's other creditors has foreclosed, and as it seems that it will only be a question of time when several will, thus placing on the market at prices lower than Lasater is now quoting several large tracts of land in the vicinity of that owned by us, we realize that our hopes for a sale lie in being able to dispose of much of our land at an early date. . . ."[24]

Those who knew Ed Lasater in 1929 saw his health failing and saw him as a harassed man, increasingly distraught by the continuing burden of his financial obligations. "The last years of his life were devoted to keeping up with his debts. Paying his obligations as they came due consumed most of his time."[25] Lasater's son Garland returned to Falfur-

[20] Ibid., September 3, 1927.
[21] Ibid., December 22, 1927.
[22] Ibid., June 19, 1928.
[23] Ed C. Lasater financial statements, December 31, 1928, Lasater Files.
[24] H. P. Drought to J. Kenneth Greenhill, June 19, 1928, Alliance Trust Company correspondence, Drought Files.
[25] Interview, John M. Bennett, February 24, 1967, and L. D. Miller, Sr., September 22, 1971.

rias in the middle of 1929. Lasater's oldest son had completed two years
at Princeton University and had graduated from the U.S. Army Air
Corps' Advanced Flying School at Kelly Field in San Antonio. The
younger Lasater attempted to assist his father, but found it difficult:
"You can't put a young fellow into a going organization with older men
who have been involved over a period of years," he said, adding: "By
then you could feel things getting pretty tense. Dad was getting old,
and he was under pressure."[26]

L. D. Miller saw Lasater several times in 1929 when his brother-
in-law stopped by Miller's Okmulgee, Oklahoma, home for visits. "He
was a worried man," Miller stated. "He was grasping at straws."[27] On
June 29, 1929, Lasater signed a note for $98,000 payable to L. D. Mil-
ler on July 1, 1934. Miller's loan was secured by 22,855 acres, that portion of the Falfurrias Jersey Dairy Company still remaining in Lasater's
hands, and by 4,300 acres known as the "Rachal land."[28] That note consolidated various advances that Miller had made earlier to Mary and
Ed Lasater. Miller described the circumstances that brought about his
involvement in Lasater's financial affairs: "On or about December, 1927,
I learned that creditors of Ed C. Lasater, the Commerce Trust Company, the Commerce Farm Credit Company and the Missouri State
Life Insurance Company, were threatening foreclosure on certain
lands of Mary M. and Ed C. Lasater, as well as on 1,400 shares of stock
in the Falfurrias Mercantile Company belonging to the separate estate
of Mary Miller Lasater." Miller said he determined that the equity in
the properties exceeded the existing debt and he advanced $75,000 "in
order to keep the interests of my sister in said properties from being
sold and entirely lost."[29]

In the late twenties, Ed Lasater was increasingly burdened by his
own business problems, but he continued to be concerned with goals
that related to the Falfurrias country as a whole: "His undoing was
caused by his determination to develop the land and the community,
to show people the way to make a living on a small acreage," the son of
a close associate remembered his father saying on repeated occasions.

[26] Interview, Garland M. Lasater, July 29, 1981.

[27] Interview, L. D. Miller, September 22, 1971.

[28] Ed C. Lasater financial statements, December 31, 1929, Lasater Files.

[29] L. D. Miller, Sr., "To Whom It May Concern," attached to Ed C. Lasater financial statement, December 31, 1929.

Lasater cotton gin, located in the block north of East Rice, between Las Pitas and North St. Mary's streets. It was operated by Ed Lasater from 1906 until he sold it in 1921. Courtesy G. M. Lasater

Falfurrias, 1910, looking west across the railroad tracks. The two-story structure in the center, the Donahoe Building, served as the county's first courthouse. To its left is Burton and Danforth's sales office for the Parrita Ranch land development. Across East Rice Street to the north is the second Falfurrias Mercantile building, and on the far right is the railroad depot. Courtesy Brooks County Historical Commission

The Falfurrias State Bank Building, constructed in 1910, at the corner of East Rice and North Las Pitas streets. The bank was purchased by the First National Bank in 1923. Courtesy Falfurrias Heritage Museum

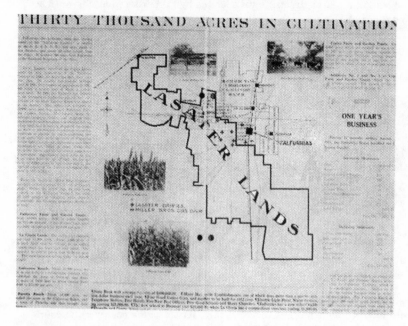

Centerfold of 1911 brochure distributed by the Miller brothers in their real estate sales promotion. Courtesy G. M. Lasater

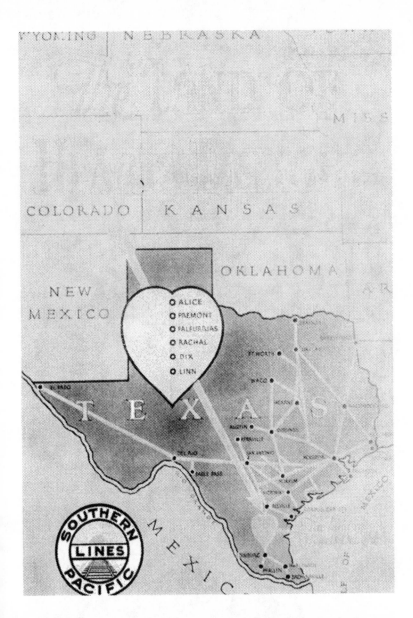

Cover of an early promotional brochure on the "Land of Heart's Delight," put
out by the Southern Pacific Railroad. Courtesy G. M. Lasater

Full-page advertisement placed by Ed Lasater in the *San Antonio Express* in 1926 to promote his farming subdivision west of Falfurrias. Courtesy G. M. Lasater

Registered Herefords on the Lasater Ranch, circa 1920. These cattle were bred with red circles around their eyes to prevent pink eye and cancer eye. Courtesy G. M. Lasater

T. S. Proctor, circa 1920, manager of the Falfurrias Creamery. This wooden churn with steel bands around the middle would turn out about one thousand pounds of butter. Courtesy G. M. Lasater

Jersey cows at the Cabezas Blancas dairy, south of Falfurrias. The silos were made of red brick. Courtesy G. M. Lasater

Early Falfurrias Creamery butter carton.

Left: L. D. Miller, Sr., youngest of the Miller brothers, 1929. Courtesy John B. Miller. *Right:* Richard G. Miller, circa 1899. The second oldest of the Miller brothers, he served as president of the Falfurrias State Bank until his death in 1922. Courtesy John B. Miller

Early-day milking, circa 1910, Falfurrias Jersey Dairy Company.

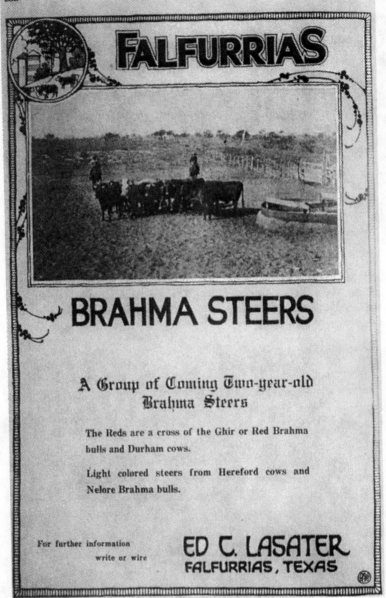

This advertisement for Brahman cattle was placed, along with three other cattle ads, in the *Cattleman* magazine by Ed Lasater in March, 1921. Courtesy *The Cattleman*

One of Peter McBride's sons added, "He gave everything he had to developing the country and improving the life of the area."[30]

Mary Lasater did not identify in the same way with the town and the farms that had been developed on part of her husband's former pasture lands. Her concerns and interests were not those of the local people.[31] But Ed Lasater never lost sight of the needs of the community he had established. Lasater's ranching neighbor, Ed Rachal, said in a speech at the school: "As you well know, Mr. Lasater had many problems in his personal business. . . . Mr. Lasater was sought as a member of the school board, and under the circumstances it would have been only the natural thing for a man to make the plea of having no time to spare . . . from his business. But far from that, he accepted his election to this position, served year after year, and maintained a never failing interest in this duty."[32]

The two houses Ed and Mary Lasater occupied during the 1920s symbolized one aspect of their relationship. Mary Lasater loved the large, white-columned house on Summit Avenue in San Antonio. That residence brought her close to her friends, the opera, reading clubs, and recitals. It also provided the means of keeping her children in contact with the offspring of her San Antonio friends and acquaintances. Ed Lasater had responded to his wife's wishes and purchased that house on Summit Avenue, but for him home was in the Falfurrias country, in the rambling ranch house beneath the live oak trees at La Mota.

Mary Lasater valued and respected social status, as well as the intellectual enlightenment and social refinement that she found among her friends in San Antonio. "Mr. Lasater felt that she valued some things that weren't essential. . . . He felt that the unity and the values that were building around Falfurrias were the true culture," Emily Edwards said. "I was sometimes puzzled by their relationship. It was as if there was a contest going on, a contest of values, what she wanted for the children and what he wanted."[33]

Like her mother, young Lois Lasater grew up surrounded by

---

[30] Interviews, William B. Gardner, Jr., March 8, 1982, and C. J. McBride, March 7, 1982.

[31] Interviews, Emily Edwards, February 25, 1967, and Matthew M. Gouger, March 20, 1982.

[32] Ed Rachal, "Address to the Falfurrias Public Schools," Lasater Files.

[33] Interview, Emily Edwards, February 25, 1967.

brothers. But unlike Mary Miller's childhood in Galveston, Lois's earliest years were spent in a world of ponies, cart races, sand dunes, and daredevil brothers in an isolated environment completely removed from early twentieth-century life elsewhere in the country. She learned to ride early, and she enjoyed the outings to Lucero, Salt Lake, and other ranch locations. Lois was a shy girl, terribly shy, and her mother was intent on promoting Lois's active association with youngsters of her own age in San Antonio.[34]

Mary Lasater spent most of her time in 1929 at the home on Summit Avenue. That year Lois joined the young ladies of San Antonio society in the annual Battle of the Flowers fete, where she appeared as the Duchess of Falfurrias. "Mr. Lasater's affairs were in bad shape; he needed every ounce of his wife's initiative and strength, but they were being dissipated on something which he considered unimportant," Mary Lasater's close friend remembered. "Mr. Lasater was sick at the time. He needed her attention, and she was caught up in that social thing. It was like a conflict."[35]

Mary Lasater longed for beauty and refinement, and she found them more readily in San Antonio than she did in the pasture land and small farms of South Texas. But she also sought understanding and knowledge through the serious study of the Bible and of individuals like Mahatma Gandhi, whose two-volume *An Autobiography, The Story of My Experiments With Truth*, first appeared in 1927 and 1929. "This simply told tale is amazing, because by seeking or hewing to the truth as he saw or understood it, he affected others in the most astonishing way. . . . Everything was his concern: diet, healing, cleanliness, and he asked no one to do what he would not do himself," Emily Edwards wrote. "Love was his weapon, and injustice his aim. . . . To me, Mary Lasater was struggling on this path."[36]

Ed Lasater believed that the earth was the basis of all wealth and that the continued fertility and productivity of the soil was a matter of utmost importance to any nation. He felt that the ranches and the farms of South Texas represented the highest elements of a nation's life. For Ed Lasater, cuture was not to be found in music, in social gatherings, in gala parties, or even in the serious volumes that filled his wife's

[34] Ibid.
[35] Ibid.
[36] Interview, Emily Edwards, June 7, 1967.

shelf of essential books. For him, the community of agriculturalists that surrounded his dairy farms and his pastures was the truest and most exalted embodiment of civilization: "Falfurrias was his creation, his dream. The Falfurrias country was a part of his being, a large part."[37]

October 24, 1929, Black Thursday, was the first of several panic-filled high-volume days characterized by precipitous declines on the New York Stock Exchange. It was followed by two days of relative calm that led many to assume erroneously that the financial debacle, though severe, was over. But that was not to be; the next week started off badly and proceeded to grow rapidly worse: "Tuesday, October 29, was the most devastating day in the history of the New York Stock Market, and it may have been the most devastating day in the history of markets."[38]

That same day, a full-page article about Ed Lasater appeared in the *San Antonio Express*. It was one of several sketches of noteworthy Texans that appeared in a special edition of the paper. It purported to recap the history of Texas as exemplified by the state's leading inhabitants. "It is largely the story of men who are cast in the heroic mold, men who refused to surrender, men who have hewn their way to their goals in the face of seemingly insurmountable obstacles."[39]

The article related Lasater's early experiences during the market decline and drought of the 1890s, the years just prior to his move into the Falfurrias country. "He had established, however, a reputation for energy, initiative and a scrupulous sense of honor, and no one was inclined to press him. He had been beaten to his knees by a succession of misfortunes, but he had no intention whatever of hoisting the white flag."[40]

The article described briefly the various phases of Ed Lasater's career—the early land purchases, the founding of the town, the subdivision and development of the farm ground, and the establishment of the Jersey herd and creamery which provided a focal point for the community of agriculturalists who settled in the area. The article described the "immense operations" undertaken by Lasater and then posed the

---

[37] Interview, Emily Edwards, February 25, 1967.
[38] Galbraith, *The Great Crash*, p. 116.
[39] *San Antonio Express*, October 29, 1929.
[40] Ibid.

question: "Has he completed his life work at the early age of his sixties? Not Lasater!" The story went on to detail a new real estate project that Lasater was initiating: "He is subdividing a 25,000-acre tract of his richest farm land into eighty-acre farms and selling on easy terms to ambitious and energetic people. Three hundred additional homes will be built among the thousand others that have found plenty and happiness in that section."[41]

The newspaper reporter waxed enthusiastic as he summarized what he had seen and heard during his visit to Falfurrias in the fall of 1929. "It is really refreshing in these days when it is fashionable to fleer, flout and rail at everybody who does not go in for a spurious aestheticism, miscalled art, to know men like Ed C. Lasater. He hasn't written a book, but he has furnished plenty of material for men who make books."[42]

The story did not attempt to give all the details of Ed Lasater's career or financial status. It did not discuss such subjects as loan balances, receiverships, or foreclosures, or any of the other harsh economic realities Lasater had to face during the 1920s. It covered only the high points of the years that had transpired since Edward Cunningham had taken his nephew in to see Colonel George Brackenridge at the San Antonio National Bank to establish the young man's first line of credit.

Ed Lasater had used his early credit to buy and sell horses and cattle. He celebrated his birthday on November 5, 1887, in Woodbury, Connecticut. He had been in the East for several weeks, traveling from town to town trying to sell his "Texas plugs" to reluctant Yankee buyers. His horse-trading venture had been slowed by bad weather and other complications and had taken more time than anticipated. In a letter to his mother, the youthful Lasater quoted his brother Tom as he described the minor adversities that had plagued the eastern outing: "I have been a little bit discouraged, but not whipped—or as Tom would express it, 'slightly disfigured, but still in the ring.'"[43]

A week after the Great Crash on Wall Street, Ed Lasater turned sixty-nine years old, and once again he was headed east. This time he was seeking new sources of financing for his ranching and dairy busi-

---

[41] Ibid.
[42] Ibid.
[43] Ed C. Lasater to Sarah Jane Lasater, October 9, 1887, and November 6, 1887.

ness, and he went carrying letters of introduction from several bankers and the governor of Texas. The bankers said the complimentary things a banker would say about a man who, despite problems and adversities, had managed to pay banks and loan companies millions of dollars in interest over several decades. The governor's letter contained the pleasing comments one would expect in a politician's letter about a noted constituent. He said that he had known Lasater for some time personally, and by reputation for a good many years. He stated that Lasater had pioneered the dairy business in Texas, and he affirmed that the rancher was widely esteemed as a man of character, integrity, and ability.[44]

In 1887 Lasater had written his mother from Ovid, New York, "I feel like starting out to hunt for something hard to do. You must have a real tough job on hand for me when I reach home."[45] In the course of the next four decades, Lasater had been able to find more than one tough job, and he was still actively managing his affairs and trying to improve the financial base for his various businesses in 1929. In December of that year, Lasater owed some twenty-five creditors almost one million dollars. Before consolidating his debts in the San Antonio Loan and Trust Company bond issue of 1913, he had owed almost exactly the same amount to ten creditors.[46] The acres of land and the numbers of cattle supporting that debt had been sharply reduced in the intervening years, and heavy operating losses in the decade after World War I had severely eroded the equity in his remaining collateral.

Ninety-eight years ago that month, Ignacio de la Peña received the Los Olmos y Loma Blanca grant. For more than sixty years he and his family owned land within that grant, land that lies to the west and north of the white hill that sits on the shores of the Laguna de Loma Blanca. De la Peña and his heirs survived Indian raids and marauders from both the United States and Mexico, but little by little the land slipped away. Taxes, drought, the lack of stock water, and the vicissi-

---

[44] Franz Groos, "To Whom It May Concern," August 13, 1929, and J. R. Scott, Jr., "To Whom It May Concern," August 14, 1929, both in Lasater Files.

[45] Ed C. Lasater to Sarah Jane Lasater, October 9, 1887.

[46] "Abstract of Title to Lots Numbers Three and Four in Block Numbered One of the Realitos Subdivision of the Copita Farm and Garden Tracts," Wright Abstract Company, San Diego, Texas, April 8, 1937, pp. 149–52. The 1913 figure excludes the $300,000 loan from the Central Trust Company on the Falfurrias Jersey Dairy Company lands that was not refinanced by the San Antonio Loan and Trust Company bond issue.

tudes of the markets for sheep, wool, and cattle reduced their resources. The falling markets of the 1880s culminating with the drought
and financial panic of 1893 dealt the final blow. De la Peña's granddaughter, Tomasa Hinojosa, and her husband, Matías García, were
among those who in 1895 could hold on no longer. Lasater's 25,000-acre
purchase from them launched him on a spectacular rise to prosperity
and prominence. Over the next two decades, Lasater bought and sold
land and cattle on an impressive scale across that region where the
Loma Blanca serves as a natural anchor; his lands once ran from that
hill thirty-five miles northwest to Realitos and twenty miles southeast
to the Quiteria pasture.

As the ninety-eighth year of the Los Olmos y Loma Blanca grant
drew to a close, the future ownership of part of that sandy mesquite-
covered plain was again in doubt. Once more the Fates were testing
the staying power of a man who claimed a portion of that tract as his
own. The Loma Blanca had changed only imperceptibly. The perma-
nence of that hill was a contrast to the stream of Indian scouts, Mexican
colonists, Anglo settlers, bankers, and lawyers who had come and gone
over the course of ten decades.

On December 17, 1929, Lasater's largest single note came due.[47]
His trip to the East had not uncovered new sources of credit, and Lasater was uncertain where to turn next to locate the capital he needed to
maintain his still extensive enterprises. On December 23, he borrowed $27,000 from a small bank in Alice, probably to pay some inter-
est and to stall his anxious creditors.[48] The new year would bring new
problems and would pose new questions. The white hill sat impas-
sively, waiting only for another year to brush lightly across its stately
countenance. It bore silent witness to those who came and went.

[47] Ibid.
[48] Ibid.

CHAPTER 14

A Train to Oklahoma

I live, but I shall not live forever.
Mysterious Moon, you only remain,
Powerful Sun, you alone remain,
Wonderful Earth, only you live forever.
—Death Song of the Texas Kiowa

In early 1930, Ed Lasater continued searching for a means of putting his business affairs on a more solid footing. On February 1, Lasater sold his neighbor Jim Cage another 16,685 acres for $123,855. The sale included an agreement which gave Lasater, still looking to the future, an option to buy back the land for the sales price plus interest a year later.[1]

Besides further land sales, Lasater saw one other possible solution for his problems: an oil strike. Exploration in the Falfurrias area had continued steadily over the years. A 1926 article related the discovery of a "mammoth" oil well in Duval County, which had caused an "undercurrent of enthusiasm" around Falfurrias, where numerous oil men were trying to negotiate leases. The story continued: "The salt dome south of town is directly in line with like formations to the west and north, and the feeling is strong that sometime in the not too distant future Falfurrias will be boasting of its oil production. . . ."[2] A team of English geologists had reached a similar conclusion after spending an extended period of time on the Falfurrias Ranch during the 1920s. They were convinced that the area around Gyp Hill, located south of

---

[1] Deed Records, Brooks County, vol. XII, pp. 173–78; Agreement between J. D. Cage and Ed C. Lasater, February 1, 1930, Lasater Files, in possession of Garland M. Lasater, Falfurrias.

[2] *Falfurrias Facts*, January 21, 1926.

the Laguna de Loma Blanca, would ultimately yield a mineral find, and they advised Lasater never to sell that part of his ranch.[3]

In September, 1929, following months of local reporting on strikes in the area, the elusive goal appeared to be within grasp when a newspaper article heralded the Houston Oil and Gas Company's discovery of a gas well west of Falfurrias. The well, drilled 4,117 feet, had an estimated pressure of 40 million cubic feet per day.[4] A few days later, local excitement reached a crescendo, and once again Lasater went out west of the headquarters to watch a well come in. The McBride family was there, as well as a number of neighbors. Several of Lasater's San Antonio bankers were also among the animated crowd that gathered on a Sunday afternoon in the Maguelles pasture to witness the event. The well produced a sensation: "Oil and gas men who were on the scene when the monster came in predicted as good for 50,000,000 to 80,000,000 cubic feet of gas per day."[5]

It was an exciting moment, but since natural gas was worthless at the time, the well produced no immediate income, even though it did maintain the promise of further exploration interest. And the Falfurrias optimism, evidently not the exclusive property of the town's founder or its real estate promoters, was quick to draw far-reaching conclusions about the area's future: "The bringing in of this immense gasser has brought an influx of oil men to Falfurrias. . . . Interest is growing as the news goes out, and no doubt Brooks County will prove the greatest oil and gas producing area in the state in a short while."[6]

Despite the steady stream of hopeful and promising reports about the prospect for oil reserves under his pasture land, Ed Lasater, twenty-eight years after he had signed his first oil lease with a Pennsylvania company, had not yet received any solid or bankable news. When concrete results had not materialized on his own property, he had begun looking further afield, and in 1927 he had formed a partnership with an oil promoter from Austin, named Campen. Lasater put $25,000 and then later another $25,000 into the Campen-Lasater Oil Company. He and Campen drilled several wildcat wells in Oklahoma, but their joint activity through 1929 had produced no finds of any consequence. Early

---

[3] Interviews, L. D. Miller, Sr., September 22, 1971, and Garland M. Lasater, February 21, 1981.

[4] *Brooks County Texan*, September 13, 1929, and September 20, 1929.

[5] *Brooks County Texan*, September 27, 1929; interview, C. J. McBride, March 7, 1982.

[6] *Brooks County Texan*, September 27, 1929.

the following year Lasater decided to go to Oklahoma to see firsthand their latest drilling prospect.[7] Campen was very excited about this one, and convinced their investment was at last going to pay off.

In the middle of March, 1930, Lasater left for Oklahoma. He stopped along the way in San Antonio to see Mary Lasater and his daughter Lois. Lois was a talented dancer, and the following day she was going to help with the dancing instruction at St. Mary's Hall. Lasater's wife had just been to the opera and had enjoyed it immensely. She was having a tea that afternoon for a friend visiting from Connecticut, and she and Molly Lupe were making arrangements for a program to be given at a luncheon meeting two days later.[8]

Lasater tried to see John Bennett in San Antonio, but they missed connections. As his train left the city, Lasater recalled the winter and spring the young graduate had spent with him on the ranch. He had hoped Bennett would stay in the Falfurrias country and enter the livestock business with him. But Bennett had decided that while he liked cattle and ranches, he preferred life in the city and had left Falfurrias to go to work for George Brackenridge. Lasater remembered his first visit to Brackenridge's bank with his Uncle Ed. He did not want to think about the problems of later years, about the disputes and deceptions, the bitterness and betrayal. At his wife's request, he had dictated a short letter outlining the early Cunningham-Lasater financial connections, but it did not explain everything. He would write another letter when he returned to Falfurrias; the children should know the whole story.

When the train stopped at a small town between San Antonio and Fort Worth, a group of boys stood on the platform pushing and shoving each other and laughing. Suddenly Ed Lasater remembered Albert and a picture of him taken only a few months before his death. Albert was standing near the pens at La Fruta with his blond hair, glasses, and a tweed coat, the same one he had worn when he had led the Grand Champion heifer into the ring at the Iowa State Fair. As the train began to move, the boys stopped their jostling and turned, smiling, to wave goodbye.

As the train moved on toward Fort Worth, Lasater recalled the

[7] Interviews, Tom Lasater, July 17, 1969, and Garland M. Lasater, February 21, 1981, and July 29, 1981.

[8] Interview, Jovita Gonzáles Mireles, March 6, 1982; *San Antonio Express*, March 11, March 13, March 16, March 18, and March 19, 1930.

trip he had made to that city to buy his first Jersey cows. He remembered how some of his ranching colleagues had joked with him about having traded his chaps and spurs for a milk pail.

During a layover in Fort Worth, Lasater went to the stockyards, where he walked around to look at the cattle offered that day. The animals were still being sold just as they had been the first time he visited the yards. Murdo MacKenzie was right after all. Cattlemen would never act in unison or deal from a position of strength. They still shipped their cattle to the point of sale and then asked the buyers what they were worth. He supposed they always would. Lasater ran into George Barse, who greeted him heartily and inquired about his health. Barse told Lasater that the cattle runs had been light; it looked like the market would strengthen and be higher by the time Lasater shipped the yearlings he planned to sell in May. While they walked along looking at the cattle and talking, they met the buyer for Swift and Company. They shook hands, exchanged views on the market, and then walked on.

After Fort Worth, the train headed north again. As it crossed the Red River into what had been the Indian Territory, Lasater thought of Ike Pryor's story of the long drive north, the cold nights, the stampedes, and the danger of swollen rivers. He thought of his own early experiences pasturing cattle in the territory with Patti's uncle, Alex Noble, and with Ed Caldwell's brother, Walter. That brought sister Ada to mind. Her daughter, Sarah, had written that Ada Caldwell was ill; he would go visit her in Corpus when he returned to South Texas.

He thought of Garland Miller, his enthusiastic assistant at Sugar Land, and of the high hopes that he had when he began the subdivision of the Falfurrias Farm and Garden Tract. He recalled the promise of the first crops, and Rob, the center of attention in any crowd, who could tell a story better than anyone in South Texas.

L. D. was different, Lasater thought, a serious young man who had gone to work for him when he was eighteen. L. D. had struck it rich and had become very knowledgeable about the oil business. After he got the latest report from Campen, Lasater mused, he would go to see L. D.; he always knew what was going on, and he would have some good advice.

After arriving in Ardmore, Oklahoma, Lasater spent the afternoon with Campen at the drilling site, going over the reports and listening to Campen's ideas about the future. When Lasater got back to his hotel room, he did not feel well. He thought it was probably the trip that had worn him out, as well as his doubts about Campen, which were weighing on him. He went upstairs to his room to spend another night alone, like so many nights at the end of other train trips he had made over the past twenty years. If this deal did not produce a strike, Lasater thought, he would quit backing Campen. Lasater no longer had as much confidence in what his partner said, even though Campen was still very positive and enthusiastic about the prospects.

The next morning Lasater awoke early, but he did not feel rested and ready as he usually did. He asked the hotel to summon a doctor. Dr. Hardy examined the rancher and decided he should be moved to the clinic immediately. Hardy called Lasater's wife in San Antonio to appraise her of Lasater's illness. Mary Lasater boarded the next train leaving for Oklahoma.

L. D. Miller drove from Okmulgee to Ardmore and was the first to reach Lasater's hospital room. After hearing Dr. Hardy describe the gravity of Lasater's condition, Miller called his nephew, Tom, at school in New Jersey. He advised Tom to catch a train for San Antonio, as he did not believe he could reach Ardmore in time. After the train carrying Tom west had stopped in Indianapolis, the conductor walked down the aisle to Tom's seat and said: "Young man, I have a telegram for you with some very sad news." Ed Lasater was dead.[9]

Amid the articles and editorials that appeared around the country after Lasater's death, and among the messages sent by letter and telegram, perhaps the words of those closest to him, his neighbors and colleagues on the local County Commissioners Court, best characterized the man from Falfurrias: "We have found him a loyal friend, a man of rare judgment in the business affairs of the county, of the highest integrity, always sacrificing his own personal interests for the benefit of the community, always planning something for the advancement of the county and its citizens. . . . an humble man, and a great citizen."[10]

---

[9] Interview, Tom Lasater, July 23, 1981.

[10] James H. Smylie, *Edward C. Lasater, A Biographical Portrait*, p. 20. Even now, a half-century after Lasater's death, a variety of rumors persist around Falfurrias regarding the circumstances of his death. None of them could be verified by anyone in a position to know the facts. The Oklahoma Department of Health death certificate states that Lasater was treated from March 17 to March 20 by Dr. Walter Hardy and that he died of uremic poisoning on March 20, 1930, in the Hardy Sanitarium, Ardmore, Oklahoma.

Epilogue

One generation passeth away, and another generation
cometh; but the earth abideth forever.

—Ecclesiastes 1:4

WHEN Ed Lasater died, he had not put his name on anything: not
the town he founded, not the county he helped create, not even the
creamery whose butter consumers all over Texas associated only with
the name Falfurrias. But even without a specific product or landmark,
many would remember the dairyman and rancher who had ridden his
horse south across the Nueces River.

Times were hard in the years following Ed Lasater's death, not just
for his family or for Falfurrias, but for countless families and communities all across the country. Lasater's ranch, already partitioned and
greatly diminished between 1920 and 1930, was reduced to a mere
trace of its former extension. His family maintained ownership of the
creamery and the mercantile store only with the help of friends and
relatives. The Great Depression appeared to eclipse the vision and
dash those dreams which had sprouted so spontaneously out of that
sandy soil. Falling markets and drought rudely jarred the pastoral scene
once again. Foreclosures, intrigue, and family disputes tarnished the
romance and glamor associated with the Land of Heart's Delight.

But more than fifty years after Lasater's death, Falfurrias is a bus-
tling community, a rural trade center for those who still live off the land
as well as for many involved in the varied business enterprises that
have brought new activity and new vigor to the town whose courthouse
sits on the hill where a lone coyote once barked. Lasater's former associates have a living legacy; descendants of McBride and Maupin,
Rachal, Miller, and Proctor are alive and well. Hilario García's numerous family has grown more numerous, and his heirs have distinguished

his memory more than once. The Treviños, the McIntyres, the Cosbys, and the Cantus carry on their proud traditions, and Sabas Pérez's descendants continue to pasture their cattle on the south side of the big lake. The Bennetts, Caldwells, and Gardners visit their friends and relatives who stayed on in the Falfurrias country. López, Cage, and Villareal, too, are all represented after several decades of change and transition.

Five decades after Lasater boarded a train to take his last trip, his former schoolboard colleague, Neil Rupp, still lives out east of town. Every day he makes his daily rounds to check his cattle—big, productive animals belonging to a new breed developed by Lasater's youngest son, that incorrigible youth who could not be interested in anything but a Brahman cow.

The Park Hotel no longer sits on the west side of St. Mary's Street across from the school. But sixty-five years after she stepped off the train and first walked along its unpaved streets to reach that place which provided respite and sustenance for weary travelers, Willie Best still lives in Falfurrias. Sitting on her front porch with her eyes half-closed, she appears unconcerned about the passage of time and unaware of her own transformation over the years into a brush-country celebrity, a living link with another era, and a quiet contrast to the modern cowboys, the urban hunters, and the oil men whose late-model pickups surge back and forth along the crowded streets of that once dusty village, which sat for so many years at the end of the line.

More than half a century after Ed Lasater's passing, the pastoral tradition inaugurated by Albert Lasater's move to Texas in 1857 is carried on by his descendants in Texas and Colorado. Southeast of Falfurrias, Lasater cattle still graze in the Loma Blanca pasture. There, on a summer day in 1981, Ed Lasater's two surviving sons, several grandchildren (including the author), and a number of great grandchildren rode horseback over that prominent white hill. They watched the whitecaps as the wind blew across Salt Lake; they built a campfire with mesquite wood and told the young ones stories of cowboys' daring deeds, rattlesnakes, border bandits, and outlaw cattle. When all the stories had been told and retold, they sat watching the fire, listening. Only the yelping of the coyotes hidden in the brush broke the nocturnal silence. All was quiet on that hill they call the Loma Blanca.

Financial Reports, Ed C. Lasater,

1910–14

TABLE 1.
Profit and Loss Summary, Ed C. Lasater

	Year Ending			
	6-30-1910	6-30-1911	6-30-1912	6-30-1913
Cattle Sales	$ 47,017.07	$212,484.18	$215,465.30	$352,414.87
General Ranch Expense[1]	(63,165.36)	(175,004.41)[6]	(118,662.64)	(80,142.19)
Interest Expense—Cattle[2]	(28,143.24)	(63,754.11)	(55,671.45)	(85,517.42)
Cash Profit (Loss)—Cattle	($44,291.53)	($26,274.34)	$ 41,131.21	$186,755.26
Cattle Inventory Value, increase (decrease) resulting from head count changes (net of purchases)[3]	173,221.93	(59,260.00)	29,607.50	(157,811.29)
Cattle Inventory Value, increase from raised book value per head		753.00	55,028.07	123,933.00
Profit (loss) on cattle, including inventory changes	$128,930.40	($84,781.34)	$125,766.78	$152,876.97
Other Income:				
Farming, Falfurrias and Realitos[4]	$ 25,916.87	$ 8,425.28	$ 2,582.32	$ 8,348.61
Profit on Land Sales		3,450.96	21,722.57	45,557.70
Rents		3,978.55	3,349.92	2,754.97
Other Sales	4,345.52	1,367.06		10,344.10[11]
Jersey operation		(6,920.82)	(10,343.67)	
Total Other Income	$ 30,262.39	$ 10,301.00	$ 17,311.14	$ 67,005.38

Expenses:			
General Expense	($21,645.44)	($34,981.55)	($32,703.64)	($30,541.97)
Interest	(9,381.08)	(32,790.68)	(29,976.94)	(46,047.85)
Personal Draw	(22,189.69)	(28,079.97)	(16,793.99)	(66,797.44)
Total Other Income and Expenses	($22,953.82)	($85,551.20)	($62,163.43)	($76,381.88)
Book Adjustment	$ 23,269.42[5]	$ 69,422.75[7]	$ 32,920.00[9]	$ 73,200.00[12]
Land Sales to Related Parties		737,170.50[8]	10,000.00[10]	
Profit per Lasater Books	$129,246.00	$636,260.71	$106,523.35	$149,695.09

[1]Labor costs during these years typically ran 25–30% of general ranch expense excluding feed, which varied widely; repairs and supplies accounted for another 20–30%, with land rents and freight being other major items.

[2]This is 75% of Lasater's interest charge in 1910, 65% thereafter.

[3]See Table 3, Cattle Inventory.

[4]In 1910: Falfurrias, $19,119.17, Realitos $6,797.70. This is the only year the two areas are separated.

[5]Real estate purchase marked up to Lasater book value of lands purchased earlier.

[6]Feed jumped to $108,315.90 from $12,181.10 the previous year and $57,402.66 the following year.

[7]Books adjusted by $29,360.50 to reflect difference between "book value and invoice" on 747 head of horses and mules, and by $40,062.25 to reflect the difference between the average purchase cost of $3.44/acre on 25,642.81 acres and Lasater's book value of $5.00 per acre on ranchland.

[8]Net profit on 40,000 acres sold by Lasater to the Falfurrias Jersey Dairy Company, a corporation owned by him.

[9]A book adjustment increasing the value of the capital stock of the Falfurrias Jersey Dairy Company. owned by Lasater.

[10]This was the profit on the sale of 2,000 acres to the Cornell-Miller Company, an entity in which Ed Lasater, Robert Miller, and Robert Cornell were principals.

[11]In Lasater's Profit and Loss statements from 1910 to 1913, the 1911 loss of $6,920.85 is the only profit or loss figure given for the Jersey operation. However, Lasater's 1913 balance sheet enters as an asset an account-receivable figure of $19,932.87 from the Falfurrias Dairy Company.

[12]Profit on issuance of 732 shares of stock in the Falfurrias Mercantile Co., a corporation owned by Lasater.

TABLE 2.
Balance Sheet of June 30, 1913, Ed C. Lasater

ASSETS			
Real Estate			
Ranch and Farm Lands:	$1,505,078.47		
(286,641.57 a. @ $5.25)			
Curtis Land: 47.02 a.	5,453.00		
	$1,510,531.47		
Improvements	22,813.98		$1,533,345.45
Falfurrias Townsite Lots & Blocks			35,213.34
Dwelling House, Stores, Etc.			27,391.27
Gin Plants: (Copita & Esperanza)			26,722.46
Investments, Stocks & Bonds			1,201,432.86
Office Furniture & Fixtures			3,488.73
Hotel & Cottage Furnishings			3,627.74
Falfurrias Jersey Dairy Co.: (Loan a/c):			19,932.87
Inventories:			
Cattle: 15,659 head	$ 546,050.00		
Horses & Mules: 739	35,752.57		
Sheep & Goats	747.45		
Wagons & Harness	3,938.01		
Agricultural Implements	3,045.93		
Stores	3,450.49		
Gin Supplies (1913)	537.50		
		$ 593,521.95	
Bills & Accounts Receivable:			
Bills	$ 144,712.72		
Accounts	130,179.11	$ 274,891.83	
1913 Crops (in field at June 30, 1913):			1,279.16
Cash			56,219.44
TOTAL ASSETS			$3,777,067.10

TABLE 2.
Balance Sheet of June 30, 1913, Ed C. Lasater

LIABILITIES		
Bills Payable		$1,009,919.29
Accounts Payable		1,851.99
State of Texas		167,927.66
Deferred Commissions (Copita & Realitos)		33,718.04
Ranch & Farm Land Sales (on contract)		52,713.19
Reserve Accounts		
Bills	$ 13,376.85	
Insurance	3,384.06	$ 16,760.91
CAPITAL	$2,344,480.93	
Add P&L	149,695.09	$2,494,176.02
TOTAL LIABILITIES & CAPITAL		$3,777,067.10

TABLE 3.
Cattle Inventory, Ed C. Lasater

| | Year Ending | | | |
| | 6-30-1910 | | 6-30-1911 | |
	Head and Value per head	Total Value	Head and Value per head	Total Value
Cows and yearling heifers[1]	9,786 @ $28.50	$278,901.00	9,761 @ $28.50	$278,188.50
Bulls	546 @ $41.00	22,386.00	555 @ $41.00	22,755.00
Calves	4,738 @ $12.50	59,225.00	3,000 @ $12.50	37,500.00
Yearling steers	1,728 @ $20.00	34,560.00	2,129 @ $20.00	42,580.00
Two-year-old steers	2,557 @ $27.00	69,039.00	1,506 @ $27.50	41,415.00
Three-year-old steers	2,481 @ $35.00	86,835.00	2,000 @ $35.00	70,000.00
Four-year-old steers				
Total	21,836	$550,946.00	18,951	$492,438.50
Increase (decrease) in dollar value of cattle inventory from previous year resulting from:				
1) Head count change		$173,221.00		($ 59,260.00)
2) Value per head change				753.00
3) Purchases		8,546.00		
Total Change from previous year		$181,767.00		($ 58,507.50)

[1]In 1910, the breakdown was 7,790 cows, two's and up, and 1,996 yearling heifers

6-30-1912		Year Ending 6-30-1913		6-30-1914	
Head and Value per head	Total Value	Head and Value per head	Total Value	Head and Value per head	Total Value
10,631 @ $32.97	$350,504.07	10,000 @ $43.44	$434,400.00	12,039 @ $43.73	$526,465.47
530 @ $41.00	21,730.00	547 @ $50.00	27,350.00	578 @ $88.28	51,030.60
4,984 @ $12.50	62,300.00	4,800 @ $15.00	72,000.00	5,569 @ $17.30	96,343.90
1,500 @ $20.00	30,000.00	100 @ $30.00	4,000.00		
2,129 @ $30.00	63,870.00	50 @ $40.00	2,000.00		
437 @ $40.00	17,480.00	162 @ $45.00	7,300.00		
618 @ $55.00	33,990.00				
20,829	$579,874.07	15,659	$546,050.00	18,186	$673,839.77

	$ 29,607.50		($157,811.29)		$ 72,700.16
	55,028.07		123,933.00		38,430.61
	2,800.00		44.22		16,669.00
	$ 87,435.57		($ 33,834.07)		$127,799.77

Bibliography

DOCUMENT COLLECTIONS

Author's Files. Dale Lasater, Colorado Springs, Colorado.

Brooks County. Deed Records. Falfurrias, Texas.

Brooks County Commissioners Court Minutes. Falfurrias, Texas.

Brooks County Historical Commission Files. Falfurrias, Texas.

Caldwell Files. Papers and letters of the late Sarah Cunningham Caldwell, in possession of Clay Caldwell, Corpus Christi, Texas.

Cattleman Files. Fort Worth, Texas. Back issues and related materials of the *Cattleman* magazine.

Drought Files. Thomas Drought, San Antonio, Texas. Historical memorandums, bound volumes of correspondence, and bound volumes of loan records of H. P. Drought and Company and Francis Smith and Company. Collection includes volumes related to business transacted with the Alliance Trust, the United States Mortgage Company, and the American Freehold Land Mortgage Company, among other English and Scottish loan companies.

Duval County. Deed Records. San Diego, Texas.

Hidalgo County. Transcribed Deed Records. Falfurrias, Texas.

Lasater, Edward C., Collection. Eugene C. Barker Texas History Center. University of Texas, Austin. Includes the following statements by Lasater: "Address at the Annual Convention of the Texas Cattle Raisers' Association," Fort Worth, March 23, 1912; "Address before the National Conference on Marketing and Farm Credits," Chicago, December 6, 1916; "Meat Packer Legislation," statement before the Committee on Agriculture, U.S. House of Representatives, March 1, 2, 3, and 6, 1920; "Policies and Practices of Mr. Hoover as Food Administrator Are Harmful to the Common Welfare," March 7, 1918; "Reply to Statement Filed by United States Food Administrator, Herbert Hoover, on May 1, 1918, with the Hon. Thomas P. Gore, Chairman, Committee on Agriculture and Forestry, United States Senate, Washington, D.C."; "Texan Says Hoover Not Efficient," unidentified 1918 newspaper article.

Lasater Files. Garland M. Lasater, Falfurrias, Texas. Letters and papers of Ed C. Lasater and his business enterprises. Includes "Audit Report," Ernst and Ernst, March 19, 1923; "Bill of Sale," Ed C. Lasater to Tom Lasater, May 6, 1921; Brooks County Abstract Company, "Lot Eleven, Block Eleven, Falfurrias Farm and Garden Tracts," Falfurrias, August 8, 1931; Dawson, W. L., "Abstract of Lands of Ed C. Lasater in Falfurrias Town Tract and Falfurrias Farm and Garden Tracts. From June 1, 1904 to May 18, 1906," Falfurrias; Kirkland, O. D., "A Complete Abstract of Title to a Tract of 640 Acres out of Los Olmos y Loma Blanca Grant," Falfurrias, 1926; Lasater, Edward C., *Some Printed Addresses and Statements in Public Service 1900–1930*; Lasater, Ed., and Falfurrias Immigration Company, "Agreement," Falfurrias, 1906; Lasater, Ed, Garland Miller, B. T. Henry, "Partnership Agreement, Falfurrias Development Company," Falfurrias, 1905; Lasater accounting staff, "Review and Analysis," July 15, 1914; Maupin, James T., "Signed Affidavit," Falfurrias, August 11, 1938; Rachal, Ed, "Address to the Falfurrias Public Schools," 1930; *San Antonio Express*, undated 1911 clipping; Seaton, Mildred, "Abstract of Land Owned by Ed C. Lasater in Grant of Los Olmos y Loma Blanca in Counties of Nueces, Duval, Hidalgo, Starr, Texas," Nueces County, December 19, 1904; Williams, A. C., Untitled speech given in Houston, 1930s; Wright Abstract Company, "Abstract of Title to Lots Three and Four in Block One of the Realitos Subdivision of Copita Farm and Garden Tracts, Situated in Duval County, Texas," San Diego, Texas, 1937.

Schuetz Files. Florence Schuetz, Falfurrias, Texas.

Starr County. Deed Records. Rio Grande City, Texas.

Starr County. Transcribed Deed Records. Falfurrias, Texas.

Texas and Southwestern Cattle Raisers Association Collection. Fort Worth, Texas.

Texas Secretary of State. Austin. Amendment to the Charter of the Falfurrias State Bank, November 10, 1911. Facts Publishing Company, Corporate Charter, April 26, 1906. Falfurrias Machine Shops, Corporate Charter, July 11, 1907. Falfurrias Mercantile Company, Corporate Charter, February 26, 1906. Falfurrias Power Company, Corporate Charter, July 11, 1907.

Treviño Files. Florentino Treviño, Falfurrias, Texas.

UNPUBLISHED MANUSCRIPTS

Anders, Evan M. "Bosses Under Siege: The Politics of South Texas During the Progressive Era." Ph.D. dissertation, University of Texas at Austin, 1978.

Bennett, John M. "Notes on Ed Lasater." 1967. Author's Files.

"Climatic Summary of the United States, Sections 30, 31, 32, 33." United States Department of Agriculture, Weather Bureau, Washington, D.C., 1931.

Caldwell, Ada L. "Recollections." Corpus Christi, Texas, 1935.

Caldwell, Edward H. "An Appreciation of Edward Cunningham Lasater." 1939.

———. "The Life and Activities of Edward Cunningham Lasater." 1937.

———. "Notes and Facts in the Life of E. H. Caldwell." Corpus Christi, 1934.

Dyer, Lloyd N. "The History of Brooks County." M.S. thesis, Texas College of Arts and Industries, 1938.

Eastwick, Edward P., Jr. "Report on Sugar Factories Owned by Ed H. Cunningham and Co. (Ed C. Lasater, Receiver), Sugar Land, Texas." February 8, 1905. Imperial Sugar Company Records.

González, Jovita. "Social Life in Cameron, Starr, and Zapata Counties." M.A. thesis, University of Texas at Austin, 1930.

"Historical Memorandum: Law firm of Terrell, Davis, McMillan and Hall, 1930-1976." San Antonio, Texas.

Lasater, Margaret K. "Edward Cunningham Lasater: His Development of the Falfurrias Country." Senior thesis, Vassar College, 1965.

Picquet, Jimmie R. "Some Ghost Towns in South Texas." M.S. thesis, Texas A&I University, 1972.

Schuetz, Florence. "Brooks County Courthouse." Undated. Falfurrias, Texas.

Tinsley, James A. "The Progressive Movement in Texas." Ph.D. dissertation, University of Wisconsin, 1953.

Wilbur, John L. "Historical Data, Texas Animal Health Commission," May, 1978. *Cattleman* Files.

INTERVIEWS

Bennett, John M. Taped interviews and conversations, February 24 and 26, 1967. Mr. Bennett (1878-1974) spent several months in 1900-1901 on the Falfurrias Ranch before returning to San Antonio to enter the banking business. He was the brother of Ed Lasater's first wife, Martha (Patti) Noble Bennett.

Bennett, John M., Jr. Taped interview, July 24, 1981. General Bennett (b. 1908), former chairman of the board of the National Bank of Commerce in San Antonio, was a frequent visitor to the Lasater Ranch in the 1920s.

Bennett, Mrs. T. R. Taped interview, July 31, 1981. When Mrs. Bennett (b. 1894) moved to Falfurrias in 1916 as a new bride, her husband was a bookkeeper for Ed Lasater. Roy Bennett later worked in the First National Bank and served as Falfurrias postmaster. Roy Bennett was no relation to John Bennett of San Antonio.

Best, Willie. April 8, 1981. Mrs. Best moved to Falfurrias to work in the Park Hotel in 1917 and was later the cook at the Lasater ranch. Her husband, Nathaniel, worked for Ed Lasater as chauffeur and in the Falfurrias Creamery Company.

Blumer, Walter. Taped interview, July 12, 1981. Mr. Blumer (b. 1899) moved to Falfurrias in 1915 after his father, Robert Ferdinand von Blumer, a Chicago doctor, had purchased land in the area.

Brooks, John Morgan. April 8, 1981. Judge Brooks (b. 1899) is the son of Captain J. A. Brooks, who served as Brooks County's first judge from 1911 to

1939. The younger Brooks succeeded his father, serving as judge from 1939 to 1971.

Cage, Richard G. March 25, 1982. Mr. Cage (b. 1909) is a son of J. D. Cage, who purchased a ranch near Falfurrias in 1925.

Caldwell, Sarah Cunningham. Taped interview, June 26, 1971. Miss Caldwell (1885–1974) was the daughter of Lasater's sister, Ada Lasater Caldwell.

Cartwright, Holman. May 10, 1971. A rancher from Dinero, Texas, Cartwright (1889–1980) and his wife, Cyrus Lucas's daughter Claire, were close friends of Ed and Mary Lasater. Cartwright served as president of the Texas and Southwestern Cattle Raisers' Association from 1944 to 1946.

Casey, Ethel Matthews. Taped interview, August 29, 1981. Mrs. Casey (b. 1887) is the daughter of J. A. and Sallie Reynolds Matthews, pioneer West Texas ranchers. In 1914 she moved to San Antonio, where she knew the Lasaters.

Cosby, A. Alonzo. Taped interview, July 5, 1981. Mr. Cosby (b. 1919) is the son of early Falfurrias residents A. A. Cosby and Otie York Cosby.

Coward, Jesse. February 24, 1981. Mr. Coward (b. 1880) worked for Ed Lasater from 1912 to 1919 at Realitos and then as foreman at Encino.

Dale, Albert W. Taped interview, August 25, 1971. Mr. Dale (b. 1894) went to work for Ed Lasater in the Falfurrias Mercantile Company in 1916.

Denman, Gilbert. October 14, 1981. Mr. Denman's father and grandfather were San Antonio lawyers and bankers. The grandfather, Judge Leroy G. Denman, purchased George W. Brackenridge's interest in the San Antonio National Bank and the San Antonio Loan and Trust Company in 1912.

Denman, Leroy G. October 15, 1981. Mr. Denman, a San Antonio lawyer and banker, succeeded his father as a principal lawyer and advisor to the King Ranch.

Drought, Thomas. January 27, 1982. Mr. Drought is a grandson of H. P. Drought, owner of H. P. Drought and Company, a major source of financing for Ed Lasater and other South Texas agriculturalists at the turn of the century.

Edwards, Emily. Taped interview, February 25, 1967. Miss Edwards (1888–1980), an artist and writer, was a close friend of Mary Miller Lasater.

Foster, Joe. Taped interview, July 9, 1981. Mr. Foster (b. 1908) began work in the Falfurrias Creamery in 1929.

Gammie, Leslie Holbrook. Taped interview, July 25, 1981. Mrs. Gammie (b. 1896) moved with her family to the Falfurrias area when it was still part of Starr County.

García, Hilario, Jr. March 22, 1982. Mr. García is a son of Hilario García who moved with his father, Julián García, to the Falfurrias area in the 1890s and went to work for Lasater in 1905.

García, Julián. Taped interview, July 25, 1981. Mr. García, a son of Hilario García, worked on Ed Lasater's ranch in the 1920s.

Gardner, William Burleigh, Jr. March 8, 1982. Mr. Gardner (b. 1925) is a grandson of Mary Miller Lasater's uncle, William A. Gardner. His grandfather and his father were associated with several early Lasater enterprises in Falfurrias.

Gouger, Matthew M. March 20, 1982. Mr. Gouger (b. 1905) grew up in Falfurrias, where his grandfather, Lake Newell Porter, was sheriff from 1919 to 1922.

Hauser, Mr. and Mrs. Lawrence. April 17, 1981. Mrs. Hauser's father, T. S. Proctor, moved to Falfurrias to manage the Falfurrias Creamery Company in 1916.

Holbrook, Martine. Taped interview, July 25, 1981. Miss Holbrook (b. 1905), a former Falfurrias schoolteacher, is the daughter of H. C. Holbrook, an early-day Falfurrias store owner.

Jenkins, Huston. Taped interview, July 13, 1981. Mr. Jenkins (1908–82) moved with his family from Paris, Illinois, to Realitos, Texas, to a farm his father purchased from Ed Lasater in 1916.

Lasater, Carolyn Kampmann (Mrs. Garland M.) Taped interview, March 24, 1982. Mrs. Lasater (b. 1915) is the daughter of San Antonio lawyer Ike S. Kampmann.

Lasater, Garland Miller. Taped interviews, February 21, July 29, 1981. Mr. Lasater (b. 1907) is a son of Ed Lasater.

Lasater, Tom. Taped interviews and conversations, January 12 and November 9, 1980, and July 23, 1981. Mr. Lasater (b. 1911) is a son of Ed Lasater.

McAllen, A. A. July 20, 1981. Mr. McAllen (b. 1912) is a member of a pioneer South Texas ranching family.

McBride, Clarence J. March 7, 1982. Mr. McBride (b. 1906), the head of the Laredo Production Credit Association for many years, is a son of Peter McBride, who was foreman of Ed Lasater's Realitos holdings from 1914 until 1930.

McBride, Dennis. Taped interview, July 27, 1981. Mr. McBride (b. 1911) is a son of Peter McBride.

McIntyre, Dick. July 26, 1981. Mr. McIntyre is a grandson of R. J. McIntyre, who moved from Arkansas to Falfurrias in 1909 and entered the lumberyard business.

Maldonado, Juan. Taped interview, July 13, 1981. Mr. Maldonado (b. 1905) began work on Ed Lasater's ranch in 1921 and later worked in the Falfurrias Creamery Company.

Miller, Bradford F. October 15, 1981. Mr. Miller (b. 1914) is a son of Richard Miller, a brother of Mary Miller Lasater.

Miller, Gardner B. Taped interviews and conversations, July 18 and July 22, 1981. Mr. Miller (b. 1920) is a son of L. D. Miller, Sr.

Miller, John C. September 21, 1971, and June 30, 1981. Mr. Miller (b. 1929) is a son of L. D. Miller, Sr.

Miller, L. D., Jr. July 2 and July 11, 1981. Mr. Miller (1917–81) was a son of L. D. Miller, Sr.

Miller, Laurence Dismukes, Sr. Taped interviews and conversations, September 21 and 22, 1971. Mr. Miller (1888–1977), brother of Mary Miller Lasater, worked with Ed Lasater for a number of years beginning in 1906. In the 1920s he became financially involved with Lasater as a creditor.

Mireles, Jovita González. March 6, 1982. Mrs. Mireles (1899–1983) spent her early years on Las Víboras, a Starr County ranch founded by her grandfather, Francisco Guerra, a cousin of Manuel Guerra.

Noll, Edena Clere Scott. Taped interview, July 20, 1981. Mrs. Noll (b. 1914) is the daughter of J. R. Scott, Jr., Falfurrias banker, and the granddaughter of Frank Rachal, pioneer Falfurrias cattleman.

Noll, Marvin. Taped interview, July 10, 1981. Mr. Noll (b. 1912), president of the First National Bank of Falfurrias, came to Falfurrias from Chicago with his family in 1918.

Pérez, Petra. March 23, 1982. Miss Pérez is a descendant of Sabas Pérez, who moved to the Loma Blanca grant in 1850.

Rupp, Neil. July 28, 1981. Mr. Rupp (b. 1896), a citrus grower and cattleman, moved to Falfurrias with his family in 1910.

Schuetz, Florence. Taped interview, April 9, 1981. Miss Schuetz (b. 1898) taught school on the Lasater Ranch at Number Five in 1918 and later for many years in the Falfurrias school system. She is chairman of the Brooks County Historical Commission.

Smith, Mildred Maupin (Mrs. L. C.). July 14, 1981. Mrs. Smith is a daughter of James Maupin, a longtime foreman on the Lasater Ranch, who served as county sheriff from 1913 to 1918.

Treviño, Juana González, July 17, 1981. In 1912, Mrs. Treviño (b. 1896) moved to Lasater's Las Conchas Dairy, where her husband, Agapito Treviño, worked for many years.

Treviño, Florentino. July 2, 1981. Mr. Treviño (b. 1895) is a son of Lino Treviño, an early resident of Los Olmos and longtime justice of the peace.

Victor, Bird McBride. March 5, 1982. Mrs. Victor (b. 1908) is a daughter of Peter McBride.

Wagenschein, Dr. Miriam. March 3, 1982. Dr. Wagenschein is a daughter of Carl F. Wagenschein (1885–1978) who moved to Falfurrias to work as an accountant in the Falfurrias Power Company in 1913. He and W. B. Gardner purchased that company from Ed Lasater in 1921.

COURT CASES

Fant v. D. Sullivan and Company et al. 124 *Southwestern Reporter*, pp. 691–93.

Fant v. Wickes. 32 *Southwestern Reporter*, p. 127.

Lasater et al. v. Fant. 43 *Southwestern Reporter*, p. 321.

Lasater v. *Magnolia Petroleum Company, First State Bank of Corpus Christi et al.* Supreme Court of the United States, October term, 1918, No. 658. Washington, D.C.: Judd and Detweiler, 1918.

Parr v. McGown. 98 *Southwestern Reporter*, pp. 950–51.

Ramirez et al. v. Lasater et al. 174 *Southwestern Reporter*, pp. 706–10.

Spark et ux v. Lasater et al. 234 *Southwestern Reporter*, pp. 717–20.

Spielhagen v. Falfurrias Immigration Co. et al. 129 *Southwestern Reporter*, pp. 164–70.

Sullivan v. Fant. 110 *Southwestern Reporter*, pp. 509–23, and 160 *Southwestern Reporter*, pp. 614–23.

NEWSPAPERS

Alice Echo, 1897–1908.

Brooks County Texan, 1929–32.

Corpus Christi Caller-Times, October 27, 1935; July 18, 1942; January 18, 1959.

Dallas Morning News, August 19, 1974.

Falfurrias Facts, 1906–30; June 15, 1934; June 30, 1939; May 11, 1961; March 19, 1980; November 19, 1981.

Houston Chronicle, February 17, 1924.

New York Times, November 13 and 18, 1917; January 27 and March 31, 1918; March 22, 1930.

Nueces County News, July 14, 1939.

San Antonio Express, June 20, 1891; November 15, 1906; February 4, 1909; March 28, 1930.

San Antonio Light, October 4, 1909.

Wall Street Journal, February 5, 1981; May 14, 1981.

BOOKS AND PAMPHLETS

About Falfurrias and Copita. Falfurrias: Miller Bros. Company, 1911.

Allhands, J. L. *Gringo Builders*. Iowa City: Clio Press, 1931.

———. *Railroads to the Rio*. Salado, Tex.: Anson Jones Press, 1960.

Bennett, John M., Jr. *Those Who Made It*. San Antonio: privately printed, 1978.

Brooks County Elected Officials 1911–1978. Falfurrias: Brooks County Historical Commission, 1979.

Brooks County Golden Fiesta. Falfurrias: privately printed, 1961.

Buckley, Priscilla L., and William F. Buckley, Jr., eds. *W. F. B.—An Appreciation*. New York: privately printed, 1979.

Casdorph, Paul D. *Republicans, Negroes, and Progressives in the South, 1912–1916*. Birmingham: University of Alabama Press, 1981.

Clark, Margaret Lasater. *On This Bluff: Centennial History, 1867–1967, First Presbyterian Church*. Corpus Christi: Renfrow and Company, 1967.

Clarke, Mary Whatley. *A Century of Cow Business*. Fort Worth: Evans Press, 1976.

Cunningham, Edward. *The Descendants of Richard Cunningham.* Saint Louis: privately printed, 1902.

Dale, Edward Everett. *The Range Cattle Industry: Ranching on the Great Plains from 1855 to 1925.* Norman: University of Oklahoma Press, 1960.

Dobie, J. Frank. *Cow People.* Boston: Little, Brown and Company, 1964.

Falfurrias, Texas Wants You. Falfurrias: Falfurrias Immigration Company, 1906.

Falfurrias: The Land of Heart's Delight. Falfurrias: privately printed, 1908.

Falfurrias, The Land of Opportunity. Falfurrias: privately printed, 1927.

Falfurrias Bulletin. Saint Louis: Falfurrias Semi-Tropic Homes Company, 1909.

Falfurrias Jerseys: Type, Production, Beauty, Utility. Falfurrias: Falfurrias Creamery Co., 1919.

Forbes, B. C. *Men Who Made America Great.* Brookfield, Wis.: Hamilton Press, 1977.

Fosdick, Lucian J. *The French Blood in America.* Boston: Gorham Press, 1906.

Galbraith, John Kenneth. *The Great Crash: 1929.* Boston: Houghton Mifflin Company, 1961.

Gressley, Gene M. *Bankers and Cattlemen.* New York: Alfred A. Knopf, 1966.

Haley, J. Evetts. *The XIT Ranch of Texas.* Norman: University of Oklahoma Press, 1977.

Haworth, O. C. *The Land of Heart's Delight.* Houston: Southern Pacific Lines, 1928.

Holden, William Curry. *The Espuela Land and Cattle Company.* Austin: Texas State Historical Association, 1967.

————. *A Ranching Saga: The Lives of William Electious Halsell and Ewing Halsell.* San Antonio: Trinity University Press, 1976.

Hunter, J. Marvin, ed. *The Trail Drivers of Texas.* Nashville: Cokesbury Press, 1925.

Lasater, Edward C. *Some Printed Addresses and Statements in Public Service 1900–1930.* Falfurrias: privately printed, no date. Copy in Lasater Files.

Lasater, George Thomas. *Members of the Lasater Family and Variations of the Family Name Serving in the Civil War.* Boyne City, Mich.: privately printed, 1970.

Lea, Tom. *The King Ranch.* 2 vols. Boston: Little, Brown and Company, 1957.

Lynch, Dudley. *The Duke of Duval.* Waco: Texian Press, 1976.

Lyons, Eugene. *Herbert Hoover: A Biography.* Garden City, N.J.: Doubleday and Company, 1964.

Mexican Texans. San Antonio: University of Texas Institute of Texan Cultures, 1975.

Miller, W. H. *History and Genealogies of the Families of Miller, Woods, Harris, Wallace, Maupin, Oldham, Kavanaugh, and Brown.* Richmond: privately printed, 1907.

Osgood, Ernest S. *The Day of the Cattlemen.* Minneapolis: University of Minnesota Press, 1929.

Proceedings of the Fifteenth Annual Convention of the American National Live Stock Association. Denver: Smith-Brooks Printing Co., 1911.

Rancho de Falfurrias. Falfurrias: privately printed, 1921.

Sadler, Jerry. *History of Texas Land.* Austin: General Land Office, 1964.

Shideler, James H. *Farm Crisis, 1919–1923.* Berkeley: University of California Press, 1957.

Sibley, Marilyn McAdams. *George W. Brackenridge: Maverick Philanthropist.* Austin: University of Texas Press, 1973.

Smylie, Vernon. *Edward C. Lasater, A Biographical Portrait.* Corpus Christi: Texas News Syndicate Press, 1968.

Sonnichsen, C. L. *Cowboys and Cattle Kings.* Norman: University of Oklahoma Press, 1950.

Southwest Texans. Publishers Edition, Revised. San Antonio: Southwest Publications, 1952.

Sowell, A. J. *History of Fort Bend County, Texas.* Houston: W. H. Coyle and Co., 1904.

Spence, Vernon G. *Judge Legett of Abilene.* College Station: Texas A&M University Press, 1977.

Sterling, William Warren. *Trails and Trials of a Texas Ranger.* Norman: University of Oklahoma, 1968.

Tarpley, Fred. *1001 Texas Place Names.* Austin: University of Texas Press, 1980.

Taylor, Virginia H. *Index to Spanish and Mexican Land Grants.* Austin: General Land Office, 1976.

Texas. *Journal of the House of Representatives, Thirty-Second Legislature.* Austin: Austin Printing Company, 1911.

Texas Almanac and State Industrial Guide. Dallas: A. H. Belo Corporation, 1969.

Texas and Southwestern Cattle Raisers Association Presidents. Fort Worth: Texas and Southwestern Cattle Raisers Association, 1962.

Texas Family Land Heritage Registry. Austin: General Land Office, 1975, 1976, 1977, 1978, 1979.

Walters, Charles, Jr. *Angry Testament.* Kansas City: Halcyon House, 1969.

Webb, Walter Prescott. *The Texas Rangers.* Boston: Houghton Mifflin Company, 1935.

Webb, Walter Prescott, and H. Bailey Carroll, eds. *The Handbook of Texas.* 2 vols. Austin: Texas State Historical Association, 1952.

Wilson, Joan H. *Herbert Hoover, Forgotten Progressive.* Boston: Little, Brown, 1976.

PERIODICALS

"A Death in Duval," *Texas Observer,* April 25, 1975, pp. 1–7.

Allen, R. Clyde. "Single-Handed He Conquered 380,000 Acres of Texas Prairie," *Manufacturers Record,* April 7, 1927, pp. 94–95.

Anders, Evan. "The Origins of the Parr Machine in Duval County, Texas," *Southwestern Historical Quarterly*, vol. 85, no. 2 (October, 1981): 119–38.

"A Review of Timely Topics," *Cattleman*, February, 1919, pp. 9–12.

Barnes, W. C. "Falfurrias and Ed Lasater," *Hoard's Dairyman*, January 25, 1929, p. 64.

Baskin, Robert E. "Archie Founded Dynasty in 1882," *Dallas Morning News*, August 19, 1974, p. 1.

"Brahma Cattle Increasing," *Cattleman*, July 1919, pp. 21–23, 38, 39.

Broyles, William, Jr. "The Last Empire," *Texas Monthly*, October, 1980, pp. 150–73, 234–78.

Clarke, Mary Whatley. "Ed C. Lasater, Ninth President of Association Was a Creative Thinker and Doer," *Cattleman*, January, 1952, pp. 20–22.

Cook, James. "Nothing but the Best," *Forbes*, September 28, 1981, pp. 155–59.

Daugherty, M. M. "Range of Prices for Beef Cattle," *Cattleman*, May, 1922, pp. 19–20.

Dieterich, Arthur. "Jerseys in Texas Date Back to '73." *Jersey Journal*, May, 1961, pp. 41–43.

"Drought Conditions," *Cattleman*, August, 1916, pp. 40, 41.

"Facts About The 'Big Five' Packers," *Cattleman*, July, 1919, pp. 9–12.

"Falfurrias, The Dairyland of South Texas," *Acco Press*, vol. 12, no. 8 (August, 1934): 1–5.

Gapen, Charles A. "Cows in Cactus Land," *Country Gentleman*, January 31, 1914, n.p.

Gould, Lewis. "Theodore Roosevelt, William Howard Taft, and the Disputed Delegates in 1912: Texas as a Test Case," *Southwestern Historical Quarterly*, vol. 80, no. 1 (July, 1976): 35.

"Government Compromises Suits Against Packers—Packers Will Give up Stock Yards—Also Groceries and Other Side Lines," *Cattleman*, December, 1919, pp. 11–13.

Gow, R. M. "Ed C. Lasater," *Jersey Bulletin*, March 26, 1830, p. 558.

Hicks, John D. "The Western Middle West, 1900–1914," *Agricultural History*, vol. 20 (April, 1946): 75–80.

Hornaday, W. D. "Dairying on a Large Scale," *Hoard's Dairyman*, June 12, 1916, p. 773.

Ingrassia, Paul. "Corporations: A Perilous Life at the Top." *Wall Street Journal*, February 5, 1981.

Jacobs, William States. "The Romance of the Brahma," *Cattleman*, December, 1923, pp. 25–27.

Johnson, William R. "A Short History of the Sugar Industry in Texas," *Texas Gulf Coast Historical Association Publications*, vol. 5, no. 1 (April, 1961): 39–83.

Kendrick, John B. "Why Uncle Sam Should Supervise the Meat Business," *Cattleman*, June, 1919, pp. 23–25.

"Kendrick-Kenyon Bills Revised," *Cattleman*, vol. 6, no. 8 (January, 1920): 11–13.

"The Land of Heart's Delight," *The Inch* (Texas Eastern Transmission Corporation), 1958.

Lasater, Ed C. "Brahma Cattle," *Cattleman*, March, 1923, p. 61.

Leuthold, Steven. "Grim Reapers: The Great Bull Market in Farmland is Ending," *Barron's*, August 9, 1982, pp. 5–7, 16.

Lloyd, Everett. "Ed C. Lasater: The World's Jersey King and His 300,000 Acre Kingdom," *National Magazine*, February, 1920, n.p.

"Low Price Reasons Analyzed," *Record Stockman*, April 30, 1981, pp. 1–2.

Martin, Harold H. "Tyrant in Texas." *Saturday Evening Post*. June 26, 1954, pp. 20–52.

"The Mexican and Indian Raid of '78." *Texas State Historical Association Quarterly*, vol. 5, no. 3 (January, 1902): 212–15.

Moses, Dayton, Jr. "Texas Begins Last Fever Tick Drive," *Cattleman*, February, 1922, pp. 15–19.

———. "Tick Eradication in Texas," *Cattleman*, March, 1921, pp. 223–26.

"Newsletter." Texas Cattle Feeders Association, vol. 15, no. 15, April 10, 1981, p. 2.

"Plant Closings Put Wilson Figures in Red," *Record Stockman*, September 17, 1981, p. 1.

Poole, James E. "Livestock Market Review," *Cattleman*, December, 1920, p. 11.

"Predicts Seven-Year Shortage of Cattle and High Beef Prices," *Cattleman*, January, 1920, pp. 31, 33.

Pryor, Ike T. "The Past, Present and Future of the Cattle Industry of the United States," *Cattleman*, December, 1924, pp. 13, 15.

"Regulation of Packing Companies and Stock Yards Again Urged by National Association," *Cattleman*, February, 1920, pp. 11–12.

"Sacred Bull of India Popular in South Texas," *Cattleman*, March, 1920, pp. 115–17.

Shellenbarger, Sue. "Tough Rivals and Volatile Market Force Companies to Abandon Meatpacking Units," *Wall Street Journal*, May 14, 1981.

Van Pelt, Hugh G. "The Man from Falfurrias," *Field Illustrated*, March, 1924, pp. 12–14.

"Washington Wire," *Beef Business Bulletin*, October 31, 1980, p. 1.

Welch, J. H. "Why Brooks County Has Eminence in Dairying," *Texas Farming and Citriculture* 13 (January, 1937): 9–10.

Wildenthal, Bryan, "Jim Cage: Cowman," *Cattleman*, February, 1942, pp. 20–30.

Index

Agriculture: and diversification, 122–23; and 1929 depression, 247–48; post–World War I, 188–89, 229–30

Alice Echo, 64–65, 76, 77

Allan, James J., 76, 91

Allen, J. J., 65, 208

Allen, Noah, 105

Alliance Trust Company, Ltd., 47

American Cattle Trust, 161

American Freehold Land Mortgage Co., 47

American National Livestock Association, 156, 164, 168, 173, 174n; Market Committee, 179–80

Anders, Evan M., 97

Armour, J. Ogden, 162–63, 179

Armour, Philip D., 162, 163

Armstrong, Jamie. *See* Bennett, Jamie Armstrong

Armstrong, John, 216

Austin, Stephen F., 4

Aycock, B. N., 132

Aycock, J. T., 29, 38

Aycock and Lasater Bros., 29

Ayre Farm, Maine, 125

Bard, Father John Peter, 72

Barse, George, 264

Bayarena, Pilar Zarate, 43

Beef cattle, 132–34

Bennett, Dr. H. M., 114

Bennett, Elizabeth Bonneau Noble, 8

Bennett, Jamie Armstrong, 57, 216

Bennett, Marybelle, 67, 89

Bennett, John M., 43–44, 52, 53, 57, 61n, 66, 263; on Cunningham affair, 245; and Lasater, 68, 238; on Lasater,
136; and Marshall Terrell, 233; on Mary Lasater, 210–11, 213

Bennett, John M., Jr., 214, 215, 216, 217–18

Bennett, John M., Sr., 7–8, 32, 43–44, 49, 51n, 142, 143n; and cattle drives, 24; on Cunningham affair, 245; and García land, 35

Bennett, Martha (Patti) Noble. *See* Lasater, Patti

Bennett, Roy, 195

Bennett, Stephan, 7

Bennett family, 5, 6–7

Best, Willie, 211, 225, 267

"Big Ranches Rapidly Being Cut Into Farms," 83

Blacks: and Texas politics, 136n

Blocker, J. R., 27

Blumer, Robert Ferdinand von, 190, 191

Blumer, Walter, 191, 193

Borden, A. P., 133

Borden, H. L., 135

Borland, Representative, 163

Borland resolution, 163, 164

"Bosses under Siege . . . ," 96

Bowen, W. C., 30

Brackenridge, George W., 8, 45–46, 90, 143, 147, 148, 258, 263; and dairy business, 123–24; interests of, 213; and San Antonio National Bank, 27–28

"Brahma Cattle Increasing," 186

Brahman cattle, 133–34, 185–86, 213, 237, 240, 267

Bridwell, J. S., 132

Brooks, Captain James A., 76, 113, 194, 195, 196

Brooks County, 113–14, 194–95

Bull, D. O., 120
Bull Moose Party, 136
Burke, E. L., 157, 177
Burnett, S. B., 135

Cabrera, Alberto, 104
Cage, Jim D., 249, 261
Caldwell, Ada Lasater, 15–17, 21, 64, 66,
    264; birth of, 9; quoted, 207
Caldwell, Edward (son of Ada), 66
Caldwell, Edward H., 31n, 65, 106, 184;
    and Ada Lasater, 15–17; and cattle,
    24–25; and crime, 29; and Lasater, 23;
    sheep ranch of, 12–15
Caldwell, Oliver, 76, 91
Caldwell, Patton, 17
Caldwell, Sarah, 264
Caldwell, Walter, 76, 77, 91, 264
Caldwell, W. E., 12, 17, 32n
Caldwell, Willie, 13
Caldwell family, 5, 11–12, 267
Campbell, Governor Thomas M.,
    108–109
Campen, Mr., 262, 264
Campen-Lasater Oil Company, 262–63
Canadian Reciprocity Treaty, 156
Canales, Manuel Garcí, 34
Carey, Joseph M., 177
Cartwright, Holman, 237–38
Cattle drives, 23–24
Cattle industry, 34–35, 171, 182n
Cattleman, 134, 186, 199
Cattle Raisers Association of Texas, 135,
    154, 158, 159n, 164, 186, 215
Clark, Margaret (Peggy) Lasater, 140n
Clayton, Charles, 164
Cleary, John, 96, 107
Closner, John, 118
Coleman, Tom, 40, 230
Colquitt, Governor O. B., 137, 154
Coolidge, Calvin, 247
Cornell-Miller Texas Farms Company, 80
Corwin, O. M., 203–204, 205–206, 242
Cosby, A. A., 89, 114
Cotton, 122–23
Cotulla Ledger, 30
Cowan, Sam H., 157
Coward, Jesse, 185
Creager, R. B., 104, 109

Creamery, 197–99, 250
Creasy, W. T., 169, 170
Crime: in South Texas, 29–32
crossbreeding (cattle), 132–34, 186
Cunningham, Col. Edward, 9, 11, 20, 25,
    79, 138, 258; business reverses of,
    57–61; and G. B. Miller, 56; and
    Lasater, 26–27, 245
Cunningham, Richard, 20
Cunningham, Richard, Jr., 20
Cunningham, Sarah Jane. *See* Lasater,
    Sarah Jane Cunningham
Cunningham Sugar Company, 59–61
Cunningham, Susan T. Dismukes, 20
Cunningham, Thomas, 9
Curtis, R. M., 120
Curtis, R. W., 248

Dairy business, 120–31, 250
Dale, Albert, 193–94, 197
Dallas Morning News, 137
Davidson, Lt. Gov. A. B., 104
Denman, Judge Leroy G., 143, 147, 235,
    237, 238, 239, 242, 250
Depression: 1893, 37–39; 1929, 247
Dickey, E. W., 248
Dickey, L. A., 236, 249
Dipping: and fever ticks, 200–201
Dismukes, Sarah R., 55n
Diversification, 122–23, 131
Dobie, J. M., 30
Dobie, James, 230
Dolores Land and Cattle Co., 34–35
Donohoe, John, 84
Don Pedrito. *See* Jaramillo, Pedro
Driscoll, Robert, 75
Drought, H. P., 231; and Cunningham
    Sugar Co., 59; and Fant, 138; on
    Lasater cattle, 132; and Lasater land
    purchases, 46, 49, 51, 53; and Lasater
    loans, 201–202, 251–53
Drought: after World War I, 199–200
Duffy, Gregorio, 95, 96, 102, 104; murder
    of, 105–106, 109
Durand, E. Dana, 170–71
Durham cattle, 61, 62n, 133
Duval, B. H., 106
Duval County, 40; and Parr, 106–108,
    115–19; politics in, 97

East, Tom, 186, 230
Eastwick, Edward P., Jr., 59–60
Edwards, Emily, 211, 212, 213, 214, 224, 255, 256
"El Colorado de Los Olmos," xvii–xviii
Elections: 1900, 100; 1906, 102–104, 108; 1908, 108; 1910, 112
Ellis, Dr. Caswell, 68–69
Ellis, L. A., 58
Encino Division, 239
Everitt, J. A., 153

Facts Publishing Company, 90
Falfurrias, 257; described, xvi, 70–71, 84–85; forming of town of, 76–80; name of, 92–93; in 1980s, 266–67
Falfurrias Bulletin, 70
Falfurrias butter, 128, 130
Falfurrias County: attempt to create, 113–14
Falfurrias Creamery, 120n, 127–28, 197–98, 204, 250
Falfurrias Development Company, 81
Falfurrias Facts, 90, 200, 248–49; Lasater-Guerra letters in, 110–12; and 1906 election, 102–103
Falfurrias Farm and Garden Tracts, 76–77, 85, 87n
"Falfurrias for Women," 88
Falfurrias Immigration Company, 81–82
Falfurrias Jersey Dairy Company, 126, 129–30, 145, 202
Falfurrias Machine Shops, 91
Falfurrias Mercantile Company, xv, 90, 145, 196–97
Falfurrias Power Company, 90–91
Falfurrias Ranch, 42, 63–64, 75, 76, 141n, 149, 156, 208, 211, 261
Falfurrias Semi-Tropic Homes Company, 80, 87
Falfurrias State Bank, 90, 228–29
Fant, Dillard R., 40, 137–38, 147–48; and cattle drives, 24; loans to, 47–48
Featherstone, W. H., 136
Fechner, R. C., 90
Federal Trade Commission: and meat-packing industry, 178–80
Fehrenbach, T. R., 18
Finances, 139–49; and land purchases,

45–53; in 1920s, 231–39; post–World War I, 201–206, 230
The Flight of the Swan, 210
Flores, Leocadió, 74
Forbes, B. C., 162
Francis Smith, Caldwell and Company, 46–50
Frank, George, 198

Gaines, Major, 3–4, 35, 70, 71
Galbraith, John Kenneth, 247
Gandhi, Mahatma, 256
García, Baltazar, 110–12
García, Benito, 34
García, Hilario, xiv, xv, 11n, 55n, 210, 222, 239, 266
García, Julia Cuellar de, 72
García, Julián, 11 and n, 239–40
García, Leopoldo, 84
García, Matías, 35, 48, 260
García, Nicolás, 11n
García, Rufino, Sr., 194
García family, 5
Gardner, Bill, 197
Gardner, William A., 79, 81
Garner, John Nance, 97, 176
Garza, Alejo de la, 48
Garza, Amado de la, 114, 194, 196
Garza, Bernardo de la, 34, 35
Garza, Domingo, 100
Garza, Francisco, 74
Garza, Homobono, 72
Garza, Juan de la, 33, 34, 35
Gelhorn, Dr. George, 214–15
George, Henry, 213
Giddens, H. W., 120–21
Giles, Alfred, 194
Gist, John M., 132
Godair, Arthur, 135
Goliad, 1, 10, 39–40
González, Juana, 127
Goodnight, Charles, 27
Gorbid, Lloyd, 185
Greenhill, Kenneth, 253
Grosscup injunction, 163
Guerra, Deodoro, 102, 105, 109
Guerra, Francisco, 95n
Guerra, H. P., 102
Guerra, Jacobo, 102, 103

Guerra, José Alejandro, 43
Guerra, Manuel, 43, 45, 215; and Brooks County, 114; and Duffy murder, 105–106, 109; and Lasater, 108–12; at Las Viboras, 95; life of, 99; and politics, 97
Guerra family, 43

Haugen, Gilbert N., 153, 154, 181
Head, R. G., 161
Heard, Dwight B., 177
Henry, B. Temple, 65, 80, 81, 90, 114
Hereford cattle, 132–35
Herff, Dr. Ferdinand, 213
Hinojosa, José Angel, 33
Hinojosa, Tomasa, 34, 260
Hockaday, Ela, 88
Hogg, Governor James, 30
Holbrook, Ada Ann, 89
Holbrook, H. C., 114
Hood Farm, Lowell, Mass., 125
Hoover, Herbert, 166–67; and Lasater, 169n; and livestock industry, 177–78
Hopkins, Judge W. B., 117
House Agriculture Committee, 181
H. P. Drought and Company, 46, 49, 201

India: cattle from, 133–34
Indian raid, 1878, 13–14

James, Henry, 201
Jaramillo, Pedro, 72–73
Jastro, Henry A., 176
Jenkins, Huston, 198
Jenkins, Wilbert, 190, 191, 198, 250
Jersey cows, 120–31, 132, 193, 236, 238, 243, 249–50
Jim Hogg County, 194–95
Jones, Captain A. C., 40
Jones, Bill, 40–41, 42, 194, 245; and new county, 113, 116n
Joske, Alexander, 234
The Jungle, 162

Katherine, Tex. (now Armstrong), xiii, xviii, 57, 75, 226
Kendrick, John B., 177
Kenedy, Mifflin, 17n, 27, 62n, 94n
Kenedy Pasture Company, 61–62, 208
Kickapoo Indians, 14

Kidd, George, 116, 117, 118
King, Henrietta M., 45, 52, 59n, 87n, 142, 190, 230
King, Richard, 3, 4, 12, 27
King Ranch, 176n, 233, 240n
Kleberg, Alice Gertrudis King, 241
Kleberg, Bob (son of Alice), 241
Kleberg, R. J., 75, 230, 233–34; and dairy business, 122; and land sale, 236, 239; and meat-packing industry, 176
Kothmann, Elgin O., 132

La Mota, 57n, 62, 63
Landergin, John, 156, 178
Landergin, P. H., 180
Land sales: during receivership, 238–39; in 1920s, 249
LaSalle County Law and Order League, 29
Lasater, Ada. *See* Caldwell, Ada Lasater
Lasater, Albert (son), 210, 221, 263; death of, 223
Lasater, Albert Hezekiah (father), 9–10, 19–20, 22, 98n, 267; children of, 20–21; death of, 25–26; and sheep business, 15
Lasater, Benjamin, 19
Lasater, Bennett (son): death of, 54–55
Lasater, Ed C., 188; accomplishments of, 149–50; and Aycock and Lasater Bros., 29; background of, 3, 9, 25–26; and Brooks County, 113–14; businesses of, 90; and Caldwell, 23; and cattle, 61–62, 132–34, 139, 141, 204; and Cattle Raisers Association, 135; children of, 210, 215–26; and Cunningham Sugar Company, 59–61; death of, 265; described, 21, 41; education of, 21–22; and 1893 depression, 37–39; and Falfurrias school, 91; as father, 215–16; financial backing for, 45–53, 142–44, 243; first marriage of, 32, 54–55; and Food Administration, 168–74; and FTC, 179–80; and García land, 35; indicted for theft, 66; and Jersey cows, 120–31; as judge of character, 64–65; land purchases by, 42–45, 137; and liquor, 86; and livestock business, 28–29, 158–61; and Manuel Guerra, 101,

108–12; and meat-packing industry, 153–82; in 1929, 253–60; and oil and gas, 208–209, 261–63; and Otie York, 89; and Parr, 116–19; personality of, 214; and Peter McBride, 185; and politics, 96, 97, 99–102, 135–37, 195–96; and rail service, 75–76; ranch of, 139, 141n, 143, 204, 243; and real estate development, 76–78, 121; receivership of, 235–41; and record keeping, 139–40; sales of, 144–45; second marriage of, 67–69, 78, 209–15, 255–56; and sheep business, 22–23; traits of, 244–46; worth of, 1909, 140–42; and voting, 196

Lasater, Edward (son), 32; death of, 54–55

Lasater, Garland (son), 209, 210, 215–17, 221, 253–54

Lasater, Lois (daughter), 210, 221, 222, 255, 263

Lasater, Lois (sister), 20

Lasater, Mary (daughter), 210; death of, 223

Lasater, Mary Miller, 55, 67–69, 78, 209–15, 255–56, 265; and children, 219–22

Lasater, Patti, 32, 55, 62, 210

Lasater, Sarah Jane Cunningham, 9, 16, 20, 25, 29

Lasater, Tom (brother), 21, 29; death of, 30–32

Lasater, Tom (son), 210, 217, 218, 219, 221, 222, 239–41; on Lasater and Guerra, 101–102; personality of, 224–26

Lasater, William A., 19

Lasater family, 5, 9–10; history of, 18–20; ranch life of, 215–26

Lasater-Miller Company, 80

Lasater name, 18

Leggett, K. K., 122–23

Lewis, C. C., 34

Liquor: and land promotion business, 86

Livestock: and Edward Cunningham, 26–27; and 1893 depression, 37–39; as industry, 158–61, 199–200, 204, 230–31; Lasater and, 28–29

Loma Blanca, 4, 6n, 23, 36, 151, 219, 226, 260, 267

Loma Blanca grant, 6n, 33, 34

López, A., 71

López, Damaso, 74

López, Lázaro, 43, 194

López, S., 71

López, Severo, 110–12

Los Olmos community, 71–72

Los Olmos Creek, 4, 11, 23, 74, 149

Los Olmos y Loma Blanca, 6, 7, 33, 34, 35, 259–60

Lott, Uriah, 75

Loving, Jim, 37

Lucas, Cyrus, 40, 186, 230

Lucas, R. P., 132

Lupe, Molly, 263

Lyon, Cecil A., 135

Lytle, John T., 161

McBride, C. J., 184

McBride, Dennis, 218

McBride, Jim, 218, 239

McBride, Minnie Alice Priour, 183, 184

McBride, Peter, xiv, 183–85, 215, 255

McFaddin, Al, 133, 178, 186, 187, 209

McGillin, Edward M., 160

McIntyre, R. J., 114, 194

MacKenzie, Murdo, 156, 157, 159, 264

Mackenzie, William, 47, 51, 132, 201

McNelly, Captain, 30

Maldonado, Placido, xv

Marketing, 158–61

Martin, Congressman S. W., 162

Maupin, Jim, 63, 65, 75, 76, 196

May Blossom Fond Pet (cow), 249–50

Meat-packing industry, 153–82; and Food Administration, 171–72

Mercantile business, 1920, 196–97

Mexican cowboys: and sign language, 218

Mexican Texans: and politics, 98–99

Mexicans: in northern Starr County, 72–74

Miller, Garland (brother-in-law), xv, 57, 79, 80, 248, 264; death of, 190, 209, 228; and Falfurrias Mercantile Store, 90; and Falfurrias State Bank, 90

Miller, Garland Burleigh, 11–12, 55–56

Miller, Harriett, xv, 228

Miller, Helen Devine, xv, 228
Miller, John, xviii
Miller, L. D., xv–xvi, xviii, 80, 207, 264;
and Falfurrias Machine Shops, 91; and
Falfurrias Power Company, 91; and
Falfurrias State Bank, 228–29; on
Lasater, 148, 254; and Marshall Terrell,
233; on Mary Lasater, 209–10; and
1906 election, 103; and real estate de-
velopment, 189, 190, 193
Miller, Mary. *See* Lasater, Mary Miller
Miller, Mary Gardner, 54, 211
Miller, Richard, xv, 57, 79, 114, 195, 209,
217; death of, 228; and Falfurrias Mer-
cantile Store, 90; and Falfurrias State
Bank, 190
Miller, Robert, xv, 79, 207, 228, 250,
264; and 1906 election, 103; and real
estate development, 189, 191; and
Spark, 192–93
Miller, Tom, 56
Miller brothers, 78–80; fate of, 189–90;
and oil business, 207–209; and real es-
tate development, 80–82, 85, 121
Miller Bros. Company, 80, 82
Miller family, 5, 11–12
Monroe, Judge John R., 102, 112
Monseratte, M. D., 75
Moody, Governor Dan, xiii
Moore, Monta J., 109
Morris, Nelson, 161
La Mota de Falfurrias, 62
Music: Lasater and, 68
Myrick, Birdie, 77

Nail, Jim, 164
National Board of Farm Organizations,
181
National Cattlemen's Association. *See*
American National Livestock Asso-
ciation
National Dairy Show, 1928, 120
Newman, M. A., 91
New York Times, 161
Noble, Alex, 264
Noble, Elizabeth Bonneau. *See* Bennett,
Elizabeth Bonneau Noble
Nobleman (bull), 125

Noel, Governor Edmond F., 123
Nueces River, 3, 4, 5, 8, 14, 71, 95

Oberwetter, H. W., 195
Oberwetter, Ray, 219
Oil and gas, 207–209, 261–63

Packers and Stockyards Act of 1921, 175
Padre Pedro, 72
Parr, Archer (Archie), 96, 97; background
of, 106–107; death of, 119; and politics,
103, 106–108, 115–19
Parr, George, 119
Parr family, 119
Parramore, J. H., 156
Peña, Ignacio de la, 23, 33, 39, 96, 259;
land of, 5–6, 7, 34–36, 44
Peña, Ignacio de la, Jr., 33
Peña family, 5, 33
Pérez, Camilo, 72
Pérez, Sábas, 8–9, 42–43, 128, 196, 267
Pérez family, 5, 197
Perredes, Eugene C., 120
Phillips, Marcus, 77
Pierce, Shanghai, 27
Pinchot, Gifford, 171, 173, 174
Politics, 94–119, 135–37, 195–96
Porter, Lake Newell, 196
Poultry: Tom Lasater and, 241
Premont, Charles, 75
Price, Waterhouse and Co., 139–40
Proctor, Sarah, 212
Proctor, T. S., 197–99, 212
Profit and loss statements, 145–47
Pryor, Ike, xiv, 156, 176, 186, 200, 204,
230, 264

Rachal, Ed, 76, 255
Rachal, E. R., 24, 88, 114, 194
Rachal, Frank, 63, 76, 77, 114, 195
Railroads, 75–76
Ramírez, Jesús María, 110
Ranch life: of Lasater children, 215–26
Ray, W. G., 91
Real estate development, 76–78, 80–93,
121, 189–90, 249
Realitos, xiv, xviii, 13, 14, 17, 23, 63, 184,
192, 208

Receivership, 235–42
Record keeping, 139–40
Requa, Mark L., 173–74
Reynolds, George T., 135
Reynolds, W. D., 156, 164
Rice, Bob, 39, 63, 64, 65, 92
Rice, R. H., 114
Ricks, Neel, 30
Ríes, Eusebio, 74
Rio Grande City, 94, 100–101, 108
Rio Grande River, 3, 4, 8, 71, 191
Rogers, Colonel C. M., 31–32
Roosevelt, Theodore: and Brahman
    cattle, 133n; and Duffy murder, 105–
    106; and 1912 election, 135–36
Ross, L. S., 114
Routt, John L., 161
Rupp, Neil, 195, 225, 267

Saldaña, Matías García, 34
Salinas, Albino, 74
San Antonio Daily Express, 29–30, 31,
    113, 235; and Don Pedrito, 73; on
    Lasater, 257–58
San Antonio Loan & Trust Company, 45,
    78n, 143, 147, 205, 235n, 236
Sansom, Marion, 135
Santa Rosa Ranch, 137–38
Schleicher, Gustave, 213
Schuetz, Florence, 196
Schuetz, Rose, 89
Schuetz, W. G., 67
Scott, J. R., Jr., 195, 229
Scott, Gus R., 90
Seeligson, Henry, 34
Sheep: business of, 24–26; and Ed
    Lasater, 22–23; and Edward Caldwell,
    12–15
Shely, W. E., 100, 102
Sherman Antitrust Act, 163
Shideler, James, 183
Shorthorn cattle, 61, 132, 185–86
Silliman, F. T., 237
Sims, W. M., 81
Sinclair, Upton, 162
Slaughter, C. C., 161
Sloan, W. W., 76
Smith, Congressman Neal, 182n

Smith, Francis, 46–50, 53, 138
Smith, W. A., 148
Sophie 19th Tormentor (bull), 125
Southern Pacific Railroad, 248
Spark, George, 192–93
Spielhagen, G. R., 81
Spindletop, 208
Spiritualism: and Mary Lasater, 211–12
Starr County, 40; politics in, 45, 94, 97,
    100–14; settling of, 70–74
Sterling, W. W., xiii
Stubbs, W. R., 177
Sturgis, Thomas, 161
Sugar: Edward Cunningham and, 57–60
Sugarland, Texas, 58
Swan Brothers, 35
Swift, Charles H., 170
Swift, Edward F., 170
Swift, Gustavus Franklin, 161–62
Swift, Louis F., 164

Taft, William Howard, 135
Tamaulipas, State of, 7
Tariffs, 157–58
Taylor, Amanda Cartwright, 211
Taylor, General Zachary, 8
Terrell, Chester, 118, 232
Terrell, J. O., xiv, 231; and dairy busi-
    ness, 125, 129–30; on Falfurrias coun-
    try, 146; on Lasater, 202–203
Terrell, Marshall, 227, 231–35, 236
Texas: crime in, 29–32; independence of,
    39–40; population growth in, 4
Texas and Southwestern Cattle Raisers
    Association, 135n, 215, 243. *See also*
    Cattle Raisers Association of Texas
Texas Cattle Raisers Association. *See*
    Cattle Raisers Association of Texas
Texas Jersey Cattle Club, 249
Texas-Mexican Railway, 66, 183, 203
Texas Sugar Growers' Association, 11
Thomas, H. D., 114
Thomas, John C., 228
Tick fever, 199–201
Treaty of Guadalupe Hidalgo, 4, 74, 98
Treviño, Agapito, 127
Treviño, Desiderio, 63
Treviño, Florentino, 197

Treviño, Lino, 72, 74, 76, 77
Turney, W. W., 243

U.S. Food Administration, 167–74
United States Mortgage Co. of Scotland, 48, 49

Vann, John, 104
Vest Report, 160, 162
Von Blucher, C. F. H., 63

Wagenschein, Carl F., 205n
Wallace, Henry C., 173–74, 177, 178
Ward, Ben Q., 27
Ward, Lafayette, 27
Water supply: importance of, 50

Wells, James B., 94, 97, 98, 118; and Manuel Guerra, 99; and 1906 election, 103; and Parr, 107
Welsh, Judge Stanley, 104
West, George W., 8, 230
West, Judge Duval, 235, 241
Wilhelm, F. E., 171
Wilson, Woodrow, 118, 137
Winters, A. J., 136n
Women: and land promotion, 88–89
Woodbridge family, 191
Wright, Wirt, 202, 236, 237, 238

York, Otie, 89

Zaragoza, Ignacio, 74

CPSIA information can be obtained at www.ICGtesting.com
Printed in the USA
LVOW120744031112

305540LV00001B/1/A